MW00477631

ALSO BY SCOTT W. BERG

*Grand Avenues: The Story of Pierre Charles L'Enfant,
the French Visionary Who Designed Washington, D.C.*

*38 Nooses: Lincoln, Little Crow,
and the Beginning of the Frontier's End*

The
Burning
❧ of the ❧
World

The
Burning
❧ of the ❧
World

The Great Chicago Fire
and the War for a City's Soul

SCOTT W. BERG

PANTHEON BOOKS · NEW YORK

Copyright © 2023 by Scott W. Berg

All rights reserved. Published in the United States by Pantheon Books,
a division of Penguin Random House LLC, New York, and distributed
in Canada by Penguin Random House Canada Limited, Toronto.

Pantheon Books and colophon are registered trademarks
of Penguin Random House LLC.

Library of Congress Cataloging-in-Publication Data
Name: Berg, Scott W., author.
Title: The burning of the world : the Great Chicago Fire
and the war for a city's soul / Scott W. Berg.
Description: First edition. New York : Pantheon Books, 2023.
Includes bibliographical references and index.
Identifiers: LCCN 2023000507 (print). LCCN 2023000508 (ebook).
ISBN 9780804197847 (hardcover). ISBN 9780804197854 (ebook).
Subjects: LCSH: Fires—Illinois—Chicago. |
Great Fire, Chicago, Ill., 1871. | Chicago (Ill.)—History—To 1875. |
Chicago (Ill.)—Politics and government—To 1950.
Classification: LCC F548.42.B474 2023 (print) | LCC F548.42 (ebook) |
DDC 977.3/11041—dc23/eng/20230201
LC record available at https://lccn.loc.gov/2023000507
LC ebook record available at https://lccn.loc.gov/2023000508

www.pantheonbooks.com

Maps copyright © Douglas Luman
Jacket image: *Chicago Fire of 1871* (detail).
Lithograph by F. Sala & Co.
Chicago History Museum/Getty Images.
Jacket design by Lauren Peters-Collaer

Printed in the United States of America
First Edition
2   4   6   8   9   7   5   3   1

Whether or not we believe that events are consciously ordered before their occurrence, we are compelled to admit the importance of Contingency in human affairs. If we believe in such an orderly and predetermined arrangement, the small circumstance upon which a great event may hinge becomes, in our view, but the instrumentality by means of which the great plan is operated. It by no means sets aside the vital influence of chance to assume that "all chance is but direction which we cannot see."

—JOSEPH EDGAR CHAMBERLIN,
The Ifs of History, 1907

Very sensible men have declared that they were fully impressed at such a time with the conviction that it was the burning of the world.

—FREDERICK LAW OLMSTED, "Chicago in Distress,"
The Nation, November 9, 1871

Contents

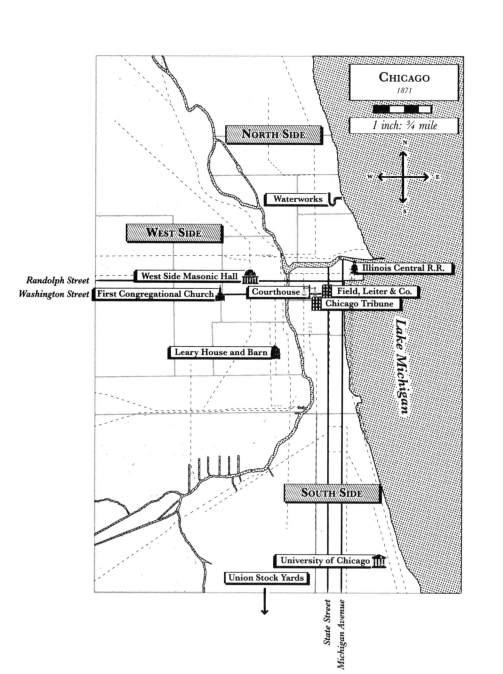

CHICAGO
1871

1 inch: ¾ mile

N
W — E
S

NORTH SIDE

WEST SIDE

Waterworks

Lake Michigan

Randolph Street

West Side Masonic Hall

Illinois Central R.R.

Washington Street

First Congregational Church

Courthouse

Field, Leiter & Co.

Chicago Tribune

Leary House and Barn

SOUTH SIDE

University of Chicago

Union Stock Yards

State Street

Michigan Avenue

Author's Note

The Chicago River cuts a wobbling line inland from Lake Michigan for one and a quarter miles, at which point the river splits into two branches, one to the north and one to the south. Between 1871 and 1874, the years covered in this book, the three land areas delineated by the river had two sets of names: the North Side, South Side, and West Side; and the North Division, South Division, and West Division. Residents and municipal offices used both names, sometimes interchanging them in the same conversation or document.

After the Great Fire, Chicago's homeowners and businesses submitted insurance claims that totaled more than $310 million, around $190 million of which would eventually be paid. While monetary equivalents across 150 years are difficult to determine, those figures translate to, at minimum, $7 billion and $5 billion today. When measured by the number of buildings lost and the amount of urban space affected, however, the cost of a similar disaster in 2023 would be many, many times greater.

Prologue

Saturday, October 7, 1871

One night before the Great Fire

From across the river the courthouse bell sounded: twice, then a pause, four times, a pause, eight times.

Two, four, eight, again and again. For months now, all through the dusty summer, the massive bell atop the Cook County courthouse in the middle of downtown Chicago had provided the cadence of the city: a warning for some, but for many more a sound like the chime that told them to take their seats at the start of a show.

The newspapers called them "firebugs." Sometimes they came in dozens, sometimes hundreds. On this night they came in the thousands, moving toward the brightening orange glow over the rooftops just west of the river. They blocked the streets, they crowded the bridges, they climbed atop storage sheds and shimmied up lampposts. They gasped, they laughed, they shouted encouragement to firemen and fire alike. They drank. They didn't represent all of Chicago, but in their appreciation of just about any sort of ready-made entertainment they were Chicagoans through and through.

The city, only thirty-four years old on this warm and windy October evening, was urban America's youngest child: full of promise and mischief, making its own way, accountable only to itself. In a city populated by more than 300,000 people, spread for miles up and down the shore of Lake Michigan, fires provided a unique sort of intimacy and knit its people together in a way little else could.

The sight of a blaze over the rooftops and the piercing cries of "*Fire!*" brought out men, women, and plenty of children, who loved to test the flames, no matter what the hour, running in close and running back out before they were shooed or dragged away. Nothing quickened the blood more than the sight of one of the sixteen gleaming cast-iron steamers of the fire department clattering past, its bell clanging as the company foreman lifted his speaking horn to his mouth and shouted, "Aside, damn you!"

Some came out into the streets because the fire had started nearby, while others were drawn from miles away. As the sense of excitement grew, a wiry and bespectacled twenty-year-old newly anointed as a city editor at the *Evening Post* hurried along with the firebugs through the West Division. With the wind up, the sky dark and clear, and many of the city's manufactories, mills, furnaces, and boilers shut down for the week's day of rest, the sound of the courthouse bell was as clear as a conversation in the same room. Something in the energy surrounding him, the number of people outdoors in the dark of night, and the unusual brilliance in the sky told Ed Chamberlin that this could be a big one. Maybe *the* big one.

Twice the bell rang, then a pause, four times, a pause, eight times. Every editor and beat reporter in Chicago carried a detailed map of the city in his head. Chamberlin knew that 248 was a fire department call box in the neighborhood the insurance men called Red Flash. Fire was always a good story. But a fire in Red Flash had the makings of a great story.

Ed lived with his older brother Everett, a drama and music critic at the *Tribune,* farther out in the West Division, away from the river, where the houses and the lots on which they sat began to get bigger and nicer. Though he'd lived in Chicago for just two years, Ed already knew many of the city's streets and alleys as he'd known the dells and country roads of eastern Vermont, where he'd lived until he was six, or those of southern Wisconsin, where he'd come of age. He was a rural boy at heart, raised in rustic little villages, come as a young man to the least clean, least painted, least charming big city in America. Chicago was all drive, ambition, movement, smell, and noise. For the tens of thousands of newcomers like him from

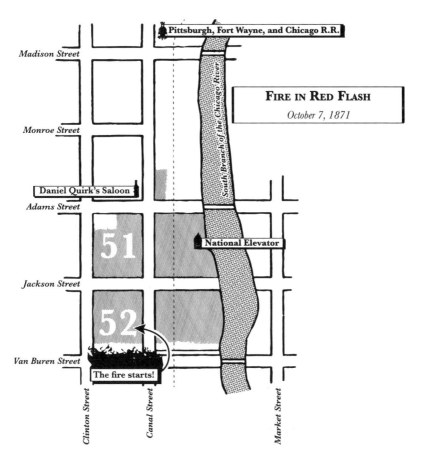

the American countryside—and for the tens of thousands who'd come from Europe—its pull was awesome and irresistible.

Block 52—just across from the South Side, bounded by Canal, Van Buren, Jackson, and Clinton—was a typical Chicago block, a mix of residences, small factories, storefronts, saloons, and empty lots arranged in a heedless jumble. Into its five acres were stuffed two sawmills, a box factory, a small lumberyard, several coal sheds, and numerous two- and three-story row houses, all made of wood. Wood shavings and wood dust filled the block's warehouse floors and floated in the air.

Ed's newspaper, the *Evening Post,* was six years old and known for its genial, all-comers Republicanism, its literary pretensions, and its lower-tier status among the city's broadsheets. But when it came to chasing fires, Ed might as well have worked for the *Tribune,* or the *Times,* or the German-language *Staats-Zeitung.* The editors of Chicago's newspapers made their money by disagreeing about politics and by catering to like-minded readerships, but they also sold papers by competing to provide the most timely, breathless, and lurid coverage of the myriad ways the city could disfigure or destroy its own inhabitants. To read the *Evening Post* during the first week of October 1871—or to read any newspaper in any of the country's fast-expanding urban centers—was to believe that to live in an American city, one must be possessed of an insatiable death wish.

In just the past few days, a dozen or more Chicago lives had been ended or forever altered. Less than a quarter mile from where Ed now ran, a boy named James had lost his left foot when it was crushed by a horse-drawn omnibus as he was picking up wheat along the track. Another boy, named Michael, seated on the edge of an omnibus, lost both feet when he swung them out too far and into the path of an oncoming trolley. A woman named Wilhemina and her three-year-old daughter were crushed to death beneath a moving railroad car when they tried to jump on. Two unnamed girls playing on the North Western Railroad bridge across the Chicago River found themselves in the path of a crossing train; both ran for the other side, but one didn't make it. Four unnamed boys went rowing on Lake Michigan and never returned; later, their boat was found bobbing upside down against the long breaker formed by the Illinois Central tracks. A man named Tomas was shot through the temple by a saloon keeper after a confrontation that concerned $2.71 in unpaid debt. Robbery, murder, collision, collapse—it seemed that every street corner was full of peril, every day an obstacle course, every minute potentially one's last.

Of all the ways to be rendered homeless, injured, or dead, fire was the most feared. In part this was because fire was, by a wide margin, the most likely. Two hundred seventy-nine days had passed so far in 1871 as Ed Chamberlin dashed toward Canal and Jackson, and during that time at least two hundred blazes had been extinguished by the city's small band of paid firemen. The last meaningful burst of rain had fallen two days after the July 4 holiday, and in the thirteen weeks since, not a drop had fallen that hadn't disappeared without a trace into the city's prodigious coating of dirt and dust. Chicago was famous for its mud, but little of the stuff could now be found.

In the course of the past week, between October 2 and October 7, the city's 193 firemen had been summoned to twenty-eight fires. Name a neighborhood, name a type of business or building, something had burned: a residential duplex, a warehouse, a box factory, a Catholic church, a barn. Careless boys with cigarettes, an inattentive tin worker, an overheated kerosene lamp, a grease spill, a defective flue, spontaneous combustion of oil-soaked rags and crackled-dry paper—it seemed during this hottest and most arid summer and fall in Chicago's history that there were as many ways for a fire to start as there were residents of the city.

More than 150,000 immigrants lived in Chicago, most of whom had arrived in the previous ten years. They came from Germany, Ireland, Norway, Bohemia, Poland, and other European points of origin. Their entertainments were modest, for the most part, and they held them close. No matter how poor, every immigrant neighborhood had its fiddler, its raconteur, its card dealer, its street-corner saloon keeper. But fire outdid everything. Fire crossed all boundaries of politics, national origin, and language. It cost nothing, required no ticket, demanded no influence, no personal connections. And no neighborhood was immune to the spectacle of the run for the alarm, the excited wait for the engines, the sweat-soaked exertions of the firemen as they battled the blaze.

From the north, a crowd pressed down Clinton Street until it reached Adams. At the center of that intersection, six horse-drawn omnibuses had converged face-to-face with no way to extract themselves. Most of their passengers disembarked, heading for the flames or walking against the crowd to find another ride or to make the rest of their way on foot. The best vantage point was the bridge over the southern branch of the Chicago River at Madison Street. From railing to railing and end to end this span was packed with traffic as those who'd come from farther away encountered those who had satisfied their curiosity and were going home. All across the Madison bridge men and women shouted at each other, in English, but also in German and Norwegian and many other languages.

A crush of people lined the southern side of the bridge, facing the conflagration. Might the sparks, cinders, and pieces of burning wood that floated through the night air in long skips and arcs travel this far? Every big fire brought collateral damage to its spectators: a ruined garment, a burn across the arm, a head of singed hair, sometimes even death. But not yet. The spectators on the Madison bridge knew that the wind was coming from the southwest. Would the fire *jump*? Meaning: Would the blaze send a piece of burning wood over the Chicago River and into downtown, where it might find the roof of a paint factory, or the top of a coal shed, or just a pile of dried shingles, and turn what was already the biggest fire most of them had ever witnessed into a catastrophe of historic dimensions?

In the twenty minutes that had passed since the first sound of the courthouse bell, the northern half of block 52, the downwind half, had disappeared in flame. At its center burned the Lull and Holmes planing mill. Inside, for many years rough-sawn wood had passed through a sequence of guides and gears on many long, low tables with saws powered by steam-driven motors, for ten or twelve hours a day, six days a week. Sweepers collected the shavings and sent them down long chutes to the bins below. A row of boilers ran beneath the floor and powered the machinery. There, in the basement, shovelers spent the day stoking the fires, using the recycled sawdust and fragments of wood as fuel. To keep the machines running, oil was poured onto and into them until it congealed and hardened into a knobbed black rime, lending the machinery a lumpy obsidian sheen. When a lumber mill caught fire, these boilers caught and held the heat, pulsing red and even blue.

On Clinton Street, on the western edge of the block, the houses seem to have been turned inside out as their residents prepared to flee. A well-dressed family patriarch sat atop a pile of bed frames, bureaus, tables, and chairs; a grim-faced grandmother guarded a great heap of clothing; a nervous-looking lad loaded an entire household into a wagon. The throng of firebugs stared at them; they stared back.

By the time Ed Chamberlin arrived at the center of the action, the situation had gone from bad to worse. From the mill, the fire spread in three directions at once: to a paper-box factory to the west, to a frame town house to the north, and to a vinegar works to the south. The wide level space between Canal Street and the Chicago River, where the Pittsburgh, Fort Wayne, and Chicago Railroad ran to and from its passenger and freight depots a few blocks to the north, was full of flammable coal sheds and lumberyards. Sparks, embers, and cinders flew overhead, launched into the air by the heat at the center of the block and then scattered by the winds.

Fires of this size were fought in one of two ways: by going in and dousing the blaze at its source, or by setting a perimeter and arresting its progress until it died down. In this case, in Red Flash, containment was the sole option. Block 52 was a goner. Now block 51, to its north, needed saving, as did the train and lumber yards along the river. But things were getting tricky. On Jackson Street, on the blaze's northern boundary, the fire engine *Chicago* was in trouble. As the wind blasted hot air into their faces, forcing their eyes shut and setting sparks to dancing on their clothes, the men of the *Chicago*'s company had to fall back in a rush, flames licking at their machine.

In that instant, a pack of citizens deputized themselves into service and in a dash wheeled the engine out of harm's way as the crowd behind them roared at their success. Every foreman of every engine company carried a speaking horn, a simple flared metal tube that allowed him to direct his own men and to press bystanders into duty. It was written into city law: if "outsiders," as they were called, were told to help fight a fire, they had to help. This was one way that a force of 193 men spread across more than ten square miles could beat back a dozen fires or more in a week. In any case, the kind of spectator who raced to a fire and stood so close that he could feel the heat on his face was the kind who needed no prodding to lend a hand. Such men imagined themselves to be heroes-in-waiting and were giddy at the chance to prove their courage.

Now, without waiting for instructions, another small squad of outsiders ventured into the space along the railroad tracks, close to the river, where they demolished coal and wood sheds along with the ramshackle residence of one "poor old woman." As the fire gathered strength and began to burn up block 51, another gang of men detached the Pittsburgh, Fort Wayne, and Chicago passenger coaches and pushed them up the tracks and out of the reach of the flames. Yet another set of spectators grabbed ahold of various spare trucks and wagons that might serve to spread the fire and pushed them into the river. When a smaller group of overzealous volunteers found itself trapped in the riverside lumberyard of Sherills and Son, the men kicked out the wall of a storage shed and tipped it into the river, then floated away on their makeshift raft.

All six of the West Side fire engines were on the scene by this time, and all six now retreated from Van Buren one more block northward, to Adams Street, where they attached twelve lines to the hydrants there and turned as one to face their adversary. In the language of the Civil War, which in the days so soon after that conflict sometimes seemed to be the only language writers knew how to use, this was their final stand. If the fire spread any farther northward, it might become uncontainable, and their summerlong war against high winds, dry air, and combustible wood could be lost.

Along Adams Street, a wall of flame now battled a wall of water. Not two blocks behind the firemen, beside the river and just south of the Adams bridge, towered the National grain elevator. Five stories high, their catwalks higher than the cupola of the county courthouse, Chicago's grain elevators were its tallest structures, and their presence up and down the river foreshadowed the city's coming mania for skyscrapers. Towering vertical shafts made of wood and full of dried wheat or corn, the elevators were also ready-made torches awaiting ignition. And once they were ignited, burning bits of pinewood from their crowns might launch themselves hundreds of feet up into the high wind. Such a brand could float for a mile or more and fall anywhere.

Meanwhile, in the streets surrounding Red Flash, the viewing party grew more raucous. Every increase in the degree of danger seemed to produce an equal increase in high spirits. On the north side of Adams Street, a saloon keeper named Quirk threw up his hands in the expectation of defeat and invited the crowd to help itself to his stock of liquor and cigars. Many of the men who now enjoyed an unexpected round of drinks and a smoke carried their own portable soda-acid fire extinguishers, copper contraptions full of water and sodium bicarbonate. In return for Quirk's largesse they doused the side of his saloon, singing as they did so.

The blaze continued hot for several hours. But in the end the wall of water along Adams Street did its job. Quirk did not lose his business. Red Flash did not become the citywide Great Fire everyone feared. The number of empty lots along the north side of Adams might have made a difference as well, by making fuel sparse and giving the firemen more room in which to operate. In any case, by the time the blaze died down early on Sunday morning, October 8, every West Side fire engine and hose cart was coated with ash and cinders, its coal reserves exhausted, its hoses split at the seams. This had not been an ordinary job: six engines spent and four dozen men overcome with smoke and heat, some now unable to open their eyes, a few unable to walk without assistance. As for the horses, the two or four needed to pull each engine, they were better off; they had been tied up away from the blaze, and substitutes were always at the ready.

Everything had almost gone wrong. Walls had collapsed, but not on top of any of the men. The National grain elevator had smoked and flared, but it hadn't caught. Flaming debris had flown for blocks, but it had failed to ignite a new blaze beyond the reach of the engines. In the end, the firemen and their civilian deputies had achieved victory, but at the cost of total exhaustion.

In all circumstances, even these, protocol dictated that the engine companies return to their stations and make ready for the next fire. Before eating, sleeping, or drinking, the men were to replace or resew the hoses, clean and restoke the boilers and keep them at a low burn, examine and adjust the fittings. On this night, though, many didn't complete their checklists. Instead, many of the firemen ate and slept. Many went home or were sent home. Some drank. One man from each company went to the roof of his station and kept an exhausted watch for more fires.

The steamer *Chicago* returned to its station house, three blocks away from Red Flash, its tall, cylindrical boiler and its many lengths of hose—not to mention its crew—in less-than-ideal condition. Under normal circumstances, as the closest machine, the *Chicago* would have stayed behind to tend the ruins of the fire. Instead, the *Little Giant,* an engine housed twelve blocks to the south and in much better condition, spent most of Sunday wetting a red glow back toward the center of the block, keeping a weary watch over tendrils of smoke, a carpet of wet ash, and mounds of charred, collapsed brickwork.

Ed Chamberlin, meanwhile, headed off to the offices of the *Evening Post,* on Madison Street, downtown. Like all the gawking citizens who'd crowded the streets of Red Flash, Chamberlin was sure he'd seen a catastrophe cut short by the slimmest of margins. It was the best fire story he'd get out of the city before winter came, and it would no doubt fill seven or eight columns, maybe more.

But Ed Chamberlin's story never appeared in print. In the end, few residents of Chicago would remember much about the fire in Red Flash—except as a portent, a prelude, a tiny taste of what was to come. The next night, the city would supply them with a much bigger fire and a much, much bigger story—the biggest story, in fact, that the city of Chicago has ever told.

PART I

Fire

≫ 1 ≪

F AR BELOW the walkway that circled the top of the Cook County courthouse, Chicago spread itself out beneath Mathias Schaefer, an ordinary fireman in the most fire-prone city in the world. Overhead, the sky was clear, the moon three-quarters full. The sun had set more than an hour earlier.

A hundred and twenty feet below his perch, Schaefer could see pinpricks of gaslight illumination, hear the occasional voices of men and women going home from the taverns, theaters, and churches that ringed the courthouse square, or watch the occasional shopkeeper lock up for the night. Sunday night was a quiet time downtown, a lull before the noisy, surging storm of workers who would overwhelm the central business district at the start of the new workweek. A warm October wind rushed across the city from the southwest, a wind that carried a tinge of the odor of the Union Stock Yards and of hundreds of small West Side factories before it piled the waves along the Illinois Central breakwater at the edge of Lake Michigan.

Schaefer was not a watchman by occupation, and this post was a temporary assignment. His usual place was not up here but out there, "on the nozzle," as they said. Pipemen were their own breed. First in, first to feel the heat and breathe the smoke, too often the first to die. Like so much of the paid labor in Chicago—jobs defined by pulling, lifting, pushing, shoving, sawing, stacking, hauling, throwing, breaking, and battering—fighting fires wore you down. Still, to be a fireman was a big step up from most menial work. It was a job

a man could brag about, one he used familial or ethnic or political connections to arrange. It paid him $75 a month or more and
earned him the respect of the men at the station, the gratitude of
the public, and the admiration of the girls and their mothers.

Walking the tight circle with Schaefer were two young women,
sisters of other firemen. They'd brought him supper from the Ble-
nis House hotel down the street and across the river, a small fee to
pay for the magnificent view they now enjoyed. Schaefer lived in
a boardinghouse on the South Side, beyond the business district,
where he roomed with a policeman, a laborer, and a sign painter.
But his true home was his station, where he often slept and more
often ate—unless he was posted here.

In this era of breakneck technological progress just before the
invention of the skyscraper—an invention that would make its first
appearance four blocks south of where Schaefer now stood—the
courthouse was an anachronism: an archaic, quasi-medieval lump
of dirty gray stone that served as a bureaucratic battlement, a vast
information warehouse, and, above all, a testament to Chicago's
rising commercial supremacy over the middle and western portions
of the United States. The courthouse was an ugly building, but a
broad-shouldered kind of ugly that Chicagoans could appreciate.
In the five stories beneath Mathias Schaefer's feet, one and a half
of which lay underground, the political and administrative engines
of Chicago churned. Here were located the central offices of the
police and fire departments, the mayor's office, the chambers of the
Common Council and the Board of Public Works, the city's courts,
its law library, its jail, and, not least, every scrap of paper bearing
every real estate and tax record for the city of Chicago.

The only piece of the building that might be described as elegant
was its cupola, a cylindrical two-story tower ringed with rounded
windows and a balustraded balcony, above which was housed the
courthouse's giant bell. Beneath the bell, down a broad stairway and
occupying the lower half of the cupola, sat the circular telegraph
room, where signals were collected from 172 numbered fire alarm
boxes scattered around the city. Attached to drugstores, saloons,
and other establishments, or placed inside fire stations, each of

these boxes operated with the turn of a key and a single pull of an iron lever. The newfangled electrical model—the old ones used an unreliable hand crank—had been installed that summer, the keys entrusted to well-known men in their neighborhoods.

The telegraph room of the courthouse held twenty-five relays that could send a signal out from the building and sound a series of tones in any or all of the city's twenty-five fire stations. All these lines, incoming and outgoing, a system of wires snaking through the city on white-pine posts, converged just below Mathias Schaefer. There, in the middle of the telegraph room, sat William Brown, the spider waiting at the center of this quivering electronic web. Brown entertained his own guest, and from below Schaefer came the soft strum of a guitar.

The two men operated in tandem. William Brown's job was to send and receive the alarm signals and to set the bell to tolling. Schaefer's task was to circle the cupola and watch over the city, to decide what was a fire and what wasn't and then to decide where the fire was. Discernment was everything. Care was needed not to mistake the orange glow of a gasworks or the smoke from a small factory for a genuine event. To call down a false alarm was embarrassing and unprofessional. But more to the point, it was dangerous.

The job was difficult enough in the day, but at night the city seen from up high, especially on a Sunday, was a sea of darkness littered with an intermittent confusion of gaslights, lanterns, and candlelit windowpanes. To round out the fire department's night watch, additional observers stood in enclosures atop each of the city's sixteen steam-engine stations during the hours after dark. But all these other sentries were as thrushes to Schaefer's hawk. His was the only viewpoint that encompassed the entire city.

Many others had walked this cupola balcony before Schaefer, but none would afterward. If this Sunday evening in October 1871 was the last moment in the life of old Chicago—its last breath, as it were—then Mathias Schaefer might be considered the last person to see old Chicago alive.

The precious few records that have survived to reveal Schaefer's life and character indicate that he was honest and conscientious.

His testimony at the post-fire inquiry would reveal that much. But in this quiet moment under the stars, suspended over the cliff edge of history, what sense did he possess of Chicago's place in the universe? Here he stood, at the center of the city that sat at the center of the United States, a country that was waking up, day by day and dollar by dollar, to the proposition that it might soon stand at the center of the world.

The city beneath his feet was awash in money. Not with money handed down through long generations, or money made on the stock market, but with money amassed through the sale and exchange of tangible things: pigs, steers and heifers, lumber, grain, land, and all the dry goods necessary to support the pell-mell growth of the city. The men who'd made the lion's share of this money were factory owners, wholesalers, merchants, railroad builders, and real estate tycoons, and they'd built their fortunes in public view, most within recent memory. They had come to Chicago well after its birth; they were a transplanted Yankee elite, a relocated eastern establishment. Most of them had arrived from New York and the New England or Mid-Atlantic states, and most of them felt that this heritage made them special, that building Chicago had been their unique task, and that they'd done it especially well. They sat on the boards of a dizzying array of organizations—railroad companies, insurance companies, banks, asylums, private charities, children's homes, libraries, schools—with memberships that overlapped so much that they became de facto social clubs of massive influence. Some were Republicans and some were Democrats, and for the first thirty-four years of Chicago's existence successful businessmen had traded the mayor's office back and forth as if it were a choice piece of riverfront land.

The growth of the city had taken place in three phases: one frontier settlement period beginning with the incorporation of the city in 1837 and ending with the coming of the railroad and telegraph in 1848; then a period, ending with the coming of the Civil War, during which the city passed St. Louis and New Orleans to establish itself as the commercial hub of the American interior; and then the period encompassing the Civil War and its aftermath, marked by an astonishing expansion in human and financial capital. Since the first shots were fired at Fort Sumter, the city had added more than 200,000 people, more than 70 percent of them immigrants, whom the Yankee elite watched with mistrust and condescension even as their businesses reaped the benefits of the influx in cheap, willing, and always-available labor. The mantra of the city's elite was a belief in the unfettered free market—the right of a business owner to pay whatever wages the supply of workers could support, the right of a landlord to raise rents as high as the demand allowed, the right of everyone to choose if and when and how they might help the less fortunate—and that mantra had gone for the most part unchallenged by rich and poor alike during the city's history. In comparison to eastern cities of similar size—and especially in comparison to the large urban centers of Europe—class conflict was a muted force in Chicago politics. The rapid growth of the city meant that the poor and foreign of Chicago could still recognize in their employers a possible version of their own future progress, from renters to homeowners, from employee to employer, from naive new settler to seasoned old-timer.

By 1871, Chicago had become the country's busiest, most populous, and most important link in a never-ending chain of goods and materials that bound the Eastern Seaboard to western farms and fields, and the United States to Europe and Asia. Chicago was a place always receiving or offering, accepting or sending, taking or giving. Up the river, down the lake, across the land came tangible goods, more than twenty million tons every day disgorged into its lumberyards, stockyards, grain elevators, and warehouses. Every day, likewise, a roughly equal amount of material moved out. No one in any stratum of society who arrived in the city for the first time during these decades of runaway growth was immune to the transactional mania of the place. Chicago processed raw materials with a hunger that excited every one of its residents and shocked many visitors. Mathias Schaefer's night-shrouded vista in this moment encompassed a fast-growing young American city. But with a small nudge of the imagination, it could also be said to include the entire country and much of the rest of the world.

To his east, past the gilded townhomes of millionaire business-men along the shore and the Illinois Central depot at the break-water, lay Lake Michigan, and beyond that, the rest of the Great Lakes, all the manufacturing East, then the Atlantic Ocean and Europe, a vast geography that fed Chicago's docks and rail termi-nals with new foods, fashions, factory goods, and people. To his west, past the modest, crowded neighborhoods of Irish and Bohe-mians, lay the prairie, the Mississippi River, and the newly settled farm and ranch country beyond, sending in its endless orders for Chicago-made farm implements, making its innumerable pur-chases from Chicago-based household-goods catalogs, satisfying its unceasing demand for Chicago-cut lumber.

To Schaefer's south lay the city's powerful business district, its banks and hotels and concert halls, and beyond those lay the post-war South, the lucrative markets in sugar, cotton, tobacco, and molasses reopened in full to Chicago at the end of the Civil War. To his north, finally, beyond the trim and tidy German blocks and the urban villas of the city's Old Settlers and business barons, lay the forests of Wisconsin and Michigan, shipping 170 million board feet of lumber to Chicago every month that the rivers were open, from April until October. Great flotillas of denuded tree trunks floated down the Illinois and Michigan Canal skirting Lake Michigan for hundreds of miles, from Wisconsin towns named Manitowoc, Chippewa Falls, Green Bay, and Peshtigo, or from Michigan ham-lets called Whitehall, Lincoln, Traverse City, White Lake, Grand Haven, and Muskegon.

The trees sacrificed to create all this lumber were magnificent, lofty soft pines that America would never see again. A hundred feet and higher they rose, five feet in diameter, sprouting from thick, endless forests full of wolves and moose and bears, species that each spring retreated farther to the north and west at the returning sound of the ax and saw. Wisconsin and Michigan pine was pliant, yielding wood with few knots: clear, soft, light, and strong, workable by hand or by even the most threadbare of mills.

The thousands of men who cut these trees in northern climes and floated them on their way down the lake were for the most part

French Canadians, Scandinavians, and former New Englanders, while the thousands of men who handled them at the docks along the Chicago River were mostly Bohemians, or Irishmen, or Blacks, almost all of them post–Civil War newcomers to the city. They worked for meager pay in teams segregated by race and ethnicity as they made plans to move on and up to better jobs as drovers, carters, draymen, railroad workers, or coal haulers.

The wood, like everything else in Chicago, *moved*. It came in on the water, it was processed, it rose in its stacks, and then it went out on the railroad lines that ran behind every lumber lot along the southern branch of the Chicago River. The market for Chicago's wood extended everywhere the railroad went, and by 1871 the railroad went almost everywhere. An order of Chicago wood sent out west was sometimes intended to build cattle fences and railroad ties, but more often it was earmarked for barns, churches, stores, and above all houses. To that customer in the hinterland, the train from Chicago carried not just an order of lumber but the future.

Chicago's lumber also built Chicago itself. Between 1850, when Chicago was home to twenty-four thousand people, and 1871, when it housed fourteen times that number, a substantial portion of this wood left the lumberyards not by barge or train but by cart, or wagon, or even hand, destined for building lots within the city itself. The endless inventory of pine just down the street, and the sizable amount of land still available within the city limits, especially on the West Side, meant that wooden sheds, barns, and town houses proliferated like wildflowers. In 1871, homeownership in Chicago was accessible to a wider swath of the population than in any other city in America.

A brick home, even of modest size, was an investment of at least $1,000, and construction in stone was reserved for the city's richest families. But $300 or $400 could buy a respectable, if cramped, lot and all the wood needed for a small cottage, while $600 or $700 bought a comfortable two-story house. Tightly packed streets encroached on the prairie to the west and to the south, while spacious, tree-lined avenues reached northward along the lakeshore. In the eastern half of the North Division, where many of the most well-to-do residents lived, three or four houses, or even just one, might complete an entire city block. In wide swaths of the West Division, close to the river, a similar parcel might contain twelve, twenty, even forty houses, in addition to a like number of barns, sheds, and coops.

Almost all the houses in the West Division were made of pine-wood. Balloon-frame construction transformed America. Unlike a timber-frame or a platform-frame building, a balloon frame was built out of long pinewood two-by-fours that ran from the founda-tion of the house to the roof, however high that roof was. This was a cheap and speedy way to build, but it also meant that many such buildings were wrapped tight in a skin that turned their walls into ready-made wooden chimneys, with no outlet for air at the top. As a pipeman, Mathias Schaefer had formed an intimate familiarity with the way such structures burned: hot and swift. A small piece of burning pine was easily lifted high into the wind. A building built of brick or stone burned slowly, stubbornly, crumbling in on itself, while a balloon-frame structure blew apart, in small pieces, like the seeds of a dandelion before a child's breath.

Many of the city's warehouses, hotels, and factories were sheathed in brickwork or stone, but these sturdy, reassuring veneers often concealed balloon-frame skeletons made of wood. Or, if yours were the rare structural walls made of brick, your neighbors' on all sides might still be made of wood. Where the poor lived, the wooden sidewalks attached to their homes might rise as many as six feet above the street, creating a dangerous enclosed airspace beneath their feet. Where the rich lived, worked, and shopped, even the street might be made of wood and elevated above the mud.

Cities visited by so-called natural disasters always turn out to have planted the fertile seeds of their own destruction, and Chicago in 1871 was no exception. The city's firefighting force was far too small, its tolerance of wood buildings too entrenched, its belief that the worst couldn't happen too sanguine. Seen from the distance of history, this ordinary pipeman walking his tight circle with the splendid view and chatting with two excited young women would make a crucial mistake, yes. But perhaps, in the end, his was only the final, and the smallest, in a long chain of mistakes.

Half a mile to the west of the courthouse lay the charred remains of the Lull and Holmes planing mill in the heart of Red Flash. Even after the previous night's blaze had been tamed, the block still smoked and smoldered. With the wind high and the night dark, no moon yet above the horizon, the remnants of the Red Flash blaze created a fitful, glowing font of rising smoke, beyond which Mathias Schaefer could be sure of little. For the length of this night's courthouse watch, he would have to remind himself not to confuse that glow and smoke for a new fire.

At some moment between nine o'clock and nine ten, as they stood on the north side of the cupola, Schaefer's guests asked him about a steady pinprick of brightness away and off to their left, over the river in the West Division, north of but not so far away from Red Flash. Together the three peered with care at a small smudge of orange in a sea of black. The People's Gas Light and Coke Company on Washington Street, Schaefer decided, running its boiler through the night. He watched for a few minutes more, and then, satisfied with his judgment, returned his attention to his guests. Turning slowly around the balcony, the companions circled to their right, to the east, as Schaefer answered questions about the imposing new clock above them, sixteen feet high with faces on four sides and a mechanism that rattled and hummed atop their conversation.

Another minute or so passed before their slow stroll brought them back to the southwestern curve of the walkway. There, beyond the smoldering ruins, to the south this time: another orange light, small but bright, beyond and to the left of Red Flash, pulsing behind the thin tendrils of smoke put out by ruins of that fire. A separate light, no doubt, in the inky black where the immigrant shanties pressed close one on another.

A fire, for certain. But just how close to Red Flash? Distances were difficult to ascertain under normal conditions, and these were not normal conditions. Schaefer now had a decision to make. He raised a spyglass to one eye, lowered it again. After a short time—for time was always of the essence—he called down to William Brown and told him to strike 342, the box at Halsted and Canalport, out toward the city's southern limit.

Brown called up to say that he'd been watching the same spot of light from his own window, also taking care to differentiate it from the Red Flash ruins, having the same troubles putting a fix on it. Could Schaefer confirm? Three forty-two? Schaefer did confirm, and Brown set the bell's mechanism. Fifty-five hundred pounds of brass and iron, in the cupola just over their heads, now came to ponderous life, operated by a small lever connected to a much larger motor.

Three booming rings, then a pause, four rings, a pause, two rings. The sound of the big bell put smaller alarms into motion all over the West Side of the city, including those inside the same station houses that had responded to the Red Flash fire the night before. In these stations, those firemen who hadn't gone home were sleeping off the previous day's work. Some had fallen asleep minutes earlier, getting their first rest in more than twenty-four hours. Too many pumps and ladders and hose still sat uncleaned and unrepaired. The men of the *Little Giant* had just come in from tamping down the last flames of Red Flash. And a few of the firemen now at the stations were undoubtedly nursing hangovers.

Schaefer would have known or guessed at all of this, and he would have worried. And as he worried, an insistent doubt itched at his mind. Was the light growing? Moving? Had he seen right? As the small illumination grew and shifted in the dark distance and smoke began to smudge the distant air, the scale of the image in front of his eyes continued to resolve into ominous clarity. Not two minutes after calling down his initial sighting, Schaefer realized he'd made an error.

Not 342. Whereas Schaefer's first call had identified the fire as two miles away from the courthouse, he now realized the flames were closer than he'd first imagined: perhaps not even ten blocks south of Lull and Holmes, a mile away from his position rather than two.

Schaefer called down again to Brown. He'd made a mistake, he said. The number ought instead to be 319, a box a quarter mile from where he now believed the fire was burning.

Below, William Brown digested Schaefer's information for a moment, and then called back up.

"I can't alter it now," he said.

For the rest of his life, Schaefer would offer no public comment, much less judgment, on Brown's decision not to change the alarm. But Brown would later testify that regulations and common practice forbade him to do so. Engines and hose carts had already been dispatched, were already on their way to Canalport and Halsted. Most would pass the fire on the way. A new alarm would only confuse them, if the alarm even reached them in time. Besides, to Brown, the new blaze didn't have the look of a big boiler fire, or a gasworks, or a lumberyard. No explosions, no tall jets of flame. A fire out there in the shanties and hay barns of the poorer class of Chicago's citizenry would be found and put out in short order. Such fires always were.

≋ 2 ≋

ONE MILE to the southwest of the courthouse, across the southern branch of the Chicago River and across a wide gulf of
wealth, language, history, and custom, lay DeKoven Street. If
Schaefer and his guests on this windy Sunday evening were granted
the spectacle of all of Chicago laid out at their feet from a splendid
height, DeKoven Street provided no view of any part of the city
other than itself. Like most of the southern reaches of the West
Side, the neighborhood was home to thousands of people who
worked long hours for low pay to nourish its ever-hungry industries. As Mathias Schaefer watched over Chicago, assuming a god's
perch, Catherine Leary lay in bed, very much a mortal.

The young reporter Ed Chamberlin would soon describe the
Learys' environs as "a *terra incognita* to respectable Chicagoans,"
a neighborhood "thickly studded with one-story frame dwellings, cow-stables, pig-sties, corn-cribs, sheds innumerable; every
wretched building within four feet of its neighbor, and everything
of wood—not a brick or a stone in the whole area." His sneering
description represented the view of many of the city's well-to-do
residents. But if life on DeKoven Street was cramped, it wasn't
small or empty. There were rough neighborhoods in Chicago,
places where a well-dressed outsider couldn't walk in safety, but
the Learys' neighborhood wasn't one of them. In fact, DeKoven
Street represented everything Chicago's Yankee establishment
said an immigrant neighborhood should be: a place full of wage
earners working long hours to lift themselves up, planning for their

own slow but sure advancement. In the Learys' city ward, eight of nine residents were immigrants, but only one in seven owned property, and this made the Learys not types but archetypes: hard and uncomplaining workers who had saved enough money to build their own small house and who rented out another for additional income. Kate fed her cows timothy hay, not the unhealthy distillery slops that poorer milk peddlers were sometimes forced to use, and she did a good business.

Two houses shared 137 DeKoven Street, the Learys' address, on the north side of the street between Jefferson and Clinton. Both were small square two-room shacks, one right behind the other, with an arm's width of space in between. In the front house, facing the street, lived the McLaughlins, who paid rent to Kate and Patrick. Patrick McLaughlin, the father, was a laborer and an ace fiddle player, while Catherine McLaughlin, the mother, worked as a seamstress. Their only child, a girl named Annie, was five years old.

Kate and Patrick Leary did not read or write, but their five children, three boys and two girls, all under fifteen in 1871, would. They expected that their children would rise in the world, and in the end they did. The family was the definition of good people—hardworking, sociable, and well liked, with friends up and down the street and throughout the blocks around them. Catherine McLaughlin said of Kate that "an honester woman I never would ask to live with," and the sentiment seemed common.

The densely populated blocks in the southern half of the West Division, close to the lumberyards and train tracks along the Chicago River, were called "Irish," and the neighborhood's surnames included Daltons, Donovans, Finnegans, Fitzpatricks, Hoolihans, and Kellys. But the names in the city directory attached to addresses along DeKoven, Taylor, Jefferson, and Clinton Streets also included Uhers and Urbans, Vaneks and Vesillis, Weatherbys and Welshes. More so than language, history, or culture, what bound these families together was *work*. Fathers worked, mothers worked, children worked.

The men worked ten- or twelve- or fourteen-hour days from Monday to Saturday at thousands of different occupations: teamsters, shoemakers, tailors, brush makers, brewers, cigar makers, varnishers, painters, wagonmakers, milliners, stonecutters, carpenters, plumbers, peddlers, dyers, blacksmiths, butchers, machinists, musicians, draymen, plasterers, clerks, saddlers, roofers, gas fitters. The neighborhood's saloon keepers owned their own businesses, as did the druggists and grocers, but for the most part the Learys' neighbors toiled for the elevation of other men's names. Many of the neighborhood's younger women joined the hordes that traveled every morning over to the South Side, to clerk in notions stores or to sit on assembly lines, while older women, mothers and grandmothers, stayed at home and took in sewing and laundry, sold milk and eggs, cleaned houses and churches.

Even by 1871, Chicago's efficiency at bringing in and making use of livestock, wheat, and lumber had become legend. But its real genius, for good and for ill, was the way it brought in and used people. Kate and Patrick first appear on the city's census rolls in 1857, after a time in Pennsylvania; most likely they were escapees from Ireland's potato blight. Every individual emigration from Europe was its own personal epic, but as far as the newspapermen and novelists of the time were concerned, an immigrant's history was something that began when she set foot on American soil. Even amid the geyser of post-fire interest in the Learys' lives, no one—not a single reporter or contemporaneous historian—would bother to delve into the past of the family they so profitably exploited.

In October 1848, when the first railroad had come through town, there had been around 4,000 foreign-born people living in Chicago. Twenty-three years later, on the brink of the Great Fire, there were more than 150,000—about half of the city's population. Add to that number the additional hundreds of thousands who by 1871 had already spent time in the city on their way to destinations farther west, and all this inflow created a polyglot, polyethnic, polymorphous city that was more immigrant in proportions and in flavor, at this moment in history, than even New York City or London.

Politics meant little to people like the Learys. Patrick, like all adult men in the city, was able to vote, and because he owned property, he was also a taxpayer. But those taxes were minimal and provided for only the most basic of public works, as well as for the departments of police, fire, and health. For the most part, Chicago's government left the poor alone, for better and for worse. If the sidewalks of DeKoven Street needed repairs, the residents of DeKoven Street would band together to pay for the materials and do the work themselves. If Patrick were to suffer a debilitating injury, private charities or the church, or his neighbors, would step in. If one of the tanneries or glue factories or lard-rendering facilities nearby were to foul the river, as happened often, the city's remedy was to try to charge the responsible business owners for the cleanup, because few public funds existed for that purpose. Landlords—a group that included the Learys—could charge whatever rent the market bore, and employers could demand whatever hours and pay whatever wages an employee might accept.

The city could function this way, with little attention to a larger public interest, because the postwar economy was strong and Chicago was full of people who for the most part believed they'd entered into a fair bargain and were destined for better things. Jobs for newcomers from afar were abundant. Those jobs might be grueling and low paying, but the bedrock of the city in 1871 was not its attention to the present but its belief in the future. A proprietorial spirit reigned. The rags-to-riches tales of Horatio Alger were read everywhere. The size of the immigrant neighborhoods and the accumulation of their needs ensured that a small businessman from Bohemia or Germany could most often find the friends and neighbors necessary to keep his storefront from going under. And the amount of raw material passing through the city meant that a job as a cart driver, lumber shover, or factory hand was almost always available.

Saturday was payday, Chicago's busiest night. The saloons were packed late into the evening, and the whorehouses and faro dens were just as full. The police—many of whom hailed from the same kinds of poor and immigrant communities that surrounded the Learys—leaned in a live-and-let-live direction. Vice laws were enforced and the most visible excesses curbed when a point needed making, but seldom otherwise. The temperance groups were always a nuisance, but no one believed that anyone in city government would—or even could—attempt to place any serious brake on the drinking habits of the Irish and the Germans, who were united by their love of a weekend mug of beer, if by little else.

On Sundays, the working-class neighborhoods took their ease. Many residents worshipped in the mornings, while others, especially the men, slept. Mothers went calling on friends and relations for blocks in every direction while their children were set free to play along the river or chase one another through the streets and alleys. In the afternoon, the men returned to the saloons to sit and socialize, where they drank, played cards, talked about ward politics and international events, and compared opportunities for advancement. When evening came, families met again at home and sat on their porches, told stories and sang, ate supper, fell asleep.

This Sunday was no different. The night was warm for October, the temperature in the seventies, enough to allow people to keep their doors and windows open and to loiter outside. The wind was up, the air dry and dusty.

The house of the McLaughlins, the Learys' tenants, was the liveliest on the block. Catherine McLaughlin's brother was newly arrived from Ireland, and the family performed the hallowed Irish ritual of welcoming the greenhorn with a beer and music party, a "shin-dig" as *The Chicago Times* called it. They'd all eaten supper at a neighbor's and were now at their own home again, celebrating yet another of the city's frequent four-thousand-mile reunions. Their guests included eight boys and two girls, a number of adult relatives and neighbors, and the newcomer. The smell of pine shavings and cow dung and cooking and dust filled the air, while the noise of laughter and singing and Patrick McLaughlin's fiddle filled the street. Other neighbors stopped by to say hello and to greet the greenhorn. Across the way, young men leaned on the sidewalk railing and did nothing in particular. The sound was pleasant and so was the night. Their houses were small, but the outdoors was not. Every so often a man emerged from the McLaughlins' house and walked down the block to the west, shoes pattering on the street's raised wooden sidewalks, soon to return with another half gallon or two of beer from Frank Schultz's saloon on the corner.

Privacy was something Chicago's poor learned to live without. Kate lay in bed, close to sleep, listening to the McLaughlins' revelry through the pinewood walls while the rest of her family also prepared to turn in. Patrick McLaughlin's fiddle went quiet early, at about eight o'clock, after which the drone of conversation next door became Kate's lullaby. At four thirty that afternoon she had fed the cows in the barn, at seven the horse. The next morning, she would need to wake up well before dawn to milk her cows, feed her children, and send her husband off to work, before heading off on her own rounds to peddle her milk. The sounds from the McLaughlins' party ebbed and rose alongside the other sounds of the neighborhood: the shutting of a door, the low of a cow, the whinny of a horse, the bark of a dog, all these mixed with laughter, conversation, the occasional shout.

As Kate drifted away into sleep, a few minutes short of nine o'clock, she and her children were startled by a panicked banging at their door. Someone was shouting. A scuffle of feet, running, other shouts. Then she heard a familiar voice in a clipped, panicked exchange with her husband: that of Daniel Sullivan, the young man with a wooden leg and nickname of Peg Leg, one of Catherine Sullivan's many boys, who lived right across the street. Something had agitated him, badly. Peg Leg knew the block well and would not raise a cry unless the danger was real. He knew his neighbors. He loved to talk; he knew everyone. He was around a lot, and sometimes he and his friends used the Learys' barn for a late-night smoke.

A clatter. More footsteps. Then Patrick was back in the room, tugging at the children.

"Kate," he said. "The barn's afire!"

Whatever myriad thoughts went through Kate Leary's head in the minutes that followed as she scrambled out of bed and outside, two are certain. One was of the contents in and around her barn. Five cows and a calf. A horse, wagon, and harness. Two tons of coal and two tons of timothy hay, laid in for the winter ahead. Another cow, tied to a fence along the alley. She also knew that the barn held a barrelful of wood shavings from one of the nearby wood mills. All the families in the neighborhood used the shavings as kindling for their stoves, and the mills were happy to give their excess away or sell it for a few nickels. To Kate, the fates of the Learys' house and that of the McLaughlins were, in many ways, immaterial. The barn and its contents represented the lion's share of the Learys' capital and a large part of their living. The house would not be possible without the barn.

The second thought was that none of it, "not five cents," as Kate would later say, was insured.

By the time she stepped outside her house, she would later testify, the fire was working on three buildings: her barn, the Murrays' barn one lot to the west, and the Daltons' storage shed to the east. These structures bordered the narrow alley that ran between the properties on the north side of DeKoven and those on the south side of Taylor. As she stood outside her house, Kate's only impression was that the blaze was already very bright and very hot and spreading fast. As she would later describe the chaos, "The wind blowed every way. You could not tell one way more than the other way. The fire went just the same as you would clap your two hands together."

She took a few steps toward her barn, thinking that she might try to save the new wagon and an animal or two, but the heat was too intense and the smoke too thick. Instead, she took hold of one of her younger children, while Patrick gathered the others, and together they all moved around to the front of the house, where they found the three McLaughlins and their new arrival outside. No greenhorn would ever receive a more memorable welcome to Chicago.

Kate didn't put together, or care, that the strength and direction of the wind, spiriting the flames northward away from her and into the alley that ran behind her lot, might very well spare her house. One of the McLaughlin brothers stood in a vacant lot across DeKoven, holding his five-year-old nephew in one arm and some of the family's clothes in the other. Others tended to Catherine McLaughlin, who had fainted dead away. Kate took in all of this and then looked down the street three lots to the west, to the corner with Jefferson. There she could see the two-story row of houses called Turner's block, occupied on its corner by Schultz's saloon. To her horror, flames began to flutter out of a second-floor window.

Several water pumps dotted DeKoven, including one on either side of her house. These were fed by the city's wooden mains and produced water of dubious quality, but in the parts of the city not outfitted for plumbing, which was most of the city, they had to serve. The previous spring, Chicago had borne witness to one of the great engineering feats of the era, when an engineer named Ellis Chesbrough had managed to reverse the flow of the Chicago River, pulling the deeper and cleaner waters of Lake Michigan through the city and depositing them into the Illinois and Michigan Canal instead of the other way around. His success was partial, and the river would take decades to fully accept the new flow, but during the summer and fall of this year families like the Learys had found fewer small fish coming through the line when they gathered water to make their suppers or take their baths. Now these pumps, their pressure far too feeble for the use of firemen, became a lifeline in the effort to save the Learys' final piece of salvageable property.

As Kate looked on, her husband and Patrick McLaughlin emerged from their houses. Both buildings were still intact but were surrounded by flames. Each man carried his wife's washtub, and both shouted at their guests and neighbors for help. Patrick McLaughlin had been sick all day with a cold, perhaps accounting for the early end to his fiddling, but he found plenty of energy now. Kate would later describe "hundreds of men" all working to pour water on the two houses. This was an exaggeration, but many in the neighborhood did what they could for the Learys. Patrick McLaughlin and Patrick Leary would draw water into the tubs nonstop for the next three hours, a scene repeated by other men at other houses on the south side of the street, at the Sullivans', and up and down the block.

When her barn was fully aflame, perhaps ten minutes later,

Kate saw men in tall hats, firemen, come running past her from the direction of Schultz's saloon. Two or three of them appeared, many fewer than she would have expected, trailing a five-hundred-foot length of hose behind them and dashing between her house and the Daltons' until they came close enough to put a vigorous spray into the heart of the fire. Kate didn't have any frame of reference to measure the speed of the fire department's arrival, though it didn't seem to her especially quick or slow. Weariness, panic, and despair had accumulated, and her wits deserted her. "I got frightened," she said later. "I got so excited that I could not tell anything about the fire."

She was in a private place, descending into shock. Her barn was gone, her animals were dead or gone, her house might burn. The arrival of the pipemen signaled hope to other residents of her block and to those living on Taylor, the next street up. The fire department was here, and the fire department always put out the fire. But whether one block or two burned, or for that matter the entire city, Kate's loss was almost complete. The first tragedy of the Great Chicago Fire was hers. Had she known there was far worse to come, who knows but that she might have joined her neighbor, friend, and tenant Catherine McLaughlin on the ground in unconsciousness. Instead, she watched her husband and tenant wet down her house, watched the fire spread, saw the sky start to fill with a rain of sparks, and waited for a second fire engine to arrive.

ALL THAT SUNDAY, before the Learys' barn caught fire, Billy Musham's *Little Giant* and its company had lingered at the site of the Red Flash blaze, wetting down the smoking detritus, watching for reignitions, and guarding against curious sightseers and opportunistic arsonists. As the ruins had cooled and calmed, one by one the ladders, hose carts, and other engines had gone away to more distant stations. Only Christian Schimmels's *Chicago* was located closer to Red Flash than the *Little Giant*, but the damaged *Chicago* had been sent home well before dawn.

At about eight o'clock at night, Musham's men decoupled their hoses from the hydrants, closed the boiler door, reeled in their lines, and hitched up their horses for the twelve-block ride back south to Jefferson and Twelfth. They returned to their station at eight thirty, twenty-two sleepless hours after the courthouse bell directing them to Red Flash had first sounded the sequence 2, 4, 8.

Too much was asked of these firemen. But then, too much was asked of many people in Chicago. Theirs was dangerous work like other dangerous work, of which there was plenty to be had. The very commonplace nature of fire made the extinguishing of any single blaze an everyday event. In the sense that no fire had ever spread to destroy the entire city, the department was a complete success.

This success had helped to convince the forty aldermen on the city council that little more needed to be done to continue the victorious streak other than to scatter alarm boxes and hydrants around the city in a somewhat regular pattern, put a watchman on top of each of sixteen engine stations, and add a couple more on top of the courthouse. The department's official budget in 1871 amounted to around $440,000, and to raise that number any further, after it had already been raised a hundredfold since the start of the Civil War, was a political impossibility, no matter how fast the city was growing.

The equipment on which Musham and his fellow firemen relied was modern and effective: shining silver-and-black cast-iron steamers, hoses made of sewn leather sections bracketed with copper fastenings, brand-new hydrants that used a spring drain valve to resist freezing. Much of this inventory had been purchased by the city council after the Civil War, as the city grew by tens of thousands of residents every year and wooden houses went up with a speed that defied imagination. But there wasn't enough of any of it. Sixteen engines with one in reserve, six hose carts, four ladders, two hose elevators, and 219 men in total, 193 of them firemen on call: a total of one firefighting company for every forty-five hundred buildings in Chicago. About the only item the department had in overabundance was horses.

Billy Musham was a Scotch-Irish bear of a man, born in the city in 1839, when Chicago had been two years old, home to a few thousand people, and just a decade removed from its fur-trading incarnation. Educated at public school, apprenticed as a carpenter, he'd joined a hose company at sixteen and never looked back. His story was common, as was the danger he'd already faced. Six years earlier, at a bad fire on South Water Street, he'd been standing between two pipemen for the *Frank Sherman* when the walls had collapsed around them. Both pipemen had been killed on the spot and a fire warden disabled for life. Musham had spent many months recuperating from his own injuries, but he'd been the lucky one.

Not at any other moment during the summer and fall of 1871 had Musham's *Little Giant* and its men been in such disrepair. In the fight against the Red Flash fire, limits had been reached. Some of Musham's crew fell asleep after returning to the station. Some went to a pump or hydrant to salve smoke-reddened eyes swollen almost shut, running their faces under a stream of cool water. Some needed to eat. Protocols demanded that certain preparations now take place, but Musham knew that most of these steps would have to wait. Instead of demanding that all of his exhausted crew tend to the machines, he sent several of his men home. To do otherwise would have been cruel.

Perhaps half of the dozen or so firemen assigned to the station had stayed behind, reclining on cots or washing their blackened clothes and ash-coated bodies. Musham did order a fresh load of wood and coal installed in the engine, while its boiler was hooked up to a steam heater that churned under the floor of the station and kept the apparatus's pressure high in anticipation of a new alarm.

Sometime shortly after nine o'clock, a crewman named Joseph Lauf climbed to the roof of the station and then climbed again into a small, raised wooden cylinder that served as their watchtower. All the stations had one of these crow's nests, in one shape or another, and all of them were manned every night from dusk until dawn no matter how quiet the night or shorthanded the company.

In a dead-flat neighborhood filled with one- and two-story buildings, Lauf was able to see through the dark for half a mile or so in every direction. It took him all of one minute to turn his gaze to the north and spot a fire about six blocks away, perhaps closer. Nothing Lauf saw gave him reason to panic; the neighborhoods in that direction were tinder dry, but all the neighborhoods were tinder dry. The streets there were for the most part residential: no furniture factories, no coal sheds, no gasworks, no dangers outside the ordinary dangers. Still, a new alarm would be hard on the men. He called down to Musham. Someone packed the engine's fire-box with wood, while the foreman himself hitched and harnessed the horses. The checklist was short, and as they gathered their gear, the exhausted men counted on this new fire to be small and inconsequential.

As the doors swung open and the company pulled out of the station, horses straining, the bell from the courthouse began to sound. In the time it took to register its three numbers, the *Little Giant* covered two or three blocks. Three rings. Four. Two. This bad weekend for fires continued to blend into their bad week, month,

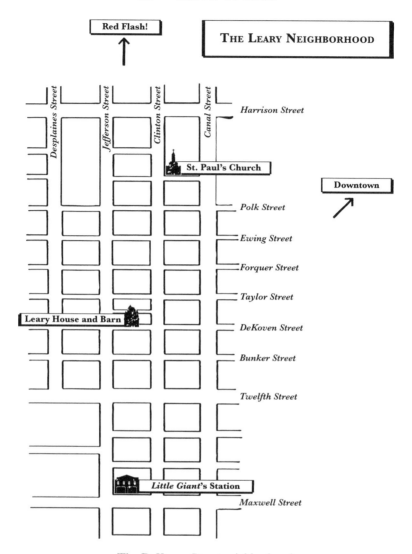

The DeKoven Street neighborhood

and year for fires, for the new sounding from the courthouse meant that the department might now be facing *two* new blazes, right on the heels of Red Flash. Box 342—the box called down in error by Mathias Schaefer—was a full mile to the *south* of the *Little Giant*'s station, in the other direction from the blaze Lauf had spotted. But Musham didn't even slow the *Little Giant,* much less turn his team around. The rule was that you went to the fire you could see. The fire Lauf had seen was to the north. Besides, people were beginning to move northward in bunches. And the firebugs always knew.

As Musham and his men shot straight up Jefferson, shouting at spectators to move aside, the glow in front of them became brighter and higher and wider. The men hung on to the engine as it jounced on the packed-dirt road, until the sudden crescendo of noise, heat, and activity all delivered to Musham the obvious message that he should stop at Jefferson's intersection with DeKoven, half a block to the west of the Learys' barn. "The fire," Musham wrote later, "was under such fierce headway that the region was illuminated almost as brightly as if by daylight."

His shorthanded crew leaped out and fixed their line to the hydrant on the southwest corner of the intersection, kitty-corner from Schultz's saloon, while the hose operators unwound their lines and fastened them to the engine. All the while, Musham assessed the situation and barked orders through his speaking horn. The placement of the fire in the middle of the block wasn't a help. Their hose would have to run a couple hundred feet down DeKoven and then back into the alley alongside the Learys' house. The longer a hose had to travel, the more sections that had to be cinched together, and the less pressure he could expect at the pipe end. Multiple sheds and barns were already ablaze, and the men of the *Little Giant* were coming at the fire from its lee side, from an upwind and not downwind direction, which meant that they could only chase after the blaze from behind and not face it head-on.

The other fire alarm, still ringing through the air, muddied the situation. Box 319 was one of the alarms for the Learys' neighborhood, but thanks to William Brown's fateful decision in the courthouse telegraph room to ignore Mathias Schaefer's correction, 319 never sounded. Musham knew that everything counted on the fact that other engine companies, more than one, would soon arrive on the other side of the fire. But Musham couldn't see the other side of the fire at all. If his was the only station so far responding from the south side of the fire, this was acceptable, as long as the opposite, downwind corner of the blaze was covered by more than one engine arriving from the north, in the direction of Red Flash.

He could, at least, count on the fact that engines from the northern stations on the West Side weren't going to continue past DeKoven to box 342 once they saw this fire.

Still, Musham would much rather have been able to see his fellow engine companies to coordinate with them. An even more immediate problem was that Musham had only two men to work his own pipe: himself and his assistant, John Campion. Rather than continue to assess the situation as foreman, he had no choice but to grab a hose and set up a stream on the Learys' barn and surrounding buildings. He and Campion ran their line in from the street, passing a dazed Kate Leary on the way. What Musham found in the alley worried him, but it didn't frighten him. A nasty fire, but not out of control. As Campion later put it, measuring the blaze in monetary terms, as Chicagoans liked to do, "One thousand dollars would have paid all losses thereby." The previous night's fire in Red Flash, they knew, had already cost a thousand times that amount.

As they put a stream on the Learys' barn, the hottest part of the fire, a familiar voice sounded behind them. This was Mathias Benner, one of three assistant marshals of the force, the man responsible for overseeing the six West Side stations. Benner's arrival meant that no longer was it Musham's responsibility to coordinate anything, which was important because the fire was "getting hot," as they liked to say. The first fire whorls, miniature cyclones of heat and smoke, began to stir, upping the force of the wind and lifting flaming debris higher into the air. Benner soon pressed several onlookers into service on Musham's hose so that the foreman himself could retreat from the alley and put a second line on Schultz's saloon. This was the first in a series of abandonments, movements out to the perimeter of the fire that left the interior of the block to its fate. Indeed, the citizens deputized by Benner soon dropped the overheated hose beside the Learys' house and ran back onto DeKoven.

Billy Musham also probably assumed that by placing the *Little Giant* on the southwestern corner of the fire, Benner knew that there were other engines to the north. Alas, Benner knew no such thing. For the rest of his life, Musham would blame the assistant marshal for making such a fateful misstep. But Benner had to play the odds. He couldn't afford the time it would take to decouple Musham's engine and move him all the way through the heat and smoke to the opposite corner of the block. Anyone in charge of fighting a Chicago fire had to tamp down thoughts of the more extreme possibilities. You could go mad pondering the what-ifs: had the hose been in good repair, had box 342 not sounded instead of 319, had there been enough men, had there, had there, had there.

If Billy Musham and Mathias Benner had known what was happening on the opposite side of the fire, their mood would have darkened. With the wind high and strong and the fire growing hotter and wider by the minute, Taylor Street, the northern boundary of the Learys' block, now became the first and, they hoped, last line of containment, playing the same role Jackson Street had the night before. But whereas the night before six fresh engines had played on the fire on Van Buren with twelve hoses, here on Taylor the job of fighting the blaze at its most dangerous point went to the most fatigued and damaged engine in the service. For ten decisive minutes, Christian Schimmels's crippled *Chicago* fought the northern line of the fire, alone and in dire need of repairs.

Schimmels was old German stock rather than Scotch-Irish, but that difference aside, he and Billy Musham seemed to be physical, temperamental, and professional carbon copies. Born in 1845 on Desplaines Street, just a few blocks away from the Learys' address, Schimmels had begun an apprenticeship as a carpenter, like Musham, had signed on with a hose company at sixteen, like Musham, and had risen to lead an engine company, like Musham. And like Musham, his boxy, powerful frame was topped by a broad, bearded face, a projection of manhood and authority that seems to have been a de facto requirement for the job. Schimmels had been in charge of the *Chicago* for three years now, commanding the engine house that sat on Jefferson Street near Van Buren, making it the closest station to Red Flash and one of the busiest in the city.

Schimmels, his men, and his machine had been on duty for seventy-two straight hours before they'd been sent home from Red Flash, and the courthouse bell sounding 342 interrupted the first sleep that many of his firefighters had taken in two or three days. Still, they were out of their station within minutes of the alarm, barreling south on Jefferson, a route that made them certain, in the telegraph operator William Brown's fateful words, to "pass the fire on their way." When they found the DeKoven fire and hooked on at Jefferson and Forquer, the fire was already bright over the center of the Learys' block. Though Billy Musham was by that time just two blocks away on Jefferson, a hundred yards straight to the south, Schimmels and the other men of the *Chicago* couldn't see the *Little Giant* through the smoke and the *Little Giant* couldn't see them.

In that moment Musham, like Schimmels, believed himself to be alone. But the *Little Giant* and the *Chicago*, at least, started the fight acting in tandem as they should have, if unwittingly. Musham from his plug across from Schultz's worked the source of the fire from its back end, while Schimmels fed a line several hundred feet eastward down Taylor, to the middle of the block, and faced the fire's advancing edge, where he hoped to draw a line of water in the dust and dirt until other engines arrived. They were "on their taps and on top of the fire," as the men liked to say. It was a hot one, but nothing they hadn't seen before.

The *Chicago*'s failure to hold the fire along Taylor Street was made of tragedy, a bit of comedy, and some irony as well. At fifty-two hundred pounds loaded with coal, it was the lightest, most mobile, and most maneuverable boiler in the force. On this night, though, the *Chicago* was in perhaps the worst condition of its life. Schimmels had a lot to accomplish in very little time, and things did not start well. After his pipemen were in position on Taylor in the middle of the block, his engineer, Henry Coleman, attached a line to the plug, cinched it tight, and opened the flow of water to test the pressure—at which the hose burst, popping its worn and weakened seams in several places all at once.

Schimmels enlisted a willing pack of outsiders to wrap the ruptures with blankets and weigh down the repaired sections with planks of wood ripped from fences and sidewalks. To no avail: the underheated boiler, fighting the leaky hose, couldn't raise the pressure to the point where a usable stream was produced on the pipe end. Coleman responded by trying to push as much water as possible through the line, but as the boiler strained higher and higher to do its job, his luck continued bad. Somewhere inside the *Chicago*'s six-foot-high cylinder of bright, polished silver steel, a solitary overworked spring came loose and brought the boiler's gear action to a stop, dropping the pressure in the hoses to zero. Schimmels sprinted back to the machine to find one of his men emptying the firebox with a small shovel, dumping the coal out onto the street, while the engineer, Coleman, faced the machine and weighed his options.

"Is it going to do any harm to run her?" Schimmels asked.

Coleman said that he didn't know. "It's running a big risk," he added. "I might smash that pump all to pieces."

"This is going to be a big fire," Schimmels said. "Smash her! We have got to run her and run the risk of its breaking her. Break her completely and then it is broke."

Coleman gave the spring a bang with his hammer to coax it back into place. The *Chicago* started to run again, but no one knew how well or for how long. Fire engines created steam by heating bituminous coal—or, in a pinch, anything else that might burn inside the "box" located under the engine's towering cast-iron water tank. To maintain the steam pressure created by boiling hundreds of gallons of water in that tank, this fire needed constant stoking and tending, even in the midst of a three-alarm blaze. Heating the box again would take five or even ten minutes, time they might not have. In front of Schimmels, the south side of Taylor Street was fast becoming engulfed in flames. Behind him lay the north side of Taylor, where the shanties and barns were letting off smoke, though none had yet caught fire. The whorls of smoke, flame, and heat from the interior of the Learys' block rose higher and faster every minute, until the sky overhead became a rain of sparks and black ash and small pieces of tinder.

Schimmels, like Musham, would maintain for many years afterward that during the first crucial, endless minutes of the fire his was the first and only engine on the scene. Both men had ignored the alarm for box 342, which was still ringing, still trying to direct them one mile to the south, to a quiet intersection at Halsted and

Canalport—Musham because his man, Lauf, had seen the fire and sent them in the correct direction, and Schimmels because his path to the incorrect location took him almost straight through the Learys' neighborhood.

Both foremen assumed that other engines had headed to the box to the south and, if there was indeed a blaze at Halsted and Canalport, would arrive at DeKoven Street late, or not at all. That was one truth. A second truth was that Schimmels and Musham were fighting in abysmal conditions—a neighborhood full of bone-dry pinewood and buffeted by a high wind—with damaged equipment and far too few men.

After twenty or so minutes, additional help finally arrived in the form of the *America,* which hooked on to a hydrant at Jefferson and Taylor, halfway on a straight line between the *Little Giant* and the *Chicago.* The problem: the *America* was a hose cart, not a steamer. A hose cart consisted of two horses pulling a large barrel coil of hose and was designed to fight a smaller fire or to supplement several engines fighting a bigger one. The *America* had no engine, no boiler, just two five-hundred-foot lengths of hose. Under normal circumstances, these carts were a crucial early element of a carefully choreographed routine. They could move quickly and start fighting the fire quickly, because their hose could be connected directly to a hydrant and did not depend on stoking and maintaining a boiler.

This is what the *America* did now, but in the absence of a working engine with which to couple, it was sacrificing more than three-fourths of the water pressure that a connection to a fully stoked boiler could provide. A hose company hooked to a hydrant could produce forty pounds of pressure, rather than the two hundred or more generated by the engines, and could throw a stream of water only fifty feet forward and perhaps twenty feet into the air. By itself, the *America* was best for wetting down buildings or keeping an overheated wood-burning stove or a smoking chimney from getting out of control, and not much more.

Still, with the *America* working in tandem with a functioning *Chicago,* and just one more engine like the *Chicago* on the scene, out of the sixteen in service, the firefighters could have run as many as ten hoses into the blaze all along Taylor between Jefferson and Clinton. With ten hoses, they could have blasted the houses and barns on both sides of the street with enough water to impede the fire's progress and take the battle to the Learys' barn until other engines arrived. Instead, the *America*, acting alone, was able to produce a few tepid arcs straight from the hydrant, its water scattering up and into the wind, turning to steam and mist before it could do much good.

Then, as the *Chicago* attached another length of hose and readied to lead in again, fear became farce when Schimmels realized that he'd left the station house with no spare supply of coal. Without that surplus of coal, there wasn't enough wood on hand to keep the new round of heat and steam up, especially since Henry Coleman, the engineer, had emptied some of the fuel out of the boiler's box before repairing the spring. Schimmels knew well that a beautiful giant heap of fresh coal sat at his station, so he sent one of his men on the nine-block dash to retrieve it. In the meantime, the rest of the company began to rip up sidewalks and fencing to stuff into his machine. Schimmels knew that this strategy wouldn't work for more than a few minutes, not for a fire that was shaping up as a three-alarm blaze every bit the equal of Red Flash.

At a point cruelly close to the nick of time, another West Side engine arrived—the *Illinois*, which had been delayed for five crucial minutes at the site of William Brown's first, incorrect, alarm. It was too little, too late. As Schimmels waited for the *Chicago* to get back to full strength, waited for his coal, waited for more engines to appear, one of the shanties fronting Taylor on the north side caught and began to blaze. This was only the second block to catch fire—Red Flash had consumed four the night before—but the advance felt much more threatening. Musham and Schimmels, still ignorant of each other, were outmanned and spread far too thin.

All along the north side of Taylor Street, other houses let off ever-thicker smoke, in imminent danger of catching. Schimmels and the *Chicago*'s men, along with the crew of the *Illinois*, turned on their heels to face north instead of south and put what water they could on the new line of fire with their underpowered boiler. More

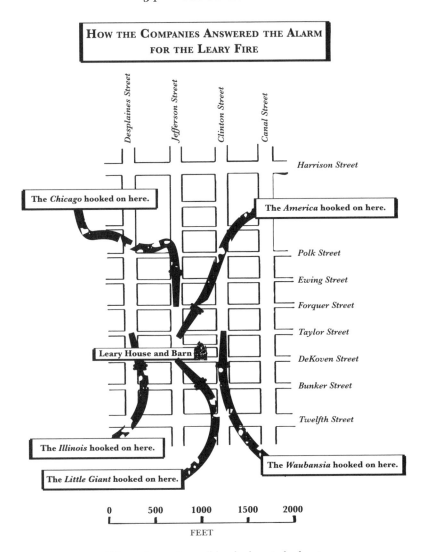

Where the engines all hooked up to hydrants

firemen began to appear out of the smoke from the east, leading in other hoses from another engine on the other side of the fire, from the hydrant at Clinton and Taylor. This was the crew of the *Waubansia*, which had been delayed by their own fruitless run to box 342, where they'd found peace and calm.

Schimmels now caught his first sight of the city's fire marshal, Robert Williams, who had arrived from his West Side home. Williams had already been on the site for some minutes, trying to ascertain the location of his various engine companies, but until this point all he'd been able to do was to bark at the men of the hose cart *America* to hang on for dear life and to spend a few minutes helping the depleted crew of the *Illinois* man its hose. When Schimmels explained the *Chicago*'s dire straits to Williams, the chief offered a few words of encouragement and ran off to check on the state of the *Waubansia*. Much would never be known about the origin and early spread of the Great Chicago Fire, but one thing is clear: fifteen irreplaceable minutes would likely have made all the difference. Bone tired as he was, Schimmels knew that had the four engines now on the site been able to take their places just that much earlier, the fire could have been quashed inside the single block where it had started.

The speed with which the houses along the north side of Taylor now began to ignite meant that the next street up, Forquer, would have to become the department's bulwark against total disaster, and indeed Robert Williams had already given the order that the line of defense be reorganized there. Four engines would now need to contain a fire raging through two full city blocks, a much less optimistic ratio than four engines to one block. And if Forquer was lost, Schimmels knew, so was the West Side, unless the rest of the force, all its South and West Side engines, should appear as if by magic in the next minute or two. He felt it as every foreman on the force would have in his situation: this cascading series of unfortunate accidents, uncontrollable elements, and insufficient preparation was adding up to an outright disaster. The danger was no longer confined to two blocks or even one entire neighborhood. The city itself, somewhere out there in the darkness beyond the flames licking at their faces, was now in real peril.

✤ 4 ✤

I N CHICAGO's municipal structure, a five-man board of police
and fire commissioners, appointed by the city council, oversaw the city's efforts at enforcing the law and fighting fires. The
board was administrative and fiduciary, tasked with the organization and funding of the police and fire departments and acting as a
political buffer between the mayor's office and the men tasked with
keeping the city safe. But when it came to staffing and running a
fire department of sufficient strength to protect all of Chicago, the
board's job consisted in tilting at windmills. The commissioners,
once appointed by the council, enjoyed immunity from interference
from the mayor's office, so they were often tarred as little political
bosses. But in most ways, their political clout was limited.

Every year, the commissioners went before the city's aldermen
to make the same set of recommendations. Every year, they recom-
mended that the city's water mains be replaced with wider, sturdier
ones; that the fire limits, the boundary within which pine-frame
construction was forbidden, be expanded; that thin, brittle Pittsburgh glass be banned from use within those fire limits; that building with brick be allowed only in the summer, when the mortar
would set more firmly and evenly; that party walls downtown contain no wood; that all buildings in business blocks contain fireproof
doors and iron shutters on their windows; that tar roofing, so easily
ignited by sparks and cinders, be banned; that the required number
of exit doors in new construction be increased; that new building
plans be submitted to the Board of Police and Fire for review prior

to construction; that firecrackers be banned; that the spots where the Chicago River met the city streets be kept clear of buildings or other obstructions; and that the city purchase a floating engine of a type already in use in Philadelphia and New York City, a contraption that would draw water from the river and throw it fifteen hundred feet in any direction.

No board member held the pipe end of a working hose or led men into a burning house. That responsibility belonged to three assistant marshals, one for each division of the city, who in turn reported to the fire chief, Robert Williams, a mayoral appointment, who cosigned the board's annual budget request and shared its bitter disappointment that none of the proposed measures over a decade or more were given serious consideration. "Private interests impel men to disregard the rights of the public," the board wrote, one year before the Great Fire, "and if we wait till everybody thinks their interests will be promoted by having fire limits, we fear we shall wait a great while, and suffer from many devastating fires in the interval." Why, asked the most powerful men of the city, should anyone pay taxes to save the uninsured, especially those uninsured who had built of wood in neighborhoods made of wood? Since 1858 the law had provided for a paid, professional firefighting force, and the law also provided for impressing citizens into duty. This was thought to be enough.

So Williams made do with the department's 193 firemen and its sixteen engines—six of which had responded to the Red Flash blaze and come home in the morning scorched and limping. Williams himself had returned to his house on the West Side from the Red Flash fire at seven in the morning, exhausted, looking for a wash and a meal and his first rest in more than twenty-four hours. Before he could settle in, though, he was called away to direct the fight against a small grain-elevator fire a few blocks distant, after which he came home again and went straight to bed while his wife went to morning church. At a quarter past two in the afternoon he woke after a couple hours' sleep, ate a late lunch, and received a family caller, before he left again to tour the engine stations hit hardest the night before. After a visit to the *Long John*'s house and an inventory of its damages, he rode back to the leveled and blackened site of the Lull and Holmes planing mill to confer with Billy Musham and see how the *Little Giant* was doing as it tamped down the blue flames that danced in the rubble of the large fires.

Finding the situation in Red Flash calm and the danger of reignition low, he'd left Musham and the men of the *Little Giant* to the mop-up. Williams stopped at home for supper before heading out yet again in search of Mathias Benner, the assistant marshal responsible for the West Side. Probably Williams wanted to share notes with Benner on the condition of the beleaguered West Side engines, but almost as soon as he'd set foot outside, the courthouse bell began ringing, for the third time that day.

The alarm turned out to be false, and an hour or so later Williams returned home again, for the fourth time that day. This was his life: one fire alarm to the next to the next. As he approached his door, he gripped his hat against the rising wind. The hat, and that wind, were details he would remember for the rest of his life. Stepping inside, he told his wife that he was going straight to bed, because he was certain that an overnight fire was bound to flare up, perhaps another big one like Red Flash. The conditions were right. He laid out a fresh set of firefighting gear and then retired, but not before asking his wife to close her door so that the gaslight she used for reading wouldn't keep him awake.

After no more than an hour, the bedroom door opened. "Robert, fire," said his wife, in a scene they'd played so many times that her announcement was routine. On went his pants, his boots, his canvas jacket, his high-peaked chief's helmet. As the courthouse bell began to ring, he picked up his speaking horn and descended to the sidewalk as the slow toll of the bell finished counting out three, four, two: 342, tolling trouble far down on the West Side.

He could see a glow to the south from where he stood on the curb waiting for the driver. The fire department was headquartered in the courthouse, three floors beneath where Mathias Schaefer at this very moment stood and pondered whether to call down to William Brown and correct a mistake, but Williams's own headquarters was his home on Madison and Peoria on the West Side, and he had a number of drivers at his call who would find him, whatever the purpose, and spirit him in whatever direction he needed to go.

Soon Williams pulled up at the corner of Jefferson and Taylor, where he found the hose cart *America* hooked to a hydrant and wondered where the rest of his force might be found. His confusion was the best evidence of how far gone the fire already was, of how much smoke, dust, and burning material already filled the air, and of how many spectators filled the streets and prevented an accurate assessment. For one block farther south Billy Musham's *Little Giant* was hooked to the hydrant on the southwestern side of the street and at that moment battling the blaze at its source, the Learys' barn. One block to the north, meanwhile, also out of Williams's sight, sat Christian Schimmels and the disabled *Chicago*, fighting a battle against its own balky boiler and its ruptured hose.

Williams jumped out and started running east on Taylor, following the *America*'s line of hose until he spotted the company's pipemen operating by themselves, directing an underpowered stream onto the houses on the south side of the street and wondering when the rest of the force would join them. This was very bad news. Already the fire had jumped the alley behind the Learys' barn and had caught in the houses on the south side of Taylor. He saw two men on the *America*'s hose, surrounded by "barns and a lot of little outhouses and fences" in the middle of "a regular nest of fire."

Reaching the *America*'s men, he stopped for a moment to call out to them, "Hold on to her, boys!" and then he kept running. He had to find other engines. Had he stopped longer to talk with the *America*'s crew, he might have learned not only that Schimmel's *Chicago* was on the scene but also that it was hobbled and capable of holding on to nothing. Instead, down Taylor he flew, to Clinton, "to see if there was anything else coming in." His worry increased moment by moment, for he didn't see any more engines "coming in" yet. Unaware that the *Waubansia* was a few minutes away, he hurried back to the *America*'s men, who in his blinkered awareness stood as the only barrier between the city and catastrophe.

"Hang on to her, boys," he said. "She is gaining on us."

Williams dashed back up Taylor to Jefferson, then ran another block farther west, where he finally encountered the men of the steamer *Illinois,* plugging in at the hydrant. This was far better than nothing, but the *Illinois* was another company short of men, so Williams had to take a position on the *Illinois's* pipe and plunge forward to a position at the rear of one of the burning buildings on the south side of Taylor, hoping in desperation to isolate the blaze to a single block. Behind him, Williams could see heavy smoke lifting off the buildings on the north side of Taylor and knew that they might go up in a matter of moments. He sent one of the *Illinois's* men to pull a second alarm that would call out the rest of the South Side companies: the *T. B. Brown,* the *William James,* and the *R. A. Williams,* which had been named after himself in honor of his promotion to chief. He then enlisted some outsiders to wet down the smoking buildings on the north side of Taylor Street.

With this decision by Williams to face north on Taylor instead of south, everything in the Learys' block was sacrificed. But the Learys and their neighbors were the least of the marshal's worries. Small, innocent errors compounded, one after the other. Seeing the imminent danger presented by the smoking buildings on Taylor and assuming, perhaps, that his engine would soon be ordered to move north a block or two, the *Illinois's* engineer cut his water off. In the minute or two that it took for Williams to relay the message to turn the water back on and continue to hold the line on Taylor, the first house on the north side of the street burst into flame.

Now, at last, Williams encountered Christian Schimmels and the handful of men of the *Chicago* who were gamely leading in another line of hose, still waiting on their fresh delivery of coal, and using wood planks in their boiler as a poor substitute. The blaze was "fast becoming a hell on earth," said one firefighter. A few minutes later, the smoke and flames had risen to new heights, the shower of burning brands and hot ash had grown denser, and most of the houses on the north side of Taylor were on fire. After a short, shouted exchange, Williams ran again, to the east. He spotted an engine on Taylor and Clinton fighting the eastward spread of the blaze, spraying water into a stiff wind, though in the chaos and smoke and sparks and dust he couldn't yet identify the company as the *Waubansia.*

It was Williams's job to believe that every fire could be contained, and his entire tenure to this point served as proof that he was right. But no fire he'd ever fought compared with what he faced that night. And now came the worst news of his career. A firefighter working one of the engines on the northern side of the blaze, probably the *Chicago*, ran up to Williams and told him in a cursory bark that the church was on fire.

The church. Williams knew enough about the West Side, and about the way this fire was likely to move, to know that his messenger had to mean St. Paul's Catholic Church, four full blocks to the north. Four stories tall, St. Paul's was visible for miles, at least under normal circumstances, absent hundred-foot-high plumes of black smoke. Williams needed no explanation. A solitary splinter of burning wood had floated northward on the high, hot wind. From Taylor Street it had glided across Forquer, Ewing, and Polk, before it found its final, fateful perch in St. Paul's pyramidal pinewood steeple.

Williams's mental map now expanded—exploded, even. The fire being fought by the *Little Giant*, the *Chicago*, the *Waubansia*, and the *Illinois*—four of the sixteen working steamers in the city's entire force—had until this moment spanned one and a half blocks from north to south. In a single instant, the danger had more than tripled. On DeKoven and Taylor, the fire's one- and two-story residential fuel was ordinary, if substantial, but St. Paul's lay surrounded by two lumber mills, a lumberyard, and a match factory. St. Paul's also lay closer to the Chicago River than the Learys' barn, close enough that a southwesterly piece of burning debris no different from the one that had escaped Taylor Street could float across the water to the South Side in search of ready fuel.

Williams now encountered Denis Swenie, a taciturn, reserved Glaswegian who captained the *Fred Gund*, which had just arrived from its North Side station in response to the sounding of the second alarm. Swenie was the oldest hand available to Williams. He'd started on the force in 1849, within a year of his family's arrival in America, as a fifteen-year-old apprentice manufacturer of hose and quickly moved up the ranks until at eighteen he was named assistant foreman of the engine company *Niagara*. By 1858 he'd been made marshal of the force, Williams's predecessor as it would turn out, and in 1858 and 1859 Swenie led the department's transition from volunteer to paid, winning out against considerable opposition. In his years on the force he had seen municipal expenditures for fighting fires go up from $20,000 to almost half a million dollars—which was, he knew, still not nearly enough to face what now lay ahead of them.

This hatred of tight purse strings and civic shortsightedness was still hot in Swenie as he fought the Great Fire and would stay with him the rest of his life. Twenty-two years later, he would say that "the whole fire was a mistake—a gigantic blunder" and maintain that responsibility for the conflagration "was more with the city than it was with the fire department." It was the city that for years had given them too few men, too few engines, not enough hose. It was the city that had placed the fire alarms and hydrants in such irregular fashion. It was the city that had decided that the manual watch system could serve as a substitute for a much larger and better-equipped department, when he and every other fireman knew that it couldn't.

Thanks to that alarm system, prone to human error, the *Fred Gund* had sat in its station for fifty minutes after the first alarm sounded, assuming that the new fire was too far to the south. Swenie had just hooked on at Forquer and Jefferson when Williams ran up and barked, "Can't you work north of this?" before telling him that St. Paul's was ablaze. Swenie understood that Williams was employing the only tactic left to him, to create a long and porous cordon that encompassed both fires, the one on DeKoven and Taylor and the one at the church. If the blocks between Taylor and Polk Streets had to burn, they had to burn. The force was down to its last option.

Swenie and the *Fred Gund* dashed to the north as instructed, arriving at the church to find the long ladder of one hook-and-ladder company already broken in two and lying on the ground as the flames spread to surrounding buildings and pushed back upriver, fast approaching the southern limits of the Red Flash fire. The crowd, presumably some of the same bunch who'd saved Quirk's saloon the night before, were back out in force and, if it was possible, in even higher spirits. A Saturday night *and* a Sunday night fire: this was the best of luck for everyone who didn't live on a direct line between the Learys' and St. Paul's. The streets were growing thick with firebugs as the news spread faster than the fire ever could.

Somewhere among that crowd ran Ed Chamberlin and the other newspapermen, back for more. All around the engine companies arriving at St. Paul's, "beer and whiskey were running like water," wrote Swenie later. Most in the mass of spectators knew it was another four-block fire by this point, something perhaps on the verge of becoming uncontainable, and this gave the crowd, many of whom had sat in saloons most of the day, a giddy, punch-drunk edge. They cheered on the engines, shouted offers of assistance, and pressed forward behind the firemen. When they got too close to Swenie's pipe, he turned and directed the hose's powerful stream at them, knocking down a dozen spectators all at once. "I expected a fight," said Swenie, "but the men who were knocked down got up laughing and wanted us to turn the hose on the rest of the crowd."

The high spirits couldn't last. As the night went on and Swenie fought his rearguard action, people continued to emerge from the neighborhoods between the DeKoven fire and the St. Paul's fire—an expanding geography of catastrophe now encompassing DeKoven, Taylor, Forquer, Ewing, and Polk Streets—their clothes and faces scorched and panic in their eyes. "Men were harnessed to trucks filled with their household goods," reported Swenie, "and sometimes the trucks were on fire." The size of the stream of refugees emptying out of the neighborhood to his south didn't give Swenie much hope. This had become the kind of fire that might kill a lot of people.

Williams found Swenie and the *Fred Gund* near the church and directed him to move northward again, to make a last stand another six full blocks to the north, at Clinton and Van Buren, which would put Swenie's back against the southern edge of the ruins of the Red Flash fire. With this instruction, Williams was sacrificing another large section of the West Side, but the logic of the order was sound.

The rubble of the previous night's blaze would make for a superb firebreak to the north, and the river would provide a wall of protection to the east, while the wind coming hard from the southwest would complete the cage inside which he hoped to capture the blaze.

As Swenie moved north up Clinton Street, he could see that flames were already spreading deep into the lumberyards and coal sheds that ran between the Pittsburgh, Fort Wayne, and Chicago tracks and the river, consuming all the fuel that had been spared the night before. The flames running along the river's bank were described later by many observers as "licking" and "reaching out" over the water like tongues or fingers. Swenie understood and concurred with Williams's plan, but he also knew that the South Side, with the lumber so close to the water going up in flames, was in greater danger with each passing minute. They were now fighting with eight engines, half of the force's available machines, and even so they were fast running low on hose, coal, and men.

Swenie and his pipemen led their hose into an alley adjacent to a furniture mill off Van Buren, exerting all of his effort on a single business because stopping *something* from burning on the blaze's northern border was about all that he could try to do. Where the rest of the fire had gone and how big it had gotten, he had no idea. His men put in an hour of hot work on the mill, coming ever closer to their own breaking point and that of their boiler, before the water pressure at their pipe ends unexpectedly trickled to zero.

Emerging from the alley at a run, Swenie discovered that Williams had directed that the *Gund* be disconnected from its hydrant and moved away from the alley for the sake of its crew's safety. Swenie argued with his chief, to no avail. Then he was pulled off the site as a squad of outsiders under the marshal's direction took hold of the *Gund*'s several hose leads and, using them like long reins, tugged the engine away from the fire. But before the engine could be brought all the way out, the men abandoned their rescue mission as the alley walls began to cave in, and Swenie's beloved machine was no more.

Drawing of the fire engine *Fred Gund*, published in *Report of the Board of Police in the Fire Department to the Common Council of the City of Chicago*, 1872

Swenie had first been given charge of the *Fred Gund* ten years earlier, in 1861, when it was called the *Liberty*. Now his engine's life was at an end, and Swenie was at a total loss. "I couldn't sleep. I couldn't sit down," he said later. "My eyes were filled with cinders and I was scorched dry." Swenie would find no solace in the knowledge that in the end the *Fred Gund*'s fate was immaterial. The West Side, at least the ten-block swath of it between the Learys' barn and the southern edge of Red Flash, was far beyond help. A total of twenty-six city blocks were now burning. The fate of the rest of the city was now the question at hand, and nothing a single engine could accomplish could do anything to change the answer.

After sending Swenie home, Williams abandoned any hope of a coordinated fight against the West Side fire and crossed over to the South Side to direct that water be played on the buildings there closest to the river, should the fire jump. No longer were there any questions of strategy. Plans had become wishes. Wishes had become prayers.

⚜ 5 ⚜

B Y ELEVEN O'CLOCK, after little more than two hours, Sunday night's blaze threatened to obliterate the limits of memory and imagination. It didn't matter whether someone was a refugee from the burning district, an unfortunate in the fire's path, a fireman, a policeman, or simply an interested observer. With the excitement from the Red Flash fire still lingering in the air, and the sense growing by the minute that this new conflagration was about to top it, alarm and hysteria traveled block by block across the city. The Great Fire, seen as a living thing, was at this moment crouched on the West Side along the Chicago River and directly across from downtown, tensed and ready to spring.

Most of the bridges crossing the south branch of the Chicago River were already impassable. The Jackson bridge, the Madison bridge, and the Adams bridge had all been blocked by the flames. These "swing bridges" were built with cast-iron rails and wooden decks that pivoted on a central pile, rotating one-quarter turn to come to rest parallel to the water's flow so that ships could pass by. The tugs and boats and tall-masted schooners making their own desperate runs away from the flames wanted these bridges held open—and for a few hours the bridges had continued to operate— but how to open and close them after their western ends were aflame and their operators long gone? So most of the crossings remained closed to river traffic as the men in their boats watched the water around them give off steam.

The Randolph Street bridge, the northernmost crossing before the convergence of the Chicago River's three branches, was still available to pedestrians, and thousands used it. The firebugs were out in larger numbers than ever before. But now many of the people out on the streets were interested only in getting as far away from the blaze as possible. Their understanding of the peril faced by the city was personal, born out of their mad rush to grab whatever of their belongings they could and run away. The things they chose to carry told the story of their lives:

> Here comes a woman with all her bed and bedding on her back. Here was a little girl with her arms full of cooking utensils. Here comes a team with a little of everything on it, and curled up on a mattress in a secure position two or three young children. One of the shafts has a tea kettle hanging to it, another a coal-hod. If any picture were being carried away, they were always the Virgin or Christ crucified. One man was hurrying along with nothing but a flatiron in his hand, another had two or three pieces of old board, and so they went, hurrying, pushing, scrambling, crowding, jostling, shouting, and laughing even.

Amid the clamor and chaos, unnoticed among "the great crowd that filled the bridge to a dangerous amount," stood a trim, tidy, white-haired man in no hurry at all. His face was gaunt, and his prominent, squared-off chin was covered with white whiskers gathered in wayward tufts and sweeps. In one hand he held a cane. He looked to be at least sixty, but he was forty-eight. He had done a great many things in those forty-eight years. Standing on the Randolph Street bridge, he seemed, as he most often did, to hold himself entirely separate from the mob.

His name was Joseph Medill. His ownership stake in the *Chicago Tribune* and his relentless editorializing on behalf of the Republican Party before and during the Civil War had made his name easy to recognize in Chicago and in national spheres, but here and now he was anonymous. He stood on the bridge, facing south, and watched the fire billow and furl as he might observe a parade or a piece of political oratory, paying no attention to the noise all around him.

Like any seasoned news editor in any big city, Medill had an unassailable sense of the moment. Filling his eyes, ears, and nose was the first chapter in the city's most consequential story since the nomination of its adopted son Abraham Lincoln eleven and a half years earlier. The next day's edition, and the extras, and the next week's papers, and their extras, would sell everywhere in the city, to everyone. An army of young hawkers would swarm the city. Out-of-town newspapers would clamor to reprint the news out of Chicago. The presses would run all day and all night for days on end, filling the Tribune building's cavernous basement with the thick smell of hot ink and the deafening rumble of its giant steam-driven iron cylinders.

Medill knew that his younger brother Sam, the *Tribune*'s city editor, would already have emptied the building of all its reporters, tossing them out into the night, anywhere they might roam for any bit of story. He also knew that those reporters who hadn't been in the building as the fire began would be skittering around the streets on their own initiative, stopping to take notes wherever they might find a bit of drama; tragedy, comedy, or trivia, it didn't matter, it would all make usable copy.

Portrait of Joseph Medill, credited to Charles D. Mosher, c. 1870

Even in the midst of this growing disaster, Medill looked across the city of Chicago from his perch on the Randolph Street bridge with a proprietorial air. Though he was no city founder or business mogul or factory builder, in other ways he knew that he was one of the makers of Chicago, part of the transplanted elite that had built the place up from a frontier town into the behemoth it was today. Here in the big city on the shore of Lake Michigan there was no impediment to such a feeling for a relative newcomer like Medill, no backlog of old families with their old money and their six-generation households to claim primacy. "There are no old men here, or old houses," one local reporter had written. "What has been is of little moment in Chicago; what is and what will be, are the only care."

He'd been exceptionally handsome in his youth: a broad torso, a square jaw, a cleft chin, deep-set, appraising eyes, black hair and brows. But by 1871, Medill had lost much of his heft and most of his youth. His mind, sharp and severe, was caged inside a body that seemed to be prematurely exhausting itself. His all-white hair made him appear to be an old hand, a sage, though he was still in the prime of life. The overall effect was one of wisdom, of dedication, of a fire contained within. But also, to many observers, of severity and joylessness.

Canadian by birth, Medill had arrived in Chicago from a sojourn in Ohio, where he'd met Kitty, his future wife, the daughter of the small-town newspaper publisher who would give Medill his start in journalism. This was the way of Chicago: no one of note in the city had been born here. The real estate barons William Butler Ogden and Potter Palmer, the richest men in a city growing ever richer, were from New York. Palmer's young wife, Bertha Honoré, was from Louisville. Cyrus McCormick, who had made his name and fortune in Chicago manufacturing mechanical reapers, was from Virginia. Marshall Field, the retail genius, was from Massachusetts, while Levi Leiter, Field's partner, had arrived from Ohio. Gurdon Saltonstall Hubbard, onetime fur trader and the town's most visible Old Settler, had been born in Vermont, as had Wilbur Storey, publisher of *The Chicago Times.* "Long John" Wentworth, two-time mayor, once as a Republican and once as a Democrat, had come from New Hampshire. Philip Sheridan, the little general, Union war hero third only to Ulysses S. Grant and William Tecumseh Sherman, hailed from New York. Medill's partners at the *Tribune*, William Bross and Horace White, were from New Jersey and New Hampshire, respectively.

All these relocated men and women were immigrants of a sort. But more than 150,000 Chicagoans had come to the city from overseas, a number that included the vast majority of the city's laborers and three of the city's most prominent political voices: Anton Hesing, publisher of the German-language *Staats-Zeitung*, born in Oldenburg; Daniel O'Hara, the city's Irish political leader, from County Cork; and the labor leader and *Workingman's Advocate* publisher Andrew Cameron, born in Berwick-on-Tweed, England. The sum of all these migrations was that there was no such thing as an old Chicagoan, no old Chicago. Medill had come to Chicago between times, well after its founding but years before the city rocketed past Cincinnati, Philadelphia, Boston, and St. Louis in population and economic influence. He was neither an original settler nor an arriviste but one of that group of strivers and climbers drawn to the city in the 1850s by its promise of raw growth and rare opportunity. Big things had been done in Chicago before Medill's arrival, but bigger things had been done since, some of them by him.

The four leveled blocks of the Red Flash blaze allowed Medill a clear view from the bridge to the neighborhoods just north of DeKoven, all of which were engulfed in flames. Close by on his right, the steeple of St. Paul's was visible, burning down to its framing. The superheated fleck of debris that had fired the church now had thousands of copies as the sky began to fill with a kind of lazy orange-and-red snow.

Medill had never seen anything of the like before, but he was familiar with the cost of fire on a personal scale: as a teenager, his family's Ohio farmstead had burned to the ground, along with any hope that he might go to college to pursue a career in the law. That seemed ages ago. On this night, Medill's personal property was safe. He didn't live in one of the tree-lined estates on the North Side, and he didn't live in one of the sumptuous stone town houses along the lake on the South Side, though two of his fellow owners at the *Tribune* did. Medill in 1871 lived as a well-to-do but hardly ostentatious West Sider, at Washington and Morgan, near the fire marshal, Robert Williams, and quite a few other newspapermen, including Ed and Everett Chamberlin. It was out of a second-story window of his house that Medill had first seen the sky lit up as if daytime had come for a second helping on Sunday, a glow that illuminated his bedroom.

If journalism was Medill's calling, politics—Republican politics—was his religion. With money provided by his father-in-law, he'd created the *Cleveland Leader* after Winfield Scott and the Whigs had been trounced by Franklin Pierce and the Democrats in the 1852 elections, and it was in the *Leader*'s offices, in March 1854, that a private meeting of Whigs, antislavery Democrats, and Free-Soilers—all opposed to the expansion of slavery into the western territories—had helped to lay the groundwork for the formation of the national Republican Party later that month. A year after that meeting, he'd come to Chicago when Horace Greeley, then the presiding spirit of Republican newspaper editors everywhere, introduced him to Charles Ray, a physician who wanted to start a Republican paper in the city. By the start of the Civil War, Medill and Ray's paper had become a powerful political shield for Republicans and a bulwark against the anti-abolitionist, anti-Lincoln, and Democratic *Times*. During the war, Medill had lived in Washington, D.C., and New York for some time, dining often with the Greeleys and sending on political news and wartime updates as an eastern correspondent for the *Tribune*.

Wherever Medill found himself in his career, he wrote opinion pieces, sometimes several each day. "He wrote countless editorials and read all others late in his house, changing and patching half the night," wrote one acquaintance. Other than a general contempt for all things Democratic, his hobbyhorses were civil service reform, unrestrained trade and labor markets, and an absolute halt to the expansion of slavery. During the Civil War, then, he became a steady voice of public support for the Union effort and for emancipation while maintaining a private correspondence with Abraham

Lincoln in which he offered a great deal of policy advice that the president, for the most part, politely ignored.

By October 1871, though, Medill's professional satisfactions had reached a low ebb. His lack of a private fortune and the financial vagaries of the newspaper business had led him to partner first with William Bross, publisher of the defunct *Chicago Democrat,* and more recently with Horace White, a zealous former reporter for the *Tribune* who now controlled the paper's editorial direction and did more to drive apart various camps of Republicans than to unite them. Medill had come up in the business as a sole proprietor of an influential newspaper with the field to itself, but now he was part of a shifting, many-headed managerial structure that left him feeling peripheral, sometimes even powerless.

The Great Fire, as it turned out, would change everything for Medill, for better and for worse, and return him to a place of public prominence that he hadn't occupied for more than a decade. The paradox of Chicago in 1871 was that it was a historic city, but it had yet few entries of its own in the bigger book of American history. A traveler from the big cities of the East, or the farms of the Midwest, or the frontier towns of the West got off the train in the heart of Chicago and marveled at the surge of growth all around, but that traveler didn't know much at all about what the city had *been.* Lots of things happened in Chicago every day, millions of individual transactions and conversations that added up to a massive influence across the continent. But before October 1871, only one really big thing had ever happened in Chicago. And Medill had been right in the middle of it.

Eleven years earlier, two hundred yards or so north of the bridge on which Medill watched Chicago burn, a makeshift meeting hall called the Wigwam tucked into the northwest corner of downtown had hosted the 1860 Republican National Convention, one of the most consequential political gatherings in the nation's history. The convention had begun with every expectation that New York senator William Seward would be nominated for president, but it had ended with the electrifying and not a little perplexing news that a gaunt and very tall lawyer from downstate Illinois had been entrusted with the fate of the disintegrating union. America marveled that Abraham Lincoln had engineered the victory, but the exact mechanism of that victory had been difficult to tease out, filtered as it had been through many factotums, representatives, and handlers.

Unknown to the public, near the heart of that effort lay Joseph Medill, who had been far more than factotum or handler. In reality, outside Lincoln himself, Medill might have been the most important of all the men responsible for the remarkable happenings inside and outside the Wigwam. The publisher's influence had been a decisive lever in the campaign to put the 1860 Republican convention in Chicago instead of in Indianapolis. Once the conventioneers arrived in Chicago, in May of that year, Medill packed the cavernous hall with early arriving Lincoln supporters bearing falsified tickets, and he seated the state delegations in an arrangement designed to keep Seward's staunchest supporters far from the center of the action while placing the most malleable state delegations in easy reach of Lincoln's tireless smile-and-a-handshake operators.

The former Ohioan Medill then parked himself next to the Ohio delegation, and at the crucial moment he leaned in to whisper a promise into the state chairman Daniel Carter's ear. In exchange for just a few more votes, he said, Ohio—in the person of the former governor Salmon Chase—would be assured an important place in the president's cabinet. Carter wanted a more tangible guarantee, to which Medill responded, "I *know*, and you know I wouldn't promise if I didn't know"—even though, in fact, he did not really know. The votes moved from Seward to Lincoln. The announcement was made. And the hall erupted with the understanding that the local boy, the Railsplitter, had, in the face of long odds, grabbed the nomination.

True to his uncompromising style—his paper's original motto was "neutral in nothing, independent in everything"—Medill never fully aligned himself with the man he'd helped move a large step closer to the presidency. Medill remained loyal to his own journalistic independence and his own politics, rather than Lincoln's, and whenever the two diverged, he made a point of expressing his displeasure in the pages of the *Tribune*. Medill spent the Civil War pushing for a comprehensive defeat of the Confederates and whipping up a froth of loyal pro-Union feeling. He also watched Lincoln with care and not entirely trustfully, castigating the president for moving too timidly and slowly in his conduct of the war and on the questions of emancipation and abolition.

That friction vanished with Lincoln's assassination in 1865. Medill now kept in his office at the Tribune building the materials he wanted to use to write a lengthy biography of Lincoln, something careful and critical but also laudatory, a project that he would not rush into publication. According to a story that was famous in political circles, Medill had first met Lincoln in the *Tribune*'s fourth-floor editorial offices in 1856, four years before the nominating convention, when the future president had climbed the steps to put his oversized boots on Medill's desk. The two men talked about slavery, but also about Chicago's place in the world, and about the prospects of any number of local candidates for lower office. Even then, Lincoln understood that for any Republican the *Tribune* was the most important mouthpiece for a thousand miles.

Now Medill stood on the Randolph Street bridge, poised in this awful, awe-inspiring moment between past and future, between the flawed Chicago he inhabited and the more perfect Chicago he believed could be. The river over which he stood divided and defined Chicago, and for a few moments longer he indulged a newspaper publisher's penchant for observation and consideration, without feeling any of the reporter's need to get someplace or the city editor's need to make a crop of quick decisions.

Just as he'd claimed to have launched the rise of the Republican Party out of the death throes of the Whigs, so too would Medill later claim to have had a presentiment that a great conflagration would soon lay waste to the city and purge it of its own past as surely as his party had reconstructed itself anew in the offices of his Ohio paper and then in the pages of his Chicago one. That very morning, in the wake of the fire in Red Flash, in words Medill might have written, the *Tribune* had warned its readers of the prospects of a great citywide blaze:

> For days past alarm has followed alarm, but the comparatively trifling losses have familiarized us to the pealing of the courthouse bell, and we had forgotten that the absence of rain for three weeks had left everything in so dry and inflammable a condition that a spark might set a fire which would sweep from end to end of the city.

Now, as Medill and thousands of other Chicagoans watched the red hail of sparks and bits of burning cinders mount into the sky, that sentence became a terrifying reality. Somewhere in that red hail, a solitary fragment of burning wood among thousands of others from the vicinity of St. Paul's arced over the river and disappeared into a jumble of buildings on the South Side, a few blocks away. A minute or two passed, and then there it was: a leaping, jittery, hungry glow on the downtown side of the river, originating from—as would later be determined—a brand-new $80,000 omnibus and stagecoach depot that was due to open for service for the first time in just three days.

Voices were raised everywhere. From one mouth to the next, the report moved through the crowd, through citizens, firemen, and policemen, block by block, every bit as quick as the fire itself could move.

The fire has jumped. The fire is on the South Side.

Medill looked one more time over the Irish sections of the West Side, down by DeKoven. Descended from severe Scotch-Irish Calvinists, he had no love for Catholic immigrants, not for their increasing numbers or their growing political influence, and he gave no time to worrying about them. Even before Medill left the bridge, the rain of burning debris had ignited the South Side in at least two more places, a gasworks and an armory. Soon, if the wind held, the fire might cross Randolph somewhere ahead of him and block his passage to the Tribune building. He leaned into his cane and moved, though not as quickly as many of the people rushing past him. These events might form a piece of the history of the world. He needed to get his newspaper out.

❧ 6 ☙

EVERY DAY except Christmas and New Year's, Marshall Field entered the marble edifice bearing his name, the most famous retail establishment west of New York City, driven by one imperative: to sell and sell well. Field, Leiter & Company was Chicago's most elegant cathedral of commerce, its most expensive rental property, and a magnet designed to attract other, lesser retailers into its orbit. The building sat on the corner of Washington Street and newly widened State. Thirty-two sixteen-inch Corinthian columns, sixteen feet high, enveloped the ground floor along its two fronts and supported four marble balconies above. In the recesses made by the columns, plate-glass window displays ran from floor to ceiling along the length of the building, each one housing a different set of eye-catching material aspirations.

A thin, trim, and unfailingly dapper man, Field arrived at his store every morning at seven in the same serene, self-possessed frame of mind. Outside his store, he was known to be aloof, rigid, even severe, but on the floor of his dry-goods palace his demeanor mellowed and his mood lifted. His thoughts were as collected and ordered as his inventory and his personal appearance, and he kept his mannerisms fine-tuned to the desires of Chicago's most loyal well-to-do shoppers, especially its women. In a cacophonous city that kept its grease-stained nose to the grindstone at almost all hours, Field stood out to them as an emblem of grace and elegant deference—a steady hand at the tiller, determined to do the thing right.

He carried in his head the wholesale price he'd paid and the retail price to the customer of every one of the more than ten thousand items in his store. He also kept a small black book in an inner pocket and made notes every day. He lived his life by mottoes and precepts. At thirty-seven, he still remembered all of his mother's, one above all: "Regard a fixed bad habit as one of the dangers always threatening success." As a result, Marshall Field had no bad habits, at least not any that he would allow the public to see. He moved in circles of successful businessmen and national leaders, and they paid him respect and attention, but at heart he was a salesman. No interaction pleased him more than the simple act of greeting a customer at the door.

Welcome, madam. Welcome, miss. How may we be of service?

Now, however, he dashed into his store on a dead run, an act so out of character that it told one of the stories of the Great Fire by itself. The young men and women who clerked for him were fiercely loyal to the store and its owners, and Field found several dozen of them already in the building, ready to do their part. And not just a gaggle of clerks, but also his partner, Levi Leiter; his bookkeeper, Harlow Higinbotham; and his chief of security, John Devlin, steadfast and tenacious as a terrier. The fire's advancing edge was still many blocks to the west, but armed guards already stood at every entrance, discouraging looters and instructing loiterers to move along.

Like Joseph Medill, Marshall Field seemed far older than his years, though for different reasons. Medill appeared to have aged prematurely; Field, on the other hand, appeared never to have been young. Field was so fastidious, reserved, and observant that the word "solicitous" might well have been invented to describe him. Where Medill had once boasted the face and physique of a stage idol, Field had always been slight. How careful and controlled and official his tone, how reassuring his presence. Women responded by becoming regular customers; for many, especially those from Chicago's wealthiest families, no other store and no other store owner would do. In this city, no name meant more to a woman working to create a little bit of home comfort, a little bit of domestic sophistication, than that of Marshall Field.

Portrait of Marshall Field,
photographer and date unknown

Descended from generations of Puritans—a fact that would have surprised no one who'd ever met him—Field had first come to Chicago in 1856 to clerk in a dry-goods store called Cooley, Wadsworth & Company after holding a similar position in a much smaller business in Massachusetts. He'd spent a decade rising through the ranks at Cooley's, all the while keeping a close eye on the nearby Lake Street store of Potter Palmer, the original king of Chicago dry goods, absorbing the older man's lessons. Palmer's sales innovations were simple, but they were revolutionary, and they had mesmerized Field: clearly displayed prices, no haggling; goods delivered on approval via horse-drawn carts; no-questions-asked returns; and most important of all, no prohibition on women shopping alone. In the first surge of Chicago's unchecked growth, Palmer had understood as no one else had that the ladies of Chicago had been cast adrift on a masculine ocean made of dust, dirt, oil, smoke, shit, and noise. He knew that all that mess had made lots of money for Chicago, but he also knew that the women of the city craved a less chaotic milieu in which to spend that money.

The Civil War came, and Chicago's businessmen had a very good war. Trainloads of lumber, livestock, and grain had been augmented by incoming and outgoing shipments of guns, bullets, field ambulances, tents, uniforms, shoes and boots, saddles, harnesses, and thousands and thousands of horses. Potter Palmer himself made few sales to the Union army—mostly flannels and blankets—but at the start of the war he used his sterling credit and massive buying power to stock up on warehouse after warehouse full of dry goods, some of which he sold as various items became dear and prices rose. Others he let sit, ready to meet any future scarcities. He'd also kept open his trade in cotton with the Confederate states for as long as he could.

Near the end of the Civil War, the city flush with money, Field was offered the chance to become a senior partner in a new firm called Field, Palmer, Leiter & Company. Shortly thereafter, in 1865, Potter Palmer sold out his share of the business to his protégés and abandoned the dry-goods business for good so that he could concentrate on buying and selling real estate and building hotels. But not before Field had perfected the Palmer way.

In 1867, with the postwar retail boom in full swing, Field and Leiter had signed a lease to rent one of Potter Palmer's new buildings on State Street—the "marble palace," they called it—for the unheard-of sum of $50,000 a year. One year after that transaction, on October 12, 1868, the city had turned out in great numbers for a grand opening that the *Tribune* described as "unparalleled in Chicago's history":

> Brilliantly lighted from garret to basement, [the store] stood in bold relief to the mere shanties which, to speak comparatively, surrounded it. It looked palatial, fairy-like, and for all the world as if it had been brought into existence by the magic stroke of an enchanter. The illuminated deadlights encircled it on the west and south, casting a lurid and subdued light upon the base of the building; but those underground rays had no sooner reached the surface . . . than they were driven back, so to speak, by the dazzling and all-powerful rays emitted from hundreds of gas jets on the first floor which [shining] through the immense and magnificent window panes, flashed across the street, making the opposite

sidewalk light as day . . . story after story, and the beautiful and tasteful French dormer windows of the attic were reached, also illuminated in the same way.

That opening-day spectacle had soon settled into an unending routine of robust sales. Now Field and Leiter were very rich men, rich enough that no one could envision a Chicago without their business at the heart of it, not even if everything east of the two branches of the Chicago River should burn to the ground. They moved $10 million worth of merchandise a year, almost all of it in cash. The line of horse-drawn cabs waiting in front of the store at the start of each day, the porters and clerks assisting the ladies across the sidewalk through the dust of a scorching summer or the snow and slush of a wind-scarred winter, spoke of a loyal clientele and a reputation second to none.

Potter Palmer had believed in the allure of a well-placed, well-arranged display, so Field created ornate, tasteful tableaux of mannequins and merchandise behind great sheets of picture glass facing the street and mounted in elaborate in-store displays. Most of all, Field learned from Palmer that nothing was so important as the projection of confidence. Buy when everyone else wasn't buying so that when the economy dipped, as it always would, a woman from the North Side could travel to his store and find not empty shelves but a promise of better times. Everything Field put on display and everything he sold was a symbol of something, most of all of optimism.

As he stepped out from Palmer's shadow, Field accumulated his own personal articles of retail belief: "Few credits and those only on short time." "No debts, cash buying only, and always money in the bank." "Get the best goods and tell the truth." "Be a little better than the demand." The bigger, older dry-goods stores in New York City—A. T. Stewart's and Macy's and Lord & Taylor—moved more volume, gave their customers an earlier look at foreign fabrics, built more grandiose buildings, claimed more international notoriety. But if there was boasting to do—and Field would never boast in person, even as the constant stream of advertisements his company placed in the *Tribune* and the *Times* did so in his name—it was true that the New York stores had taken advantage of circumstances that any number of businessmen could have noticed and turned to a profit. New York, after all, was the first off-loading point for European goods and, for that matter, Europeans. As well, New York was located along north–south connecting routes to Boston, and Philadelphia, and Washington, D.C. For two hundred years people had shopped in New York City, the nation's locus of finance, fashion, and culture. How could a well-capitalized company run with a sharp eye for merchandising not succeed in New York?

But in Chicago? This city had been no sure thing. Chicago had been planted less than forty years earlier on a plot of ground known by white men for a fetid canal route, a small and poorly armed fort, a sleepy fur-trading post, and an odiferous onion field. It had emerged from that soggy wilderness as an incorporated city in 1837, which meant that on the day of the Great Fire the city was three years younger than Field himself.

Other American cities trumpeted their long history, their place in the original colonial fabric of the country, but Chicago was far too young for all of that. Fifty years earlier, in 1821, "Chicago" had been a Native American word for "onion" and nothing more; forty years earlier, in 1831, it had been a remote and weather-beaten trading post; thirty years earlier, in 1841, it had still counted no more than twenty-five hundred residents, a good many of them land agents and speculators. Now, in 1871, more than one hundred times that many people lived in the city, and amid all this clamor Field & Leiter was an oasis. Needs were met. A woman's status as a person with a brain, a purse, and a capacity to make independent decisions was not only acknowledged but celebrated, granting the store a rare aura of loveliness.

Field loved the provision of things, not things themselves. His one cold comfort as he ran into his store after the breakneck carriage ride from his lakeside home was that Field, Leiter & Company was no longer situated on Lake Street, which ran west to east beside the main branch of the Chicago River, one block north of Randolph. Had Field and Leiter not made their move then, they would have found themselves in the line of the fire already, surrounded by the crowds fleeing the courthouse and its surrounding streets and waiting for the flames to arrive. Without question, were Field, Leiter & Company still on Lake Street, much of its inventory would already have burned. The garish light and mountainous billows of smoke to the northwest told them so.

On his way to the building, Harlow Higinbotham, the accountant, had detoured to the firm's car barns at Twentieth and State, eleven blocks to the south, where he'd instructed every driver he could find to line up every delivery cart they could commandeer in front of the imperiled store. Higinbotham's plan was not complicated: the biggest and most expensive goods, the most that could be saved in the fewest trips, would be the first items to be spirited away. Levi Leiter lived on the far South Side, upwind and distant from the line of the fire, in an expansive residential property that could hold more inventory than even Field's own mansion on Park Row. Field and his partner knew they would lose millions of dollars' worth of inventory, but they also knew that they had a great deal of ready cash in reserve, and they knew that others knew. However this disaster ended, they could bargain for a makeshift warehouse, covered stables, an empty school building, even a vacant house, set up what merchandise remained, and put in large new orders with their eastern suppliers before any other retail concern in the city could do the same.

The decisions were made quickly, Field's announcements and actions as precise and decisive as always. Most clothing would be abandoned, as would all notions, anything whose value was in bulk sales of smaller items. Saving a portion of these inventories would not help, and besides, most clothing was sold on the third and fourth floors, which would take too long to evacuate. The second floor, the first floor, and the basement level were filled with many choice candidates for salvage: carpets that sold for $1,000 and more apiece, cottons and other linens by the bolt, silks and muslins, flannels and blankets.

The clerks and drivers engaged by Higinbotham soon had a

fleet of carts lined up along State Street, and the rescuers set up their own kind of bucket brigade. Field, Leiter, and Higinbotham pointed out the merchandise, the clerks shuttled the items hand to hand to hand, out the door and to the carts, while Devlin, the security man, stood outside the main entrance and watched for looters, his coat pulled back and his firearm in prominent view.

So it went, as orderly as possible given the circumstances. The beauty of the building was still evident, as was its opulence, perhaps even more so because of its precarious state. The first floor represented the city's retail apotheosis. Frescoed walls framed walnut counters with kaleidoscopic displays of silks, which were now bundled and brought outside. In the northeastern corner of the first floor, in a carpeted and mirrored alcove set off by a railing, were sold the ladies' cloaks, where in normal times a shifting cast of young female clerks explained "all the little curlemagigs": striped plushes, lambswool, velvet, bedouin opera cloaks made of sable fur and sealskin, on and on. Many of these expensive cloaks were brought outside, stacked as high as the men could carry them. Elsewhere on the main floor, mostly consigned to the flames, were shawls, curtains, men's and women's suits, poplins, linens, damask cloths, ribbons, laces, gloves, hosiery, underwear, cravats, neckties.

Hour after hour, as the fire marched toward them block by block, the carts drove off, two or three at a time, each sortie guarded by a clerk or security man riding shotgun. The next set of carts were then rolled into place, and the next pile of merchandise loaded in. Here was the very essence of Chicago as viewed in a fun-house mirror: a race against time and disaster, driven by one sober actuarial computation after another. All these decisions were made by fantastically wealthy men and carried out by junior clerks who recognized in Mr. Field a man who fifteen years earlier had come to the city to take just such a subordinate position as theirs.

The women of Chicago who desired these items would be back soon enough, wherever the next Field & Leiter storefront might be housed, as would the visiting shoppers from the West who relied on Chicago to provide them with their own sense of eastern grace. It didn't take a leap of faith to believe that Field, Leiter & Company would survive, just an understanding that money and people would continue to move in and out of the city because, in the final analysis, where would they go instead? Even if all of Chicago were to burn, Marshall Field believed he would come out of it stronger than ever. The demand would never abate, while the supply would be forever his.

PART II

Flight

❧ 7 ❧

A s Marshall Field arrived to direct the rescue effort in his store, just after midnight, Joseph Medill continued to make his way eastward down Randolph Street, his progress slow and halting among the panicked crowds. A multitude had watched the Red Flash fire the night before, wondering if it would cross the river to the South Side and imagining what they would do if it did. Now, twenty-four hours later, that nightmare scenario had arrived. Most of the people surrounding Medill rushed westward against his path, or away to the north, to his left, crossing the main branch of the river to get to the North Side and away from the growing walls of fire and smoke that threatened to close around them.

Medill had walked Randolph Street often. The South Side block closest to the river as he stepped off the bridge was known for its saloons, clothiers, employment agencies, and cigar manufacturers, but it also housed a sign engraver, assembly hall, grocer's, barber, and manufacturers of pianos, awnings, saddles, shoes, brushes, and bedsprings. On this night, Chicago's usual unceasing movement of goods and people had taken on a surreal aspect. All along Randolph, layered many deep against every building, an overcrowded line of carriages, wagons, hacks, and liveries waited in many different stages of loading.

A countless number of men and women poured out of doorways and alleys laded with sacks and handcarts and luggage. Some dragged merchandise on sheets. Many of the carts and carriages that scurried in every direction were owned by the businesses along

Downtown environs

Randolph, while others were the property of opportunists who had hurried to downtown from the safe zones of the city, the far West and South Sides. Some asked for $10 a load and found takers right away, some asked for $50 until they got it, but all were soon employed. Most of these drivers discharged their duty with honor, while others abandoned a load in the middle of the street when a better offer came along or waited until the wagon was loaded and the renter back inside and then drove off with the goods, never to be seen again.

By this point, it was impossible for Medill or anyone in the crowd around him to understand exactly where the fire had been and where it was headed. An awareness existed in the frantic crowds along Randolph that the fire had jumped the southern branch of the river and was now burning in their own district, but they had no idea how close or how fast. Had they been able to rise above the street-level chaos and achieve a balloon's-eye view, they would have seen a ten-block-long broil of fire on the West Side, between DeKoven and Red Flash, along with two brightly burning blocks on the South Side: one centered on Parmelee's omnibus depot and stables, close to the river across from Red Flash, and another on the city gasworks, at Monroe and Market, a few intersections farther north. Medill kept moving until he reached Randolph's crossing with Madison, on the northwest corner of the courthouse. A tall black cast-iron fence, lined on top with pointed finials, surrounded the square. The gates at each of its corners had been opened.

Instinct told many that the courthouse square might be a refuge, what with the oversized block's open spaces on all four sides of a fireproof brick building at its center. Medill rested for a moment and watched as the effort to save the city's records went into full swing. "The city and county officers and police, and many citizens were carrying out and trying to save in wagons and in their arms papers and documents," he wrote later. "The roar was terrific; the smoke drifted over me in huge volumes; sparks and pieces of burning wood were flying through the air by millions, and there was a strong wind blowing, apparently from every direction." Medill and the others in the square who bothered to look upward understood that no place on the South Side was safe. Four stories over their heads, they could see little tufts of flame on the courthouse roof. Illuminated by the ever-thicker downpour of sparks, a small dark figure moved like Quasimodo on his cathedral, holding a broom and bucket and beating at the flames.

Medill had no way of knowing it, but this was the watchman Mathias Schaefer, whose night had only deteriorated since he'd sounded the mistaken alarm that set the great bell to ringing. For an hour and a half after calling down box 342, Schaefer had acted as spotter while the telegraph operator William Brown had sent out a second alarm, which sent signals to all six of the firehouses on the West Side, and then a third, which rang a bell in every fire station in the city. After that third alarm, discussions of what box to strike were academic. The entire department had been engaged, and in any case the blaze would no longer be difficult to find. Just before eleven, the flare of the steeple of St. Paul's church catching fire had drawn Schaefer's attention. He'd called down the sighting to Brown, and with that action the official portion of Schaefer's night was complete, because the fire department was nothing if not regular in its rotations.

At eleven, another watchman, Dennis Deneen, had climbed into the cupola to relieve Schaefer, even as more of the city burned below him. There were now two jobs to be done: monitor the fire and protect the courthouse. For the time being, Deneen would do the one, Schaefer the other. After the lumber mills and match factory surrounding St. Paul's had caught fire and begun to shoot hot debris into the sky, all bets were off. Now the entire western edge of downtown was ablaze, and it was frightening to see how far and high the burning shards of wood could float. The roof of the courthouse was covered with clay shingles beneath a layer of soft black tar and ringed by a wooden balcony railing. Mortal danger from above had never been part of any fireproofing calculation, not for a building of this height.

Just before midnight, Schaefer descended for a street-level reconnaissance. As he made his way out of the building, he learned that Chicago's mayor, Roswell Mason, had arrived at the courthouse and commandeered a ground-floor office, where he was dictating telegrams to nearby cities, asking that any firemen or equipment that could be spared be sent to Chicago by the fastest possible express train. One glance outside told Schaefer what he needed to know: the fire was perhaps four blocks away on a diagonal line to the southwest and headed for the courthouse. Time was short and getting shorter.

Amid the press of people filling the building's square, Schaefer encountered a fellow fireman named George Fuller, William Brown's midnight replacement. Schaefer followed Fuller up five flights of stairs and said good night to Brown. Over the next hour, Schaefer and Deneen watched as their peaceful cupola, where they'd entertained many a guest, became a crow's nest perched at the eastern edge of a growing sea of fire. The scattered bits of flame that Medill described in his own account of the night continued to enlarge and multiply, and Schaefer and Deneen had to run about the surface from one end of the roof to the other, the tar growing softer under their shoes. Every downtown building that called itself fireproof based that description in part on the great steel cylinders of water situated on their upper floors or roofs, and Schaefer and Deneen used these reservoirs to wet the upper surfaces of the building as best they could, as fast as they could. They dashed about, beating the flames with brooms, throwing buckets of water on flare-ups, and sometimes stamping their feet, hollering encouragement at each other all the while.

Their footing ever more unsure, Schaefer and Deneen did their best. And for some time, they succeeded. But like almost every building in the path of the fire that night, great or small, the courthouse had a fatal flaw. A row of glass ran under the eaves of the building. A decorative element, many of its panes were missing and had gone unreplaced. The beginning of the end came a short time after one o'clock, when Schaefer made the discovery that fire had scurried under the rooftop through one of these gaps and was now in among the wooden frame that held up the roof. Schaefer knew that the attic spaces of the courthouse were airy and crisscrossed by wooden beams. Fire taking hold in that cavernous space meant that his available time had shrunk to minutes. The heated air would already be billowing underneath the roof in horizontal gusts, creating a broil of black smoke that might burst out around them all at once and at any time, causing the upper floors of the building to collapse onto the lower.

Schaefer abandoned his efforts and called to Deneen that they must make their escape. He also called down to Fuller, the man who'd replaced William Brown, telling him to abandon his post. Then Schaefer went back up into the cupola to set the mechanism that would ring the bell automatically. This action was quixotic in the extreme: no one needed the sound of the bell to tell them the city was on fire, but set the bell he did. In the few minutes it took Schaefer to set the mechanism, the uppermost portion of the building began to burn fiercely. Getting down and out in the next few minutes became a matter of life and death. A curved stairway hugged the wall descending to the telegraph room, which was filling with thick smoke. Fire had traveled through the walls and collected under the wooden stair treads, which also began to smoke, so Deneen rode the railing, collecting splinters all the way down. A panicked dash got the two men through the telegraph room, where, Schaefer said, "the plastering was then dropping down in that room, and I could see the fire all above through the cracks." He ran down the building's central staircase four flights, into the basement, where he found the jail and twenty-two men locked behind its bars, all of whom listened intently to his report on the chaos above them. The jail keeper insisted on waiting on instructions from someone with more authority, so Schaefer provided some advice: the prisoners' lives depended on letting them loose.

Schaefer didn't take the time to wait on the jailer's decision. He dashed upstairs and burst out onto the street. By this time, it was after one o'clock. A few minutes later, before he had much of a chance to get away—but after he saw the twenty-two men from the prison dash out of the building, along with their keeper—he noticed the sudden absence of the bell's sound overhead. Then he heard a rumble, then a noise like an earthquake, then a cascade of ever-louder crashes. Like most of the more expensive buildings on the South Side, the courthouse was robust in appearance but frail at its core. The housing of the bell had burned away, and down fell two and a half tons of nickel alloy and brass, straight through the wooden center of the building, obliterating the staircase down which he'd escaped minutes before.

The biggest, strongest, most imposing building in Chicago was now a shell, burning down into ruin. For many out on the streets, no other image of the Great Fire would be as memorable. Even those dashing by the courthouse on their way to safety stopped for a moment to stare. As one observer present in the square after the bell's collapse would write, "The strong southwest wind was driving the heat in sheets of flame from the hundreds of burning buildings to the west of it, upon the southwest corner of the building, with such terrific effect that the limestone was melting and was running down the face of the building with first a slow then an accelerating movement as if it were a thin white paste."

A blaze that melted buildings made of stone was nothing that a fireman could be expected to extinguish, but still the members of the force fought on. Distinctions between hero and fool were no longer material; all that was left was work. Having avoided death, Schaefer crossed Randolph Street, where he found the fire marshal, Robert Williams, and the South Side steamer *Economy*. Both had abandoned the battle on the West Side and now played a hopeless stream of water over the burning Sherman House hotel, another one of the city's fireproof landmarks.

Williams spotted Schaefer and handed over his spot on the hose, and then the marshal ran off to find other men and other engines. Schaefer soon found that the *Economy* was already attended by two foremen and a full contingent of pipemen, so there was nothing for him to contribute. Besides, Schaefer noted, the wind was now whipping around the open spaces surrounding the courthouse with such an intensity that the engine's stream of water on the hotel was knocked down before it could reach the second floor. Little more could be done here, so Schaefer dashed away, like Williams, in search of another company in need of men. Whether he found one is unknown. His part in the larger drama of the Great Fire was now finished, the historical record of his involvement now complete—at least until the embers would cool, the stone would cease to melt, and the question of blame would take center stage.

≈ 8 ≈

JOSEPH MEDILL DIDN'T loiter in the courthouse square long enough to witness the bell's demise and the building's implosion. One thought continued to crowd out all others and give him purpose: publish the next day's edition of the *Tribune.* Eastward movement was no longer possible on Randolph, the crowds too thick and the air too full of sparks, cinders, and burning debris flying over the courthouse, so Medill set out north on Clark Street toward South Water Street, which bordered the main branch of the river. He hoped to then proceed east to Dearborn, and then head south eight blocks to his paper, but his walk doubled in length as he took unplanned turn after unplanned turn to follow a maze of passable streets to his newspaper's home.

Two years earlier, *Harper's Weekly* had gushed of the newly constructed Tribune building that "it is constructed of Athens (Illinois) marble and is fire-proof in every part." Floors of cement, party walls of brick, and iron ceilings, stairways, and cornices gave the building an ornate solidity. When Medill arrived, around one o'clock in the morning, he was gratified by two sights. One was the building itself, still standing, as yet unmolested by any flames. The second sight, no less reassuring for being expected, was the buzz of human activity inside. "I found the printers at work setting up the report of the fire as far as it had been prepared," he wrote later, "and learned that all of the reporters were out getting fire news, and that the pressmen were ready to start up as soon as the forms were sent down."

Horace White, the paper's editor in chief, presided, along with

Sam Medill, who as city editor was best equipped to deal with the chaos of reporters dashing in and out of the building at all moments, handing in their notes, and looking for further instructions. The arrangement of the floors of the Tribune building formed a tidy diagram of the process of putting out a metropolitan newspaper in post–Civil War America. Business offices, mostly sales and advertising, used the third floor. Editorial functions happened one flight up, and then, another flight up, rewrite and copy. In the basement, the paper's gigantic cylindrical rotary presses operated. But on an all-hands occasion such as this, reporters and editors physically compressed the spread of tasks, congregating on the second floor near the great racks where type was set, emending and proofing stories even as the type was fit into place.

Once Medill had ascertained that Horace White, his brother Sam, and the other editors of the paper were busy transferring raw copy into the forms, he took charge of the battle to protect their work from the disaster unfolding outside. The uppermost floor of the building supported giant steel tanks that held the water that cooled the presses, served the building's plumbing, and waited on just such an eventuality as this. A squad was detailed to fill any receptacle on hand with water, which was to be poured in as constant a stream as possible on the walls and windows on the west side of the building.

Medill then climbed up to the building's roof. "I had a bird's-eye view of the ravages and the spread of the flames," he wrote, and that view consumed him to such a degree that he didn't do anything but watch the conflagration for long stretches of time. The *Tribune* was situated a little farther to the east and closer to Lake Michigan than most of its journalistic competitors, and that distance made all the difference during these hours when the rest of the South Side was running for its life. Now that he was five stories in the air, and not hobbling his way through streets packed with evacuees, Medill could see the blocks around him clearly enough and catch useful glimpses of what was happening farther away.

To his west, Medill saw fire and smoke bright and thick and high in the air across most of downtown. To his southwest, he could see that something big had caught on fire along the southern edge of the business district, its light shining with a special intensity. As he guessed and would later confirm, he was witnessing the death of Conley's Patch. Chicago was full of neighborhoods like Kate Leary's, decent places derided as slums when in fact they were simply crowded and poor, but Conley's Patch was the real thing: downtown's headquarters for paid sex, bootleg liquor, unlicensed gambling, and other, more exotic vices. The buildings were low and rickety and shoddy, packed in against one another so closely that many freestanding structures still touched their neighbors. The Patch ran for many blocks east to west, centered on Monroe Street, and now that it had caught, the fire would spread fast and hot toward Lake Michigan.

The streets below him were full, and not only with people. Great mischiefs of brown rats swarmed out from unseen crevices, while flights of pigeons madly sought escape from the rising smoke. Pigs, goats, cows, horses, dogs, cats, and chickens scurried about; Chicago was full of animals from corner to corner, and almost all those animals had been left to their own devices. Every business and residence in sight was either wetting down its walls or evacuating its contents, or both. Those hotels near the Tribune building were emptying out like beehives before the heat and smoke, producing a mad rush of well-dressed travelers heading for the lake, bearing their trunks and valises. Occasionally something like a gunshot sounded, and often Medill heard a muffled explosion as the contents of some fuel repository gave in to the flames. The variety of household goods that continued to move through the streets was astonishing, laded in carts or carriages or carried by hand: papers and books, chandeliers, jewelry boxes, safes, sofas, pianos and other musical instruments, firearms, mirrors, toys and dolls, sackfuls of silks and linens, barrels, family portraits, carpets, cookware and silverware, on and on. Men and women wore as much of their wardrobes as they could manage, covered with layer after layer of suits or dresses that made them wobble and sweat as they ran.

Somewhere on the Tribune building's roof was an anemometer, and if Medill had stopped to read the gauge, he would have discovered that the wind was gusting forty, fifty, even sixty miles an hour. This wasn't some kind of cruel prairie zephyr come to aid the fire in its task of destruction; this gale was the work *of* the fire itself, which formed convection whorls made of rapidly rising, superheated air. Such whorls were called fire devils and weren't well understood, because they required unique conditions that only big cities and great forests could provide—tall, narrow canyons inside of which the flames could whirl and collide, agitating the air and setting it in a spin that became a funnel of rising wind many stories in height, carrying the mounting heat along with it.

Medill hadn't fought in the Civil War, though as a strong Union man to the core he'd pushed the war forward with all the force of his paper and personality. He'd lost a younger brother in the aftermath of the Battle of Gettysburg as the Union men chased Robert E. Lee's forces back across the Potomac River. Now, without warning, he was caught in the middle of his own war, and his recollections of the Great Fire reveal a keen satisfaction in this strange sort of battlefield promotion. As he would write later, he set out "to organize a corps to make such a defense as was possible." His description of the action continued in this vein as he wrote of organizing the fight into "fronts." Two fronts were the northern and western sides of the building, facing the fire, and another was the roof. Perhaps his earlier vision of the courthouse catching fire from the top down, and of Schaefer fighting the flames, contributed to his understanding of the problem. But it didn't take a career's worth of experience as a fireman to see the threat from above.

Medill spent well over an hour watching the scenes on the streets below while the rain of sparks and flying shards of wood lit up the roofs of many buildings to his west, one by one. Despite his opposition to the new Tribune building's cost, he knew as much about its construction as anyone. He knew that the Cincinnati cement that covered the roof was warranted to 250 degrees Fahrenheit, but he'd also looked out over the city from the roof many times, under happier circumstances—it was an old and comfortable perch—and in the heat of summer he'd felt the surface soften as he walked across it, from the force of the sun's rays and nothing else. The Great Fire, at this moment, was still many blocks to his west and north and the wind was still working in his favor, pushing the blaze north of them on a diagonal line that pointed at the Illinois Central terminal and other unlucky targets in that direction. But the fire didn't have to come straight at them for the wind to pour flecks of hot material onto that soft cement.

At about three o'clock the roof started to catch fire, in small flares and smolders. Medill directed a detail of more than a dozen employees to douse the flames and shovel the burning brands off the edges of the building. Some of his men, short on buckets or shovels, ran around stomping out flames as they appeared. But whatever good feeling the employees of the *Tribune* nurtured as protectors of their building soon ran headlong into the reality on the streets around them. A reporter ran up to the roof to tell Medill that the Grand Pacific Hotel, under construction west of the courthouse, had been entirely consumed—yet another brand-new, sturdy, "fire-proof" behemoth bedecked with the latest in modern firefighting materials and apparatuses lost to the fire. All the while, the rain of flaming debris got thicker, the pieces bigger and hotter. The fire devils were multiplying, raising cyclones of smoke and heat more than a hundred feet into the air, transporting raw hot air into their faces.

Such heat was dangerous enough for firemen whose bodies had grown accustomed to it, who wore thick canvas outfits designed to keep it out. Medill and his employees had never fathomed a wind so hot it hurt. Still they pressed on. "There were half a dozen chimneys," Medill wrote, "and we would run behind these and stand with our backs against the east side to get a little air and recover from the effects of breathing smoke"—eyes stinging, throats raw, hair singed. Pressed against the brickwork on the lee side of the wind, they would rest until they felt a bit of energy return, then leap out and tamp down the flames for a bit longer.

What had once seemed impossible—that all three divisions of the city could be in peril at the same time—was now fact. As Medill watched through the light and smoke, he could see with disbelief that the fire had taken hold of the North Side. Smoke rose from two spots well to his north, across the main branch of the Chicago River. Then, shortly after three o'clock, he saw something that made his heart race, even amid all the other dramas unfolding below him. Far across the river, close by the lakeshore, sat the city's celebrated waterworks in a complex made of two buildings. The first was the tall, octagonal water tower, rising high into the air like an obelisk, described by Oscar Wilde in later years as "a castellated monstrosity with pepper boxes stuck all over it." The second was an equally ornate but much more sturdy-seeming pumping station, square and squat.

These two structures were Chicago to the hilt, the city's most whimsical architecture reserved for its most basic of material needs. They were easy for Medill to see because they were set together in a small green, about a mile and a half away, and little fire yet filled the intervening blocks. Now, to his horror, he saw that the roof of the pumping station had been set ablaze, presumably from an especially far-floating shard of burning wood. Medill was an avid amateur engineer, and he knew very well that once the pumping station burned, all pressure in the system would draw to zero, which meant that no more water would flow in the mains. Which would mean no more water would replenish the stock in the Tribune building's rooftop water reservoirs. No more water would be available to the fire department anywhere in the city, outside the blocks adjoining the river or the lake. All of Chicago understood that the Great Fire had hours earlier outgrown the capacity of the fire department to do anything but peck at its edges. But it was still a shock to realize that all firefighting efforts, any attempt to check the progress of the flames, however small, would soon all but cease.

With each passing minute, the sights beneath Medill's perch became ever more surreal. He could look east straight down Madison to the lake. Dearborn Street, running north and south, had become a nightmare of its own, a great compressed mass of people, carts, and horses. An old cemetery occupied one block along Dearborn, and, as Medill wrote, "I saw the wooden palings around the graves on fire and also masses of furniture, bedding, and other property burn up." The noise continued to grow. "Over all this terrible scene there was a sullen roar, much like that one hears when close to Niagara Falls," he added, "but mixed with crackling sounds and constant reverberations loud as thunder."

The superheated air of the fire created ever-higher whirls and vortices and gales that reached sixty, seventy, even eighty miles an hour in short bursts, flinging sparks, ashes, and debris across the faces of hapless evacuees. Medill several times descended to the lower floors along the west side of the building, where a group of employees was watering down the walls with what was left in the tanks and watching with foreboding as the window glass developed ever longer and wider cracks and the furniture began to smoke. They'd shut the iron shutters on the east and south sides of the building, but as the clock ticked past three, they found that they had to take care of the wooden shutters on the west side of the building by dashing in the room, hurling a bucketful of water against the window, and dashing back out before the heat rendered them senseless.

All the while, Medill was aware, and amazed and gratified, that reporters were still coming in with notes, editors were barking out sentences to printers who set and reset type as fast as their fingers could fly. The exertions of the long night had become a desperate race against time. The next story told by the *Tribune* might turn out to be one of its own destruction.

❧ 9 ❧

BY FIVE O'CLOCK on Monday morning, Ed Chamberlin's considerable enthusiasm for the enterprise of journalism had been extinguished. As the heat pushed Joseph Medill and his crew to ever more frantic exertions in the Tribune building, a mile and a half to their northwest Chamberlin paused his pell-mell travels across the burning city to become nothing more than a spectator. He sat on a tall pile of lumber in Avery's lumberyard, on the west side of the turgid and muddy T where the main branch of the Chicago River split north and south, and watched. It was a splendid vantage point, the clearest ground-level panorama of Chicago to be found anywhere in the city, a view full of masts and grain elevators and warehouses and lumberyards. On this night, however, it was a picture window looking out on hell: terrifying, numbing, and yet strangely beautiful to Chamberlin, who was out of danger's reach and past the point of exhaustion.

He'd arrived at the lumberyard half an hour earlier. Somewhere in that miasma of flames, ashes, scorched and crumbled masonry walls, on the South Side, lay the Evening Post building, four doors to the west of the Tribune's. His assumption was that his paper's home was gone. The night before, he'd been awake until dawn at the Red Flash fire, and his sleep had been short. He described his mood now as "listless." "All solicitude for the remaining portion of the city, and all appreciation of the magnitude of the tragedy that was being acted across the river, had left me," he wrote. "I did not care whether the city stood or burned. I was dead, so far as my sensibilities were concerned."

Half a mile to his southeast, the remains of the courthouse burned, its cupola and bell having hours earlier plunged into oblivion. Down the south branch of the river a few blocks, Chamberlin could see that the National grain elevator, spared the night before, was now a collapsed, smoking heap. Small tugboats still navigated the water in front of him, trying to move larger vessels to safety while skirting half-sunk and still-burning ships. All three branches of the river were still illuminated well into the distance by the burning rigging of large vessels, visible through the haze as drooping red traceries of fire. To his left, the North Side was going up in smoke as the fire began to march toward the prairie and Lake Michigan. He told himself that he would get up in a few minutes to see what was happening there.

The day before, Joseph Medill's *Tribune* had given three full-length columns to the Red Flash fire, a Battle of Gettysburg proportion of the paper's available quota of words. How many columns the *Evening Post*, Chamberlin's own employer, would have devoted to Red Flash, and how many of his own observations would have made it into that reportage, he would never know. The *Evening Post* didn't publish on Sunday nights. And there would be no Monday paper this week. And whenever his paper did resume its run, the story wouldn't be Red Flash.

He'd reached the scene at DeKoven Street within a few minutes of the fire's ignition, even before the blaze first crossed Taylor. He was still a twenty-year-old, and no matter what his skill with a notebook and pen, he jumped to conclusions the way the Great Fire jumped across streets, alleys, public squares, and rivers. In young Ed's simplified conception of the world, everything had a simple explanation. The panic that had surrounded him as he watched was, to his mind, the special condition of the immigrant poor. "The wretched female inhabitants were rushing out almost naked, imploring spectators to help them on with their burdens." It didn't occur to him that fate or bad planning could play a decisive role in affairs, and so the people of DeKoven were to blame, as well as the firemen for being "enervated by the whisky which is copiously poured" after a fire such as Red Flash.

He'd watched the action on the West Side from a shed along Ewing Street, three blocks north of DeKoven, until that shed began to smoke. Then he'd moved up the street, toward Red Flash, and watched again, notebook in hand, a sequence of sentry and retreat that would repeat itself again and again over the next hour. Chamberlin had moved northward along Jefferson with the fire's western edge until he reached the ruins of Red Flash. Along the way, he wrote, "two boys, themselves intoxicated, reeled about, each bearing a small cask of whisky, out of which they insisted on treating everybody they met." He watched the engine *Titsworth* work the fire on Van Buren. "Suddenly the horses were attached to the engine, and, as soon as the hose was reeled, it disappeared, whirling northward on Jefferson," he wrote. "What did it mean? I caught the words, 'Across the river,' uttered doubtingly by a bystander. The words passed from mouth to mouth, and there was a universal incredulity, although the suggestion was communicated through the crowd with startling rapidity."

So Chamberlin had run, again, to the Adams Street viaduct and eastward across the river, to discover the South Side ablaze. In that moment he'd made up his mind to keep moving, to run everywhere he could in order to witness as much as possible of what he called "the doom of the blazing city." By one o'clock in the morning he was pelting down Monroe Street, just ahead of the fire in Conley's Patch, overwhelmed by the scale of destruction around him. "I contemplated the ruin that was working, and the tears rose to my eyes," he wrote. "I could have wept at that saddest of sights, but I choked down the tears, and they did not rise again that night."

Then Chamberlin had decided to head for the Evening Post building, on Madison, but was arrested in his progress by the sight of the courthouse, its upper floors consumed by flames. The burning cupola, he wrote, "presented a scene of the sublimest as well as most melancholy beauty." As Mathias Schaefer completed his narrow escape from the building, Chamberlin witnessed the death of the great bell and reported the "dull sound" and "heavy shock" as it reached its final resting place in the building's basement. His hat pulled low, his collar raised high, Chamberlin began a sweep of the South Side, traveling down every thoroughfare he found clear of fire, skipping through falling sparks and over fallen debris. Arriving at Lake Street and LaSalle, with the fire a block or two away, he recorded what he called "the scene of confusion at its height":

> As large as was the number of people who were flying from the fire, the number of passive spectators was still larger. Their eyes were all diverted from the scurrying mass of people around them to the spectacle of appalling grandeur before them. They stood transfixed, with a mingled feeling of horror and admiration, and while they often exclaimed at the beauty of the scene, they all devoutly prayed that they might never see such another. The noise of the conflagration was terrific. To the sound which the simple process of combustion always makes, magnified here to so grand an extent, was added the crash of falling buildings and the constant explosion of stores of oil and other like material.

"All these things," he added, "the great, dazzling, mounting light, the crush and roar of the conflagration, and the desperate flight of the crowd, combined to make a scene of which no intelligent idea can be conveyed in words."

Then he'd zigzagged back to the west, scribbling hasty notes, until he reached the Randolph Street bridge, the same perch that Joseph Medill had occupied many hours earlier. By this time, approaching four o'clock in the morning, Chamberlin wrote, "whatever excitement we had felt during the night had passed away." For a time he sat on the railing of the bridge and watched the city burn as "a torrent of humanity" passed by him, and took note of the strangest tableau of his evening: "I saw an undertaker rushing over the bridge with his mournful stock. He employed half a dozen boys, gave each of them a coffin, took a large one himself, and headed the weird procession. The sight of those coffins, upright, and bobbing along just above the heads of the crowd, without any apparent help from anybody else, was somewhat startling, and the

Crowds on the Randolph Street bridge, published in *Harper's Weekly*, October 28, 1871

unavoidable suggestion was that they were escaping across the river to be ready for use when the debris of the conflagration should be cleared away."

Soon the heat of the South Side fires had driven Chamberlin off the bridge and back into the West Side. After a short walk to the north he stopped at Avery's lumberyard, where he now lay atop a large pile of wood, watching the city burn and chatting with a few other men who had discovered the same improvised box seats. As they watched, the Wells Street bridge connecting South Side to North Side caught fire, "affording something novel." The south end of the bridge, closer to the flames, burned more quickly, and soon "the whole structure tipped to the northward, and stood fixed, one end in the water, at an angle of about sixty degrees." They continued to watch, fascinated, as the bridge burned until it "looked like a skeleton with ribs of fire."

At around five o'clock, Chamberlin stood up, bade his companions adieu, and kept walking. He might not have cared any longer if the city stood or burned, but the story was now in the North Division. He crossed the river and followed the fire there

for a short while, gathering what information he could, until about
seven, when he decided that thirty-four hours of fire reportage had
given him sufficient material to satisfy his employer—whenever his
employer might find itself in business again.

As Chamberlin crossed back over to the West Division and
walked home in the hazy morning light, he noted that the streets
were full of "scores of working girls on their way 'down town' as
usual, bearing their lunch-baskets as if nothing had happened."
Like Chamberlin, these young women found that the view in front
of their faces was impossible to square with their customary reality.
Chicago could not be destroyed, at least not on a scale that would
bring it to a complete halt. "They saw the fire and smoke before
them, but could not believe that the city, with their means of livelihood, had been swept away during the night." To watch them
march into their jobs was one of the saddest and most peculiar
moments of Chamberlin's life. But in another way, the sight was the
most Chicagoan thing he'd ever seen.

≋ 10 ≋

B Y SEVEN O'CLOCK on Monday morning, ten hours after the Learys' barn had ignited, the fire was so big, so broad, and so hungry that it had obliterated not only large sections of the city but also any sense of a single, shared experience. In fact, the Great Chicago Fire was never one fire but several, each with its ultimate ancestry on DeKoven Street but each proceeding with its own character and life span. Some of these separate fires still raged; others had spent most of their energy.

On the West Side, one fire had consumed the Learys' neighborhood, while another had consumed the blocks surrounding St. Paul's. Then, on the South Side, separate fires that originated at Parmelee's omnibus depot, the South Side gasworks, and Conley's Patch had over the hours joined together to envelop the city's central business district. Now the North Side burned from three more points of origin: a paint shop along the main branch of the Chicago River, a set of train yards a few blocks farther east, and the waterworks along the lakeshore. In this manner, at first, at least eight distinct fires raged, each with its own pace and path, before they slowly combined into one citywide conflagration. Each one, by itself, was far larger than any fire the city had ever known. Knit together, they formed a disaster for the ages.

By the time the morning sun began to show as a low, pale disk through the smoke and haze drifting above Lake Michigan, the fire on DeKoven Street was all but out, the Learys' neighborhood all but destroyed. The courthouse from which Mathias Schaefer had fled in the nick of time was no longer anything more than a set of cragged stone pillars emerging from a pile of rubble still aflame. The Palmer House, Grand Pacific Hotel, Tremont House, and Sherman House, all "fireproof," were no more, and fire had destroyed the offices of the *Times*, the *Republican*, the *Evening Mail*, the *Evening Journal*, the *Staats-Zeitung*, and *The Workingman's Advocate*. The upper floors of the *Evening Post*, Ed Chamberlin's paper, had collapsed well before dawn. The First National Bank, the city's most august financial institution, was a ruin. The Field & Leiter building was gone—much of its merchandise now transferred two miles to the south—as were the spacious warehouses of John V. Farwell, the company's closest wholesale competitor.

In the central and eastern portions of the North Side, where a great many of the city's wealthiest residents lived and where the fire still blazed, no longer did the flames move in great whirling leaps as they had in downtown the night before. Here, where a single house might sit alone at the center of half a city block, the fire's ability to form towering cyclones of heat and flame was negated. Instead, the tree-lined lots and fine flush wood sidewalks burned low and hot and slow as disaster now marched northward in a low broil of flame toward the city's uppermost borders. A second low column of fire flew faster, like a flanking cavalry maneuver, up the more thickly populated western part of the North Side, beside the north branch of the Chicago River. Here the blaze ripped through the city's thickest German and Scandinavian sections, which were packed with trim, well-kept shops and smaller wooden homes.

Steam engines and other equipment had begun to arrive at West Side rail stations in response to Mayor Roswell Mason's frantic telegrams of the night before—three full companies from Milwaukee were the first to arrive—but all they and the bedraggled Chicago force could now do was to peck at the edges of the fire, working to save a few blocks here and there along the north and south branches of the river. As the fire spread, it widened, and thousands of North Siders evacuated to Lincoln Park along Lake Michigan, where they stood huddled with thousands of displaced Chicagoans ranging from the penniless to the very, very rich, some of them knee-deep in warm lake water. Others gathered in the adjacent Catholic cemetery, sitting atop the graves and gravestones of Confederate prisoners of war and unclaimed indigents, among others. All wondered when they'd go home, if there were homes to go to, where they would sleep.

On the West Side, arrested in its northward progress by the ruins of Red Flash and prevented from spreading to the west and south of the Learys' neighborhood by the mounting southwesterly wind, the fire had long ago satisfied itself with consuming the lumberyards against the south branch of the river and now burned slowly and sluggishly. Meanwhile, on the South Side, the fire continued to shift and turn and move through downtown in new and unpredictable directions. One of those vectors took the flames on a slow march northward across Madison, right into the heart of the publishing and bookselling district of the city, where the Tribune building still stood. Any and all measures of greatness would serve Chicago's boosters, and now Joseph Medill was living through the biggest and most destructive disaster the country had ever known. The points of comparison that would soon be offered by all of the city's newspapers were world historic: Moscow in 1812, London in 1666, Pompeii in AD 79. The Great Fire was a catastrophe, but also a wonder.

Medill and his fellow owners were served by a staff who ran perhaps the best-organized paper in the country. Certainly it was the best organized in Chicago. Its circulation numbers might have run a close second to those of the *Times,* but its influence in important rooms and among important people was so much greater than Wilbur Storey's paper as to eclipse all other sources of journalism west of Washington, D.C. Medill had tried to dissuade his partners from taking a large loan to construct the new building, but he also knew that the resulting edifice was a testament to the newspaper's success, and that fact gratified him. In this era, the first heyday of modern, telegraph-driven journalism, newspapers came and went. To plant the paper in its own five-story fireproof building was an homage to the power of the press and the preeminence of the *Tribune.*

The problem was, Medill was more aware than anyone that

"fireproof," as applied to their new building, was just a word and nothing more. On his walk into downtown, he had seen the gargantuan courthouse catch fire, and he knew that it had collapsed with little resistance from its outer walls made of three-foot-thick Indiana stone. Then he'd stood on the roof of the Tribune building for some time and watched as other, similarly touted buildings, including some of the grandest, smartest, strongest hotels in the city, lost their lives to the flames.

Perhaps the Tribune building's own stonework walls might withstand the heat, but by the time the dim and smoky light of morning arrived, the building's window glass had formed innumerable cracks, the coating of tar on its roof had melted, and too much heat had gathered in some of its western rooms, those on the side of the fire, for a man to stay and wet down the walls more than a few moments without scorching his own hands and face. The rush and roar of noise outside told its own awful tale. It was an act of defiance, of stubbornness, of foolishness, to demand that the paper put out an edition that night, but Medill received little resistance to the charge from his employees, who possessed a valid excuse not to come in but who had come in anyway.

Medill's luck did not hold out. He was left alone to lead the fight against the fire now: his co-owners, William Bross and Horace White, were long gone, tending after their own homeless families, who had been caught in the path of the flames and had made their own narrow escapes. At seven o'clock, an ashen-faced man ran upstairs from the basement presses to deliver news of the fire's coup de grâce. The paper's iron rollers had "melted into a mass," he said, and with them had disappeared any hope of putting out a Monday special edition. And even if the presses had remained intact, the man gasped, the smoke in the basement was too thick for breathing. And even had the basement been free from smoke, he finished, to make sure Medill took the point, the depleted water supply would have prevented the steam-powered machinery from working for more than the shortest of print runs.

Really, to have imagined at any point in the long, awful night that a Monday morning edition of the *Tribune* could appear was a delusion. "The printing of any papers containing an account of the great fire had to be abandoned," Medill wrote later, his pedestrian prose belying the deep-seated emotion that had driven him to fight with such desperation for so long. It was a sore blow for a man who believed that getting the news out under all circumstances was the highest calling in life.

Medill now traded in his concern for printing a morning edition for the survival of the building. But soon another of the paper's employees found him to say that the fire outside had jumped, skipped, and whirled so that it now approached the building along Dearborn from the *north*, against the prevailing wind, as well as from the south—a fiendish pincer move that startled Medill into a flurry of action. He hurried as best he could down four flights of stairs and out a back door, into the long alley that ran between their building and McVicker's Theatre, whose windblown and trampled sidewalk placards advertised the holdover for a second week of a popular Irish melodrama called *Elfie*. What Medill saw was clear enough. The Conley's Patch blaze had spread toward the lake faster than he'd thought possible. There was fire to the south of him and another wall of flame coming from the opposite direction, heading down Dearborn toward the Tribune building, cutting off what he'd expected to be a reliable escape route and leaving his building with minutes to live.

Medill rushed back inside and moved from room to room to gather his men and order them out of the building. Some of the paper's employees had worked themselves to exhaustion in the westernmost rooms of the building and now lay prone on the floor, barely conscious. Medill and his companions from the roof dragged the men to their feet, sometimes none too gently—for, as he put it, "there was no time to coax a man to get up."

Only now, when Medill at last abandoned the thought of putting out the next day's news, did he stop to think about the previous day's. All the firemen on the continent, it seemed, could no longer save his city. And he couldn't save his building. And his printers couldn't save the next day's edition. But what he could do was try to save the inestimable treasure that lay in a set of sewn leather binders in an inner office of the building: a complete run of the *Tribune*, every issue from June 10, 1847, to the present, bound month to month in full-sheet size at twenty-eight inches in height and each weighing twenty pounds or more. Words—old words—were now more important to Medill than bricks of any age.

A duplicate set of binders, covering the past eleven years, lay in Medill's West Side house, beyond danger, so he shouted at his men to grab only the editions prior to 1860. Another one of the night's innumerable hand-to-hand brigades began, in conditions that made the effort seem less noble than mad. They now operated in air that was superheating in advance of the fire moving toward them just a block or two to the north, south, and west, a press of heat that began to singe their hair, clog their nostrils, and toast the bottoms of their feet.

As they hurried to the building's exit, their hands pulsed in the heat, and the binders themselves began to smoke, the old newsprint so dry and brittle that their cargo threatened to catch fire in their grasp. The couriers got outside, only to drop their bundles on the sidewalk, swearing and shaking their hands. Over their shoulders, less than a block away now, the fire and smoke mounted in a wall that seemed to rise higher than the Tribune building itself. Medill and his men started to scramble eastward down Madison Street in as straight a line as they could, in the direction of the lake, leaving the pile of binders behind.

There, then, on the sidewalk, a large swath of Chicago's history burned. In the future, a second stash of the *Tribune*'s run from 1860 forward would be discovered in another editor's home, in addition to the one lodged with Medill. In this way the day-by-day history of Lincoln's nomination, of the decisive moment of South Carolina's secession, of the brutal battles of the Civil War, of the disquieting and disappointing years of Reconstruction in the South, all was preserved in minute detail. But from the first few years of the paper, perhaps one in three issues was ever discovered, tucked away in various offices, archives, and homes.

The loss was substantial. Created in 1847 as a daily offshoot of a negligible Sunday magazine called *Gem of the Prairie*, the *Tribune* had been born just in time to witness the events of 1848, which had been Chicago's best year, its annus mirabilis, a year no other American city could or would ever duplicate. Events that in a city like New York, Philadelphia, Boston, or St. Louis were spread across decades had in 1848 occurred in one compact rush in Chicago. At the end of 1846, five months before the *Tribune* had launched and eleven years before Medill arrived to become the paper's managing editor, no canal connected Lake Michigan to the Illinois River and the Mississippi River beyond. Not a foot of telegraph wire ran in the city. There were no cattle yards, no grain elevators. No Board of Trade operated to regularize the exchange of commodities and associated contracts. No Atlantic Ocean–going vessel had ever docked at a Chicago wharf. No railroad had ever run into, out of, or through the city.

But two years and a day later, by New Year's 1849, all of that had changed. This was part of the myth of Chicago. Everything was different in Chicago because everything had seemed to happen all at once. With the destruction of the *Tribune*'s full run of back issues, the city's year of wonders, its sudden birth into the modern age, faded that much further from the record and shone forth that much brighter as legend.

The night would be very hard on all sorts of historians. Many of the documentary materials for the biography of Abraham Lincoln that Medill planned to write had been stored at the newspaper and not at his house, a choice he would regret forever. The courthouse was destroyed, along with all its legal documents, its real estate records, its legislative ledgers. An original copy of the Emancipation Proclamation was kept in a public library on the North Side, now in flames. All in all, much of the official record of Lincoln's involvement with the state and with the city was going up in flames, along with the personal histories of most of the founders of Chicago. William Bross, Gurdon Saltonstall Hubbard, William Butler Ogden, Ferdinand Peck, the McCormicks—their homes lay on the North Side or near the lake on the South Side, and all were now being consumed. Many men of the generation one ahead of Medill's had turned to reflection as age worked on them and their day-to-day responsibilities shrank, consulting the correspondence they kept in home libraries to write their autobiographies, memoirs, and recollections. In these heady postwar days, setting down the stories of their lives was a popular pastime for the men who'd made Chicago. And now those memoirs, and memories, were burning.

At the same time he lamented the city's lost past, though, Medill was able to look at its future through a stubborn ahistorical lens. London's fire of 1666 had destroyed fourteen centuries of history. Here in Chicago? Less than forty years, that was all, so little that there were hundreds of residents who still carried in their own heads the all but comprehensive story of the city's past. A fortune in capital had gone up in flames, but Chicago's true wealth did not come from its inventory of money or goods or ideas. It came from the *flow* of money and goods and ideas, which was a very different thing. And what had flowed the previous day could and would continue to flow the next day, and the day after that, and the next week, and into the future. At some point between the first minutes of the DeKoven fire that he saw from his second-story windows and his escape from the Tribune building to the Illinois Central breakwater along the lakefront, a kernel of thought formed, not only that the city would rise again, but that it could do so in a new and different and better way.

Medill believed a lot of things and he believed them absolutely. He believed that Chicago could not be killed, that individual fates were nothing compared with the city's collective energy. He had the rigidity and assurance of the true disciple. He believed in temperance, and he believed in probity, and he believed that a small set of influential men were fit and obligated to make important decisions for everyone else. He believed that professional politicians should follow and not attempt to lead these best men. And he believed, most of all, in taking hold of opportunity.

Less than half an hour after Medill and his charges escaped with their lives and little else, the Tribune building's roof and floors gave way. Even as they did, Medill began to make his slow, circuitous way back to his own neighborhood. On the far reaches of Wash-

Ruins of the Chicago Tribune building, published in
C. R. Clark photograph book, 1871

ington Street, a full fourteen blocks to the west, far away from the
river and the edge of the fire, there were no screams, no running
crowds, no awful illumination, no choking smoke. For all outward
appearances this was an ordinary Monday. The young women
Chamberlin had seen earlier that morning, the ones heading off to
South Side jobs that no longer existed, were still moving along the
sidewalks, but fewer of them. And some were now walking in the
opposite direction, heading back to their own residences, awestruck
and bewildered.

When Medill reached his own home at last, his voice was hoarse
and his clothes singed and covered with soot. He didn't take long
to comfort his wife or his two young girls, or to sit with them and
together ponder their good fortune, or to tell them stories of what
he'd seen. Nothing was more characteristic of Joseph Medill than
what he did next. This was a Monday morning, and like any Monday morning there was business to attend to. His plan, much like

that of Marshall Field, had a clarity born of simplicity. Fetch a couple hours' sleep. Gather together what staff he could. Find a West Side print shop that could operate at high volume on short notice. He couldn't get a paper out this morning, but he could do his damnedest to get a paper out before Wilbur Storey and the *Times* did.

PART III

Aftermath

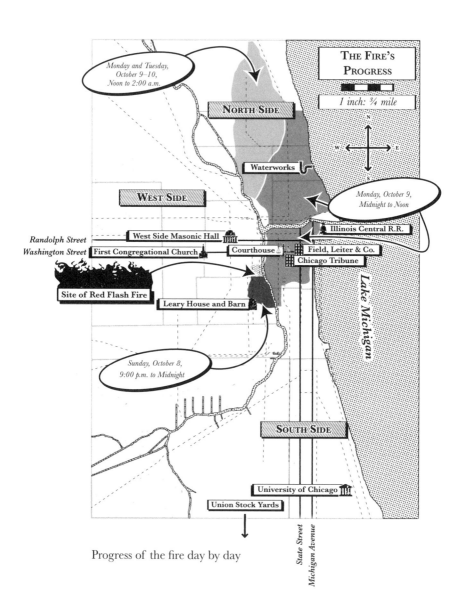

THE FIRE'S
PROGRESS

1 inch: ¾ mile

Monday and Tuesday,
October 9–10,
Noon to 2:00 a.m.

NORTH SIDE

N
W   E
S

Waterworks

WEST SIDE

Monday, October 9,
Midnight to Noon

Randolph Street   West Side Masonic Hall   Illinois Central R.R.

Washington Street   First Congregational Church   Courthouse   Field, Leiter & Co.
Chicago Tribune

Lake Michigan

Site of Red Flash Fire

Leary House and Barn

Sunday, October 8,
9:00 p.m. to Midnight

SOUTH SIDE

University of Chicago

Union Stock Yards

State Street
Michigan Avenue

Progress of the fire day by day

≈ 11 ≈

A S THE MONDAY MORNING sun rose behind thin clouds and smoke on a city decimated in one part and still burning fiercely in another, a stout, extravagantly square-jawed forty-four-year-old man named Charles Courtney Pickney Holden summoned his driver and climbed into a carriage outside his West Side home. He lived on Aberdeen Street, well outside the reach of the fire, in the same well-to-do area straight to the west of the courthouse inhabited by prominent city administrators, newspaper editors, factory owners, clergymen, and others of more than moderate success. Far enough from the conflagration to avoid any thought of flight, Holden aimed to turn the tables and follow in the fire's path instead.

His would be one of thousands of tours of the city that day, but no other tourist had Holden's unique power to do something about what he saw. For twenty years now he'd held a well-paid job as a land assessor for the Illinois Central Railroad, determining property values along the company's right-of-way, but history would not remember him for that work. Instead, it would remember him as one of the two aldermen from the Tenth Ward of the city and as the president of the city's Common Council, a position that made him the person more responsible than any other in government for taking action to help the wounded city heal.

Given the sometimes-extreme political gyrations of Chicago, Holden had no assurance that he'd be an alderman past November of the next year. But in this moment he, more than anyone else,

Portrait of Charles C. P. Holden,
credited to Charles D. Mosher,
date unknown

held what reins of political power the city had to offer. This morning, in both official and personal capacities, Holden intended to
ascertain the damage to the city on what he called a "mission of
observation." He knew that the North Side still burned—he had
eyes to see the wide billows of smoke still rising across the river—
but he didn't know yet how much of the city was gone, how long the
recovery might take, or just how much raw need existed.

As for where the fire had been: anyone could understand that.
Its path was made obvious by looking at the blackened city blocks
and registering the force and direction of the wind, still blowing
warm, dry, and strong from the southwest. Holden rode against
that wind, moving south along Jefferson Street, keeping his carriage on the west edge of the fire's line of damage. The sky was full
of scudding clouds, the dirt roads dry and smooth. To his right he
saw untouched homes on small, tidy lots, local businesses still open,
gawkers gathered on every corner, residents of the west side of the
street counting their blessings.

To his left, as far as he could see, everything was a dark junk-
yard of desolation. As his driver led him down Jefferson and across
Harrison, Holden saw in the southwest corner of the intersection

eight forms shrouded in white: eight dead bodies arranged side by side, like a row of piano keys. He didn't stop. Holden knew that the "harvest of death" would be impossible to comprehend, that eight corpses represented a fraction of those that would have to be found, gathered, identified, and laid to rest. Still, those dead Chicagoans were his first glimpse of the fire's true violence, and he would never forget the sight.

Another six blocks brought him down to DeKoven Street, the southern rim of the barren ground. All the while the crowds grew thicker while the mix of human despair, restlessness, and excitement grew ever more potent. A few weeks later, Holden would describe the scene for a reporter:

> Great living masses met our vision in every direction. There were the sick and the crippled, the aged and the infirm, great numbers of whom had been injured in various ways by the fire; and all were appealing most piteously for help, although thankful that their lives had been spared. Scores of little children clung to their mothers, while the mothers knew not whither to go or what to do. Women in every station of life were rushing about hither and thither, hunting for their lost little ones; husbands were searching for their wives—wives were hunting for their husbands; and children were crying as though their hearts would break—orphans, indeed, so far as we could judge.

This description says as much about Holden, who was never above a little melodrama, as it did about the mood of the ever-growing crowds on DeKoven. While plenty of sadness and exhaustion were on display, the dominant emotion on the West Side, even just half a day after the fire had swept these blocks, was curiosity.

The sight of the Learys' pair of cottages, standing intact, was as arresting to Holden as the bodies a few blocks to the north. The survival of the two structures at 137 DeKoven would be commented on as long as Chicagoans would talk about the Great Fire. Like sentinels huddling shoulder to shoulder on the edge of a ruined battlefield, the Learys' fragile frame house and the one rented by the

McLaughlins still stood, alone on the entire block. Behind the two buildings, to the north as far as the eye could see, there was nothing but smoldering ashes, rubble, and charred shapes that included stoves, kilns, hydrants, livestock, pets, and the occasional human being.

The full scale of the ongoing disaster was too vast for anyone to try to comprehend, but the very human scale of its opening moments could be absorbed. After all, everyone in Chicago had witnessed or experienced a barn fire, or a cookstove fire, or a warehouse fire, or, for that matter, a big fire like the one that had consumed Red Flash on Saturday night. A Great Fire four miles long and two miles wide, moving like a living thing in its speed and malevolence—that was something out of a Jules Verne novel. But any resident of the city could imagine themselves on DeKoven as the fire took hold: the first jitter of the flames in a window, the first plumes of smoke pouring out, then the sudden presence of fire-

The Learys' two closely spaced houses at 137 DeKoven Street, after the Great Fire. The house on the left, fronting the street, was rented by Catherine and Patrick McLaughlin.

men, the foreman barking through his speaking horn and the pipe-men on their taps and leading long lengths of hose into the blaze. Here at 137 DeKoven, at least, was a fixed and identifiable spot that everyone also knew would become a permanent part of the world's history. To stand on DeKoven and ponder the Learys' cottage was a unique opportunity to stand next to immortality.

If Holden stopped for a few moments to listen to the conversations all around him, he would have heard many of the voices, even those of the children, lit with excitement. *It started in the barn! It started in the barn!* they shouted, and pointed to a charred rectangle of ground thirty feet north of the Learys' house. *Mrs. Leary was milking her cow!* they said, though they had no idea if that was true. *She knocked over the lamp!* said someone else. It was a good story and people seemed to like to hear it. Where anyone had first heard it, though, no one could ever say.

Another curious phenomenon had already taken hold, in the morning after the city had caught fire on this very spot. While the vast plain of fuming ruins between DeKoven and wherever the fire might be burning now was understood to be *terra non grata,* off limits to explorers, the Learys' humble property was an exception. Here, all restraint and decorum were forgotten. A legend was even now being born: barn, cow, lamp, flames. An immigrant Irishwoman was already becoming a blank slate on which could be written the story of the beginning of—and blame for—the Great Fire.

People circled the two houses. They climbed the short stairs to the McLaughlins' front entry, which faced onto DeKoven, and tried the door: locked. They tried the Learys' door: locked. They stood over a rectangular mass of charred ashes forty feet behind the house, the remains of the Learys' barn, and pointed northward to indicate the direction of the fire. Reporters from several different newspapers were on the scene and gave credence to anyone who claimed to have been present at the fire's ignition, all the while scratching in their notebooks. Who was this Mrs. Leary? She milked cows for a living. She was Irish. Can we speak to her? Where is she now? No one knows. Did she milk the cows at night? Certainly she did. Was she in the barn when the fire started? Did *she* start it?

The answers they received were as varied as the questions, none of them reliable, but all of them useful if you were a reporter who needed copy. Few called her "O'Leary," not yet. The most entertaining tales of how the fire started were written down with the most enthusiasm, soon to be presented as fact in the post-fire editions of the *Tribune*, the *Times*, the *Evening Post*, the *Inter Ocean*, the *Staats-Zeitung*, the *Republican*, the *Evening Journal*. The Learys and the McLaughlins themselves were nowhere to be found, having absconded—so everyone assumed—with the true story of the fire's origin.

The full scope of the fire that had started on their street was impossible to fathom for the spectators milling along DeKoven. It was like guessing the progress and location of a distant oceangoing vessel by standing on the pier at its point of departure. Where was the blaze now? What were its farthest limits? Had it really jumped the river *twice*, once to ignite the South Side and then again to light the North Side, where each home destroyed might represent the value of every possession in the Learys' entire neighborhood? Had the well-heeled fancy cats there suffered the same fate as the cottage dwellers here?

Holden kept his visit to DeKoven short. His purpose that day was not to find out how the fire had started. The Board of Police and Fire Commissioners would assume the responsibility of an investigation. Holden's self-appointed charge, as president of the city's Common Council, was to ascertain the scope of the disaster and engage the machinery of city administration to respond in kind, and to be sure that every class of resident in the city was taken into account. After all, every class of citizen needed help. And every class of citizen voted.

Holden crossed the river to the South Side, where the wide roads were mostly hard-packed dirt and the progress surprisingly easy in the absence of the usual Monday morning bustle. In short order, he passed the ruins of Conley's Patch, the courthouse, Field & Leiter's, and the Tribune building, among all the other vanished downtown standbys, the hotels and the churches and the theaters and the storefronts. At one point he encountered the fire chief,

Robert Williams, who told Holden that "the thing had gone up" and that with the final destruction of the waterworks, at about four in the morning, his department had been rendered "powerless" as the water pressure dropped to nothing in the mains. The realization was more symbolic than anything else; the firemen of Chicago and their compatriots from other cities could continue to work along the river, using its water, but the Great Fire had escaped their grasp well before the loss of the waterworks. After a short and fruitless search through the ruined downtown for any other city officials, Holden crossed the river to the North Side, observing the boats and bridges sitting charred in the water and moving through the wreckage of the city's wealthiest sections before he ended his tour along the lakeside at the still-intact, nonfunctioning water tower and pumping station, dark smoke still rising from the neighborhoods a mile or so to the north.

In the coming weeks and months, Holden would be credited for some things and blamed for many others. He'd experienced plenty of success and defeat in his political career, and he held a position of influence. He was not easy to dislike, for up to this moment he'd moved with unusual ease between and within the city's panoply of classes, ethnicities, and political parties. Of all of Chicago's public figures, in fact, he might have best embodied all the contradictions and vying factions of the city. He had money, and he owned several properties around town, but he owned no business of his own and earned a salary paid by far wealthier men. He was an old-timer, but he was not an Old Settler. He'd first visited Chicago in 1836 at the age of eight, one year before the city's incorporation, as the son of a farmer passing through, traveling from New Hampshire en route to a land claim in southern Illinois. On that trip the Holdens stayed a night at a rowdy and rustic hotel on Lake and Canal Streets, and Charles had never forgotten the experience.

Growing up in rural Illinois, to the southwest of Chicago, Holden had walked six miles round trip to a school lodged in a "rude log hut" and read elementary history and mathematics and grammar. After seven years of this rough isolation, he'd returned to Chicago to work as a clerk, first in a grocery and then in a bookstore. Then a call to fortune sounded somewhere in his soul, for he'd spent the next decade living his own miniature version of the history of the American West, the kind of unheeded miniature epic that constituted so many of the minor biographies of the nineteenth century. He enlisted in a company of Illinois men to fight in the Mexican-American War, but arrived too late to see real action. Instead of coming straight home, he rushed for gold in California and tended a yeoman's farm in the Napa Valley, before he headed back to Chicago in 1853.

On his return trip Holden had survived the wreck of his passenger vessel on the shoals off Anacapa Island, just north of Los Angeles. Soon thereafter he landed his post with the Illinois Central and toiled diligently and well, reaping the benefits of the federal land grants that generated so much income for the railroads through lean and lucrative economies alike. Then, during the Civil War, Holden had discovered politics. In 1862 he'd run for mayor and lost by 8 percent to the father of a well-known Union soldier, but one year later he'd won the vote for alderman in his West Side ward. In 1870, after seven years of service, he was chosen by his fellow aldermen to head the Common Council.

A centrist Republican who could poise himself between Democrats and liberal Republicans, immigrants and natives, poor and rich, Holden balanced constituencies with as much aplomb as anyone could. He was genial, of high but not unseemly ambition, and he loved his city. Eight years was a long run as an alderman, and whatever hunger for office he might have possessed seemed to be sated by his work representing the Tenth Ward. His power had increased, via his election as council president, but his political survival was still subject to the whims of his own ward's voters and not those of the entire city.

Municipal governments in the nineteenth century didn't align neatly—or at all—with national parties or ideologies. The most vocal argument to be had was not between Democrat and Republican—many prominent Chicagoans had been both during their lives—but rather between those who felt that the mayor and council, of whatever party, should have a firm hand in the running of the city and those who felt that a city was, in essence, a public "corporation" that should be run more like one of Chicago's many revered private firms. The key question, above all, was not who was a voter or who was a citizen but who was a "stakeholder." Property ownership was held to be the highest personal aspiration, but also the most important qualification for making decisions about the city's political direction. Or, put another way, for many of the city's better-off citizens, the ability to make good economic decisions—as expressed in a person's visible accumulation of wealth and property—was held to be hard evidence of one's ability to make good political decisions.

Voters, in this model, chose the city's "managers," but weren't expected to have too much say in their managers' choices. What voters needed, therefore, were trustworthy and credible candidates who could be expected, once in office, to leave most of the running of the city to private enterprise. Tax rates were to be kept low, the professional fire and police forces kept small, while charity was to be farmed out to dozens of private providers. What happened on your street was your concern, and yours to do something about. The city's primary responsibility was to stay out of the way.

Prior to the Great Fire, most of the residents of Chicago, those living in shacks and those living in mansions, had bought into this philosophy to one degree or another. Now, all of a sudden, a very different contingency had emerged. It was plain—at least as Holden saw it—that the government of Chicago would have to act on very short notice and on a far larger scale than ever before, and it would have to act for the city and all its people as for a single organism. As he wrote later, "Action, immediate action, was wanted. The situation was thoroughly understood, and something should be done at once, or dire disaster would befall the suffering people." After his carriage tour, his estimate of the population rendered homeless by the Great Fire was seventy-five thousand. In the end, that number would be too low by at least twenty-five thousand. Chicago—the incorporated, administered municipal entity formed less than forty years earlier—could not sit on the sidelines during this emergency, no matter what the cost.

To help his city help its residents, Holden would need to gather quite a few key people in a hurry. But despite his position as council president, he held no power of executive fiat and neither did anyone else. Chicago's government had been carved up and subdivided over its short history—"segmented," in the language of urban historians, but "weakened" served just as well—in ways designed to diminish any one person's access to power. Most executive power rested with the Common Council, but spread among its forty members, two from each city ward. Chicago's mayor could advise the council, put in nominations for certain posts, and submit an annual budget, but he did not even have the power to break ties or appoint or dismiss police, fire, health, and public works commissioners, who were appointed by the council and operated within their meager budgets as independent managers—or, according to some, as political bosses.

Functionally, then, Mayor Roswell Mason acted as a voice for the entire population, in contrast to individual aldermen, who answered to the political desires of a few dozen city blocks. This left Holden, the president of the council, in his agenda-setting and majority-representing role, as an executive equal to the mayor. But whatever measures Holden implemented needed to be implemented in conjunction with the other nodes of power in municipal government, not dictated to them. Under most circumstances, proclamations and public orders in Chicago tended to work more effectively with multiple signatures affixed, not one. Holden understood that a sense of unity, of collective action, was of the greatest importance.

The first order of business that morning was to find the city's elected leaders a home. Holden needed a command post to stand in for the destroyed courthouse, and he needed as many members of the government there as soon as possible. And, given his estimate of the magnitude of need in the city, he would need a whole lot of other help as well. There was in American history no precedent for the Great Fire, no existing system of response. A new kind of intervention would be needed, at a scale never before imagined. And it would need to commence not in weeks, or days, but in the next few hours.

E VEN AS the fire continued its march through the upper reaches
of the North Side, Charles C. P. Holden re-formed the city
council at the First Congregational Church on the corner of
Washington and Ann Streets, in the middle of the West Division, a
few blocks short of Union Park. A squat Romanesque box, fronted
by a lofty stone facade and topped by a gem-encrusted cruciform
halo, the church now became, in Holden's words, "a nucleus, or
headquarters, of relief, around which all sufferers from the fire
could cluster."

The church was "requisitioned" with the blessing of its clergy.
Once Holden found the place, news spread that city government—
and the center of relief efforts for those in need—had relocated
twenty-seven blocks to the west of its former home in the courthouse. Holden put out word that he would need runners, lots of
them, and soon a pack of willing boys from the neighborhood was
dispersed in every direction to gather and return with the mayor
and aldermen, the police and fire commissioners, and any and all
"prominent citizens" who might be able to offer particular help in
these uncertain moments. In this way the structure of governance
would be transplanted on the fly from one division to another.
In Holden's mind, the church now "was the city, in its corporate
capacity, from top to bottom."

The West Side, which was intact except for the two dozen
blocks along the river between DeKoven and Red Flash, now acted
as a new downtown. Real estate agents prepared new advertise-

ments featuring higher rental rates for every available West Side room, building, and vacant lot they could wrangle. Hundreds of retail stores were already making their move across the river to new quarters in the division, one wagonload of rescued merchandise at a time. New telegraph wires were already being tied to the remnants of the old ones and strung to new telegraph offices. And newspapers—including Joseph Medill's *Tribune*—were already setting type in makeshift offices on the West Side.

Wrote Holden, "as if by instinct, as soon as the doors were thrown upon, people began to come" to the First Congregational building: the destitute, the curious, the generous, the weary. More eager young boys were gathered, happy to have a part to play on this historic day, and on their winged feet more notices were carried, as well as a charge to find any policemen who could be found and instruct them to gather at the church. One of the earlier deputations returned with the news that the mayor was too occupied to come, so Holden told the runners to go back "and not to return without him."

Thomas Brown, head of the Board of Police Commissioners, arrived soon after noon, and he and Holden huddled and at once agreed to grant the city's police officers the immediate authority to swear "trusted citizens" into the force to act as temporary peace-keepers. Nothing would be achieved, Holden believed, without a visible expression of order and vigilance in the streets, whatever the actual threat of mischief might be. A sixteen-year-old boy with a toy printing press at home offered to print the new police badges and was granted the job, producing small strips of cotton cloth stamped with the word POLICE or SPECIAL POLICE, assisted in his task by fifteen-year-old Kate Medill, whose sister and mother were helping to organize matters elsewhere in the building.

Another alderman was dispatched to a sizable vacant church building on Green Street, seven blocks closer to downtown, to set up a relief kitchen to feed what Holden knew would soon be a swarm of hungry, homeless residents. When the owners of the building objected, they were removed from the premises. Within an hour a team of women from the neighborhood was setting up cookstoves and gathering staple ingredients in bulk. More orders were sent via more runners to bakeries throughout the unburned portions of the city, granting their owners written permission to stoke fires even as a general ban was put in place. In exchange, the greater portion of everything they baked was to be turned over to the as-yet-unnamed relief organization formed in the commandeered church.

Holden and Brown directed two aldermen to seize any unoccupied land anywhere on the West Side they could find it and impress the men and material needed to build two thousand temporary houses. Holden then prepared an announcement that stated that the city of Chicago itself would meet "all expenses" incurred for relief and order. He had no doubts that the money would appear. By the time the sun rose on Monday in Chicago, crowds had gathered all over New York City, and Brooklyn, and Boston, and Atlanta, and everywhere else the telegraph reached, to absorb the brief, awful messages. *Chicago is on fire. The city is lost. Send help.* The news created a feeling of civic sympathy that almost no other circumstance could, and the promises of supplies and money already pouring in by telegram from around the country and around the world assured Holden that such materials and funds would be in ample supply—and the council's to control.

Considering the thoroughness of Holden's planning and the swiftness of its execution, one might think he had spent his entire career planning for the Great Fire. In a few hours, he'd enacted a complete curriculum in disaster relief, and still he wasn't finished. Couriers were to spread out to the edges of the burned district on its west, south, and north sides to "hunt out those in the greatest need" of food and shelter and bring them in impressed wagons to the First Congregational Church and other buildings like it. Directives were issued to open all public schools as shelters for the homeless while temporary housing was under construction.

With no pressure in the city mains and days or even weeks to go before the waterworks functioned again, still more wagons were to be impressed for a system of manned and wheeled brigades to collect water from Lake Michigan, and yet more wagons were to be commandeered to stand in reserve for unanticipated purposes.

A volunteer guard made of men and women in small groups was sent into the South and West Sides as a visible discouragement to looting, horseplay with the fires still smoldering in the ruins, or any other crimes and misdemeanors born of malice or mischievousness.

By mid-afternoon, the flow of people into the First Congregational Church became a flood. Men and women and children poured in to look for aid, or to make themselves available to provide aid, or just to have a place to rest under a sturdy roof and be among people in similar straits. Others were out of options and wanted a way to get out of the city. Holden and the other aldermen were only too happy to oblige, issuing hand-signed passes for free rail transportation to anyone who asked. A great many of Chicago's burned-out residents had friends or family in Milwaukee, St. Paul, Rockford, Cairo, St. Louis, or any of hundreds of other middle-of-the-country towns and cities, and given the pressing shortage of housing and food, it was in their best interest and Chicago's that they leave, at least for a while. Anyone who could go to get help from some other people in some other city, at someone else's cost, would make Chicago's response more effective.

At two thirty in the afternoon, finally, the mayor himself walked in, extracted from his own ad hoc command post in the far South Side. All the previous evening, until he'd been warned out of the building by the watchman Mathias Schaefer, Roswell Mason had toiled in the telegraph room of the courthouse, sending personal appeals to every mayor of every large city within a few hours' train ride of Chicago, messages that now brought in car after car full of people and other assistance, in the form of clothes, shoes, blankets, cookware, construction tools, medical supplies, and hundreds of other items.

After a few hours' sleep at his Michigan Avenue home, more than a mile below the southernmost edge of the fire, Mayor Mason had spent the later part of the morning huddled with various deputies and businessmen, trying to set up depot stops for incoming supplies and working to relocate telegraph offices. Now he found Holden and the half-assembled council in the church's largest common room, in the basement, where a piece of paper was put into his face for his immediate signature. Handwritten with underlinings and cross outs, it would be the first official message about the fire from the city of Chicago to its citizens:

PROCLAMATION: Whereas, In the Providence of God, to whose will we humbly submit, a terrible calamity has befallen our city, which demands of us our best efforts for the preservation of order and the relief of the suffering, *be it known* that the faith and credit of the city of Chicago is hereby pledged, for the necessary expenses for the relief of the suffering. Public order will be preserved. The police and the special police now being appointed will be responsible for the maintenance of the peace and protection of property. All officers and men of the Fire Department and Health Department will act as special policemen without further notice. The Mayor and Comptroller will give vouchers for all supplies furnished by the different relief committees. The headquarters for the City Government will be at the Congregational Church, corner of West Washington and Ann Streets. All persons are warned against any act tending to endanger property. Persons caught in any depredation will be immediately arrested. With the help of God, order and peace and private property will be preserved. The City Government and the committee of citizens pledge themselves to the community to protect them, and prepare the way for a restoration of public and private welfare. It is believed the fire has spent its force, and all will soon be well.

In reality, no one in the building knew if the fire had "spent its force." But they did know that just about everything that could be destroyed in the northeastern quadrant of the city, where the wind still pointed, was probably gone by now. In that direction, lake and prairie were all that was left.

As for the assurance that "all will soon be well," that was pure Chicago: chin up, jaw firm, attend to business. It was a noble sentiment, one that had served the city well during its formative era and during the four bloody and lucrative years of the Civil War. But in no way was it true in this moment. Perhaps all might soon be well in the realms of trade and business, given Chicago's geographic advantages and its financial importance to the rest of the country, but more than a hundred thousand lives had been disrupted. The mayor signed the document after his first reading, as did three other men: the city comptroller, who would now count and control the money coming into the state from parts elsewhere; Holden, in his capacity as president of the Common Council; and Thomas Brown, the head of the Board of Police.

With this action, the hydra-headed power structure of the city was set in motion. The four signatures invoked the power to persuade, in the case of the mayor; the power to execute, in Holden's hands; the power to accept money and move it around, given to the comptroller; and the power to enforce the city's laws and guard its property, in the person of the police commissioner. The proclamation was sent out for printing and distribution, and then the four men chose another large meeting room in the basement of the church where, with seven of the city's forty aldermen present, they declared an emergency quorum in order to constitute an active Common Council.

The first act of this re-formed authority was to send out a directive, under the signature of the mayor, forbidding the sale of liquor in any saloon until future notice. Well into the evening, telegraphs continued to arrive from Mason's fellow mayors around the country, hand delivered to the church from several relocated and rewired telegraph offices on the West Side. Less than twenty-four hours had passed since the Learys' barn had caught fire, but already the entire wired world knew what had happened, as far away as England, Russia, and India. The newly interconnected planet was a marvel, and the conflagration in Chicago was one of the earliest tests of its speed, efficiency, and scope. The telegraph and train weren't new inventions, but the nationwide networks that tied them together were. Distant tele-typed conversations could be held almost as if two people stood in the same room, and the trainfuls of people, supplies, and money were already on the way.

In the absence of the usual municipal boards and departments, many of the members of which were picking through the debris of their own homes, Holden and the mayor created new city offices to operate out of their West Side church headquarters. Several doctors on hand were formed into an impromptu commission of health, while other volunteers organized themselves into a water force, to collect water from the lake, parks, and artesian wells and transport it to the burned districts, where people might have nothing to drink. Joseph S. Reynolds, a Union general who'd accompanied William Tecumseh Sherman on his march to Atlanta—and who was also the brother of Holden's wife, Sarah—was appointed superintendent of the lost and found, a crucial responsibility in that the title referred not to things but to people. Some time later in the day, Joseph Medill visited his wife and daughters at the church before leaving again to attend to the *Tribune*'s first post-fire issue.

At six o'clock, as smoke continued to rise in dark plumes from all three divisions, supplies from other cities began to arrive at the church from the two West Side train depots a few blocks to the east, alongside the river. "Barrels and boxes came pouring in," wrote Holden, "filled with cooked hams, roasts of beef pork, veal, turkeys, chickens, and indeed everything in the way of meat and bread." All this provender was routed to the city kitchen on Green Street, where "many hundreds had a good substantial supper" that night. Clothing, blankets, and bedding were sorted and distributed by a committee of women that included Kate Medill and Sarah Holden. Reports and requests for help continued to come in from the burned district, and in response volunteers were sent far and wide with cooked provisions and water, along with squads of the new "special police."

The hastily arranged session of the city council adjourned well after dark. Somewhere to their northeast, a few fire engines still fought to extinguish burning buildings along the banks of the Chicago River. Past those fire engines, somewhere out on the prairie, a large camp continued to fill with thousands of bedraggled, frightened, and exhausted people who huddled close together against the wind and looked over the burning city. In Lincoln Park, along the lakeshore in the far reaches of the North Side, another several thousand residents stood and sat on the shore and in the

Refugees in Lincoln Park, published in *Harper's Weekly*, November 4, 1871

shallow water, soaked and flecked with sodden ashes. Wrote one refugee, "Hundreds and thousands of people lay out on the sand in the wind strong enough to blow a chair left alone clear across the park. The air was so full of dust and sand that it was impossible to see the fire, and there, utterly exhausted, lay the lowly and the proud." Another observer marveled at the sight of "some nuns marshaling a long line of little children from some orphan asylum that had been burned." To the south and west of the burned district, people robbed of their homes and businesses gathered in parks or in schools or churches, where smaller, neighborhood-based relief efforts echoed those around the First Congregational Church. Where homes still stood and food was still plentiful, grateful prayers were uttered around much-appreciated dinner tables and beds. And the railroads, at least those whose cars, tracks, and depots had not burned, sent out car after car full of people on the council's free passes.

Soon after midnight on Monday, a light autumn rain began to fall. No opening of the heavens, not much more than a drizzle. Far too little and two days too late. But real drops. Everywhere in the city, faces turned skyward in gratitude and even in wonder. Chicago was not the kind of city to curse the tardiness of the help, to complain that the rain hadn't fallen the day before, or the day before that. They'd gone months without rain, and this was soon enough. The fires still burning on the North Side began to sizzle and sputter, while the ruins elsewhere continued to smoke.

৯ 13 ৫

O N TUESDAY AFTERNOON, October 10, less than twelve hours after the Great Fire burned itself out, a rotund, pugnacious man with a famously bushy mustache sat in his house in full dress uniform and considered a most unusual request made by an unexpected group of visitors. It was an odd fact of Chicago in 1871 that its most recognizable resident had lived in the city for only four years. In offices and clubs around the country, people knew the names Ogden, McCormick, Field, Palmer, Wentworth, Pinkerton, Honoré, but only one Chicago name resonated in America's North, South, East, and West, in small-town shops and urban business blocks alike. He was the city's shiniest ornament, its grace note, its favorite adopted son.

Whereas it seemed that everyone else of renown in the city had been chosen *by* the city, elevated to greatness by its geographic and economic advantages, General Philip Sheridan, legend of the Civil War, had chosen Chicago. He was the victorious Union army's most legendary embodiment of pluck, dash, and that most treasured of military chestnuts, "audacity." Indeed, there was something permanently martial to him, wound up and ready to explode in consternation, mirth, or violence, depending on the situation. His verve for battle and his ruthless efficiency in the field had been demonstrated in eighteen months as Ulysses S. Grant's cavalry commander, during which time he'd routed Jeb Stuart, taken the Shenandoah Valley for the Union, and blocked the escape of Robert E. Lee before the Confederate surrender at Appomattox. Six years after the end of the war, the South hated Sheridan as much as it hated anyone, even William Tecumseh Sherman and the late Abraham Lincoln, and that gave Sheridan a cachet no other Chicagoan could match.

Even at forty, Sheridan's spirit and energy—and inclination to introduce long bursts of profanity into almost every sort of conversation—were wonderful or terrifying to behold, depending on whether one was allied with his interests or opposed to them. His unglamorous physical appearance was a considerable part of his appeal. Chicago was a place for stout, serious men, and Sheridan fit the bill, so much so that he might have been a caricature of the type. Many a postwar memoir or history had paused to consider him at length.

"Not an ounce of superfluous flesh was to be seen on that energetic frame," wrote one subordinate. "He bore in every line and motion the outward evidence of concentrated energy, while his face and head were the picture of vitalized mental power. The likeness in mold and line to Napoleon Bonaparte at Sheridan's age was being generally commented upon." His unusual appearance had even been given the special attention of Abraham Lincoln, who once wrote that Sheridan was a "chunky little chap, with a long body, short legs, not enough neck to hang him, and such long arms that if his ankles itch he can scratch them without stooping." In New York or Boston, those lines might have hit the recipient as a bald-faced insult, but in Chicago they were without doubt a compliment. Sheridan had taken them as such. He and his wartime mount, Rienzi, were the subject of a famous poem, "Sheridan's Ride," written in 1864 about his arrival at the Battle of Cedar Creek:

> *Under his spurning feet the road*
> *Like an arrowy Alpine river flowed,*
> *And the landscape sped away behind*
> *Like an ocean flying before the wind.*
> *And the steed, like a bark fed with furnace ire,*
> *Swept on, with his wild eye full of fire.*

Portrait of General Philip Sheridan,
credited to I. W. Taber, date unknown

Unmarried, Sheridan lived down Michigan Avenue in the South
Side, a mile below the line of destruction, where he shared lodgings with his youngest brother, Michael, who acted as his military
secretary, along with several other aides-de-camp, a steward, and a
coachman. The setting was tranquil, within an easy omnibus ride
of downtown but possessed of a pleasant atmosphere of suburban
remove. Sheridan's mode of interior decoration, both of house and
of office, tended toward the self-aggrandizing; he'd sat for any number of portraits, sketches, and busts, many of which were prominently displayed.

The people gathered in his house on Tuesday could be classified as members of the city's business elite, but given the eventual
trouble that would come out of this meeting, only a few of their
names were ever made public. It is clear enough that they were
some of the most prominent residents of Chicago and included
a city attorney or two and several wealthy downtown merchants
who lived outside the burned district. But if their identities would
remain shrouded to history, the content of their conversation was
unambiguous. They wished to negate a large part of the work that
Holden, the mayor, the commissioners, and the aldermen had done

over the past twenty-four hours. All of them were here together to make an extraordinary request: they wanted General Sheridan to take control of the security of the city and of the efforts at public relief.

The proposition, coming as it did from a group of men whose open disdain for municipal government was woven into the city's political fabric, was not surprising. And neither was it surprising that Sheridan was wary of their request. He'd been through more of war than anyone else in Chicago. A city burned to the ground was something to be written into the annals of history, but it wasn't beyond the imagination of the man who'd led Grant's cavalry at Five Forks, Waynesboro, Sayler's Creek, and Appomattox. After the war General Grant had appointed Sheridan the army's point man in Louisiana and Texas, which made him the despised northern face of Reconstruction. He'd soon become a hero of the Radical Republicans by refusing to bow or even bend to southern politicians and their attempts to deny the Black population its full freedom, removing a recalcitrant governor in Texas, and vigorously enforcing the right of Blacks to vote. He'd also earned applause from the Union states—and more hatred from the South—by reputedly saying, "If I owned Texas and hell, I would live in hell and rent Texas."

Sheridan was relieved of duty by Abraham Lincoln's successor as president, Andrew Johnson, who preferred to let the southern states have their way, however oppressive, cruel, and violent, with former slaves. The move out of his assignment in the South didn't bother Sheridan much, and not long afterward, in 1867, he was ordered by Grant to St. Louis, where he was put in charge of the mounting conflict with the Plains Indians. The assumption was that the ruthlessness and efficiency he'd demonstrated in the Shenandoah Valley could be just as successfully applied to hostile members of the Cherokee, Cheyenne, Apache, and other Indian nations.

Whether or not Sheridan said "the only good Indian is a dead Indian" or "the only good Indians I ever saw were dead"—both were attributed to him—as a military leader he often seemed to act on those beliefs. In short order he became a hero to whites in the West, who didn't care how their lands were rendered free from

Indian depredations, so long as they were, and a malign spirit to most Indian tribes and to white peace activists and social organizations in the East, who prioritized Christianization efforts and cultural assimilation over generals with guns. Sheridan didn't want to Christianize anyone. He was opposed to anyone who opposed what the Union had gained, or assumed it had gained, by its victory in 1865. His work in support of freed Blacks in Texas and in opposition to the Indians of the western plains came from the same place in his mind and made Sheridan one of the most morally complex—and morally confounding—figures of the day.

In 1868, Ulysses S. Grant's election as president had bumped everyone in his chain of command one step up the ladder of authority. William Tecumseh Sherman took Grant's old position as general in chief of the army, and Sheridan was given Sherman's former command of the Military Department of the Missouri. This meant that Sheridan's responsibilities now encompassed the entire American Northwest and made him the second most important military officer in the country. His first significant decision in the job had been to move the department's headquarters from St. Louis to Chicago, a place he believed would soon eclipse all other American cities, even New York, in size and influence. And Chicago loved him for that belief.

With this promotion, the news of which brought tears to his eyes, Sheridan's days of leading men from the saddle were finished. Now, as a surprise delegation of visitors stood in his drawing room the morning after the Great Fire, he'd been off field duty for more than two years. In Chicago, he lived a new kind of life: he went to parties, mingled with eligible young ladies, and took dance lessons alongside Marshall and Nannie Field—though he still swore an awful lot. But for the most part he traveled: hunting trips, fishing trips, trips of exploration, trips of observation, all of which coincided with a period of relative peace with the western Indian nations.

In early 1870, when he heard the news that France's emperor, Napoleon III, had declared war on Prussia, Sheridan had asked leave of Grant and Sherman to go to Europe to witness what parts of that conflict he could witness. While riding alongside Otto von Bismarck, prime minister of Prussia and architect of the recent German unification, he'd expressed his admiration for the efficiency and organization of the Prussian soldiers and his disgust with the French for their clumsiness and lack of a killer instinct.

After his trip to witness the Franco-Prussian War and a whirlwind tour of Europe, Sheridan had returned to Chicago in early 1871 in time to dash off on an expedition known as a grand hunt, in the European tradition of well-appointed luxury. During the six weeks just before the Great Fire, he and a group of military officers, newspaper editors, and businessmen had hunted buffalo in Nebraska and game from Fort McPherson to Fort Hays, hopping from river to river, most of the while guided by a young Buffalo Bill Cody. On the way out from Chicago, Sheridan and his companions had been granted use of the director's car by the superintendents on the Chicago and North Western and the Union Pacific, and on the way back they'd been given free transportation in a palace car on the Kansas Pacific line along with free passage on all Chicago railroads.

Sheridan had returned to his Michigan Avenue home on Thursday, October 5. Three days later, the city caught fire. Miles below the southern line of the fire, he'd had no fear for his house. Around midnight, as Mathias Schaefer had worked without hope to save the courthouse by beating and stamping out the flying debris collecting on its roof, and as Mayor Mason sent the last of his desperate telegrams seeking help from other mayors in other cities, General Sheridan conducted his own rescue mission on the southwestern corner of the courthouse square.

There sat the Merchants Insurance building, occupied on its ground floor by the Military Division of the Missouri, where his brother, the division secretary, kept its records from the Civil War and the struggle against the Plains Indians, as well as the postwar pay and personnel records for many of the division's officers and enlistees. When the *Tribune*'s editor in chief, Horace White, ran into Sheridan in front of the post office at about midnight, a grim Sheridan said that his own Civil War papers were lost. The two men expressed optimism that the fire was not likely to spread much more to the south or east, and they separated.

It was a testament to Sheridan's fame and reputation that stories circulated even when the fire was hours old about the little general's heroic efforts to check the fire's southward progress once it had crossed to the South Side. If all the separate accounts were to be believed, he'd organized citizen patrols, teamed with the mayor to send telegrams, torn down buildings with his own hands, procured gunpowder, blown up city blocks to create firebreaks, and led citizens along precarious escape routes, among other things. Sheridan, for his part, never left a record of his movements that night. The most popular story was that he'd gone to collect powder from one of the city's armories and been refused until he'd cursed the man into submission.

Some confusion seems to have arisen regarding the efforts of his unrelated namesake, the police commissioner Mark Sheridan, in locations that weren't so far from those occupied by the general. The most that's certain is that General Sheridan played some part in blocking the southward progress of the fire at Harrison Street, either by helping to blow up buildings or by helping to tear them down. Horace White told of fleeing citizens calling out, "Where is General Sheridan? Why doesn't he do something?" and then, at the sound of dynamite detonating somewhere out of sight, assuming that the noise had to be the general's work. "Think of people feeling encouraged by the fact that somebody was blowing up houses in the midst of the city," added White, "and that a shower of bricks was very likely to come down on their heads."

Few of Sheridan's admirers would ever know, though, of the awful personal toll this night exacted from the general. For at some point after midnight Sheridan lost Rienzi, who had been stabled near the courthouse, when the animal's quarters burned to the ground along with all of the dozens of horses inside. This was a grievous blow, a deep pain that any cavalry officer understood. A gray pacer three inches taller at the shoulder than Sheridan himself, Rienzi was a spoil of war from the Battle of Missionary Ridge, one that had been commended for "great strength, an easy gait, and wonderful endurance." They'd been together through five major military campaigns, and before the fire Sheridan had still taken Rienzi for regular rides around Chicago and the surrounding prairie.

So it was with his own cause for a heavy heart that Sheridan had woken well before dawn on Tuesday, to find and speak with the mayor. As a light rain fell and the city came to understand the fire was losing its force, Sheridan offered Roswell Mason the use of six companies of regular U.S. soldiers from Leavenworth, Milwaukee, and Toledo in keeping the peace and enforcing whatever dictates might soon emerge from the mayor's office. Relief supplies were arriving from cities across the country, creating an obvious need for protection of large depots. Patrols of burned districts were a necessity, especially where safes might still be intact or where household valuables might have been left behind. And the presence of uniformed and armed soldiers on the streets under the city's control might serve as a useful deterrent to any new arrivals determined to use the chaos of the Great Fire's aftermath to criminal advantage.

Mason had accepted the general's offer on the spot, and then, at some point in the morning after their conversation, he'd left for the First Congregational Church on the West Side at the summons of Charles C. P. Holden. But over the course of the day other citizens on the South Side got wind of the general's meeting with the mayor and wondered if it had gone far enough. That's why they were in Sheridan's house—even as seven hundred federal soldiers were on their way to Chicago on special express trains, along with several carloads of supplies from U.S. Army depots.

Sheridan knew what his guests wanted. They wanted his power, and they wanted that power elevated above the mayor's and the city council's. Even in these first few daylight hours after the fire died, as people dug out, searched for loved ones, and pondered utter ruin, the business establishment of the city sensed opportunity. And they wanted the Little General on their side. They wanted his soldiers in the city under the command of Philip Sheridan, the famous army general, and not under the command of any mayor-appointed police chief or council-appointed commissioner. They wanted the tons and tons of donated supplies soon to arrive in the city to be put under Sheridan's control so that, by extension, Charles C. P. Holden and the city's aldermen wouldn't get to decide who received what aid and how.

Sheridan also understood that the people in front of him were not all of one shared motive. Given later events, at least three agendas seemed to be in play. For some of his visitors, there was a genuine sense of unease, a perception of shaken civic foundations, and having a conversation with Sheridan helped to allay that feeling. For some, who knew that the attention of the nation was on the city's financial affairs, the goal was to prevent a descent of the city's credit into dangerous territory, and putting the Little General in charge of the city would send a reassuring message far and wide. And for many, the concern was order and continuity, a reaction to things happening elsewhere: to violence between native-born Americans and immigrants, to the rise of a less docile labor class, to the emergence of ethnic political machines. In this view, whatever agitations Chicago's workers and any outside forces seeking to influence them might have in mind—whatever advantage they might seek to gain from the chaos of the Great Fire—the sight of Sheridan's soldiers would give them pause.

The general heard them out. He considered their request. And he said no.

First, he pointed out that his visitors were asking him to place his own authority above that of the city's. Underneath everything, Sheridan was—and understood himself to be—a representative of the federal government, pure and simple. And not only was he a representative of the federal government, but he was third in the nation's chain of military command, a man whose actions would always receive close scrutiny in Washington and elsewhere. Like that of so many Union generals, his opinion of Abraham Lincoln had evolved over the course of the Civil War from wariness to near worship, to the point that Sheridan had come to respect if not embrace the principle of civilian control of federal forces.

In the South, during Radical Reconstruction, he'd chafed at politics and the need to be politic—when he'd said he'd been through hell in Texas, he meant it—but he believed in their necessity. His faith wasn't in individuals but in the structures of government and the rightness of the Union cause. The previous morning, when he'd suggested that Roswell Mason bring in federal infantry to guard the city, he'd made it clear that he intended to place those forces at the disposal of the Common Council and the mayor's office. Clear and definitive lines of command, the power of yes and no in the field, the maintenance of unambiguous power relationships: these were pillars of his world, and he wouldn't knock them away because a few anxious or opportunistic businessmen asked him to.

Sheridan told his audience that he saw no legal basis for the suggestion made by his visitors that a federal officer, and by extension the federal government, could supersede the authority of city officials. He told them that he felt it was important that the city itself be seen as the entity that got them through their trial, that the army be viewed as an arm of the mayor's office; as he testified later, "It was my earnest desire that the civil authorities should, if possible, bring the city through its troubles with such aid as the army could give."

The men left his house, rebuffed. But they weren't finished. Because, for many of them, a fourth motive operated. Though it was never made explicit, two years of actions in the wake of the blaze would demonstrate that much of Chicago's business aristocracy saw the Great Fire as a golden chance to shift the locus of power in the city away from its elected political bodies and into private hands—theirs. They believed that what the city needed, now and forever, was not the mutual-back-scratching, ward-based, special-interest-bound setup of the Common Council and its aldermen. They wanted to cut off the "bummers," as they loved to call them, at the knees, and the Great Fire gave them an unexpected way to do so. In this pursuit, thick with distrust of the growing immigrant populations of the city and their access to the machinery of raw democracy, Sheridan, whether witting or unwitting, would not be their leader so much as the vehicle that could help them reach their destination.

≥ 14 ≤

A LL TUESDAY, the players continued to assemble, taking new roles in a drama whose audience was as large as the country itself. By mid-morning, as General Sheridan received his private delegation of concerned citizens, the work at the transplanted *Tribune* offices in a West Side job-printing office on South Canal Street, belonging to the company that created Chicago's annual directories, was in full swing. "One after another, all hands turned up," wrote Medill's fellow owner William Bross, "and by the afternoon we had improvised the back part of the room into our editorial department, while an old wooden box did business as a business counter in the front window." The editor in chief, Horace White, the city editor, Sam Medill, and the rest of the *Tribune* staff were working triple shifts to conduct the operations necessary to prepare a curtailed Wednesday edition for a public desperate for news, racing to put a small mountain's worth of reporters' notes into readable, printable form.

More than 300,000 people waited on a detailed description of this indescribable thing that had happened to their city. Any report, however tenuous, would be better than nothing. One page, two pages, four pages—whatever the *Tribune* could produce, it would. The contents of the first post-fire edition of the paper would by necessity be curtailed, so Horace White and Sam Medill kept it simple: an open request that businesses and homeowners submit a list of their losses for printing in future editions; a long, breathless, and mostly hearsay description of the fire; a list of people so far known to be dead or missing; a list of other municipalities offering aid; a request that those capable and desirous of leaving the city via free rail pass do so; and a chest-beating editorial often credited to Joseph Medill, but much more likely the work of the Chicago booster extraordinaire Bross, under the headline CHEER UP.

In the midst of a calamity without parallel in the world's history, looking upon the ashes of thirty years' accumulations, the people of this once beautiful city have resolved that CHICAGO SHALL RISE AGAIN. With woe on every hand, with death in many strange places, with two or three hundred millions of our hard-earned property swept away in a few hours, the hearts of our men and women are still brave, and they look into the future with undaunted hearts. As there has never been such a calamity, so has there never been such cheerful fortitude in the face of desolation and ruin.

The recipe invented on the fly by Sam Medill and his fellow editors was elementary and born out of journalistic necessity, but it was sound. The next day, Wednesday, a four-page edition would appear and close out the only time in the paper's history that it had gone more than a single day without publishing. The *Evening Journal* had published one page on Monday night, and Ed Chamberlin's employer, the *Evening Post*, would manage a small Tuesday night edition, using the same presses procured by Medill, but the *Tribune* beat every other morning paper, including the *Times,* back into print. As soon as the first issue was in the forms and on the way to the presses, Bross prepared to take a train to New York City and Wall Street, where he hoped to reassure investors that not a single one of their investment dollars need be moved out of Chicago. Two days later Bross would tell a reporter from the *New-York Tribune* that "everyone" in Chicago "was bright, cheerful, pleasant, hopeful, and even inclined to be jolly in spite of the misery and destitution which surrounded them and which they shared."

Other players continued to shift places, leaving and arriving, arranging and rearranging. As Bross rode out of the city, another

Chicago titan rode in the opposite direction, racing home at the miraculous pace of the expanding railroad network. This was Potter Palmer, the original dry-goods king of the city, Marshall Field's mentor and guiding star. Palmer had been away from the city on the day of the Great Fire for the funeral of his sister, but also to court investment capital in New York, and so had missed the great event of his city's lifetime. By Tuesday afternoon, he was rushing home to assess the damage to his hotels, to his bank account, and to his real estate holdings.

Palmer also sought to reassure his young wife that all would be well, though he had ample reason to believe that she would be the more optimistic of the two. Even in the Chicago of the nineteenth century, where life often seemed to amount to the accumulation of a million separate business transactions, some small and some very large, the marriage of Potter Palmer to Bertha Honoré struck many as a financial arrangement designed to cement together the interests of two of the city's most powerful real estate moguls. Bertha was twenty-two, Palmer was forty-five, while Bertha's father, Henry Hamilton Honoré, was forty-seven. The couple was well aware of the gossip, knew that many viewed Bertha as an ornament, a prize, and they didn't care. Their marriage was already shaping up to be extraordinary and would continue to do so.

Their personal story, of a growing family empire interrupted in its breakneck expansion, seemed to stand in aptly for the story of the city itself. That very month, Bertha had been set to take possession of the largest suite at the Palmer House, providing her with unchecked access to two distinct and desirable Chicago lives: one at her husband's hotel on State Street in the heart of the city's business district, along the greatest retail row for a thousand miles in any direction, and the other in their home on a leafy West Side lot distant from the noise and clamor—reminiscent, as little else in Chicago could be, of her bucolic southern upbringing.

Palmer's hotel on State and Quincy had been completed for guests one year earlier, and since then men had been working on Bertha's personal suite, the most ostentatious wedding present the city had known. Six stories high, clad in Cleveland brownstone, and topped by a mansard roof, the Palmer House had been considered safe from all forms of destruction, but most especially from fire. Brick party walls ran through the building from front to back, and the entire edifice rested on heavy iron columns buried in uncommonly deep foundations.

Other hotels in Chicago were bigger, but none had had this one's collection of first-class accoutrements: Parisian carpets in all of the public rooms, water closets and baths in all of the guest lodgings, first-floor parlors outfitted with Knabe pianos from Baltimore, and, in the basement, a billiards parlor and several barrooms serving liquor whenever a traveler might desire a glass, no matter how late or early in the day. The three hundred feet of street frontage on State and Quincy had been filled end to end with stores selling shoes, cigars, umbrellas, and other items designed to appeal to weary travelers and to add to the growing retail cachet of State Street.

Most impressively, the building containing Bertha's magnificent wedding present was to be the first of *two* Palmer hotels on State Street. Just two weeks before the Great Fire, Potter Palmer had signed a set of contracts to begin work on a second Palmer House, across State and three blocks to the north, at the intersection with Monroe. This new Palmer property would not be an attempt to surpass "any hotel west of New York"; it would be an attempt to surpass every other hotel in the world. It would be bigger, more expensive, more luxurious than anything Chicago had known. By itself, it would tell the world that Chicago was second to no other city.

Every part of the couple's tale seemed to say something about the city's endless ability to absorb fascinating lives transplanted wholesale from destinations in every direction. Bertha's father had been a successful storekeeper on Pearl Street in Louisville, selling imported kitchenware and cutleries. Her grandmother Mary had freed the family's slaves, and this contributed to the ease with which the Honorés moved to Chicago in 1855, when Bertha was six. She became aware at a young age that real estate money was flowing into Chicago and that her father had gotten into the business at an advantageous time, before the speculative bubbles of the Civil War

Portrait of Potter Palmer,
credited to John Carbutt, 1868

Mrs. Potter Palmer
(Bertha Honoré Palmer),
by Anders Zorn, 1893

era drove up prices but after the city had proved itself as a never-tiring hub of worldwide commerce. She learned that her family's position in Chicago was much more fluid and full of potential than it would have been had they stayed in Kentucky. Bertha was smart enough and self-assured enough to understand that the many different regional and international accents she heard on the streets of Chicago, in place of the constant buttery drone of Louisville, created opportunity as much as they could cause confusion.

From the first, the Honorés entertained at home whenever they could, and Bertha grew up at the heart of a high-spirited social circle that included some of Chicago's most notable residents. She was a studious, attentive girl, and her family encouraged her musical and intellectual prowess, along with her independence. One day in 1862, with the Civil War well under way, a friend of her father's had come to the family house on Reuben Street for a party. Bertha was thirteen. She'd heard Potter Palmer discussed as a genius of retailing. She always remembered what she wore that day: a white muslin dress and black lace gloves, most likely purchased from Palmer's store, where Bertha and her mother were frequent customers.

When Bertha first saw him that day in 1862, Potter Palmer was making a fortune by amassing and reselling great reserves of cotton, wherever he could find it, purchasing the fruit of slave labor in an effort to outfit the army that would eventually end slavery. He was thirty-six and had never married, a hard-driving man focused on his store and his wholesale concerns to the point of making himself ill. He was quiet, reserved, watchful, and prone to short bursts of droll wit, but never outpourings of emotion or unguarded expressions of enthusiasm. At the war's conclusion, Bertha had left Chicago for Catholic school in Georgetown, and at her farewell soiree she'd said a personal goodbye to Potter Palmer. Shortly afterward Palmer himself had left the country for Europe, in need of recuperation. He was worth $7 million, but he'd worked long hours on little sleep for so many years that his face was worn, his body stiff and sore, his heart weak.

Soon the studious convent student had become the stunning and much sought-after debutant. After the war, Henry Honoré had moved the family to a spacious, marble-fronted townhome on Michigan Avenue with a spectacular view of Lake Michigan, a vista uninterrupted by any human creation except the breakwater tracks of the Illinois Central Railroad. Bertha had her coming-out party, convinced her mother that waltzing should be allowed, and was courted by many of the richest and most good-looking young bachelors in the city.

Then, in 1869, Potter Palmer had returned to Chicago from his tour of Europe and a short sojourn in New York City focused less on a pile of smaller endeavors than on a few big things. He'd already sold out his share in the Palmer dry-goods emporium to Marshall Field and Levi Leiter and forever stepped out of the retail business in a financial handover that was the talk of the town. The rents on his State Street properties alone would keep him comfortable for the rest of his life, but he was done selling things and now turned to buying and building them.

The transfer of his dry-goods interests to Field & Leiter and the construction of that firm's new store were calculated to emphasize the rising cachet of State Street, impress people with the resources of Marshall Field, and get them talking. There was also the real need to defray the cost of the new building's construction and of his considerable plans for the future. By the close of 1869, Palmer had purchased or put in thirty-two buildings as part of his State Street project. At the same time, the first Palmer House was going up. Early in 1869 he had let slip that that building's most opulent residential suite *and* its bridal suite were being built with a single individual in mind.

The wedding had taken place in July 1870, fifteen months before the Great Fire, in the largest of the drawing rooms in the Honoré family's new home on Michigan Avenue. Bertha knew that Potter Palmer's heart had been given to State Street as much as it had been given to her. She knew how much property he owned and how much their fortune depended on the rents from that single long stretch of hard-packed dirt. And she knew how much he'd invested in the two Palmer hotels, in the completion of her wedding present, and in the initial contracts on the new building. Now the pet project at the heart of the second act of his professional life—and of his marriage—had vanished into a sea of char and rubble.

State Street was a ruin from the Chicago River down to Harrison, twelve blocks of pure destruction. His losses, Palmer understood, would cap out at some multiple or another of a million dollars, with little hope that insurance would cover much more than half. The Palmer House, two years and $1.5 million in the making and open for little less than a year now, had been leveled, yet another fireproof victim of the Great Chicago Fire. As for Palmer's other properties on State Street, an unexpected reckoning would now occur. Would that strip of land remain the shining commercial magnet he'd created over the past five years? He'd have to take care that the reconstruction of State Street happened his way. The buildings—and their lucrative rents—were gone, but would the real estate hold its worth? Or would that worth decrease as retailers decided to leave for better offers? Or would those values in fact increase as retailers and shopkeepers competed to move into—or back into—comforting and familiar haunts? Palmer's credit was sterling, his financial friends close, dear, and loyal. Money given, lent, or paid to Potter Palmer, it was understood, was good money.

Of all his many renters along State Street, Palmer would watch Marshall Field with the keenest interest. One of his first priorities after reuniting with Bertha would be to probe his protégé's situation. He knew that Field, for all their outward similarities, was much more of a pragmatist and less of a dreamer than he was. He guessed that Field would look to reopen his store as soon as possible, wherever he could and with whatever merchandise he and his employees had managed to cart away in the dark hours of Monday morning.

And indeed, Field and his partner, Levi Leiter, were thinking in two directions, neither of which yet involved Palmer's ruined property on State Street. They'd already contracted to build a new wholesale warehouse on Madison and Market, in the rubble of the South Side close by the south branch of the Chicago River, and they were well on the way to opening a temporary retail branch south of the burned district on State Street and Twentieth, in an old omnibus barn near Leiter's house. The company's clerks were busier than they'd ever been. Some counted financial losses, some conducted a careful inventory of salvaged merchandise, while others prepared advertisements for the post-fire editions of the newspapers.

Field and Palmer both believed it, and so did the rest of Chicago: Field & Leiter's rapid return to glory would become a symbol of the success of the city itself. The work on the new retail store, under such improvisational conditions, transported Marshall Field back in time to his beginnings, to smaller business concerns in smaller locations. He'd worked himself up from a small dry-goods store in Pennsylvania, and now he would work himself up again. His credit, like Palmer's, was immaculate. And Palmer would watch all of it closely, but above all he wouldn't allow Field the smallest chance to get too comfortable in his new quarters and thereby dictate a new commercial orientation of the city, away from Palmer's consolidated real estate holdings on State.

In the meantime, at the First Congregational Church, even as the city's business leaders adjusted and readjusted their plans day by day, Charles C. P. Holden kept busy on the second day after the fire with his own kind of reconstruction project, concocting a new kind of ad hoc government, working in his own way to project confidence by always showing the machinery of the city in motion. By ten o'clock on Tuesday morning there was no room in any of the church's spare spaces for more supplies, so a West Side skating rink and several other buildings were commandeered for the purpose and put under the guard of the police. Kate Medill and her daughters, Kate and Elinor, worked side by side with Sarah Holden and other women to organize and distribute a small mountain of donated clothing according to gender and size, along with train cars full of dishes, silverware, pots and pans, and other kitchenware. All the while people streamed into the lost and found department, either lost themselves or looking for loved ones, and, in Holden's words, "many affecting scenes" played out as they found their hopes crushed or their prayers answered.

Holden, Mayor Roswell Mason, and the city comptroller counted the money coming in, a bonanza of aid that represented the largest outpouring of charity in the country's history. Separate donations of $100,000 had already been promised by Boston, Brooklyn, Philadelphia, Pittsburgh, and Cincinnati. With the addition of smaller promises from smaller cities and towns and individuals, more than $1 million of relief aid had been pledged on Monday and Tuesday alone, most of it able to be drawn on the mayor's signature from deposits in Chicago banks. All school buildings and churches were to act as shelters, and supplies were sent to them as outposts of what they called "special relief," meaning help offered on a street-by-street and neighborhood-by-neighborhood basis.

The president of the Board of Trade was given a desk at the church and put in charge of recording and directing the flow of all supplies coming in. More single-sheet proclamations, one after another, went out with more young runners, who traveled the streets of the city nailing their messages to fences, telegraph poles, trees, benches, unoccupied buildings, and other public surfaces. No use of kerosene and no smoking in public areas until the water flowed again. No raising of prices for bread, bricks, or transportation. No use of wood-burning stoves or fireplaces. Another notice announced the organization of a "dead house" in a livery stable on the West Side, where the most awful and unrecognizable of human remains would be brought in the absence of the city morgue for the purpose of identification.

Chicago liked to congratulate itself at a rate that sometimes seemed to emphasize, rather than minimize, its fifth-place size among American cities. But there was no doubt that the city was so far doing very well during this most trying three days of its history. At a neighborhood level, the fire had produced heroes, and the near absence of serious crime in the wake of the disaster was both an accomplishment and a relief. Even as the fire burned itself out, Bertha Palmer had opened her West Side home to fire refugees, as did hundreds of other well-to-do residents. And for each of the names recognized as leaders in the relief and rescue effort, there were thousands of other people who were not so famous but whose efforts did much to reduce the level of suffering.

Behind the business and political elites of Chicago operated an army of unsung workers. Chicago mapped its urban personality by layering large strata of people: a wealthy mercantile aristocracy made up of well-known names, the crop of Old Settlers that had been present for the city's charter in 1837, and a growing population of merchants and small-factory owners, all buttressed by a massive working class. All these groups were present at the First Congregational Church, and together they represented a unified city in motion, an assurance of safety and reawakening and activity. In some ways, the scene at the church represented an ideal Chicago, its most attractive face, despite the awful circumstances. But as with every other moment in the city's history, before and after the Great Fire, disruptive forces moved just beneath the surface, ready to burst forth given the smallest opportunity. If the wooden

city of 1871, in retrospect, seemed to be a Great Fire waiting to happen, so too did the immediate aftermath of the Great Fire contain
its own troubling portents. And as with everything in Chicago, the
hurry-up capital of the country, those troubles would not wait long
to appear.

❧ 15 ❧

INTO THE DARK of Tuesday evening and on into the earliest hours of Wednesday, the trains continued to move. Two of the city's five passenger depots had burned to the ground, and many miles of track had deformed within the fire's boundaries, but even that scale of destruction left a dozen rail lines and many small stations still in operation beyond the reach of the flames. At all three of these surviving depots—even at the large Illinois Central and Michigan Central terminal along the lakeshore, which had been damaged but not disabled—a motley collection of travelers and indigents grew ever larger.

People with no place to sleep and no possessions and no way to contact relatives who lived elsewhere were getting on a train and riding out. Behind them they left leveled and uninsured houses, jobs that had no guarantee of resuming, lost pets, lost heirlooms, lost greenbacks, lost hopes. Men and boys rode on top of the departing trains, while others stood in the aisles or lay on the floors. Many large families traveled with one trunk containing all their possessions, sleeping huddled together in some corner of a depot until the next set of departing passenger cars was announced. Fellow evacuees gave cake and candy to footsore and bone-weary children. Some passengers bore visible marks of the fire: scorched clothes, singed hair, scarred flesh, bloodshot eyes, lined and worn faces.

A week later, the city council would estimate the number of post-fire departures from the city at fifty thousand people. At least ten thousand of these had gone out in the first three days after the fire on written passes. But in the end, no one could measure the true scale of Chicago's post-fire diaspora, not in the moment or at any point afterward. The census of 1870 had counted 298,977 people within Chicago's corporate limits, but the city's year-over-year growth was so great that perhaps that many remained in the city even after the mass departures, after accounting for visitors, temporary residents, and new permanent arrivals over the past year.

Not everyone in this first wave of departures bore a free pass, or, for that matter, yet knew that passes were available. Some paid. Some talked a conductor into letting them on board without a ticket. Some of those riding out on the rails in the days after the fire planned on a temporary exodus, while many others never looked back. For some who had intended to leave the city anyway—temporary workers, farmers in town to sell a crop or conduct business, jobbers picking up a stock of samples for a return to the small towns where their buyers lived, travelers who'd been bundled out of their hotels in the middle of the night—the pass was a free ticket out, and they used it gladly.

And for others still, the surviving depots and stations served as places to stay the night in the company of other afflicted people, a night's home for the homeless before the railroads brought back their private police and sent the squatters off to the church buildings and schools that now served as emergency housing. "Men, women, and children huddled together," wrote Charles C. P. Holden, "covered with soot, cinders, and ashes, almost destroying their human appearance."

Starting early on Tuesday morning, a few hours after the fall of rain began, the incoming trains were no less full. The clamor and noise in the surviving stations and depots was yet more evidence of the new, astonishing, interconnected postwar world. An overnight response in cities hundreds and even thousands of miles away was now taken for granted. Trains and telegraphs together created a speed of response that for older residents of Chicago felt as impossible as the magnitude of the disaster. The trip from Milwaukee aboard an express train shorn of most of its usual load and pushed to its limit took two hours. From Indianapolis, five. From Cincinnati or St. Louis, ten. The Learys' barn had caught fire less than forty-eight hours earlier, but already in came carload after carload of heavy equipment, linens, food, and everything else one might require to rebuild a city—including hundreds of people ready to fight fires, keep order, and help with a massive relief effort.

The first trains carrying fresh fire engines and firemen had arrived even before the fire jumped to the North Side, at around three in the morning on Monday. From that point forward, the assistance hadn't stopped pouring in: "every imaginable article fitted to aid the sufferers of our city; such as clothing, boots and shoes of all sizes and for both sexes, ladies' and children's apparel without stint, bedding of every description and in vast quantities, household goods in endless variety." The first relief supply train arrived from Indianapolis late on Monday, its chief of police stepping out of the passenger car to stare out at a vision of hell, bringing with him two carloads of cooked provisions and two fully manned fire engines that had immediately wheeled off to fight the flames that even then licked the streets within blocks of the terminal.

Outgoing telegrams hadn't originated solely in the mayor's office or in the buildings that housed the city's prominent newspapers, all of which were wired for instant communication. Chicago was also home to four private telegraph companies, whose offices clustered around the courthouse, and until the fire overtook them, they had operated with lines of customers and at full tilt. The large passenger depots and most of the smaller train stations contained relays as well, though many of those had stopped operating early in the fire's progress. The telegrams from these offices spread with unbelievable rapidity to other stations in other cities, and thence into public squares and company offices and private homes.

The outpouring of messages had served to pack the incoming trains. Not everyone riding into Chicago was a fireman or policeman or someone sent to help with relief. Many of the people arriving at the Illinois Central and other depots had reversed the flow of exile, determined to come to the city and learn the fate of loved ones. Some might have unwittingly crossed paths with those they'd hoped to find. Many others were out-and-out gawkers who hoped to catch a glimpse of history, boarding a train to go look at the ruined city still in the process of being ruined, a wonder of the world. And some headed for Chicago to take advantage of the situation, as entrepreneurs, hustlers, criminals, or a combination of all three.

In the midst of this mass of humanity riding the rails into Chicago sat another icon of the city, a man who, more than any other—more even than Potter Palmer, who was making his own rushed return home—would consider the wounding of Chicago like the wounding of his own child. If General Sheridan was the city's favorite adopted son, William Butler Ogden, first mayor of Chicago and its wealthiest man, could claim as much as any other man to be the city's founding father. His was a famous name, full of intimidating associations. But at sixty-six, the tall, well-postured, handsome man of his youth in Chicago had been replaced by the softer, more melancholy, less powerfully built man of his retirement in New York City, and few of his fellow passengers would have recognized him on the train. But everyone would have recognized his name.

As a young man Ogden had spent one term in New York's state legislature in order to focus on a single item of business: the effort to get a railroad line run across the southern half of New York state in order to keep families like his, woolen and lumber millers, from losing all of their commerce to similar towns along the route of the Erie Canal. When Ogden had left New York for Chicago, in 1835, it had appeared that the water route had won. Now he was coming from New York to Chicago again, but there was no doubt: the train, not the canal, had emerged victorious. And along with it, because of it, so had Ogden.

Like many travelers by rail from the Northeast, Ogden came into Chicago straight from the south, clattering along the curve of land formed by the southernmost tip of Lake Michigan and then making a sharp turn to the northwest and to true north to come into the city along the waterfront. As Ogden's train passed the outlying canal district and entered the city proper, not too long after midnight, the world bifurcated, much as it had for Charles C. P. Holden as he rode down Jefferson Street from his house to DeKoven Street.

Portrait of William Butler
Ogden, photographer and
date unknown

Everything out of the train's windows to Ogden's right was a dark expanse of water. With a simple turn of his head in the other direction, everything became a smoking, stunted ruin, made up of thousands of shadowed and unrecognizable shapes in the nighttime gloom. Under other circumstances Ogden's train might have come all the way in along the Pittsburgh, Fort Wayne, and Chicago line, running a parallel course to the Illinois Central about a mile to the west, along the southern branch of the Chicago River and into the West Division of the city, but the tracks of that line ran over DeKoven and past Red Flash, through the heart of the fire's early progress, and many were now twisted, warped, and pitted, or covered with debris. In some places, they were melted into the ground. The Illinois Central tracks, on the other hand, ran along the breakwater and terminated on a flat very near the spot where Fort Dearborn, symbol of Chicago's beginnings as an Indian trading post, had once stood. From Ogden's vantage point, it seemed that everything else to the north, west, and south—everything not in the direction of Lake Michigan—was gone.

The familiar shape and arrangement of the city, the grid of streets and the geometry of buildings imprinted in every resident's mind, was now invisible to Ogden's eyes. But it wasn't invisible to his memory. As he traveled the final half mile of his long trip from New York, a narrow inlet separated him from the waterfront boulevard called Michigan Avenue. Two days earlier, here had stood the massive and elegant set of residences called Terrace Row. These were the towering lakeview town house mansions of many of his wealthiest friends, including the *Tribune* co-owner William Bross. The largest part of Ogden's fortune had been made through Chicago land deals, and Terrace Row represented the city's most prestigious residential real estate. Now even the grandest and most towering of these houses were misshapen piles in the dark. Beyond and above them, the shell of the courthouse was visible from the windows of the train as a jagged silhouette.

Ogden had always been a nostalgic man, but now, in declining health and feeling his mortality, he was deeply so, and not just in the matter of the city he'd helped to build. Thirty-six years earlier, he had ridden west as a land agent for his brother-in-law's firm, convinced on his arrival that the onion bog beside Lake Michigan was a financial dead end. But after a week in which he turned $100,000 of the company's landholdings into six times that amount, he saw a future of unlimited promise. Chicago in 1835, two years before its incorporation as a city, was a western boomtown of a different sort: instead of a vein of precious minerals to bring speculators, con men, and brokers on the run, the attraction was the potential of a canal route connecting Lake Michigan, through twelve miles of genuine swamp, to the Illinois River and the Mississippi beyond. With a canal in place, goods could flow into and through Chicago from all over the globe: coffee from Brazil and tea from India, sugar from the West Indies and cattle from California, all this bounty passing along the sandy, sluggish river near the southern tip of Lake Michigan.

When Ogden first arrived, the dubious treaties that had removed the last of the Potawatomi tribes from their homeland were not yet a year old. His brother-in-law, Charles Butler, and the rest of the partners in the land-sale endeavor sat in their oak-paneled offices in New York and realized staggering returns, but Ogden possessed enough of his own money from his father's businesses, along with his share of Butler's pooled investment, that he was able to do what few else on-site in 1835 could: watch the rapid-fire exchanges of land and money between other speculators and then throw larger amounts at just the right parcels at just the right times.

Ogden's patient, level temperament and his experience running his late father's many businesses had served him well, as had a calculating eye. Within weeks a large chunk of land on the north side of the main branch of the Chicago River was his, along with his portion of other plots owned by Butler's New York consortium. Within months, Ogden was building a magnificent house overlooking both lake and river on a plot he called Ogden's Grove: the same house, in a later incarnation, that he would now be hoping against hope to find intact after his train pulled in. After Chicago incorporated as a city, Ogden was elected its first mayor. And in the time since, the realms of the city he'd affected were so many as to seem the work of a dozen men.

He'd drawn the first designs for the swing bridges that for thirty years now had spanned the Chicago River, and he'd also been the force behind the construction of the city's two tunnel crossings. He'd helped to found the city's Boards of Trade, Health, and Education. A street was named after him, as was a business block, a baseball and skating park, a school, and a shipping vessel. All of the thousands of people who lived or worked in a four-block strip north of the main branch of the Chicago River stood on land first purchased by Ogden. Anyone who bought lumber in the city stood a good chance of buying lumber from one of his company towns in the North Woods. Anyone who rode in or out of the city stood a good chance of riding on a railroad he'd helped to develop. Goods shipped down the canal to the southwest of the city went past Ogden Slip and traveled through a low, boggy, odor-ridden area called Ogden's Ditch.

Now, after receiving news of the fire, he'd traveled a full day and a full night from New York City to get to Chicago, contending with his emotions as new bulletins were posted at each stop and transfer point along the way. Every platform was full of talk of the calamity, every new rider on the train bore the latest reports or rumors of unimaginable destruction. Reliable information was scarce, but even before Ogden had reached the Illinois border, he knew for certain that the fire had touched the West, South, and North Sides, and also that many a "fireproof" building had already gone up in flames. The first wave of passengers leaving Chicago, likewise, had already made it to Gary, Toledo, Cleveland, and even Pittsburgh, and their stunned and breathless accounts rippled through the train stations and into Ogden's ears.

By the time Ogden had boarded his first train on the route west, New York City knew far more about the fire than did most small towns in Illinois and even many residents of the outskirts of Chicago itself. The train carried him west, but it was a single tendril of the telegraph reaching east with its news of tragedy that had brought Ogden out of his sleep and changed his life forever. Two nights earlier, late on Sunday, a butler whose name is lost to history had climbed a flight of steps in a house that would have been the envy of every one of Chicago's richest residents, bearing three telegrams full of bad news.

Villa Boscobel, the New York country home Ogden had left in the wee hours of Monday morning after receiving his terrible news, was as removed a place as could be from his former life in Chicago. The grounds on which his mansion sat consisted of bluff-top frontage measuring more than half a mile along the Harlem River, dotted with wisteria, clematis, woodbine, oak, and ebony. A three-gabled Gothic Revival designed by Calvert Vaux, Frederick Law Olmsted's partner in the design and building of New York's Central Park, the mansion rose stately and cool gray, its facade 160 feet long and its quoins, arches, and other details fashioned out of olive-tinted New Brunswick sandstone, while the grounds sported a broad veranda and offered a spectacular view of the thin line of water that separated Manhattan Island from the Bronx. A steep cliff face descended on both shores, his own and the opposite. Below, on warm days, sails dotted the view.

The entire property was an ideal spot for children, and the house contained within it a schoolroom built for the large family of the previous owner. But Ogden was childless and measured his legacy in different ways. His life in New York was less busy than the one he'd lived in Ogden's Grove, but he kept his hand in a number of Chicago businesses from afar and he still entertained. Henry David Thoreau was a regular visitor and spoke of Ogden as one of the great men of American history, equal to Daniel Webster and Ralph Waldo Emerson. Olmsted and John Muir also stopped by when they could and considered Ogden a close friend. In these later years of his life he'd come to treasure the growing of fruit trees. He would spend entire days tending his orchards, pruning, cultivating, cross-breeding, and harvesting their bounty.

During his own youth in Walton, New York, a small, picturesque mill town along the Hudson Valley a hundred miles to the northwest of this spot, Ogden had consumed the great adventure stories of Walter Scott, Daniel Defoe, James Fenimore Cooper, and Miguel de Cervantes, and he had proved adept and eager at hunting, swimming, skating, and riding. Even at a young age, echoing Joseph Medill's early desires, he'd planned to study law and make his way in New York or some other large city, but then, when Will was fifteen, a stroke had laid waste to his father, Abraham.

Almost overnight, as a boy, Will had to become the full-time manager of a thriving lumber and woolens concern. Any dream of making his own way in the world had been squelched, but the family tragedy paid lifelong dividends by accelerating his business acumen. By the age of seventeen, as the Ogden mills continued to thrive, he'd learned the intricacies of supply and demand, of hiring and wages, of billing and invoicing, of deal making and negotiations. In this manner Ogden grew up in a hurry, and by the time he was twenty, he was a significant figure in Walton.

In 1829, ten years after his father's stroke and weeks before he'd been set to marry Sarah North, a childhood friend turned the love of his life, she had caught an aggressive and soon fatal case of pneumonia. For years afterward Ogden had supported Sarah's siblings and parents as if they were his own, and in Chicago he'd been a gregarious, loving uncle to the twelve children of his brother, Mahlon. He kept Sarah's letters and other mementos, and guests at his Chicago house even up to the time of the Great Fire remembered that he would sometimes take them out and sift through them, lost to the conversation around him.

Early on Tuesday morning, Ogden churned into the lakeside train depot in the deepest dark the city had ever known. Though the rails were intact, only the massive front wall of the depot, with its three soaring masonry arches, still stood, like Roman ruins. No gas ran through the lines to illuminate the lamps along the platforms, and few torches or candles were permitted beyond those allowed to the fire and police forces. In the Illinois Central station, Ogden saw no one he knew, which surprised him. He hired a hack and crossed the Chicago River, headed for the once-familiar surroundings of the near North Side, land he had so long ago purchased for himself in anticipation of a future that looked very much like the present, at least before the fire.

"The burning district had no lamps," he wrote, "thousands of smoldering fires were all that could be seen, and they added to the mournful gloom all around." The short trip to his house from the depot, a route ingrained in memory, took him more than an hour. The signposts were gone, the landmarks burned beyond recognition, and the streets sometimes impossible to find. "I was lost among the unrecognizable ruins and could not tell where I was," he wrote. "Not a living thing was to be seen." Finally, he turned onto Ontario Street and came face-to-face with the personal cost of the fire as he looked over "the ruined trees and broken basement walls—all that remained of my more than 30 years pleasant home. All was blackened, solitary, smoldering ruins around, gloomy beyond description, telling a tale of woe that words cannot." Thirty-four years earlier, Ogden had welcomed Chicago's first high-society community into that house for all-night gatherings he'd enlivened with reminiscences of his childhood, tales from old adventure novels, songs on the piano, and plans for the city's future spun out of thin air. Now his mind raced along paths full of loss: material, financial, emotional.

And those thoughts were a pleasant exercise compared with what awaited him to the north, a tragedy that in its own awful way was more complete and all encompassing than the one that had befallen Chicago. For only two of the telegrams delivered by his butler had spoken of Chicago. The third had read, "A whirlwind of fire is sweeping over Peshtigo." This was Ogden's lumber town in Wisconsin, 250 miles to the north, and if Chicago was vulnerable, made as it was of wood, how much more prone to destruction was Peshtigo, built of wood to receive, process, and transport wood, in the middle of a vast pine forest? That both Chicago and Peshtigo could have caught fire on the same night seemed impossible. But they had. Whatever lay in front of his eyes here in the city was dwarfed by the imagination's visions of a fire set loose in the villages and mills of Wisconsin's lumber country.

Before heading to Peshtigo, though, Ogden would spend a few days in Chicago, huddled with his brother, Mahlon, and other business leaders of the North Side, men who were also counting losses that, like Ogden's and Potter Palmer's, would run up to and into the millions. Whatever measures the city would take, the scope of the disaster was so large that each division, each neighborhood, would need its own plan of action. For men like Ogden, the city council, mayor, and even the state and federal government were at most ancillary sources of assistance. What good would be done for his own interests would be done by himself—and by whatever insurance companies were able to make good on policies that ran well into the millions of dollars.

Still, even as he counted his losses in Chicago, a persistent pull on Ogden's heart came from the North Woods. More than a thousand people worked in his lumber town, most paid by him and all depending on him now. The news from Peshtigo suggested the worst: that all was lost, that while much of Chicago had escaped the flames, no part of his lumber enterprise and the town surrounding it had been spared. That Chicago would prosper once again was in his mind beyond doubt. What he would do about an obliterated Peshtigo was a much murkier question. He'd always been a builder. But now, at a time in his life when his drive and energy had been replaced by quieter, more contemplative impulses, the task in front of him seemed bigger, harder, and far more personal.

≫ 16 ≪

A T EIGHT O'CLOCK on Wednesday morning, October 11, less than thirty-six hours after the fire had died out, a line began to form around a livery stable on Milwaukee Avenue in the West Side, just across the river from the visible desolation of the most heavily German neighborhood on the North Side. The "dead house" that Charles C. P. Holden and the council had arranged as a gruesome extension of their lost and found department was to be opened at noon, and the attention was intense. Here was the most simple, true, and graphic measurement of the catastrophe's toll.

The mood of the crowd was a thick mixture of anticipation, dread, sadness, curiosity, excitement, and weariness. Only men of age would be allowed inside, ten at a time, one hundred every twenty minutes, three hundred per hour. Many of those in line were Swedes and Germans whose nearby North Side homes had vanished in minutes in the morning hours after the winds had achieved cyclonic volume and speed. And not only were their dwellings gone, but friends and family members had vanished as well, and now they were living in dread of what they might find. Others came from other portions of the burned districts with the same mission in mind. And many others, of course, came to gawk.

The population of the city was now subdivided according to the three invariable demographics of disaster: the living, the dead, and the missing. Most of the living considered themselves lucky, whatever they'd lost. Some were grateful, some relieved, some even excited and full of new purpose. The dead were mourned and pitied, their deaths imagined and reimagined, told and retold, in escalated tones of horror and awe. As for the missing, the search for loved ones was as desperate and quixotic as it always is after a world-changing cataclysm.

If the effort to locate a loved one through a neighborhood watch, through the church, or through the lost and found department that Holden and the city council had set up at the First Congregational Church didn't work, there were more individual approaches available. Depending on one's means and available time, a searcher might hire a private detective, place a classified ad in the newspapers, post a sign in the burned district, or roam the streets, avoiding police and peacekeepers and ducking through smoke and cinders and the still-burning rubble that would send up small, desultory jets of blue flame for many days to come. He could add his own name to the list of the dead by investigating a basement with a weakened ceiling, or by moving down an alleyway where the smoke from the ruins gathered thick enough behind him to knock him down and out. He could lose a hand or an arm by reaching into the wrong pile of rubble. And should he stay out too late after dark, he might get shot by one of General Sheridan's newly arrived federal soldiers or by a member of Pinkerton's Police or by the citizen militia that was even at this moment being organized. Everyone knew that.

As a last stop, the anxious searcher could travel to this livery stable at the edge of the untouched northwestern portion of the city. Police officers stood inside and outside, enforcing decorum and guarding against mischief. The remains were laid out on tables, propped up in chairs like hideous puppets, or heaped on the floor. Dignity was no one's concern. At one end of the high, dark space, in a small recess, were stacked seventy or eighty individual bundles of char, only a handful of which might be recognizable. Elsewhere in the room lay a "man of far above the ordinary size," dead of suffocation; another body lay intact and unmolested but for the head and face, which had "melted"; a third was displayed in pieces, arranged with some care so as to present an intact individual, but who knew.

By the end of this, the first day that the dead house was open, eight thousand visitors came to stare at fewer than 150 sets of human remains. This was a horror house for the ages, a lurid and grue-some carnival attraction, a once-in-a-lifetime opportunity to stare indiscriminate death in the face and go home to wife, to children, to fellow workers and tell the tale. People flocked to the improvised morgue out of "a morbid curiosity and a feeling of certainty that they, at least, could recognize what no one else could." Nothing provided by P. T. Barnum could match it.

Almost everyone who entered the dead house with an actual hope of finding a lost loved one found himself disappointed. On the first day of viewing, only two bodies were identified, both belonging to laborers newly arrived in the city. Still, this represented two fewer unidentified victims of the fire, and such a determination mattered to Chicago, a city that believed above all else in counting things. Everything that happened in the city was an increment of some larger total: sacks of grain, heads of cattle, flats of lumber, immi-gration of people. And money, of course; Chicago loved to count money. In a city that had yet to produce its own Walt Whitman, its Mark Twain, its John Singer Sargent to help it present itself to the world in the form of figurative words or impressionistic images, numbers stood in for other evaluations, other ways of measuring things.

It helped that the numbers that mattered had only risen dur-ing the thirty-four years of the city's existence: population, receipts, tonnage, acreage. Many of Chicago's most successful men, in fact, would leave behind little record of their lives other than box after box of financial ledgers and receipts. Nothing about the city stood still and nothing went backward, until now. After the fire, Chi-cago made an obsession out of counting losses: buildings, property value, insurance claims, and the dead. In great detail, the news-papers recorded the circumstances of individual deaths, sometimes a dozen or more in one article. Less than two days after the fire had been doused by a light autumn rain, the discoveries were ongoing.

A man who didn't survive his leap from a high window on Dear-born Street; six men killed when a retail building collapsed on Clark and Madison; five men caught in a wagon, crushed by a falling wall on State Street near Washington; a young clerk for a lightning rod manufacturer on Fifth Avenue, burned to death when he tried to carry out the company's ledgers; a "drunken man" who failed to outrun the flames on Michigan Avenue; on Ontario Street, in a cellar, the "charred trunk of a human body," surrounded by wine bottles. At Lill's brewery, near the waterworks, the charred "skull and limbs" of one brewer were found on Tuesday "lying some distance from the body."

The dead, it seemed, could be found everywhere and in every manner of posture and situation. On Bremer, a family of eight, no survivors, trapped in an upstairs bedroom. On South Water Street, the bodies of two "notorious cracksmen," assumed to have perished in the act of looting a store. Near the waterworks, a corpse stuffed, presumably at the victim's own volition, inside a large pipe. On Dearborn, an insurance salesman found on the pavement in such a posture as to suggest he had leaped from a fourth-story window and perished upon hitting the ground. In the six blocks between Townsend and Wesson on the North Side, where the fire had burned hard, hot, and fast, more than forty bodies, all unrecognizable. And on Jefferson and Taylor, the eight shrouded corpses that Charles C. P. Holden had seen on his Monday morning tour of the city.

Meanwhile, lists of the missing published in the city's newspapers ran into the hundreds every day during this first week after the Great Fire. Each morning, some names were added and some subtracted, but most were printed again and again, poignant reminders of a heartache that might linger far into the future. "The wife and two children of Chaz. Herzog, missing"; "Gust. Johnson's wife and child, missing"; "George S. Clarke, missing"; "Tommy Jackson, ten years old, missing." On and on the names went, filling as many as three entire newspaper columns.

Not all of these names represented fatalities. Some people had been separated from loved ones during the chaos and had no home left to host a rendezvous or had been wounded and were lodged in a hospital or charity. Many of those people turned out to have taken refuge on the prairie outside the city, along the lakeside, at the homes of strangers, or in a church or school building. Perhaps a few were even using the Great Fire as cover to make a break from their past life and start anew. But many of the people listed would never be reunited with loved ones. And in the end, absent a verifiable set of human remains or evidence of a permanent residence within the city, many would never be counted. Of the 132 bodies buried by the city itself, most of them transported later in October to the Cook County Cemetery, 117 were impossible to identify.

Of all the accounting Chicago performed in the wake of the Great Fire, the death toll would be the least certain and the least credible. In the days following the blaze, newspapers tossed many different numbers about, anywhere between "hundreds" and "thousands." Eventually, the county coroner would announce his own tally, ending the official discussion at a figure of three hundred dead. In the immemorial tradition of counting the dead after war, accident, and disaster, it was low. But in Chicago's case, it was laughably low.

Counting bodies was an exercise in gross overconfidence in the wake of a fire that had melted steel, marble, and glass. Bone begins to disintegrate at eighteen hundred degrees Fahrenheit, and there is little doubt that the Great Fire sometimes exceeded that temperature, especially on its run through the more densely populated neighborhoods and business districts of the South and North Sides. On the West Side, north of DeKoven, the population had been rendered skittish and ready to flee by the Red Flash fire of the night before, but the South Side was a different story. The fire's progress through Conley's Patch and then the newspaper district, both of which had believed they would remain out of the fire's path, was quick, volcanically hot, and brutal. Furthermore, on any given weekend, the 330,000 people who called Chicago home were augmented by as many as 20,000 visitors, many of whom would never have been considered in the official count, for lack of any way to confirm their status as living or dead. Movement of people at that scale was impossible to track, and no one tried to do so.

The role of illiteracy and poverty in answering the question of how many had perished was just as complex. A good portion of the city's residents spoke no English, lived unrecorded, or moved so often as to be untraceable. The real problem was less that three hundred was too low a number—though too low it was—than that it was too specific. A true count wasn't possible, and by offering one, the coroner and other counters were telling a lie, if one that they knew the public would swallow. Three hundred was just an actuarial baseline, a panacea to the city's desire to know the unknowable. Chicago's reporters knew this, its residents knew this, the city's leadership knew this. But no one objected, not in any public way. The count of the dead was another way that an unfortunate populace could close the door on the true cost of its Great Fire and consider itself fortunate instead of horribly unlucky.

Chicago was a quintessential American city in the sense that for all the raw materials flowing through its veins, it placed its bets on people more than things. Any financial loss could be absorbed, and the count of that loss was coming in day by day. Eventually, the tally would include 2,100 acres of burned ground, 17,500 buildings, and more than $220 million in property. Next to these numbers, three hundred dead sounded like a stroke of unbelievable good fortune. The count would stick, and fill history books into the twenty-first century, because it was the only number available. Buildings could not rebuild people, but people could rebuild buildings. To question the assertion that only three hundred people had died in the worst urban disaster in American history was to deny the good fortune of Chicago's population, and to so many of Chicago's residents the city's good fortune was its most essential fact.

≈ 17 ≈

FTER THE DESTRUCTION of the Merchants Insurance building on the courthouse square, home to Philip Sheridan's military command, he'd taken an office on Wabash Avenue, on
the South Side, below the southern edge of the fire's destruction.
Next door to him worked the mayor's staff in their own new quarters, along with the city treasurer and other staff, even as the city
council continued to work out of the First Congregational Church
on the West Side. On Wednesday, October 11, one day after the
general had rebuffed the delegation of South Siders at his home, a
larger and more insistent group of men came to Sheridan's office
door to renew the request that the protection of the city be put in
his hands.

No longer did his visitors base their arguments on the need
to protect safes and supply depots. Now they pressured Sheridan
by conjuring a verbal image of a city being consumed by chaos:
burned-out streets full of looting, robbery, mugging, arson, and
murder. In this vision, the city had descended into a state of lawlessness, even barbarity. The impression of anarchy was helped along
by the city's all-too-willing newspapers, most of which were starting
to publish again, fighting tooth and nail for readers. As if gripped
by a collective fever dream, the editors and reporters of Chicago
would have had their readers believe that in the midst of the fire's
progress and during the two days afterward, hundreds of people
had been shot, or lynched, or beaten to a pulp, all of them on the

spot as the flames danced nearby, and all for looting, or for trespassing, or for starting copycat fires.

INCENDIARIES KILLED or NO MERCY FOR THIEVES, read the headlines, followed by strange, unreliable paragraphs:

> An excited crowd gathered round the West Division Police Station, about 5 o'clock yesterday afternoon, intent upon making an application of lynch law to a man who was alleged to have tried to set fire to a house on Milwaukee Avenue. Three or four ropes were flourished in the crowd, and several speeches were made by parties urging them to rescue the incendiary from the hands of the police.

"Whether the report is or is not correct is not known," ran the last sentence of one such article, but, spoken or unspoken, this seemed to be the basic premise of most. Wrote the *Evening Post* on the same day in the same secondhand vein, "We hear that a fellow in the remaining portion of the South Division was caught trying to fire a building on Sixteenth Street and hung to the nearest lamp post." Fires flickered in the ruins for days after the big blaze, and all it took to create a flare-up or even a small explosion was a new gust of wind, or a mound of coal to reignite, or a bubble of leftover gas to come through the lines. Even so, woe to the curious bystander or burned-district tourist seen retreating from the flames. Every new fire, however small, was viewed as the act of an arsonist. More than one hastily fingered suspect was taken away by the police—not for justice, but for protection from a small mob.

The breathless writing in the papers had no basis in reality. There was no hard evidence that any sort of crime wave beyond the city's usual portion was under way. Sheridan himself didn't believe the reports, not least because war had taught him to be wary of the proliferation of exaggerated secondhand stories in the wake of cataclysmic events. But he knew that the fear behind the stories was real. Sheridan knew from the start that the federal soldiers he'd already ordered into the city were there for reassurance more than for any practical purpose, and if more reassurance were needed, he would listen.

The men in front of him that day asked the general to accompany them to the basement of the First Congregational Church, where Charles C. P. Holden and the city council were sequestered with the mayor, the comptroller, and the fire and police commissioners. Even as he acquiesced, Sheridan knew what was sure to happen next. As soon as this new delegation of "best citizens" arrived at the church, they announced their desire to Roswell Mason that he make General Sheridan solely and entirely "responsible for peace and order in the city." They added a request that an order be issued to that effect on this same day.

The mayor agreed on the spot. The mechanism of the appeal to Mason was tailor-made for Chicago's mish-mashed municipal structures, tapping as it did into one power the mayor did possess: his power to abdicate, rather than exercise, his authority. Mason had no standing to issue orders to the city council, but he could issue proclamations, and by doing so throw the problem out into the wider realm of public sentiment. In this case, he sent out a statement over his signature that he'd be turning his own and the council's authority for law enforcement over to General Sheridan. With the mayor's agreement, the business establishment of the city achieved checkmate. The means were blunt, even crude, but the maneuver was perfectly suited for the moment.

The two police commissioners on-site, Thomas Brown and Mark Sheridan, didn't give in without a fight. Voices raised, they argued that the people best qualified to reassure a skittish population and keep trouble to a minimum were the policemen already under their supervision, men who had walked among the people of Chicago, talked with them, and lived among them. And the best people to command those police, they argued, were their superiors, not a veteran of the Civil War whose experience of command had taken the wishes and needs of a civilian population into little account. In Chicago, police commissioners were appointed by the city council and were not subject to the control of the mayor's office, but at the same time, if the better-off portion of Chicago's populace with property left to lose supported Roswell Mason's proclamation—as they would—there was very little the commissioners, or Holden and the city council, could do in protest, short of having Chicago's police officers engage in open battle with U.S. soldiers.

The argument continued until General Sheridan himself spoke up. He set aside his usual brusqueness and profanity and addressed the assembled aldermen and other officials in a quiet, conciliatory tone. He didn't dispute the point made by the police commissioners. Were the matter in his own hands, he said, he wouldn't even be here at the church. He was acting not at his own behest but at that of others, he added, people whose financial interests in the city's reputation and stability made them worth hearing out. Then, having made a fine point of his reluctance, he brought out his heaviest artillery.

"There can be but one hand in this," he said. He would be happy to stand aside, but if not, sole control of the forces guarding the city would be an absolute condition of any arrangement that involved his participation. Then he added, should no one have taken the point, that unless the question came to resolution soon, he might have to send all of his federal troops home to their forts in Kansas and elsewhere rather than subject them to a struggle for their control. If on Tuesday morning Sheridan had declined the request to take charge of post-fire Chicago, now, twenty-four hours later, his every recorded motion, act, and word belonged to a man who was happy to assume the job.

Brown and Mark Sheridan continued to object, but Holden and the other aldermen knew their case was lost. If news that control of the city had been offered to Phil Sheridan, and that in response the council had sent all of the general's troops away, got out in the *Tribune* and *Times*—both of which had published sensationalistic articles about the supposed depredations being practiced all over the city—the council might as well disband now rather than wait to be voted out in the coming fall elections. As a longtime lawyer for the Illinois Central Railroad, Mayor Roswell Mason was a close friend and ally of many of the men now facing off against Holden and the commissioners. And though no proof exists, Mason might very well have encouraged the second request to General Sheridan himself.

The mayor's proclamation went out within hours of the meeting and was published in every newspaper in the city the next morning. Its first sentence read, "The preservation of the good order and peace of the city is hereby intrusted to Lieutenant-General Philip H. Sheridan, United States Army." Promises of cooperation with the city's police force were added, but the police commissioner Thomas Brown's own written account of the decision makes it clear that General Sheridan was given the final say on the protection and policing of the city, allowed the use of federal troops however he wanted to use them, and granted full oversight in the creation and deployment of a Chicago regiment of volunteer soldiers. The police would still answer to their commissioners, but the new federal soldiers in town would not, in direct contradiction of the original arrangement between the mayor and the Little General.

The *Tribune* made no bones about its happiness with Sheridan's new role, writing the next day of the general's headquarters on Wabash Avenue that "here the head of the city has planted a pine table, and entertains his numerous friends." The "head of the city" in that sentence was not Roswell Mason, the mayor, or Charles C. P. Holden, president of the city council, or any other elected official, but rather the unelected and un-deputized general Sheridan.

Less than forty-eight hours after the fire had cooled, the city had in effect two executive departments. One, run by Holden and other members of the council, was still collecting money and supplies and still controlled a police force under the supervision of the city's police commissioners. But it was a force that had been neutered, ordered to stand aside and not interfere with U.S. Army regulars and city militia in their midst. The other executive arm, ostensibly under the control of the mayor but controlled by the Yankee elites behind him, was also collecting its own donations of money and supplies, supported by a military presence that was made up of young men from afar and that operated independent of any state or local control, under the direction of the third most powerful man in America's chain of military command.

This was not a minor distinction. Martial law had been declared, to the great satisfaction of the city's business establishment and to the general approval of its wider populace. The unexpected opportunity to strip the city council of one pillar of its municipal power had presented itself, and Chicago's men of money and influence had taken fast advantage.

And, as soon became clear, these "best citizens" who had precipitated the transfer of authority from the city administration to General Sheridan were far from finished. The next day, a second meeting took place at the First Congregational Church, when Charles C. P. Holden and the council were visited by a second deputation. These were officers of the Chicago Relief and Aid Society, who occupied an economic stratum far above even those men of influence who had brought General Sheridan the day before. The society's president was Wirt Dexter, one of the city's richest and most successful lawyers—who, by the end of his career, would be described as the leader of the bar in Chicago—while its treasurer was George Pullman, who had over the past decade achieved great wealth and national fame as the inventor of the Pullman sleeping car. The society's board included several of the wealthiest merchants in the country, Marshall Field and his closest competitor, John V. Farwell, most prominent among them, along with commission merchants, lumbermen, meatpackers, ironworks owners, lawyers, bankers, and others of an elevated financial stratum. On this day the society was represented by Dexter and two other board members, all of whom spoke for a small group of ultrapowerful men, worth many millions altogether, who ran enterprises that employed thousands of men and women throughout the city.

However visible Sheridan's soldiers and militia were, the distribution of charity would turn out to be a far more consequential battleground in post-fire Chicago than the protection of real estate or the physical security of the streets. There were, after all, a hundred thousand or more people who had no home to burgle or set alight, no safe full of company earnings to guard, but the control and distribution of relief was something that affected every one of them.

Holden's plan for policing the city had been simple: add to the size of the police force by deputizing special volunteers and leave the details up to Commissioners Thomas Brown and Mark Sheridan. His plan for administering relief, on the other hand, had many tendrils and relied on thousands of individuals who had already done three days' worth of grueling work to get a system of organization and distribution up to speed. And now the Relief and Aid Society wanted to step into the middle of that work, dismantle all of it, and start over. Wirt Dexter and the society's other executives came to the First Congregational Church on this day supposedly for an exchange of ideas and ready for compromise, but in fact they were girded for battle. In their eyes, a second pillar of municipal power was ready to come down.

Prior to the Great Fire, the Relief and Aid Society was just one of many charitable associations in Chicago, and nowhere near the most active. Every denomination of Christianity ran its own relief effort, in addition to the YMCA, the Ladies' Christian Union, and the United Hebrew Relief Association. More charity flowed from more specialized groups that included the Hibernian Benevolent Society, the United Sons of Erin Benevolent Society, the Union Benevolent Society of Italians, the Chicago Sick Relief Association, the Bethel House, the Société Française de Bienfaisance de l'Illinois, the Slovanska Lipa Benevolent Society, and the Chicago Home for the Friendless.

With jobs in Chicago prone to drastic seasonal and yearly fluctuations, filled so often by an ever-growing immigrant population who lived on a financial cliff edge, and so often rife with physical dangers, this outpouring of private assistance was a necessary part of the civic weave that held the city together in the absence of any full-scale government welfare or unemployment programs. The Chicago Relief and Aid Society was neither the biggest, oldest, nor most well-funded charity in the city. But it was led by well-connected and influential men who believed civic respectability was best established in private and not public spheres. For years the society had modeled itself after New York's Association for Improving the Condition of the Poor. The idea was moral uplift of the destitute according to rigorous scientific and actuarial principles, and in America in the nineteenth century moral uplift meant self-sufficiency, especially in the eyes of those who had self-sufficiency to spare.

The society's offer of "cooperation" with the city was not a surprise, at least not to Holden, who understood that the gesture was not at all what it seemed. The day before, after the meeting that had installed Sheridan's forces as a military protectorate independent of municipal control, Wirt Dexter had buttonholed Holden at the church to suggest that the Relief and Aid Society take over the entirety of the collection and distribution of food, supplies, and money, framing the gesture as a kind of favor to the city. Holden had politely rebuffed the offer. He'd told Dexter that all the city's private charities had a role to play, but that the city itself was best positioned to conduct relief on the scale of a hundred thousand people and several million dollars, that in fact the relief effort was already well under way.

Now, on Thursday, outwardly mollified, Dexter at first didn't ask for complete control of the relief effort. Rather, he suggested a coordination of efforts, the merging of Holden's General Relief Committee with the board of the Relief and Aid Society. Holden expressed hesitance, unsure of how such a merger could be effected on the fly, after so many gears of relief had been set to moving. Still, he didn't reject the offer outright. So it was all the more surprising when, two days later, on Saturday, October 14, without warning to Holden and the council, another announcement over the mayor's signature was published in the paper:

> I have deemed it best for the interest of this city to turn over to the Chicago Relief and Aid Society all contributions for suffering people in this city.

Two years earlier, Roswell Mason had been elected atop the Citizens Party ticket, a reform-minded group of businessmen that sought to slow the growing strength of the city's working-class and immigrant wards and check the influence of the city council. That same group of businessmen had now been given an unexpected opening, and they took advantage. This was the second of Mayor Mason's two complete transfers of power away from Charles C. P. Holden and the council in two days, neither of which involved the exercise of any actual executive authority vested in the mayor's office. With his latest proclamation, Mason, who had sole signatory power over most of the donations that were pouring into Chicago's banks from across the country, had cut Holden off at the knees. All the money and all the material items sent to Chicago now belonged, with one stroke, to the Relief and Aid Society to do with as they pleased. Given the trainloads of supplies and millions of dollars rolling into Chicago—a windfall that made up a large percentage of the city's entire economy—this was giving entities outside city government control not only of law enforcement and indigent relief but of the entire reconstruction.

The members of the city council wanted their objection put on record, so a vote was taken at their next meeting and the mayor's resolution defeated. But this was a symbolic gesture without any means of enforcement unless Holden wanted to try to use the police to forcibly seize supplies from the Relief and Aid Society and the federal forces that would guard its depots. One sentence near the end of Mason's proclamation had sealed off any hope of undoing the mayor's action: "General Sheridan desires this arrangement, and has promised to cooperate with the association."

Holden's objection to the new arrangement had less to do with the kinds of work that the society might perform and more to do with the society's inexperience in managing public money. Commitments of aid totaling $2 million had already been received from New York, Cincinnati, Boston, St. Louis, and dozens of other American cities, as well as from London, Paris, and Munich. Not all of this money had been sent to the mayor's office—some was given to the city council, or to individuals, some to churches, some to fraternal organizations—but most of it had been. And in all of its previous years of existence the Relief and Aid Society had disbursed a tenth of what it now proposed to manage during one winter.

The mayor's resolution had offered a concession to the society's limitations: "The regular force of this Society is inadequate to this immense work, but they will rapidly enlarge and extend the same, by adding prominent citizens to aid this organization in every possible way." The introduction of the resolution and the debate surrounding it would later be painted as amicable in the newspapers and in early histories of the Great Fire, but it wasn't. Holden, especially, would never forget Wirt Dexter's duplicitous maneuvers. The society's board of directors, essentially its entire workforce, was tiny; the government of Chicago, involving hundreds of administrators, was large; the need, gigantic.

And even if the society did "rapidly enlarge," it would have to teach itself all kinds of new tricks in a short period of time. It was not in the business of handing out food, clothes, and blankets by the hundreds of thousands. Sometimes in the past, the city had given the society money, but by vote of aldermen and only in very small sums. The rest was raised from wealthy donors outside the view of city government. Wirt Dexter's entire operating balance, entering 1871, had been $12,890, and in normal times individual contributions to the society ran from twenty-five cents to a few hundred dollars.

For Holden it wasn't a question of the intelligence and competence of the society's directors, which he didn't doubt. And he knew that the city had never distributed so much charity all at once, either. Rather, it was a question of who was best set up to deliver relief on a massive scale to people who had no resources of their own to fall back on, and to do so in a hurry. People needed help now. The society would, Holden knew, do more to tighten rather than loosen the screws on eligibility for aid. Who was "deserving" now? How to measure their need, multiplied by so much? Tens of thousands, maybe eighty or ninety thousand, up to a quarter or even a third of the city's residents were homeless, and many of them hungry. By taking all the relief money, the society would put an end to Holden's efforts, mothballing a great many plans already in motion and making hungry and homeless people wait days or even weeks before new ones were drawn up.

The Relief and Aid Society belonged to no one political group, at least in theory, and was fronted by men of sterling reputation. But if Holden didn't doubt the competence of the society's directors, he did question their motives. This was a second action in just a few days designed to raise up unappointed and unelected men in the place of appointed and elected officials, actions that would have been impossible to take under almost any other circumstances. The city's own police force had been superseded by Sheridan's guards, who answered through a military chain of command to the general, who was empowered now to make decisions without subordination to any state or local authority. And now this: a tiny extra-governmental authority would be given millions of dollars that had been sent to the city itself and to no one individual. The entire scope of Holden's own relief plan, already set in motion via the General Relief Committee, relied on funds that didn't exist in the city's, county's, state's, or country's coffers, but would have come instead out of the sums that were pouring in from national and international destinations. Without access to that money, the council would be rendered inert, a powerless bystander in the effort to heal Chicago's gaping wound.

As Holden and a great many other Chicagoans would come to understand, the actions of the men behind Sheridan's and Dexter's assumption of control weren't a necessary response to the fire; they were, rather, a show of political force. After the publication of the mayor's two proclamations, the apparatus at the First Congregational Church broke up after a "continual session" of six days. No longer in need of such a large space, the city council removed to a nearby police station on Madison and Union, while the mayor remained at his improvised Wabash Street offices next to Sheridan's command in the far South Side. Only Holden, with a few others, remained in a smaller set of rooms at the First Congregational, "doing what he could to carry out the original intention in taking possession of the church." He still controlled some supplies that had been donated to the council and not to the mayor, and there were still decisions to make and edicts to issue. But in the wake of Mason's resolutions, there was much, much less left for him, and by extension the city, to do.

In one week, two citywide models of security and charity had fought it out in Chicago, one public and one private, and the private model had won, hands down. But the story of the aftermath of the Great Fire isn't complete without the inclusion of a third model, one that in its unassuming way would cause more consternation for the Relief and Aid Society than anything Charles C. P. Holden might ever have imagined. This model was introduced by the city of Cincinnati, whose Chamber of Commerce and Common Council had met on Monday afternoon, while the Great Fire still burned, to select nine officials to "go in charge of the supplies" to Chicago. Their train left at seven that night; after several delays, they'd arrived twenty-four hours later and headed straight for Holden and the First Congregational Church headquarters, bringing with them $110,000 worth of supplies and $10,000 in cash.

One of the train cars that transported the Cincinnati contingent had been unhitched and used as a temporary kitchen on the North Side. Four thousand dollars of the cash they'd brought in was used to start a soup house on South Peoria Street, in the West Side, beside the Pittsburgh, Chicago, and St. Louis tracks. Up and running by Saturday morning, four days after the Great Fire subsided and the same day that Roswell Mason's proclamation shifted responsibility for relief away from the city, the Cincinnati soup house opened at eight o'clock each morning, serving four thousand gallons of free soup each day to more than thrice that number of people.

The catch? Nothing, other than a strict policy that limited visits to one a day and stated that all soup must be taken off-site for consumption. "Persons wishing soup will bring buckets or other vessels," read Cincinnati's announcement, "as it cannot be eaten on the premises." No ticket was necessary. No age restrictions were established. No application, no review, no interrogation. Only a container was required: a cup, a bowl, a bucket, a barrel, all filled for free, no questions asked.

This charity was offered independent of the city *or* the Relief and Aid Society, whose self-drawn charter included many things, but not the provision of free food or supplies or housing—of *anything*—without a thorough examination of the recipient's worthiness. It was a simple, concise contrast: charity in its purest form, as practiced by the representatives of the Cincinnati delegation, as set against something else, as exemplified by the Chicago Relief and Aid Society. For a very short while, these modes of offering aid existed side by side without friction. But in short order, the competing visions of relief would serve as the first sign of much larger problems.

The subject of free soup seems a strange candidate to be the first small link in a chain of conflict that would overturn the post-fire hopes of the city's most influential citizens and forever establish the political power of the city's booming immigrant neighborhoods. But that was the role it played. Despite Chicago's belief that it stood as one in the face of catastrophe, the Great Fire would soon expose a great many bitter and heretofore hidden fault lines.

PART IV

Election

≈ 18 ≈

IN THE CACOPHONY of talk that filled the first weeks after the Great Fire—talk of rebuilding, of fire limits, of reform and relief, of the face Chicago would present to the world in its new incarnation—one voice was absent, a void in the city's discourse more conspicuous than any other. While Chicago sifted through its piles of rubble, William Butler Ogden was five hundred miles away, lost in an incomprehensible second tragedy. Only four days after a westbound train had brought him into the city from his home in New York, another train had departed to take him northward into the woods of Wisconsin, where he found a nightmare that exceeded even Chicago's.

The remnants of the Great Chicago Fire that would go on to cling most tenaciously in the popular imagination—the melted and misshapen courthouse bell, the defiant water tower, and, above all, "Mrs. O'Leary" and her cow—don't include the strangest thing about the burning of Chicago: that the Great Fire was only one of several great fires through the northern reaches of the country on the same night. And not by any measure but financial ruin was Chicago's the most destructive. In the woods and prairies of southern Minnesota, northern Illinois, and all of Wisconsin, massive, unchecked wildfires had been the story of much of 1871, and those of October 8 and 9 remain the most widespread in the history of America.

For months before the Great Fire, the weather all over the western half of the country had behaved in strange and worrying ways.

A ridge of low pressure had hovered over the Arizona Territory in July and August, spiking average temperatures across most of the western two-thirds of the United States as much as three degrees in the late summer. By early October, that ridge had migrated up to the northeastern corner of the Colorado Territory, a vast and sluggish weather system—what meteorological scientists of the time called a "cyclonic storm"—resting on a diagonal and tilted rightward with one end of its gigantic oval touching Lake Superior and the opposite end touching the Pacific Ocean near Los Angeles, two thousand miles away.

For weeks without end, epic winds had whipped counterclockwise around the eye, sweeping over vast landscapes in straight lines that seemed to stretch on forever. On the western side of the system, away from Chicago, a steady barrage of twenty-mile-per-hour winds brought subfreezing air down from Canada and onto the Dakota Territory, Montana, Wyoming, and Utah, where daily temperatures sometimes dropped twenty degrees below normal. On the eastern side of the oval, warm, dry air traveled up from Mexico, New Mexico, and Texas, and swept across the plains until it arrived at Illinois.

Conditions might have been ominous in Chicago, but in the pine forests of Michigan and Wisconsin an awful confluence of factors made a great cataclysm almost inevitable. Dramatic news reports aside, nothing was "sudden" or unique about the catastrophe that struck all over the upper Midwest on the night of Chicago's Great Fire. During the first week of October, as two dozen small blazes had caught in Chicago, prairie and forest fires were burning unchecked across eleven counties in Minnesota and eight in Wisconsin. The clear-cutting and grading associated with thousands of miles of new woodland rail lines had eliminated natural windbreaks, flattened rises in the land, and created dangerous wind tunnels in the gaps between the trees. The prairie and forest fires racing along these lines displaced people thousands at a time, some of whom escaped far to the east and west, while others sought closer urban destinations like St. Paul, Milwaukee, St. Louis, and Chicago. Before October 8, hundreds of thousands of acres had already burned, but still the entire region of America north of Missouri and Kentucky was primed for something to happen.

By Wednesday afternoon, the day after his arrival at the Illinois Central depot, Ogden was sure of two things: most of his wealth in Chicago had gone up in flames, and, as unfathomable as it seemed, his largest financial investment anywhere else in the world had also perished. Though he was eager to get to the North Woods, he'd still lingered for a few days in the city, counting his losses and meeting with partners and managers of his Chicago businesses to form recovery plans. Speaking at the relocated Chamber of Commerce on Saturday, October 14, three days after he arrived, Ogden cautioned against the temptation to let any temporary move of the city's municipal functions to the West Side become permanent. He decried "efforts said to have been made by certain parties," a statement that seemed to find in Charles C. P. Holden's establishment of the continuing government at the First Congregational Church a scheme to remove city hall from the central business district forever.

Men like Ogden, whose financial health depended on long-established business structures, trade networks, and personal relationships, had the most to gain by discouraging change. The pieces had been knocked off the chessboard, and to proceed fairly, he said, those pieces needed first to be returned to the places they'd occupied before catastrophe struck. In his address at the Chamber of Commerce, Ogden also spoke with enthusiasm "of the early history of the city" and told a story about Chicago's first swing bridge, a device of his own design built in 1840, which he now used as a metaphor of unity that did double duty as a warning. "There is room enough for all sides to grow up again," he said, "without the people of one division trying to steal that which belongs to another."

If his property holdings had included any significant portion of the West Side, which was enjoying a bonanza of new business, his tone might have been different. This was the way Ogden spoke, thought, and lived—mingling the interest of the city's population and his own interest, always placing the public good hand in hand with his own personal gain. That Ogden should get all the richer through whatever actions he performed at the city's behest was such an established principle in Chicago as to be incontestable. In public and on social occasions, he was an earnest, quiet, and persuasive speaker, and he closed at the Chamber of Commerce by reminiscing about the poverty of the city in its formative years. He reminded his audience that in the 1830s and 1840s they'd built Chicago up from much less than what still stood and that they'd done so in seemingly no time at all.

That same night, after his address, Ogden left for Wisconsin and his logging interests there. Chicago's grain came from 770 million acres, its hogs from seventeen states, its lumber from pine forests that spread for thousands of miles. And Ogden had his hand in some part of all of it. Over his history and Chicago's, Ogden was founder, owner, shareholder, president, or director of more companies and organizations related to crossing and profiting from the land than seems possible. This was not to mention his seats on the boards of many dozens of insurance companies, manufacturing companies, charities, and civic institutions. The sum of these affiliations meant that Ogden attended a lot of board meetings while participating in the day-to-day management of no one organization. He was free with his associations but choosy about his bedrock commitments, and in 1871 the town of Peshtigo and the Peshtigo Company were by far his largest active concerns outside Chicago.

Forty-five miles north of the town of Green Bay on the western shore of the body of water also called Green Bay, the town of Peshtigo and its nearby harbor funneled the harvest of a million acres containing a billion towering white pines, each tree worth a potential $100 or more to his company. The word "Peshtigo" was yet another of the era's uncountable, vaguely attributable Indian names, here given to the river with a providential set of rapids that sped Ogden's logs out toward Lake Michigan and provided power for a set of mills that made a manufacturing powerhouse out of an otherwise unremarkable, if picturesque, corner of northern Wisconsin.

After the Civil War, Ogden and his partner, Isaac Stephenson, of nearby Marinette, had built a lumber town, bankrolled its public buildings and many of its private residences, and fitted it out with hard-packed roads, telegraph lines, and commercial docks. After only six years Peshtigo could claim a brand-new bridge, Lutheran and Presbyterian and Congregational and Catholic churches, two hotels, and a new watch and jewelry shop. The town still had no paid police force and no jail. All of its most lucrative businesses bore the Peshtigo Company name: a sash-and-blind factory, a gristmill, machine shops, the company store, and the giant wooden-ware factory, which turned out wheels, tools, all manner of furniture, and a hundred other staple items.

For Ogden, the entire milieu of Peshtigo—its sights, sounds, smells, and seasons—was reminiscent of his childhood home of Walton, New York. For a man as nostalgic as he was, the romantic qualities of mill rivers were powerful, setting aside their awesome potential to generate income. As he told one biographer, "I was born close by a sawmill, was early left an orphan, was cradled in a sugar-trough, christened in a millpond, graduated at a log-schoolhouse, and, at fourteen, fancied I could do anything." The truth was, however, that in 1871, Walton, New York, did not much match Ogden's sugarcoated vision of rustic authenticity, because it was too well established and cultured, its well-to-do citizens able to attend philosophical readings and gala social events and join genteel hunting parties, not to mention able to get to New York City in a day. Peshtigo, Wisconsin, lay far closer to his fictionalized and idealized rough-and-tumble childhood, and its fate affected him deeply.

Two thousand people lived in the town, and every one of them received their pay from Ogden and Stephenson or worked for someone who did. Peshtigo had no saloons or brothels, but there were some to be found a short ride away in Marinette or Appleton, and this helped to establish a steady flow of available labor. The town absorbed several dozen new residents each week, many of them immigrants, a blend of the pious and promiscuous, lumberjacks, loggers, and railroad workers. Here on the shore of Green Bay, as in Chicago and everywhere else, the core paradox of the age held fast: the overseas newcomers were desperately needed to keep the money flowing, while at the same time they were scorned, assumed to be inferior to their supervisors and to the men who paid their wages.

Many of the loggers were itinerant workers, traveling from Maine, New York, Vermont, and Pennsylvania after the seasonal harvest there was complete. The mills of Peshtigo were populated by people speaking Swedish, German, and Norwegian, saving their pay for the day when they might own their own patches of property, hoping to rise in the Peshtigo Company or to get away to start their own businesses. Ogden might have inherited cash, connections, and a sizable company on the death of his father, but the bootstrap myth he embraced spoke loudly to other men who'd come to America under that same spell.

All summer Peshtigo, even more than Chicago, had whistled past its own graveyard. The summer's drought had drained the river and made logging hard and slow. While under other circumstances the decreased pace of production might have allowed the company to make up for its low volume by raising its prices, the forests in Michigan, across the water, were bearing the fruits of wetter weather and saturating the market with their own logs, driving the workers of Peshtigo to a frenzy of activity in the dust and heat. With annoying regularity, high September winds knocked down telegraph poles and cut contact with Green Bay, Milwaukee, and Chicago for days at a time. By early October, the river was at its lowest level in memory. The town contained no fire station or organized fire company, though it did possess a single hand-pump fire engine donated by Ogden himself. When Peshtigo's own fire did arrive, hours before the Learys' barn caught, that single piece of apparatus proved worthless.

It took Ogden almost three days to get to Peshtigo by train, a trip that under other conditions would have involved a single night's stopover. No passenger rail line yet ran all the way into the town, so Ogden disembarked in Marinette and rode a carriage the rest of the way, a slow ride that served to ease him into the reality of the catastrophe. Large swaths of forest had been replaced by smoking craters, creating a landscape dominated by acres and acres of pitted and blackened ground as lingering fires cooked the soil to a light, ashy uniformity. This was a preview of hell, but what Ogden found in Peshtigo when he rolled into town assaulted the senses and defied even the most lurid of imaginations.

Some of the first people he saw were the members of burial teams who still shuffled through a small sea made of ash and the vague outlines of building formations. Even a week after the fire the teams were searching for victims. They'd already collected hundreds of sets of charred remains, human and animal. Some were solid, and some would come apart when lifted. Many were fleshless skeletons found in their last pose: a mother shielding her child, a girl fallen while running, a man huddled in the corner of a barn, a couple under the bed. The town's fire bell sat on the ground, a shapeless lump, its housing burned away. An entire row of train cars had vanished except for their iron wheels. Some bodies could be identified only by a small set of metal items a person was presumed to have carried. Some bodies could not be identified at all. Fifty horse carcasses lay in a row, conforming to where their livery stalls had been, the stable's location outlined in ashes around them.

More than a thousand people were unaccounted for. As Ogden toured the damage, he heard the reports from the supervisors and foremen who'd survived. He asked for and appreciated the details. For a man of his business and engineering bent, such details provided refuge from the horror and provided him with a thin coating of understanding. Even more than Chicago's blaze, what hit Peshtigo had been a firestorm, not a fire, and the name told the story: it was neither storm system nor fire but the combination of both, as three separate fronts collided and the winds built and swirled so that when the spreading prairie fires of the previous weeks encountered the tall timber stands, they exploded. Within minutes of hitting the pinewood stands, the fire reached two thousand degrees and higher and was pushed along by bursts of wind reaching 120 miles per hour.

The center of the storm had traveled in an unquiet eye thousands of feet in diameter, and that eye hit Peshtigo dead on. The Chicago fire had produced fire devils on the updraft created in the building canyons, but that is not what happened on the shores of Green Bay. This had been a full-blown and full-sized tornado made of the hottest fire nature could produce. Buildings caught fire and flew apart in the same instant, and a human being caught outdoors hadn't stood a chance.

The arrival on Monday, October 16, 1871, of "Mr. O.," as the locals called him, was to the executives and workers of the Peshtigo Company as the coming of a savior. True to his history, Ogden didn't shy away from the sights of destruction or the physical labor of reconstruction. On his first night in Peshtigo, he gave an impromptu speech. "We will rebuild this village," he declared, "the mills, the shops—and do a larger winter's logging than ever before." And his workers, as devastated as they were, cheered.

Like Chicago's fire, Peshtigo's own disaster might have been incomprehensible, but it was not quite as complete as the earliest reports had suggested. A fire that took the form of a tornado also had something of the arbitrary destructive path of a tornado. Much of the town's harbor had survived, and now the sawmill there ran its machinery day and night to churn out a thousand coffins. Public, state, and federal dollars were soon to arrive. General Sheridan, in Chicago, had directed federal troops Ogden's way, though in Peshtigo they would not enforce martial law but rather lend their hands and backs to the cleanup and initial rebuilding. The harbor took in survivors and served as a staging ground for medical care and transportation. Telegraph lines were soon restored, and Ogden insisted on the rapid rebuilding of the rail line to nearby Menomonee.

At sixty-six, many years removed from the athletic peak of his youth, Ogden joined the cleanup and rebuilding with a manic intensity. One foreman described his relentless pace this way:

> At daylight in the morning he was up, and worked with the men till dark constantly exposed to the rain and sleet and snow. When night came he would go on an open car, drawn by mules, eight miles to the harbor. All the evening until late in the night he was engaged with his clerks and assistants in drawing plans, writing

letters, and sending telegrams to his agents and the next morning break of day would find him again at the head of his men at Peshtigo.

Another observer noted that Ogden seemed to throw off "at once thirty years of his age, becoming a young man of exhaustless energy, untiring industry, and contagious enthusiasm." Ogden would stay in Peshtigo for two months, and in that time the town would get back to its feet and make itself ready for the spring logging season. But the physical work and the responsibility for so many damaged and departed souls wore him down. One of the company's overseers would years later say of Ogden that "he was cheerful and pleasant and inspired everybody with courage and faith in the future. This terrible strain upon him, and overwork for a man of his years, probably shortened his life."

When Ogden was able to count his total losses in the lumber town, the numbers were staggering even for a man of his wealth. He knew that more than $1 million worth of property and inventory in Chicago was gone, and now he could add at least another $1.5 million in Peshtigo. He had faced adversity before, lost great sums, but like many enterprising men of his kind in the early years of the era, he had always relied on his name, reputation, and considerable credit to buoy him. Above all, he had depended on his belief in the future and the energy that came along with that belief. Now, for the first time, the opportunity waiting in his future seemed to pale beside the past he'd lost.

≥ 19 ≤

C HICAGO'S REPUTATION as a center of vice and violence was well deserved, a natural by-product of its rapid growth, its yawning divide between rich and poor, and its position as a transportation crossroads of astounding variety. Where so many kinds of people came together in often temporary proximity, crime was easy. Since the city's inception in 1837, murder, robbery, and arson had been a regular part of the weave of life, along with gambling, prostitution, and graft. Books were published for visitors from east and west with titles like *The Spider and the Fly* and *The Tricks and Traps of Chicago*, most often aimed at young women and all bearing the same message: you'll never in your life see anything else like this city, but watch out for yourself. As one such treatise advised, *"The prevention of evil is always better than the cure."*

The belief in a widespread fire-abetted crime spree continued strong into the next week, and fanciful headlines poured forth, but in reality the opportunity for mischief was slim. Outside the burned district, the city was more densely inhabited than ever, now protected by General Sheridan's soldiers, or by property owners bearing rifles, or by private security forces, or by the police. The burned district was charred into rubble, unstable, and prone to new fires. Its safes might seem an ideal target for a burglar, but the fire had burned so many safes so hot that their contents had vaporized, and most of the rest had been removed from the premises by their owners within days or were under armed guard. Inside the burned district, life was far more dangerous for a looter than for his target.

Without doubt, over the long Monday of the fire and into Tuesday, some people had taken advantage of the chaos to dash inside an abandoned storefront or warehouse and make off with whatever might be had before the flames arrived. But by the second week after the fire, that chance was gone.

Still, the continuing fear of disorder ran high enough to be called paranoia. The fifty-two-year-old Allan Pinkerton, personal guard to Abraham Lincoln and founder of the nation's most famous detective and armed-guard agency, was suffering through the aftermath of a stroke, and his two sons now ran the Chicago branch of the famous family business out of temporary quarters on the West Side. Newly styled Pinkerton's Police, they advertised themselves with pride as "independent of Government or municipal control." They'd been the first to patrol the burned South Side after the fire cooled, and soon their handbills, signed by the elder Pinkerton, were visible throughout the division:

> Any person Stealing, or seeking to steal, any of the property in my charge or attempt to open the safes, as the men cannot make arrests at the present time, they shall Kill the Persons by my orders, no Mercy Shall be shown them, but Death shall be their fate.

The *Tribune* trumpeted its support for any and all security measures: "The doubter must remember that the most extensive residence portion of the city is now far more at the mercy of its own inhabitants than, please God, it ever will be again." A long parade of men was detained for acting suspiciously, and the residents of the city still repeated many rumors of copycat arsonists being hanged, but in the end there were no corroborated accounts of vigilante lynchings or summary executions. In their allegiance to pure invention, the reports in the papers of a post-fire crime bonanza had a great deal in common with the reports about Kate Leary and her cow. The motivations were similar: to sell papers, of course, but at the same time to confirm to readers frightened by the pace of growth and change that the fabric of Chicago could be shredded by its lowest, poorest, roughest elements. That is, if the city did not remain vigilant.

The concern with crime represented a post-fire fear of threats to the city's political structure, to its divisions of class, to its sense of hierarchy according to country of origin. The fearful response was born less out of a desire to safeguard the upper classes from the lower classes than out of a fervent desire to keep those distinctions in place. An emphasis on "protection" divided the city into those with things to protect and those without. For what measure of theft could now happen to the tens of thousands like the Learys of Chicago? What reason did the poor have to be afraid now? A big fire that gutted their thinly insured homes and businesses was their greatest fear, and no new fire could ever match the one that had now decimated their neighborhoods.

In truth, the people running things saw a mostly peaceable city. General Sheridan himself discounted all the reports of post-fire violence, telling the mayor after the declaration of martial law, "I am happy to state that no authenticated attempt at incendiarism has reached me, and that the people of the city are calm, quiet, and well disposed." This was part self-promotion, because Sheridan's job was to keep the city calm and quiet, but a few days later he added an emphasis: "There has been no case of violence since the disaster of Sunday night and Monday morning. There has not been a single case of arson, hanging, or shooting—not even a case of riot or a street fight. I have seen no reason for the circulation of such reports."

From their vantage point at the church, Charles C. P. Holden and the police commissioners agreed that "the roughs, the incendiaries, and bad characters of all classes and kinds, as a rule, gave Chicago a wide berth during those days of great excitement and peril." The city's police blotter backed them up; one week after the fire, few individuals were in custody for vandalism or violence committed since the spark in the Learys' barn. The jails were not overfull. General Sheridan's appointment as law-enforcement baron had been intended to assuage fears of what might happen, rather than to counteract any real and present danger.

The truth was that in the immediate aftermath of the fire Chicago's streets had become safer, quieter, and more harmonious than at any point in the city's history. If someone was going to guard supply depots and patrol burned-over districts that resembled recently cleared battlefields, why not a man who'd first made his name as a ruthlessly efficient quartermaster and then as the greatest cavalry officer in the history of the U.S. Army? But even if there was little argument about Sheridan's character and experience, the necessity for subverting civilian authority to military rule was much less clear. Still, many in the city told themselves that it was Sheridan and his boys who kept the streets safe.

Until, on October 20, 1871, the second Friday after the fire, they didn't.

Twelve days after the fire began and ten days after Sheridan took control, the city was crawling with soldiers, militia, policemen, and various other sorts of guards. The men patrolling with their rifles were a temporary fact of life, and for the most part they inspired confidence and didn't create problems. These were bored men on boring duty, and in fact far more ink and attention was given to the federal soldiers' off-duty adventures in the saloons and brothels than to their on-duty presence on the streets. Sometimes a group of soldiers on patrol would cross paths with a policeman or two, and when that happened, jibes might be hurled back and forth, but no physical confrontations occurred, and questions of jurisdiction were most often decided in favor of the army patrols. Sheridan's authority soon expanded, by consensus of the business leaders of the city, to include Pinkerton's men and numerous other private-guard companies, along with men like John Devlin, the head of security for Field & Leiter, who'd guarded the company's caravan of goods as they were taken away from the store.

Sheridan also oversaw a new city militia under the immediate command of Colonel Francis Sherman, who'd served under General Sheridan in the Civil War and who was the son of the man who'd defeated Charles C. P. Holden in the 1862 mayoral election. This militia was made up of volunteer "companies" that operated within neighborhood boundaries and combined to form the "First

Regiment Chicago Volunteers," adopting such names as the Mulligan Zouaves, the Sheridan Guards, and the Hannibal Zouaves. The entire arrangement had a special appeal for young men who'd missed out on the Civil War and appreciated a taste of the regimental dash they'd heard described by their uncles or older brothers.

Theodore Newell Treat was one such young man, a volunteer member of the University Cadets. Twenty years old, a sophomore at the University of Chicago, he hailed from Janesville, Wisconsin, a prosperous farming hub just across the state line, best known for Abraham Lincoln's visit there when Treat was six. He was enrolled in the university's "scientific" course of study, as opposed to the "classical," the only other degree offered. This meant that his program set aside any Greek and most Latin and focused on advanced mathematics, English, German, history, physics, rhetoric, and natural history. Eighteen professors taught 253 students. To be admitted to a full course of study required rigorous preparation in English grammar, ancient and modern geography, U.S. history, and algebra. Theodore was a smart, earnest boy who came from a family with enough money to pay the university's yearly room, board, tuition, and incidental fees, which totaled around $300.

The campus lay on the South Side at Cottage Grove and Thirty-Fifth Street, three miles below the lowest progress of the fire and a mile beyond the neighborhood that General Sheridan called home. Built on lakefront land once owned by Stephen Douglas, Abraham Lincoln's famous debate opponent, and conferred to the Baptist church for formation of the city's first university, the institution had opened in 1856 on ten acres shaped like a baseball field's home plate, surrounded by a high iron fence and centered on an imposing V-shaped four-story stone edifice that housed one of the country's best-equipped observatories. Sometimes called Douglas University, the school was not quite national in reputation, but it had garnered attention one year before the fire by graduating the nation's first woman and first Black man to earn law degrees.

Shortly after the fire and General Sheridan's initial meeting with the mayor, Colonel Sherman had enlisted Richard T. Colston, a former Union officer taking a part-time slate of classes, to take charge of the young men guarding the university grounds and sur-rounding neighborhood, where a relief supply station was located. The idea that anyone would attempt to break into a well-secured supply depot so far from the burned district was fanciful at best—but not as fanciful as the idea that anyone would want to cause mis-chief near the campus, where a few hundred students daily went to their under-attended post-fire classes.

Every night at seven o'clock, the twenty or so boys who made up the University Cadets met with their captain and classmate to receive their arms and patrol assignments and to confirm the evening's countersign, the password that allowed the cadets and residents of the neighborhood to identify each other in the dark. A popular choice on many nights was "Sheridan." On the night of October 20, ten days after the fire, Treat learned that it would be his turn to patrol the perimeter of the campus.

A mild and pleasant Friday turned damp and cold before night-fall, and by midnight the streets were populated only by the odd omnibus rider or a student coming back in from his studies, hud-dled and hurrying against the chill. Autumn had arrived, as if the Great Fire had burned away the heat and dryness that had seemed to linger so long with such oppressive, ominous persistence. This far south of downtown, the fire hadn't touched the visible world. The moon was bright, and as Treat made his slow rounds at the periph-ery of the university, the streets were peaceful and unthreatening.

Soon after midnight, his boredom was broken when a single fig-ure, a tall man, approached out of that darkness. As the unknown pedestrian passed the front gates of the university, the young mili-tiaman stepped into the street, raised his rifle, and issued two com-mands: halt and provide the countersign.

The unknown man didn't stop and he didn't provide the coun-tersign. But this wasn't criminal behavior. In fact, if anyone other than a policeman or soldier embodied law and order in the city, it was this stranger making his way home. As the city's police court prosecuting attorney, Thomas Grosvenor was the scourge of rogue restaurateurs, brothel owners, building code violators, olfactory offenders, and other miscellaneous scofflaws. The Colonel, as he was known, had been a Union officer and was wounded at Harpers Ferry. Though he was not the most famous veteran in the city, he was respected and liked, at least by his colleagues in the city offices.

Grosvenor's night had been as pleasant and quiet as Treat's. He'd spent time at a friend's house on the North Side and left at about eleven o'clock, taking an omnibus down State Street to Twenty-Fifth. He lived on Bryant Avenue, another eight or nine blocks farther to the south, but he liked the long walk. So it had been without concern or fear that Grosvenor strolled past the university.

As to why he didn't answer Treat's command, perhaps he was tired. Perhaps he didn't know the countersign, which he was supposed to have asked for before leaving the neighborhood. Perhaps he'd been drinking. Perhaps he bore a feeling of proprietary confidence: it was his neighborhood, after all, and he was the fifth-highest ranking member of the staff at city hall, a man of some authority. In fact, in the night's deepest irony, it's very possible that he had been one member of the anonymous deputation that visited Sheridan to ask him to take control of the peace and safety of Chicago. And perhaps the age difference contributed to the misunderstanding: Grosvenor was thirty-seven and the boy was twenty. Or perhaps several of these factors taken together contributed to the tragedy that now unfolded.

In any case, Grosvenor didn't say anything to Treat and kept walking. After he'd passed, Treat again told him to halt and said that he'd fire if he didn't.

"Go to hell," answered Grosvenor, and continued on his way. "Bang away and be hanged."

The boy fired.

It's not clear what damage or mischief Treat imagined this well-dressed, solitary gentleman walking through the streets of the far South Side of Chicago in the rain, however impertinent, sought to accomplish. The boy's later testimony made clear that he was enforcing order for the sake of enforcing order. He was to shoot anyone who failed to give the countersign or otherwise disobeyed orders, both of which had happened in this case. At no point, he would later testify, had he felt any danger to his own person.

The ball took flight and smashed through the attorney's left arm, a rib, and his stomach, before coming to rest in his liver. The wound was fatal, but not immediately so, and Grosvenor was able to scream—"Oh God, oh God, my wife!"—a noise that brought out several residents of the neighborhood and reached the watchman on duty on top of the nearby station of one of the fire department's hose companies. Grosvenor got up and fell, got up again and tried to run several paces, dropping blood onto the wooden sidewalks, and fell on his face in front of a shoe store, never to rise again. Several firemen carried him into their station house, where Grosvenor lay moaning and calling out for his wife and family for a time.

Brought home a short time later, Grosvenor died in his bed at five o'clock in the morning. No quoted conversation or testimony, then or later, ever recorded Treat's whereabouts at the moment of the attorney's death—whether he'd run back to his room at the university, followed Grosvenor to the fire station, or went to get help. "The boy sentinel," *The Chicago Times* called him. Did he know in that instant that he'd killed a man? Did he think of himself as a soldier in that moment, or at any time thereafter? Had the peace been kept?

Later that day, Treat would be detained in a police holding cell. But he would never be tried for a crime. Grosvenor's death was nothing more than an unnecessary confrontation with a tragic ending. No one would ever argue otherwise. And with that single episode, like a spigot turned from on to off, broad public support for a federal military occupation of the city vanished. The *Times,* which had opposed the mayor's decision to abdicate power to Sheridan from the start, was unmerciful: "Who is General Sheridan? Is he some imperial satrap in whose favor the city of Chicago or the state of Illinois have abdicated their functions? Who gave General Sheridan authority to put muskets in the hands of a parcel of crack-brained college boys?"

Not two weeks earlier, Medill's fellow publisher William Bross had written of the sight of Sheridan's army companies marching into the South Side on the morning after the fire, "Never did deeper emotions of joy overcome me. Thank God those most dear to me, and the city as well, are safe." But now even the *Tribune*, an ally of the law-and-order crowd if ever there was one, performed a temporary about-face to join the chorus of indignation, writing that the "thoughtless manner in which" Grosvenor "came by his death, growing out of the present disturbed condition of municipal affairs, has occasioned a strong feeling regarding the manner in which our semi-military protectors have been permitted to discharge their duties."

As much as the mayor and the business barons of Chicago wanted to pretend that Sheridan's martial authority was a normal state of affairs, there were plenty of important people who never agreed. Earlier on the same day that Thomas Grosvenor went for his fateful night out with a friend, Illinois's governor, John Palmer, had written and dispatched a pointed letter to Mayor Roswell Mason, enclosing an admonishment. "It excited the greatest surprise, and has occasioned me the profoundest mortification, that you failed to inform me," wrote the governor, "of the necessity, in your judgment, for the employment of military force for the protection of the city." This was strong language, and an important objection. Chicago was still part of Illinois, its affairs still intertwined with the state's.

The governor continued, "It has pained me quite as deeply that you should have thought it proper to have practically abdicated your functions as mayor," and added that the presence of U.S. troops unanswerable to civil authorities was, in his reading of the situation, illegal, that it was improper and unconstitutional in any case for Sheridan to act in anything but a subordinate role to the city's police commissioners. He closed by asking the mayor to relieve General Sheridan so that the city could receive the money the legislature had that day set aside for extra police.

Timing was everything. Letters such as this one between Springfield, the state capital, and Chicago were most often sent via train and not by telegraph, to save money and to maintain a sense of decorum and a separation between state powers and city authority. This custom meant that Mayor Mason received Palmer's message just hours before the shooting at the university, or perhaps the next day, just hours afterward. Had Grosvenor not been killed, Palmer's message might have initiated a legal argument between governor and mayor; after all, nowhere was the relationship between federal, state, and city governments in the wake of a catastrophe such as the Great Fire well established.

But now that a public figure, a city attorney, was dead by the hand of a college student under federal jurisdiction, things moved to a conclusion rapidly and with no public objection. On Saturday, October 21, as Grosvenor's stunned family and friends gathered to make funeral plans, Roswell Mason began an exchange of letters with General Sheridan, who was headquartered next door. After the usual thanks for service rendered, Mason told the general, "I would like your opinion as to whether there is any longer a necessity for the continued aid of the military." To which, a day later, on Sunday—presumably after a set of face-to-face conversations— Sheridan wrote back to the mayor, "If Your Honor deem it best, I will disband the volunteer organization of military on duty since the fire, and will consider myself relieved from the responsibility of your proclamation."

At six o'clock on Sunday evening, October 22, less than forty-eight hours after Treat had pulled the trigger, Sheridan's time as military ruler of Chicago was finished, as quickly and as shrouded in secrecy as it had begun. An announcement was sent to the papers and entered into the official record. The Chicago Volunteers stood down, while the seven hundred members of Sheridan's federal infantry made haste to collect their belongings and board trains that very evening back to Louisville, Fort Leavenworth, Fort Hays, and Omaha. The city's police chief and commissioners were put back in charge of law enforcement. The SPECIAL POLICE badges came out of storage.

As for the incident that had precipitated this sudden withdrawal, one of Holden's special policemen might well have made a similar mistake, in this or a different part of the city. What Treat did was not unprecedented in the history of police work, but the fact that he was doing it as a citizen volunteer under martial law made it less than ordinary. The speed of the shutdown demonstrated that the people running the show, including General Sheridan and the mayor, knew that thorny questions had been raised. In fact, the general himself had raised those questions with the first group of businessmen to approach him, a group that most likely included Grosvenor, whose death now hovered over the city like a chastening ghost.

Two days later, Sheridan reported to William Tecumseh Sherman, general in chief of the army, his past and current commander and close friend, with a brief summary of his involvement in the post-fire protection of Chicago. The duties of the federal companies had concluded on October 23, he wrote, and the men sent away. All militia volunteers were discharged. The letter didn't mention Grosvenor's murder or Theodore Treat at all. It didn't have to. Part of life in the military was that mistakes were made. General Sherman's response was intended as nothing less than a preemptive acquittal:

> The extraordinary circumstances attending the great fire in Chicago made it eminently proper that General Sheridan should exercise the influence, authority and power he did, on the universal appeal of a ruined and distressed people, backed by their civil agents, who were powerless for good. The very moment that the civil authorities felt able to resume their functions, General Sheridan ceased to exercise authority, and the United States troops returned to their respective stations. General Sheridan's course is fully approved.

Governor Palmer would soon seek to indict Sheridan and Roswell Mason, though not Treat, for the murder of Grosvenor, with the hearty approval of the *Times* and the stern disapproval of the *Tribune*. But no grand jury was about to pursue a trial for such a famous and highly decorated Civil War hero, and the case soon went away. Together Sheridan and Sherman had helped to save the Union. At no point would the city's business barons acknowledge that they had brought to bear a level of force that far exceeded the needs of the situation. Just a few days later, in fact, they would ask that Sheridan's soldiers return, setting off a long round of argument between city and state authorities. In their eyes, a man was dead, a prominent man, and that was a tragedy to be regretted, but the streets were quiet. And all was well. More than ever before, they believed, the city was theirs—an outcome that in their eyes justified the mistaken loss of one man's life.

ᴥ 20 ᴥ

O N THE MORNING of October 31, 1871, perhaps in a small nod to the encroaching spirits of Halloween, one of the *Tribune*'s editorialists—though clearly not Joseph Medill—published a column titled "The Phantom City." Far more like something Ed Chamberlin might have written at the more lyrically inclined *Evening Post*, the piece was a kind of rhapsody on a classical theme, subtitled "A Moonlight Stroll Through the Shades of Chicago," while a second subtitle lamented the "Rapid Disappearance of the Poetry and Romance of Our Ruins." It began by comparing the Great Fire to "the red flames that blotted out Ninevah, or the sword of the Assyrian or Roman when he devastated conquered Jerusalem," and its prose only became loftier after that.

Insofar as the *Tribune* was the mouthpiece of the hard-nosed, full-speed-ahead business interests of Chicago, the column was a strange piece of work. The Great Fire had indeed produced impressive ruins. Photographers flocked into the city on trains for weeks afterward and dotted the streets of the burned district with their darkroom wagons, producing haunting images of ruined brick walls that were published and sold everywhere from California to Russia as stereographs and framed mementos. But for a pro-business paper in a pro-business city that was focused on rebuilding, the classical allusions and sense of melancholy added up to a rare and remarkable moment of what might be termed civic self-awareness:

So little regard have we for the past, and so constantly do we turn our thoughts to the future, that the very appearance of those ruins, which we gazed at so sorrowfully and wonderfully twenty days ago, will soon be effaced from our minds, and we will forget that this new city, in this new country, has had its ruins, as well as Italy or the east, though ours were once the homes of merchant princes, and theirs of Emperors and barbaric Kings.

The sentiment was also strange because in all its other writing, from the Wednesday after the fire, when the paper first published again, until this Halloween day, the *Tribune* exhibited not the slightest twinge of melancholy about the loss of anything. To the contrary, the *Tribune* and the other papers of Chicago were full of suggestions of what might be done by the city to clear away those romantic ruins and what might be built on top of them, all in the greatest possible hurry. "Soon be effaced from our minds," indeed.

In fact, the newest pastime of the city's residents, expressed in a

View of the corner of State and Madison Streets after the Great Fire, photographer unknown, 1871

geyser of excited letters to the editor, was to propose how Chicago might best use the fresh start it had been granted. What might the city do differently, do better, more wisely, more efficiently in this second incarnation, this unanticipated rebirth? The newspapers were full of unsolicited descriptions of new types of fireproof windows, shutters, roofing, fire extinguishers, and more. One writer, oblivious to the aftershocks of Grosvenor's murder, proposed the formation of a Citizens' Guard, a corps of civilian militia ten thousand members strong whose job it would be to impose martial law whenever necessary, a duty that would by some political miracle or madness be made "obligatory by a municipal enactment, conformable to the constitution of the State." One proposal lamented private control of the Chicago River's waterfront and asked that the city seize the chance to exercise eminent domain in order to create a series of public dock accommodations along its main branch. An "engineer" wrote to suggest that the rebuilding include more than two hundred miles of underground pipe dedicated to a citywide system of steam power, to be used for ventilation, heating, cooking, and power. And from another engineer came the proposition that houses in the most valuable precincts of the city be heretofore built only out of cast iron.

None of these unsolicited suggestions, other than one calling for "loftier reservoirs" on top of downtown buildings, would ever become reality. Chicago in the immediate aftermath of the fire was interested not in creating a new self but in duplicating the old one. As adjusters from hundreds of insurance companies near and far combed over the burned district of the city, a steady stream of announcements appeared that spoke to the city's eagerness to get back to business as usual. Every day the Board of Public Works issued permits for five, ten, even fifteen new structures. The most popular new buildings were brick warehouses and brick business blocks, going up on every street in downtown. The pace of construction was breakneck, with work continuing well into the night, lit by calcium lights burning lime as fuel, all in anticipation of the higher lease rates available to the first to rebuild.

As the sound of saws and hammers roared on, rumors spread

of possible wildcat strikes by bricklayers, some of whom were asking for a dollar's raise from $1.50 to $2.50 per day, but this news put no dent in the pace of reconstruction. The property owners of Washington Street, who never before would have engaged in any concerted thinking about the arrangements of the stores on their block, now banded together into an official association, determined to "rebuild in first-class style" their portion of the South Side as a unified advertisement to potential renters. Charles C. P. Holden got in on the action, announcing his plans to build a block of his own on Madison Street, in the West Side, hoping to entice a permanent stay out of some of the businesses that had decamped over the river in the wake of the fire. Construction on the new Chamber of Commerce and Board of Trade building, across from the courthouse, was already under way, as were new editions of several of the city's biggest banks and hotels.

In the meantime, the Irish and Bohemian neighborhoods near Kate Leary's cottage celebrated a cold and wet holiday in what meager style they could manage. In 1871, Halloween wasn't yet embraced by all classes and nationalities, but it had begun to leave behind its Catholic origins in Ireland and Scotland and spread throughout the wider working-class and immigrant communities in American cities. Neighborhoods like the Learys' had over time turned the holiday into a genial evening during which friends visited friends, family visited family, and permission was given to the children to stay up late to take part in "innocent exercises." The telling of ghost stories and fortunes went on well past midnight, along with apple dunking and hazelnut roasting. Some families or groups of children went door to door exchanging food and conversation, and some wore homemade costumes of ghosts, witches, and other creatures, but these travels weren't yet the centerpiece of the night.

That Halloween, in the wake of the Great Fire, it was easy to believe in ghosts. Whether an intentional or unintentional nod to the day and the mood, the piece in the *Tribune* ended on a bit of poetry that represented some of the best writing that had ever appeared on its rag-paper sheets:

By the starlight one can see only the vague forms of objects near at hand. The river has gone from sight, and the buildings beyond are swallowed up in the darkness. Far away are the blazing coal heaps, burning up like mimic volcanoes, and farther yet, the gas lamps of the West Side; but they seem infinitely remote, and on the verge of the horizon of the night. All other sights, all sounds, have died away, and there remains only a sense of desolation and ruin, so great and terrible that one can linger no longer, but gropes his way as best he can back to the light, and the homes of men.

The "homes of men," for many, were in this moment nothing more than overcrowded barracks or temporary wooden shelters. The Relief and Aid Society had constructed three large barracks even as it made no bones about its opposition to their use—out of concern not so much for the health and comfort of the "vagabonds," as they called the recipients of temporary relief housing, as for the inconvenience to the citizens who lived nearby. These poor property owners, said one writer, might suffer from "throwing pell-mell into the heart of the city a crowd of idle and vicious characters, whose barracks will be the hot-bed of vice and sickness." The North Side barracks held six hundred people, while the two raised in vacant lots on the West Side had room for a thousand each. Surrounding these structures were encampments dotted with tents requisitioned by Phil Sheridan from U.S. Army depots around the Midwest.

Charles C. P. Holden's original plan—to give anyone who needed them the materials for a rudimentary frame house, no questions asked—had evolved over the past three weeks, after the transfer of the relief effort to the Relief and Aid Society. Decisions about help were now made according to a concept called "scientific charity" that had been put forth for the past four years by the new *Journal of Social Science.* Not that Wirt Dexter and the business barons of Chicago society who populated the board and staff of the Relief and Aid Society were reading the *Journal of Social Science,* but they were following in the footsteps of the leaders of New York's

Association for Improving the Condition of the Poor, who did. And that organization's directors believed in the ability of numbers and theories to determine the proper level and modes of distribution of citywide assistance. In this era of massive industrial and corporate growth, cities like Chicago ran on the proposition that *everything* could be counted, rated, and ranked, including a family's need in the face of a disaster no one could comprehend.

The principles of scientific charity were simple. Emotion was useless; reason was useful. Impressions meant nothing; measurements meant everything. Christian charity was fine for churches, but a secular relief authority must render strict and final judgments without falling prey to religious sentiment or an overactive largesse. Charles Dickens, no favorite in Chicago after he'd skipped the city on his final lecture tour of America three years earlier, had skewered the philosophy of scientific charity in his novel *Hard Times* in the person of the skinflint teacher Gradgrind, who begins the book by lecturing his students on the folly of empathy and emotion: "Facts alone are wanted in life. Plant nothing else, and root out everything else. You can only form the minds of reasoning animals upon Facts: nothing else will ever be of any service to them." Wirt Dexter would have seen none of this as satire.

Residents of the temporary barracks lived under one long roof in three-tiered bunk beds, sharing a handful of privies. "The intention and desire," wrote the society's directors, "is to move the low class of people as quickly as possible from the barracks, and convert their present quarters into storehouses." But the process for receiving housing assistance was logjammed by rules and anything but quick.

First, the person who desired housing filled out an application that asked eleven questions. After providing his name, the address of his former residence, an explanation of his current quarters, and the number of people in his family, the applicant was asked if he had formerly owned or rented his lodgings, what types of lodgings those were, where his new lot was located, how he supported himself or what skills he possessed, if he carried insurance and if he'd been paid on said insurance, and how much money he had in the bank. Finally, he was asked to make his specific case for assistance and to provide a reference from "some reliable and well known citizen."

This last requirement was tough for many applicants to manage, not least because there were almost a hundred thousand residents without a roof overhead and only a few thousand who fit the definition of "well known": a phrase meaning, in this case, well known to the investigating officers of the Relief and Aid Society. Then, even when the reference was provided and approved, the petitioner still needed to submit to an "investigation" by a society "visitor," who came to wherever the applicant was staying and confirmed what could be confirmed and inferred the rest, with absolute veto power over the application.

If the society visitor stamped an applicant as worthy, then came the bounty: an order for precut lumber and a set of plans for a twelve-by-sixteen-foot house for families of three or fewer, or a fifteen-by-twenty-foot house for families of four or more, no matter how big the family. In general, no workmen came along with the wood. Exceptions were made for widows and the physically impaired, but otherwise the society's assumption, not too far off the mark in the Chicago of 1871, was that everyone and anyone could construct a house by themselves or knew someone who could. The practical effect of this assumption was that of the tens of thousands of houses going up in the burned district, most were built sturdy enough for the fast-coming winter and some were not. And all were built out of very flammable pine.

All the time, the society tallied like mad, whatever it could tally: board feet of lumber delivered to building sites, number of applications filed vis-à-vis number of applications approved, number of visitor visits made, number of blankets distributed. Two hundred thousand three-person meal packs were issued, each consisting of an impressive daily ration of one peck of potatoes, three pounds of pork, one pound of sugar, one pound of cheese, three loaves of bread, one pound of crackers, one bar of soap, one candle, one cabbage, and two quarts of onions.

It was also about this time, at the end of October 1871, that two other counts were made official. One was the county coroner's far-cical final estimate of three hundred dead as a result of the Great Fire. The other count was the more accurate summation of insur-ance so far paid and unpaid. The numbers were unheard of by nineteenth-century standards, anywhere in the world. A little more than $310 million had been claimed in insurance, of which an esti-mated $190 million would be collected. Those whose property was insured through policies spread among a number of companies in larger cities in the East could expect a satisfactory settlement. Those whose property was insured through Chicago firms—and this group of policyholders included most of the smaller shopkeep-ers and individual homeowners who had any insurance at all—were in greater trouble.

Much of the hometown Merchants Insurance company's li-quidity, for example, was generated by the rents payable in its own building and in other Chicago real estate, most of which no longer existed. Counting their assets and examining their liabilities, the company's accountants knew from the first look that bankruptcy was on the way. Most of the other insurance firms based in the city were in similar straits. An industry tottered as many firms paid out whatever they could, however meager the amount, and then closed their doors forever.

Other industries, however, continued as strong as ever. Many were unscathed. And some realized a bonanza. Chicago could present itself to the world as so resilient and optimistic in the face of unfathomable damage because so much of the city was *un*dam-aged, doing business as usual with little or no interruption. Reading the earliest dispatches from Chicago, the rest of the country could be forgiven for believing that the city had been destroyed. But in fact, more than 70 percent of its street grid was untouched, and that didn't include the suburban districts beyond the city limits. Chicago had lost hundreds of millions in capital, but it still had many, many times that amount to fall back on. Forty percent of the city's stock of lumber had burned up, but that left millions of board feet avail-able to use, with more coming in from the forests of Michigan and Wisconsin every day.

Likewise, more than a dozen of the city's grain elevators still stood, and if the main branch of the Chicago River was lined with ash and char, the dockage farther down the south branch toward Bridgeport still received all kinds of raw materials and sent out all kinds of manufactured goods, its dockhands working extra shifts to supply the sudden increase in demand. The Union Stock Yards, vast and never resting, lay outside Chicago's corporate limits to the southwest of downtown, three miles beyond the Learys' neighborhood, and this city within a city was operating at full volume, as were the railroad tracks that brought in livestock and sent out cured meats. And any business on the West Side that supplied provisions, groceries, hardware, medicines, clothes, or other essential goods found itself more popular than ever.

Finally, purveyors of vices great and small enjoyed boom times. The city's intact saloons, which had been given the all clear to reopen just two days after the fire, were more full than ever. People were in the mood to drink. Prostitution had taken a hit, because many madams and their employees had left town in every direction rather than wait out the rebuild, and gambling houses had experienced a similar scaling back—it was easier to run a faro den out of sight than to rebuild one out of sight—all of which meant that those that survived experienced profits in rare proportions.

But the most visible post-fire entertainment in Chicago, combining vice and virtue as always, was politics. As Halloween night passed and gave way to the cold winds of the coming winter, the city seemed to wake up all at once to the fact that a municipal election was set for November 7—just one week away. Well before the rebuild could gain a full head of steam, the next step for Chicago was to decide who would lead it out of its wilderness of destruction.

Before the Civil War, mayoral elections in Chicago had happened in the spring, every year. In 1863 the city had switched to two-year terms, and in 1869 it had moved the elections to November, which meant that the contest of 1871 would be only Chicago's second to take place in autumn. Here was another what-if: had the fire struck with a new city administration already in place, the bitter battle about the way the city should run that was about to erupt would have been dampened. For all of its history, Chicago's elections had been intramural battles more than interparty contests: since the start of the Civil War, the mayor's office had gone Republican, Democratic, Republican, and then, two years earlier, Roswell Mason had been elected over a fellow Republican as a representative of an amorphous reform-minded group called the Citizens Party that promised to keep a closer and more critical eye on municipal expenditures and not much else.

As the year's electoral maneuvering got under way, Joseph Medill found himself in an old and familiar king-making role, canvassing other prominent citizens, participating in backroom conversations, harnessing the power of the *Tribune*'s editorial page. He was known for it and took pride in it, and it was his words on October 23 at a meeting of Cook County Republicans that had begun to guide the city toward its eventual consensus. At that meeting, thirteen days after the Great Fire, he told the assembled officers of the party that "he believed that a ticket of the very best, ablest and purest men of both parties—particularly our Mayor, Aldermen and Commissioners—would be of more benefit to our city" than partisan ballots. "Let the country see," he continued, "that we are united and harmonious in our municipal politics, and it will redound to the credit of the city, and aid in securing that confidence and assistance which we shall need to get out of the ashes and ruins that now envelop it."

Messengers were sent to the Democratic Central Committee to request a joint meeting to determine a ticket. The Democratic response was lukewarm, but the idea took hold in the imagination of the city's political and business elite, then its middle class, and would not be let go of. Under Medill's experienced hand, something called the Union-Fireproof ticket now came to life. For an audience in New York or Cincinnati or St. Louis, went his thinking, the word "Union," with its echoes of the recent victory in war, meant that the city could be counted on to rebuild as one, while "Fireproof" meant investors and insurers could put new money into the city without fearing a repeat of the losses from the Great Fire. This was not a party affiliation; it was a coalition, to comprise men of all political stripes who agreed that the face Chicago showed to the outside world was much more important in this moment than its internal agreements or disagreements.

At this same meeting, Medill and his fellow Union-Fireproof proponents selected as their mayoral candidate Henry Greenebaum, who had emigrated from Germany in 1848 and then had risen, with a financial boost from several family members, to a prominent position in banking and civic affairs. Greenebaum was a remarkable choice, even a historic one, given that he was German and Jewish, a most uncommon combination for an American mayor in the nineteenth century. At the same time, it didn't take a political genius to understand that Germans, who made up almost 20 percent of the city's population in 1871 and were the wealthiest of its larger immigrant groups, were a key building block in whatever new political structures the Union-Fireproof coalition wanted to build in the wake of the Great Fire.

The city had many public primary schools but only one public high school, out on the West Side, close to Medill's home. This was where, six days later, on the morning of October 29, 1871, the Union-Fireproof supporters met to make their final decisions about the men who would put their names forward in the municipal elections of this unusual fall season. The makeup of the campaign and party committees was a warning to anyone who might run against them, a who's who drawn from every strain of Chicago politics: Democrats, Republicans, liberal Republicans, reformers, temperance men, even socialists. It also included an unusual mix of native-born Protestants, Irish Catholics, and Germans.

In this single room, in fact, gathered the greatest combination of political talent the city had ever known, representing a comprehensive history of city administration going back to the city's founding. Among them were the Democrat Carter Harrison, a prominent young lawyer who would later serve two terms as a U.S. representative and four full terms as the city's mayor; the former Democrat and now Republican "Long John" Wentworth, already a six-term U.S. representative and two-term mayor; the Republican Anton Hesing, owner of the German-language *Staats-Zeitung* and the foremost political broker in the German community; Medill's fellow publishers at the *Tribune*, Horace White and William Bross; the lawyer, philanthropist, and early railroad builder J. Y. Scammon; the Democrat Daniel O'Hara, a political leader in the growing ranks of Irish Catholic immigrants; and Andrew Cameron, publisher of the national labor-union paper *The Workingman's Advocate*.

This was an alliance as politically diverse as any American city could have put forward in 1871, and its makeup did indeed send an unmistakable signal to the rest of the city and the country. With unusual gravity, the men horse-traded positions in the new administration. They selected candidates for each of the twenty open alderman positions. Then the top of the ticket was announced. At some point between the Union-Fireproof meeting on the twenty-third and the meeting on the twenty-ninth, for reasons that went unrecorded in any public record, Henry Greenebaum's name had been removed and replaced with that of Joseph Medill.

Greenebaum's removal from the ticket was a real loss to history, but in the moment the choice was a savvy one, most of all because no one believed Medill had any ambitions in the field of politics. He was no one's idea of a Democrat, but his dual associations with Abraham Lincoln and with Horace Greeley, who'd started him on his career in journalism, helped him to appeal to a broad base of Republicans, those who were supportive of President Ulysses S. Grant and those who weren't. His paper had sometimes been hard on the Irish poor, but with less of the viciousness showed by the *Times*, and Medill had generally gotten along with the publisher Anton Hesing and the German community, even without his recent role in putting Greenebaum forward.

Medill was very much a behind-the-scenes operator, by habit and by temperament. Stepping out in front of the curtain would test him as nothing else ever had in his life. Much as General Sheridan's seeming reluctance to take the reins of law and order in Chicago made people trust him all the more, so too was Medill helped along by the widespread belief that he didn't want the job. But there was an important difference: Sheridan always believed he was the best man for the position, while Medill was full of doubts. He was well suited for the work of influence and opinion, but he understood even as he accepted the top spot on the ticket that he would win. And then he would have to place himself inside the political ropes. And inside the political ropes was not a place to which he was accustomed.

☙ 21 ☙

THE QUESTION OF who would become Joseph Medill's opponent resolved more slowly. Less than a week before the election, the Union-Fireproof campaign was still complaining that their opponents "change their ticket daily in order to confound us" and to deny the *Tribune* a clear target for its editorial fire. But they knew quite well, as did the rest of the city, that the election of a Union-Fireproof mayor was a fait accompli, which made drumming up enthusiasm among potential rival candidates difficult. Also, with widely popular representatives from every political faction of Chicago propping up Medill, it was difficult to define a single faction as the opposition.

Meetings in opposition to the Union-Fireproofers did happen all over the city, but they were muted affairs, held more out of disgruntlement that Medill should have the playing field to himself. "The Democrats and sorehead Republicans," the *Tribune* called them, while the *Times* just used "Dem-i-Reps," and those names did vaguely describe the two coalitions facing Medill. "Sorehead" was just the latest iteration in a long line of names given to postwar, pro-Grant Republicans. "Barnacles," "bummers," "stalwarts," or "regulars"—all referred to those Republicans who essentially stood and voted against the civic reform platform that animated the newest wing of the party, the self-styled "liberal Republicans," whose core sense of themselves was how very far they believed they stood above the muck and mess of business-as-usual politics.

Going through the motions of ward caucuses in Chicago was

always a good idea, because much could change in two years, when the next mayoral race would be held. On November 2, 1871, only five days before the election and with little fanfare, the opposition ticket placed Charles C. P. Holden at its head. Holden was a well-seasoned political veteran, having served as an alderman for ten years, and he'd already lost a mayoral contest, so it seems strange that he would offer himself as a sacrificial lamb at the altar of the gathering Union-Fireproof consensus. But he had his reasons.

From that point until the election, Holden seems to have had no designs on winning. Instead, he was portrayed in the press as part political martyr and part political operator. The *Times* referred to Holden's "anxiety for office in the present emergency, when no good citizen would ask for it." In the end, Holden's motives for running in a hopeless cause would become clear: to give himself a vehicle to deliver the message to Chicagoans that he and the council had not received proper recognition for their work in the wake of the fire; to protect the council from the more fervent of the Union-Fireproofers' reformist urges; and to maintain what energy was present in the local organizations with an eye on the next set of elections.

In Chicago's swirling and shifting political climate, this was a sensible plan. The campaign documents Holden submitted to reporters and the content of his few public addresses that week were not statements of why he would make the best mayor, or why Medill should not be elected. Rather, they served as testimony, or even depositions, a way to enter a form of evidence into the public record that the city council was a positive force and not the obstruction to good government that the Union-Fireproofers made it out to be. Holden believed that everything he'd done beginning the Monday of the Great Fire was done as a practical, levelheaded response to the fire. The actions of his opponents—of the men of the Relief and Aid Society and of the overlapping cohort that had drafted Philip Sheridan to take control of the city—seemed to him less an effort to do what needed to be done than a shot across the bow of Chicago's poor and foreign citizens. By running for mayor,

Holden would have a chance to make this case in public, when otherwise he might have been ignored.

The centerpiece of Holden's editorial barrage was his long narrative of the activity at the First Congregational Church in the days following the fire, while another important letter, also published in several of the city's newspapers, offered a series of testimonials from various state delegations extolling their faith and trust that Holden and the council would have used donated money wisely and distributed supplies fairly, had the Relief and Aid Society not snatched that money away. This was an important point to make at a time when the Union-Fireproof supporters and many of the town's newspapers were talking about the effect of an untrustworthy city council on the city's ability to get credit and good rates on insurance from faraway observers.

Nowhere in any of the material that Holden distributed did he say a word against General Sheridan, nor did he disparage Joseph Medill, either by name or by inference. The opposite was also true, but only on the surface. The record of the election of 1871 can be scoured top to bottom without uncovering a single instance in which Medill vilified his opponent. But Medill was, of course, part owner of one of the most powerful newspapers in the country. And over the election's single week of all-out campaign activity the *Tribune* overflowed with smears, suggestions, and outright slander against its part owner's opponent.

The Union-Fireproofers might have proclaimed lofty goals, but their tactics were low. Never mind that Holden's wife, Sarah, and Medill's wife, Kate, had spent several days together at the church coordinating the distribution of supplies and that their husbands had long been friends and occasional allies. According to the hard-and-fast rules of Chicago politics, a sharp, even vicious contrast between candidates was necessary, however thin their ideological differences might be. And the editorialists of the city were happy to oblige.

In normal years the closing stretch of a Chicago municipal election was a free-for-all, involving raucous rallies and aggressive editorials as the opposing sides sprang at each other from their respective corners. But this year's contest was more of a pile-on, all against one. In the compressed time frame imposed by the distraction of the Great Fire, the haymakers were saved for three days, spanning Saturday, November 4, to Monday, November 6, the eve of the election. Nine separate columns in the *Tribune* alone beat the drum loud and clear. The effort in every instance was to turn Holden into the living emblem of the bummers and soreheads, the "ward loafers" and "dead-beats" who, according to Medill's surrogate editorialists, were a clear and present danger to the very survival of the city and evidence that politics as usual would destroy Chicago's best chance at a full recovery from the disaster.

It seemed that every item in the news, however small, provided a chance to pour derision on the opposition. Someone in government had proposed the construction of a commemorative fire memorial, and the *Tribune* used the suggestion as an opportunity to take a shot or two at the opposing party and at Holden himself:

> LET US COMMEMORATE. How a Neat, Appropriate, Fire-Proof Monument may be Obtained for Chicago—A Good Use for the Old Safes, Insurance Policies, and Discarded Office-Holders.

The Great Fire had left behind "several fire and burglar-proof safes, which were overtaken by the fire late at night, and, before they could make proper arrangement to resist the enemy in a body, were rendered worthless." Here came the sarcasm: this lump of melted safes, said the *Tribune*, has "solved the question of a neat, allegorical, imposing, and cheap monument." By way of the sheer number of burned safes available, such a commemorative edifice could rise "many thousand feet above the level of the sea." To self-satisfied readers of the *Tribune*, this was funny. "Pedestals might be constructed at intervals all the way up, upon which could be placed for variety the whole Police and Fire Departments, the present defunct Common Council, and Board of Supervisors, Mayor Holden, and the other dead members of the Bummer faction."

The editorial concluded with one last poke at the presumed loser of the upcoming mayoral election:

> Such a monument would, without doubt, become rapidly famous, and eclipse in beauty even that of London. No one could mistake it for the fitting tribute of a grateful city to Mayor C. C. P. Holden, and being built and adorned with what is confessedly worthless, would be a monument to economy, as well as to the fire, beside removing the rubbish to one particular spot. Let the work be commenced immediately.

The most oft-repeated charge against Holden was that of nepotism, a hardy perennial whenever Chicago's business interests wanted to attack the council. And to be fair, it took at least two hands to count the number of Holdens working in city government, although most could be found only in obscure crannies. Charles C. P. Holden himself held three elected or appointed posts: alderman, president of the council, and West Side park commissioner. One cousin worked in the city's internal revenue office, while another, Charles N. Holden, was city tax commissioner, a trustee of the state insane asylum, and a member of the Board of Education. Another Holden worked as a clerk in the post office, and yet another collected water taxes for the Board of Public Works. General Joseph S. Reynolds, Charles's brother-in-law, held posts at the Custom House and Board of Education. B. F. McCarty, brother-in-law of Charles N. Holden, was the city's fire warden, while Jesse Holden, son of Charles N. Holden, was a map clerk at city hall.

In a city where General Sheridan's brother served on his staff, a position paid out of federal taxes, and where Sam Medill was hired as his brother's city editor, the force of the accusation that Holden's family had too many men in office was somewhat diluted. The charge was also full of bitter irony for Holden himself, because through two marriages that had brought him to forty-four years of age, he had fathered no children, though he and his wife, Sarah, had adopted a girl. He might someday be in a position to find sinecures for a grandchild or two, but his ability to practice nepotism in the virulent form attributed to him by the *Tribune* would always remain far out of proportion to the vehemence of his accusers.

The other barbs, though no less sharp, were covered in a thick rust of silliness. "Chief Caucus Packer Holden," he was called, a play on his initials, and in this incarnation Holden was accused of scheming to use his aldermanic and ward-level connections to stuff ballot boxes and "grab" the mayoralty. This logic stretched past the breaking point, because everyone knew that there were no effective party caucuses to be found this year, not while most of the city was busy rebuilding their homes, and anyway that by putting his name in the mayoral hat, Holden, the council's president, was asking to *reduce* his authority. Setting the council's agenda and determining the makeup of its various committees were the responsibilities of its president, and probably the most tangible political power a person could wield in Chicago. Also, mayors, by tradition if not by law, served single terms, while council members often held their seats much longer. In truth, trying to "grab" the mayor's seat was one of the least power-hungry political actions Holden could take.

To throw up more smoke, the Union-Fireproof supporters on staff at the *Tribune*, with the help of the Relief and Aid Society officers George Pullman and Wirt Dexter, combed the society's ledgers and pulled out a set of receipts that supposedly showed Holden riding about the town in high style and charging the cost to the society. "If it costs him $240 a week to keep him in carriages when he is only an Alderman and a Park Commissioner," wrote the *Tribune*, "what thousands will be required to keep him equipped and mounted after he becomes Mayor?" This charge was weak, in that the documents entered as evidence of Holden's wastefulness were invoices that represented reimbursement for out-of-pocket expenses for himself and several city officials for their own work on the relief effort, invoices submitted and thus entered into the public record by Holden himself—invoices that had, in fact, already been reimbursed to him by the society.

The next accusation was even softer and related to a $15,000 donation from private citizens in Detroit after the Great Fire that had come to Holden instead of to the society. According to the society's chairman, Wirt Dexter, Holden had put the cash "in his breeches pocket and he didn't propose to part with it to the Relief and Aid Society." When Holden replied that he had in fact turned the money over to the city treasurer, David Allen Gage—a man who worked in the same Wabash Street office as Mayor Mason— the *Tribune* didn't miss a beat, dropping its original accusation and changing the charge against Holden from one of withholding the money to one of not producing a proper receipt for the money. The *Times*, usually wary of any alliance with Medill, piled on with glee. "Holden," it wrote, "says he is made of 'steel.' Holden is not good at spelling, and evidently meant 'steal'—in which he is an acknowledged expert."

Never mind that it had taken three weeks for the society to offer the first accounting of its own harvest of more than $2 million in relief money from other cities—Holden's $15,000 was made into evidence of gross impropriety without the smallest shred of evidence. And the Union-Fireproof men didn't stop there. Should Holden be elected, wrote the *Tribune*, "nature will assert itself, and the bummers will either swoop down in a ravening pack upon the fund of the destitute fire-victims, or else they will bring the whole influence of the city government to bear to stop the forwarding of relief to Chicago."

These attacks were widely read, impressively worded, and, seen from the distance of history, pointless. Holden was never going to win. Chicago had a way in many of its elections of coalescing around an individual, independent of party politics. And it was clear that, however improbable the circumstances, Joseph Medill's turn had come. The Germans, the Irish, the *Times*, the *Tribune*, workingmen, and businessmen, all wanted continuity and consistency until the fire's effects began to recede, but they also wanted someone who seemed to provide a break from partisan politics, and with his coalition ticket Medill gave them both. Medill could also be counted on to be personally boring, at a time when the city had experienced enough drama. From the point of view of the average voter, a vote for Medill was apolitical: they were selecting an emergency government, nothing more or less.

Besides, Holden himself was tied to voters with a loose knot. The president of the city council was selected by its aldermen, not by the general public. He had no voice, no journalistic "speaking horn" to wield during election week. With a strange-days alliance of the *Times,* the *Tribune,* the *Staats-Zeitung,* and even *The Working-man's Advocate* stumping for Medill and the Union-Fireproof ticket, Holden didn't have a platform on which to refute the charges against him, couldn't bring any charges of his own if he'd wanted to, couldn't lay out any substantive differences with his opponent. In fact, he might not have had many substantive differences to lay out. For the most part, he wanted what Medill wanted—a robust and efficient rebuilding above all—but where they differed was in Holden's belief that the city itself, in the form of the Common Council, should be in charge of that rebuild. He was proud of the council's work under his leadership, and he wasn't going to let that council go out without rising to its defense.

Subsequent events would absolve Holden of all the charges leveled against him in the week before the election except that of nepotism, which was a political tradition in Chicago in any case and would not go away because of a single disaster, no matter how historic. In reality, every one of the accusations was bunk, as most of the citizens of the city understood, even as they readied to select Joseph Medill. Few believed that Holden was a political boss involved in runaway fraud or embezzlement. Among the portion of Chicago's citizens who would vote this year, there was simply a sense that Chicago needed to stand facing the world with a unified front, and Holden couldn't offer that unified front to the same degree that Medill could.

In any case, the opposition to Holden wasn't about Holden himself. For the Yankee elites backing the Union-Fireproof ticket, an opportunity had presented itself most unexpectedly in the form of the Great Fire, and they took it. Larger questions hovered over the mean-spiritedness that pervaded Chicago's one-week sprint to the political finish line. One related to the fact that a new party projecting a new brand of political harmony was engaged in a very old kind of smear campaign. Another question had to do with the changing face of the city, which in its earlier days had been far more northeastern, white, and Protestant, but was now increasingly Irish and Catholic, German and Scandinavian, Bohemian and Black. Another set of questions surrounded the economic relations of Chicago to the rest of the country, its perception as a safe home for investment capital in the wake of the Great Fire. But perhaps the biggest question, not for the long haul, but in this moment, was that of what—and, in the end, *who*—constituted good government.

Whose city was it, after all? What did Charles C. P. Holden have to do with all of this? Where did this animus for the well-behaved and genial council president come from? The answer came not from Chicago but off the telegraph wire. In this new era of amazing mass communications, a city such as Chicago could import its political concerns from other places just as easily as it could import livestock, wheat, and lumber. The eyes of Chicago, or at least the eyes of that group of Yankee elites who wanted to use the ashes of the Great Fire to make a show of taking control of the city, were fixed on events eleven hundred miles to the east.

Every day, all through 1871, Chicago's newspapers had brought reports from New York of the latest revelations surrounding William Tweed—"Boss Tweed," as he was far better known—and his iron grip on the political machinery of New York City. Beginning in January, several of Tweed's lieutenants had turned state's evidence on him, and what a pile of evidence it was, highlighted by the count of kickbacks paid to Tweed himself that totaled in the millions of dollars. As the news arrived in Chicago over the wires one sensational scandal at a time, it became clear that New York City was run by a vast and tightly organized "ring" that gorged itself on political patronage, graft, and special favors of all kinds, a system that thrived because it was able to distribute those favors so comprehensively throughout the city's immigrant communities. Fraud and embezzlement on such a scale—Tweed's enormous mansion on Fifth Avenue and Forty-Third Street by itself was a kind of open confession—were shocking.

What else was shocking was the speed with which Tweed had taken control of city hall by way of his working-class constituency. Three years earlier, in 1868, Tweed had been a junior member of the state senate, a not entirely aboveboard lawyer, an emerging real estate mogul, and grand sachem of Tammany Hall, but in no way could he have been described as the most powerful man in New York. Just one year later, in 1869, by way of innumerable illegal movements of money along with a shrewd and encyclopedic understanding of the structures of city government, he had taken complete control. The city's mayor, its comptroller, its parks commissioner, and the governor of New York, John T. Hoffman—all were Tweed men through and through. Charles C. P. Holden was no Boss Tweed, but not so long ago Tweed had not been "Boss Tweed" either. How quickly things could change, how quickly could a city's politics be corrupted. Not by the longest stretch of the imagination was Holden a genuine threat to Chicago's business barons, but that didn't stop the *Times* from referring to the "Chicago Tammanyites" and adding, "Boss Tweed and Boss Holden are correlative and nearly convertible terms."

This is what Medill and the Union-Fireproof men feared most: not a Democrat or the wrong kind of Republican in office, and not Charles C. P. Holden himself, but the use of city office by someone outside the downtown locus of wealth and influence to consolidate power through a complex web of individual connections spun at ward level, all to the decided disadvantage of the traditional plutocratic establishment in Chicago. The question of civil service reform, of making government *good,* in the mind of Joseph Medill, cut at every facet of the post–Civil War city: the role of the police, the distribution of relief, the rise of the working class, and the direction of the leadership in the rebuilding city. Medill might have cared about the city's credit rating as much as Ogden, Palmer, and Field did, but what the presumptive mayor most believed in was keeping the decision-making apparatus out of the hands of professional politicians. Holden was not a professional politician— the job of alderman paid very little and was very much part time—

but he had been an alderman for almost a decade, and in the minds of Union-Fireproofers that made him fair game.

Later in his life, after his time as mayor of Chicago, Medill would become a hard and bitter voice in opposition to the city's immigrant population, its poor Catholics most of all. The son of Calvinist Irish parents, he never shook his ancestral prejudices. But in this moment it was not populism or popery Medill feared, not even tribalism, but rather something that might be termed "localism." Chicago was a city of neighborhoods, focused around church membership, ward politics, fraternal orders, corner stores, co-ops, and, not least, saloons. And this was where, to the Union-Fireproofers, the danger lay. Their complaint against the growing influence of the working class was not that they were grasping and pushy when it came to winning office but rather that they sought election for local or even personal reasons and ignored a larger good—which, to Medill, made them ripe fodder for the growth and spread of a Tammany-style political machine that could and would destroy the city's reputation, crush its credit rating, and set leaders like Medill and his socioeconomic ilk aside, to Chicago's never-ending misfortune. The Union-Fireproofers *had* to win, he felt, and whoever might find himself in the way—in this case, Charles C. P. Holden—had to be pushed out of the way with a hard political and even harder rhetorical shove.

≥ 22 ≤

B Y 1871, Illinois had outlawed prizefighting, along with dog-
fighting, cockfighting, and "other such brutal sports." But like
the card games and the billiards houses, the brutal sports had
a vigorous life after dark and almost out in the open. Traveling
fighters fought bare-knuckle matches in tight, close rooms off alley-
ways, matches that sometimes ended in death or, short of that, a
lifetime of physical or mental debilitation. Habitual winners might
make the trip down the Mississippi to New Orleans and the myriad
championship matches there, where the fighting was rougher, better paying, and a little less illegal.

In the realm of legal, aboveground amusements, horse racing
had saturated the North after the Civil War, a southern entertainment transplanted and given a heightened emphasis on wagering.
But already by 1871 the preferred spectator sport of the Union
North was baseball. For fifteen years since the sport's introduction
in New York state, Chicagoans had fielded their own slate of local
teams, as many as twenty-four of them at a time competing for a
vaguely defined city crown, until, in 1870, the Chicago White Stockings were formed as a professional team to compete at a national
level.

Men who'd come back from the Civil War were in less of a
mood to watch an owner keep all the gate receipts, and in 1871 the
game of baseball and its players had split into two strata, one paid
and one amateur. The American Association of Professional Baseball Players comprised fifteen teams, including the White Stock-

ings, while the American Association of Base-Ball Players, which retained its amateur identity, had twenty-four. Only months before the Great Fire, the city treasurer and White Stockings owner, David Gage, had built the Union Base-Ball Grounds near the lakeshore, shoehorned into a rectangular block that brought the right-field fence so close to home plate that any ball hit over it was scored as a double and not as a home run. When the blaze had run through the ballpark, at about six in the morning on Monday, the grandstand and fencing went up like a tinderbox, but more important, the fire destroyed the team's precarious financial footing.

In the three weeks since the night of the fire, when a visiting team from Forest City had been forced to turn around within sight of the baseball ground, the Chicago nine had played just two games, both in Brooklyn, winning one and losing the other. And now they had one more to go. The White Stockings had gone 19-9 on the season, enough for second place. By the rules of the new league this gave them a berth in a final game against the first-place Philadelphia Athletics, the winner to be crowned champion.

All of which put the team in Williamsburg, Brooklyn, on October 30, 1871, playing in the first professional baseball league's first title game as representatives of the avid baseball-watching Chicago public, most of whom didn't have the slightest idea that the game was even going on. The smart money was on the opposition. As one writer put it, "The speculators eventually made their calculations that want of practice would tell severely on the Chicagoans, and, so far as their batting was concerned, it did." For a game of such supposed importance, the White Stockings presented a motley sight. "Not two of the nine were dressed alike, all their uniforms have been consumed at the fire. They presented a most extraordinary appearance from the parti-colored nature of the dress. All who could get white stockings did so, but they were not many." The six hundred people in the grandstand represented the team's lowest attendance of the season, and in that spirit the White Stockings scored the fewest runs they'd ever scored and lost 4–1.

News of the team's gallant effort against the Philadelphia side didn't reach Chicago for four days, because baseball, such an important part of the city's fabric that year that crowds of ten thousand had been common at the Union Grounds, had become an afterthought. Meanwhile, their season over, the Stockings played on. The championship decided, they stayed in Brooklyn to play the New York Mutuals in an exhibition game, losing 11–3 in front of a crowd larger than the one that had witnessed the championship. The players were distracted and playing out the string, already tired of having no home, no club.

Back at home, other popular amusements found their feet again. The unheralded Globe Theatre won the race to become the first South Side theater to reopen, when its owner, John H. Wood, snapped up an old warehouse on the West Side and refitted it with a crude stage so that he could begin reemploying actors and charging admission as soon as possible. The night before the election, November 6, 1871, as the opposing tickets held their final rallies and the newspapers typeset their final editorials, the Globe premiered a new play called *Divorce*. The plot was breezy and non-topical, centering on two rich and marriageable sisters, one of whom marries a "wealthy old widower" while the other marries the much less well-to-do "lover of her youth." Both marriages are threatened in unexpected ways, a great many twists and turns ensue, and the sanctity of both marriages is reaffirmed in the end. A preferential nod is given to the young woman who weds for the money, because, after all, this was Chicago.

Down on State and Twentieth, meanwhile, the biggest news of the season—bigger than the reopening of the Globe, far bigger than the news that the White Stockings had come up short, and bigger, in many ways, than the imminent election—was that Field, Leiter & Company was back in business. "Among the prodigies of pluck which many of our businessmen have achieved," wrote the *Tribune,* "it would seem at first invidious to select any one in particular, but the magnitude of the business, and the almost world-wide reputation of the great dry goods house of Field & Co. deserve a notice even among the number around us."

Just four weeks after the fire, this jump on his competitors was a coup of priceless value for Marshall Field. He'd been able to reopen so quickly because he and Levi Leiter had millions in available credit all over the country, because they'd saved a considerable load of merchandise on the night of the fire, and because they'd implemented an ingenious system of storage that held post-fire shipments of goods from New York in an Indianapolis storage facility, able to be moved in overnight once the new building was ready. And now the new building was ready: a car repository belonging to South Side Railway Company, leased at a rate so far below Potter Palmer's $50,000-a-year State Street rent as to allay all fears about the store's balance sheet.

The thousands of visitors on this new kind of opening day experienced a convincing simulacrum of the State Street store, and they spent. The sky was dark and threatening, but still the carriages arrived from all over. It was time to thumb one's nose at the Great Fire, and Field & Leiter's customers obliged with glee. Ladies wore their best dresses and brought their umbrellas, their pocketbooks, and even, for a change, their husbands. They marveled at the grace and sophistication with which Field and Leiter had outfitted their temporary omnibus warehouse.

"Good thick brick walls" and a "stout, 16-inch wall running down the center" of the hall reassured customers that the new place wouldn't easily fall prey to another calamity. The building ran 130 feet on State and 150 feet on Twentieth, while the interior wall served as a convenient divider between the retail store on the north side and the wholesale department on the south. Thus was made more visible than ever the dual nature of Field, Leiter & Company: on one side, the wholesale and jobbing business—providing merchandise to individual retailers in Chicago and all over the West—which provided the firm with the majority of its profits, and on the other side, the retail space that made the store the most beloved and most recognizable in the city.

Two entrances accommodated visitors, one for carriages on the north side, on Twentieth, and another for foot traffic around the corner on State. The ceilings and walls had been painted white, and a large display window on Twentieth had been filled with mannequins and furniture. On the main floor, near the carriage entrance, where the "finer ladies" were likely to enter, were sold the expensive silks and laces: the $59 handkerchiefs, the $200 scarves. Opposite the State Street door sat the glove counter, specializing in calfskin and kid glove models; in a city whose dirt and mud were now covered with soot and ashes, and which was about to enter the winter season, gloves like these were no longer only a sign of wealth and leisure but also a promise that the city would soon return in a more genteel and opulent guise.

In the back of the store an interior window looked onto the examiner's department, where "the clerks examine the articles, measure every yard of goods, make everything tally with the check, wrap them up, and dispatch them through the rear door." To allow customers a full view of the firm's famous delivery service in operation, the foundation of its policy of "sales on inspection," was a new idea, a small burst of retail genius in the wake of the fire. As always, spectators mingled with shoppers. Some wanted to buy, some wanted to buy extravagantly, some just wanted to watch, and Marshall Field was fine with all of it.

The message to the city was clear and plain, and Field & Leiter operated as the perfect speaking horn. Sales were brisk. Wrote the *Times*, "The store was thronged with ladies from early in the morning till the hour of closing, rejoiced to avail themselves again of their favorite 'shopping' resort." The world of retail would thrive. The carriage house on the far South Side was one prong of Field's three-pronged plan, which conspired to work the fire, and his sterling credit, to his competitive advantage. While contractors had swarmed to the renovation of the new store, thrilled to have the work, Field had also been negotiating the quick and very visible purchase of a large lot at Madison and Marshall, in the middle of the burned South Side near the branching of the river, as a promise to the city and to all of the city's commercial hinterlands that the company's full-scale wholesale department would soon be up and running.

All that activity was public information. But Field had something else up his sleeve. As the third part of his plan, he'd been meeting with Potter Palmer since the day of the older man's arrival from New York after the Great Fire, guessing that Palmer would look not to cash out on his real estate holdings but rather to rebuild and expand on an enormous scale, so as to use the disaster to extend his supremacy as the city's wealthiest and most important retail landlord. Repeating what he'd already done would not be enough for Palmer. Another announcement was made on the same day of Field's reopening: "It will be a gratifying item of intelligence to the entire community to learn that Potter Palmer has determined to rebuild the old Field & Leiter store at once, on its old site." The contracts, Field revealed, had been signed one day earlier, and workmen were already clearing the rubble and stacking bricks and lumber. Their new store would be a showpiece, a demonstration to the world. But as opulent and expensive as their plans were, as important as his footprint on State Street was to him, Potter Palmer was, as always, aiming much higher.

❧ 23 ❧

THE NIGHT BEFORE the election settled in cold and rainy, with
no trace of the weather that had lasted all summer and created
such ideal conditions for a catastrophe. In the town's largest
Baptist church, Robert Collyer, the best-known clergyman in Chicago, delivered a talk on the theme of "Our Loss and Our Gain."
Collyer, like so many in the West, had come to Chicago for a fresh
start, in his case from Pennsylvania after his conviction for heresy
in refuting the Methodist Church's pro-slavery stance. That move,
away from the faith of his youth and into the Unitarian church,
was the seedbed of everything he did now. He was known for his
courage in advocating unpopular positions, for being unafraid of
wading into public life and even politics. He had discovered himself in Chicago, where he had built a life as an orator of surpassing
charisma and intensity.

Now, on the eve of the vote, he let fly. He talked about the forces
of good and evil, about the feeling in some Christian hearts that the
Great Fire had rendered a judgment on Chicago for its embrace of
the forces of sin. Collyer was having none of it. "I do not believe
that God wanted to burn up the poorest shanty within the city limits," he said. He lamented not the loss of buildings and raw materials, he said, but "the destruction of home treasures," and told a joke
about the possibility of being reunited with personal heirlooms and
keepsakes in heaven. He talked of the danger of measuring losses
in monetary terms, and then he turned to political affairs, where
the specter of Boss Tweed now stood in for the specter of the devil.

The language bore a heavy theological tint, but Collyer's basic message might as well have been printed on a flyer for the Union-Fireproof ticket:

> Crush out, with the splendid enginery of the ballot-box, every-thing that offends or maketh a lie, and let us see if we cannot ward off the danger and disgrace that has fallen on New York. Then shall our fair city rise out of her ashes, and sit beside this lake for ten thousand years to come, beautiful for situation, joy of the whole earth.

On the morning of Election Day the weather turned sunny and calm, while the continuing offensive in the *Tribune* against Charles C. P. Holden and his allies was anything but. The paper went through a list of aldermanic candidates ward by ward and issued dire warnings. Would not the voters of the Third Ward, it asked, "endeavor to-day to relieve themselves of the disgrace they have sustained for two years in their Aldermanic representation"? About the Eleventh Ward and its candidate, "the notorious James Walsh," it wrote, "Has the ward become nothing more than one of Walsh's saloons, to be governed and controlled by him and his barkeepers?" The election of the Union-Fireproof candidate in the Ninth Ward, meanwhile, "would, in a peculiar manner, be a return to the original theory that honesty and competency are requisites for a faithful discharge of official duty." Reverend Collyer offered more support for Medill in a morning editorial, writing, "I think he has no equal in the Northwest, either for insight or ability about all questions touching good government, and he has certainly no superior in intrinsic worth."

For all of the urgent alarms sounded by Collyer, the *Tribune*, and Medill's other mouthpieces, however, turnout was light. People were still busy reconstructing their lives, and the assumption that Medill would win was nearly universal. By the end of the day, a little more than twenty-two thousand male citizens eighteen and older, those who owned property and those who didn't, cast votes, down from thirty-one thousand two years before. In total, about one of every ten adults in the city had a say in the selection of the post-fire city government. The Board of Trade suspended its meeting for the day so that its members could vote, as did many other downtown organizations and employers, but as much as the members of the Union-Fireproof ticket proclaimed otherwise, the mind of much of the city was on something other than politics.

That night, once again, the Union-Fireproof leadership congregated at the city's lone high school, where the earliest returns told the tale in full. As expected, Medill had no chance of losing. After seven o'clock, when the polls closed, only two questions remained to generate any suspense: Would the Union-Fireproof ticket elect enough of its candidates for alderman to create a majority on the city council, and would Medill's margin in the mayoral vote be the widest in the city's history? The answer to the first question was no—seven Democratic or "sorehead Republican" candidates were chosen, out of twenty open seats. In combination with eleven anti-Union-Fireproofers among the twenty councilmen not up for election, plus an additional three or four aldermen who didn't identify with either side, this result left the Union-Fireproof ticket at least two short of a functional majority. But in the contest for mayor, Medill mopped the floor with Holden, receiving more than 70 percent of the vote, a level of support that had been achieved just once before in the city's previous thirty-one elections, eclipsing even William Butler Ogden's landslide 489–217 victory in the city's first year, 1837. Chicago had in essence split its ticket, voting decisively for the bipartisan emergency coalition's candidate for mayor while denying that same coalition control of the city council.

No gathering with dour and half-deaf Joseph Medill at its center could be considered lighthearted, but the mood at the high school was upbeat. The well-to-do of Chicago liked to drink liquor instead of beer, and plenty of liquor flowed, even though the victorious candidate was a teetotaler and sometimes a temperance advocate. When Medill addressed the crowd, toward midnight, his speech was, true to form, devoid of triumphalism or sloganeering. He'd spent more than a decade lecturing the residents of Chicago on the best way for government to run—through "wisdom" and "intelligence" and "prudence" and "restraint"—and in this moment he sought to project the first three qualities, while the fourth he threw out the window.

He dispensed with any notion that he would be content to serve, as so many mayors had before him, as a figurehead. To this end, he started by outlining his plan to acquire more power than Chicago's previous mayors had ever held. Describing his new office as "one whose moral influence is disproportionate to its municipal power" and one that had been "reduced to an ornamental appendage to the city government," he announced that one of his first actions as mayor-elect, even before taking office, would be to insist that the Illinois state legislature push through a dramatic and unprecedented expansion of mayoral powers in order to facilitate the quick and coordinated rebuilding of the city.

In the "Mayor's Bill" Medill would propose, he would ask the state for the power to nominate all nonelected city officials, to unilaterally remove all of the same, to preside over the council and break tie votes, to determine the makeup of the council's standing committees and to serve as an ex officio member of all, to wield a line-item budget veto, and to be given special police powers that under certain conditions could supersede the authority of the police commissioners and the department's superintendent. Only with this set of powers, Medill said, under his firm and unfettered hand, could the city be rebuilt in proper and prosperous fashion without breaking the municipal bank. Taxes would be reduced, city payroll would be cut, tariffs would be lowered or eliminated, and ineffective commissioners would be removed from office if they didn't produce measurable results, all to create confidence and to speed along reconstruction.

"The affairs of this city must hereafter be conducted as a prudent and wise man manages his own affairs, and that must be our model," Medill said, articulating his core political belief—that the best government should look to, and look *like*, what he considered the best people—to cheers and applause. He painted the city's dispersed form of government as a many-headed monster, each head trying to gobble up its maximum possible portion from the public trough. He then played his ace, the same card General Sheridan had played one month earlier: should the lawmakers of Illinois not expand his authority according to his list of demands, he said, "I would feel at liberty to resign the office and slip down and out." And no one in the room doubted his word.

Medill had for many years been writing editorials about reform and good government, and he had the necessary rhetoric at his fingertips. He spoke about fiscal responsibility, and good credit, and disinterested public service, painting a picture of a stronger, better, more sensible Chicago. But he also punctuated his address to the Union-Fireproof gathering with a gloomy personal forecast of his time in office. "As its requirements during the next two years will tax to the utmost whatever executive ability, industry, and patience which I may possess," he said at one point, "I shall need all your forbearance, sympathy, and support to carry me through the ordeal before me." By the standards of victory-party oratory in any age, this was bleak stuff—especially for a man who'd won such an impressive majority. But Medill was no fool when it came to under-standing the massive task ahead of him and of the city.

Elected office was not Medill's realm and never would be. His personality—straightforward, uncompromising, low on ebul-lience—was made for running a tight ship at a large newspaper, where he and a few other men answered to no one but themselves. But he was self-aware enough to understand that the same traits could cause him problems in public life. He could now no longer lob rhetorical shells at the messiness of politics from the safe dis-tance of his editorial seat. A crusader for reform all his life, he knew that to clean up a mess, one had to come into close contact with the mess. When he predicted that he would experience his time in office as an "ordeal," he would be right.

Still, Medill's sober speech didn't last for more than ten minutes, which represented a victory for all involved. The man who addressed the crowd next, Anton Hesing, was a stocky, heavy-browed Ger-man with a pleasant, round face and closely groomed beard who looked nothing like the gaunt, wild-haired mayor-elect. But in other ways, Hesing was a doppelgänger of Medill with a much more animated foreign accent. Both men were former Ohio Whigs turned early Republicans. Owner and publisher of the German-language *Staats-Zeitung*, Hesing was in a position to act as arbiter for a very broad and important immigrant constituency, just as Medill was the Republican business class's most vocal mouthpiece.

Of the approximately twenty-two thousand men who had voted, more than sixteen thousand of them chose Medill. The city, or at least that small percentage that had been able and willing to participate in the election, had in essence chosen private leadership over public politics. This was something of a tradition in a city that regularly elected businessmen, lawyers, executives, and newspaper-men to positions of leadership. Medill versus Holden had been a mismatch from the start, but still the *Tribune* crowed, "To have found a Holden man in that crowd would have been a tougher job than to have found the woman who milked the cow that kicked over the lamp that set fire to the barn that burned up Chicago."

The city seemed for the moment unified, politically. But in many other ways it was still the place it had become during the Civil War, which was several political entities side by side and lay-ered one atop the other: a Protestant business aristocracy supported by an army of assistants and clerks; a shop-keeping middle class dominated by Germans and Scandinavians; a populous class of laborers that was more Irish than anything else; and the publishers, writers, and editorialists for Chicago's newspapers, who were small in number but enormous in influence. These groups agreed that for the moment unity and single-mindedness were the tools most needed for the rebuild to come, and the first result of that unity was Medill's election.

But when Medill said in his speech that "every candidate, entrusted this day with office, must perform his part to carry into effect the public wish so unmistakably expressed at the polls," he was kidding himself. The unmistakable "public wish" for unity, law and order, a levelheaded approach to rebuilding, and a firm hand on the financial tiller had been an accident of timing and the larg-est emergency anyone could imagine. It also depended on a nar-row definition of who constituted the "public." Immediately after the fire, the energy for dissension and division was tempered, put off until the city could rebuild and leave the residents free to start shouting at one another again. Medill would never have run for mayor but for the Great Fire, and he was depending on the unexpected novelty of his election to hold off the usual sniping, backbiting, mistrust, and outright indifference that the city's politics usually generated. But the mayor-elect's assumption that the "public wish" was "unmistakable" and would therefore coalesce into a set of definite policies, that he would always read the nature of that wish correctly, and that that wish would remain unified and unchanged for the two years of his term was absurd.

In truth, the "public wish" at this moment had little to do with electoral politics. More than 300,000 residents hadn't voted. Most of Chicago was still hurting from the fire and still trying to determine what kind of future lay ahead. Visitors to the city flooded in, and many found Chicago subdued, serious, even stunned. On November 15, one week after Medill's election, subscribers to the city's newspapers read excerpts from an article titled "Chicago in Distress," published in the November 9, 1871, issue of *The Nation* and written by the landscape architect Frederick Law Olmsted, that provided a unique and clear-eyed view of the city's mood. Olmsted had made his name as a journalist as a young man, and still dabbled in the trade, but his great fame had come from his work with Calvert Vaux to design and build New York's Central Park, a massive project well into the latter stages of its construction. Olmsted had a close connection to Chicago through his long friendship with William Butler Ogden and his work on the planned community of Riverside, a model suburb placed in a picturesque pin oak forest four miles southwest of downtown at the nexus of the river canal and the existing Chicago, Burlington, and Quincy rail line.

No planner or designer in America was in greater demand. Along with major projects under way in Buffalo, Prospect Park in Brooklyn, Niagara Falls, and Madison, Wisconsin, Riverside was in the early stages of development. In Chicago, Olmsted had in mind a demonstration to the world of what suburban living could be. He'd been slated to visit the city later in October to work on his project, and when news of the fire clicked through the telegraph to his hometown, near Boston, he'd headed for the train station and brought along his pen.

Olmsted was a very different kind of writer and editorialist than Chicago was used to. His literary mentality belonged to the East, not the Midwest. His aesthetic frame of reference, cultivated from his travels but also from his chosen profession of landscape architecture, was a novelty in a world dominated by businessmen and laborers. Olmsted lived to bring beautiful order to chaos and wildness, much like the builders of Chicago, but his kind of order was far less rigid and far more accommodating of nature, its curves and asymmetries, its sense of spirit and play. His work involved sculpting rather than leveling. In this sense, the Great Chicago Fire itself, thought of as a living thing, was the very opposite of Olmsted, which might account for the sense of melancholy clearheadedness pervading his article, so different from the *Tribune*'s cheery calls to rebuild, rebuild, rebuild:

> For a time men were unreasonably cheerful and hopeful; now, this stage appears to have passed. In its place there is sternness; but so narrow is the division between this and another mood, that in the midst of a sentence a change of quality in the voice occurs, and you see that eyes have moistened. I had partly expected to find a feverish, reckless spirit, and among the less disciplined classes an unusual current setting towards turbulence, lawlessness, and artificial jollity, such as held in San Francisco for a long time after the great fire there—such as often seizes seamen after a wreck. On the contrary, Chicago is the soberest and the most clear-headed city I ever saw.

Whatever the "less disciplined classes" might think of their characterization, the people of Chicago, as a whole, would have recognized themselves in Olmsted's writing. In this moment in the city's history, they were indeed a sober lot, no matter how much they enjoyed their alehouses and liquor cabinets.

Joseph Medill was hoping to take advantage of this spirit of determination to make long-lasting change. Many of the town's residents hoped along with him, especially those downtown merchants and factory owners who felt that one of theirs was now in charge. Medill wanted a new city, run in a new way. He wanted city government to be moral, and thrifty, and coolheaded—not the ward-based, special-favors arrangement of growing immigrant coalitions he felt he saw it becoming. But whether what Medill and the Union-Fireproofers wanted to do and what Chicago was determined to do coincided, no one could yet know. If the desires of the greater part of its citizenry matched those of its new mayor, his term might be a successful one. If not, a great deal of trouble might be brewing.

PART V

Inquest

≥ 24 ≤

T HE FIRST SIX WEEKS after the fire were spent clearing away the rubble. In the residential districts on the North and West Sides, wooden shacks and barracks were rising, hundreds every day, but downtown the effect was of an erasure. Hired crews of laborers worked day and night to break up stone, brick, and iron and cart it away, along with mounds of broken glass, to the long, deep, and stagnant inlet that filled the space between Michigan Avenue and the Illinois Central tracks along the eastern edge of the South Side. By mid-November, many of the blocks downtown were free from debris and had been leveled and tamped down to a tabletop flatness. A number of new buildings were under construction already, but many other sites contained tall, neat piles of bricks or building stones, some under tarps, that waited on the spring construction season.

At the same time, the city had other matters to resolve, other debris to clear away besides the rubble of downtown. On November 23, forty-four days after the Great Fire, Kate Leary sat in a cushioned chair inside Chicago's second precinct police headquarters, surrounded by five men. On her lap she held her youngest child, two-year-old James, who "smiled good-naturedly and kicked his bare legs around in great glee." The men's names were Brown, Sheridan, Gund, Chadwick, and Williams. Outside, the wind was up and biting. Inside the "captain's room," as they called the office, it was cold, cramped, and crowded. In addition to the tableau of

236 · SCOTT W. BERG

witness, child, and interrogators, a stenographer sat nearby, along
with reporters for at least two of the city's dailies.

Though Kate Leary had lived most of her forty-four years in
obscurity, she was now known by name—if by a name she seldom
used, Catherine O'Leary—to every resident of Chicago and to
much of the rest of the world. Four of the men standing over her
were police and fire commissioners, while the other was the fire
marshal, Robert Williams. In most ways, Williams's story could
not have been more different from that of the woman in front of
him, but in other ways, in this moment, it was similar. He was a
civil servant, with real, if limited, powers, but, if the newspapers
were to be believed, an imbecile, a drunkard, a fool. She was many
things—wife, mother, immigrant, homeowner, entrepreneur—but
in the eyes of Chicago's remorseless press she was a demon, a vil-
lainess, a harridan, an "old hag."

Like Leary, Williams and the rest of the men of the fire department had spent the six weeks since the Great Fire ended buffeted
by the winds of public suspicion, mockery, and contempt. Beginning on the day after the conflagration died out in the rain, Chicagoans demanded an explanation of what had happened, and the
department still hadn't provided one. The drumbeat had sounded
loudly: the *Tribune* accused the commissioners of "having failed in
their duty to investigate to the public, whose servants they are, the
origin and progress of The Great Fire, and the conduct of the Fire
Department on the fatal night of October 9," while the *Evening
Journal* was even more blunt:

> If, as is generally believed, the flames succeeded in getting the
> mastery of the Fire Department because of the drunkenness or
> inefficiency of its officers and employees, the fact ought to be
> established, or, if not a fact, disproved, by a thorough and search-
> ing investigation into all the circumstances of the beginning and
> early stages of the conflagration.

Marshal Williams, as the man in charge of the force during the
Great Fire, had become a choice target. The *Evening Journal* im-

plored that "the investigation be thorough and complete, especially into the management, condition and conduct of the Fire Department, and the alleged incapacity of the Chief of the Department as exhibited on that terrible Sunday night." An opinion in the *Times* castigated the commissioners' foot-dragging as cowardice, implying that the board was stalling the inquiry to protect itself "for employing a man so totally unfit to fill the very responsible position of chief of our fire department."

Two days after the election, on November 9, with reform and accountability the watchwords of the new mayor, the commissioners had moved to conduct an inquiry into the cause of the fire. After promising to start the next day, they hadn't, and then day after day passed with no interviews, no depositions, no investigations of any kind, until on November 22 they began to collect their evidence, in a series of interviews that was expected to take two weeks.

The end of November was late to begin the investigation of a fire that had caught on October 8, and indeed there was every reason for the reading public to believe that the commissioners had been goaded into the inquiry. On the first day, the investigators had spoken with the fire department's telegraph operator, William Brown, and the watchman, Mathias Schaefer. On this day they'd already questioned two firemen, both engine captains, before ushering Kate Leary into her seat. Six more witnesses would follow before they adjourned that night, which made each interview a scribbled-down sprint instead of a careful retelling of events. Leary's turn took only thirty minutes, even if her testimony was the testimony the citizens of Chicago most wanted to read.

Just after two o'clock in the afternoon, Commissioner Chadwick began the session by asking, "What do you know about this fire?"

What did Kate Leary know about this fire? She would have needed days, not minutes, to properly answer the question. She knew everything and she knew nothing. It had begun in her barn but had left her house unscathed. It seemed that a lifetime had passed since she'd been roused out of bed by her husband, shouting at her that the barn was on fire. Within hours, every house, barn, shed, fence, and sidewalk to the rear of her house was gone, replaced in what seemed like a blink by a never-ending army of sightseers and journalists with notepads, asking anyone—but most of all the young people dashing around the streets—how did it start? Someone said it started in the Learys' barn. Someone said, which barn is that, but of course the barn was gone. Someone else said that the Leary woman kept her cows and her horse there, that she milked the cows there. Finally someone said that she'd been milking her cow that night. And so it had gone.

At the fire's beginning, she'd crowded her children, all five of them, across DeKoven, to the southern side of the street, where Mrs. Sullivan lived, knowing for certain that she and her family were safe but that her living was gone. She knew that within a day the sightseers had begun to come, to gawk, and then, soon enough, to crawl all over her home, ascending to her roof via ladders, striking jocular poses on the porch for photographs. The Learys knew that they would soon sell the place or rent it out, but in any case they would never return as residents.

She knew that she had been as scared as she could be. She knew that Sunday night had been warm for mid-October. It had been the kind of night when things moved more slowly, when most of the neighborhood loitered outdoors. She knew that the McLaughlins, who had rented the larger, front house for two years, were entertaining a greenhorn fresh off the boat. The husband worked in a foundry, played the fiddle. Now the McLaughlins were gone as well.

A few days after the fire, as fabricated descriptions of Leary's appearance, indolence, slovenly habits, and even supposed glee over the fate of the city began to fill the papers, her friend Michael McDermott, city surveyor and a notary public, had arrived at her new lodgings farther to the southwest, near the stockyards, to take a statement. How McDermott knew the Learys is unclear, but he might have been one of Kate's customers. He was disgusted by the coverage in the *Times* of the fire's first moments and wanted to set the record straight. The Learys, he wrote, "have been known to me personally for several years as of irreproachable character. Mrs. O'Leary is neither haggard nor dirty."

"An honester woman I would never ask to live with," Mrs.

McLaughlin would say later, in her own testimony, adding, "She is neither filthy nor haggard." Leary might never have read either McDermott's or McLaughlin's assessment in print, but she would have been happy that someone had said such things. In truth, she was honest, neat, hardworking, a good mother. They could say about the Irish what they wished, and they did, but her own life had now been given to the public as a fat string of lies.

What had happened to her over the past six weeks had never happened to anyone in America, because such a tarring had been impossible before the age of the coast-to-coast telegraph network. She had become a bug under a national magnifying glass, her name familiar to every family that took a big-city newspaper in America and in much of the rest of the world. Chicago resented the Learys, not least because the Learys' house still stood while so many didn't, even as the fact that their entire livelihood had burned up with their barn and wagon remained unremarked. Had the Learys' house not survived, in fact, it's likely that they would not have been so cavalierly and callously blamed for the fire. All over the city, they were triply resented: as culprits, as survivors, and as the possessors of too much apparent luck.

And even amid the destruction of their working capital, they *were* lucky. They were alive. The Learys had no insurance, but they still had the two houses and the lot. Even if one takes at face value Kate's statement that the family had no savings, that still left rental income or a potential sale in the range of hundreds of dollars. All around them, neighbors were rebuilding. Much of the wood in the city had burned, but much hadn't, and those eligible for relief were putting up small sheds while they made plans to rebuild with the wages of their resumed employments.

All the while, Kate Leary became the target of a media onslaught that knew no boundaries, no shame, and no allegiance to the truth. Only the *Evening Journal* had managed to publish on the Monday of the fire, and only a one-page extra. Fifth or sixth place among the city's papers, for a few evening hours the *Evening Journal* had the entire city's attention. And in the fourth paragraph of that one-page edition, below the headline THE GREAT CALAMITY OF THE AGE, the onslaught had begun. "The fire broke out on the corner of De-Koven and Twelfth streets," read Chicago's news-hungry public, never mind that such a street corner didn't exist, "at about 9 o'clock on Sunday evening, being caused by a cow kicking over a lamp in a stable in which a woman was milking."

The most credible explanation for this assertion is that the *Evening Journal's* reporter heard the story from the neighborhood's excited children, even as the fire still raged in the blocks north of DeKoven. The next paper to publish, on Tuesday morning, was Ed Chamberlin's *Evening Post,* which added more confusion and rumor to the mix, placing the Learys' barn on "Farquahr" Street, which was properly spelled "Forquer" and was located two blocks to the north of the blaze's actual point of origin. Then the *Post* tried to have it several different ways all at once: "How these flames originated, we do not know, though rumor has it that they were the result of incendiaryism and also that they sprang from a carelessly used pipe or cigar."

By Wednesday, Joseph Medill's *Tribune* had joined the parade. Leary remained unnamed, and no blame at all was assigned. The only detail provided was that "at 9:30 a small cow barn attached to a house on the corner of DeKoven and Jefferson streets, one block north of Twelfth street, emitted a bright light, followed by a blaze, and in a moment the building was hopelessly on fire." The barn was not in fact attached to any house, and most of the block had been aflame by 9:30, but otherwise the report hewed to what was known, which made the *Tribune's* first stab at the origin of the fire a model of restraint in comparison to everything that was to follow.

To that point, two days after the fire, the damage to the Learys had been mild: minor factual errors and innocuous rumors and not much else. That is, until *The Chicago Times* published its first post-fire edition on October 18, a week after the *Tribune's*. The *Times,* after ten years under Wilbur Storey's direction, was a different kind of newspaper from any other in America. Storey believed that people read a newspaper to be told stories with the power and immediacy of fiction, and his reporters were instructed never, ever to let the absence of facts get in their way. His paper was a purely populist publication, most often Democratic, but a friend or enemy as necessary to immigrants, political parties, and members of every social stratum. Storey believed that what people wanted most after the Great Fire was not to know the facts but to have someone to blame, because a good villain made for a better story. And give them someone to blame he had:

> The contemptible cow barn, on De Koven street, whose owner is nameless, and whose existence was yesterday as utterly unknown as the individuality of any one of the vermin which haunt our streets, is, to day, an initial point as famous as the Vesuvius whose hot rage so inundated and buried two great cities that nearly eighteen centuries have been required to discover their sepulchre.

The *Times* introduced Kate Leary to its readers as "AN OLD IRISH WOMAN" living on relief whose "very appearance indicated great poverty. She was apparently about 70 years of age, and was bent almost double with the weight of many years of toil, and trouble, and privation. Her dress corresponded with her demands, being ragged and dirty in the extreme."

It's very likely that no *Times* reporter had spoken to Leary, or had ever seen her, for that matter. If one had, he'd ignored everything he'd heard and seen. The paper's story went on to invent out of whole cloth a despicable motive fit to the current moment. The unnamed Irishwoman, it claimed, had for some time pretended poverty and dressed in rags so as to collect her ration of county relief funds. Exposed in her deception, the *Times* reported, "the old hag swore she would be revenged on a city that would deny her her daily ration of bread and bacon."

For good measure, Storey's paper added a made-up "confession." There had been no accident. No cow had kicked any lamp. The old Irish hag set the blaze herself, said the *Times,* and was happy to have done so. The reporter's disgust at this act of a woman's selfish vengeance, her wanton disgust that the city had failed to support her in her indolence, mimicked the resentment of visitors to DeKoven who found that the house "on the corner, owned by the old hag who had caused all the desolation, was untouched."

Still, all through this barrage of character assassination, neither the *Times* nor any other source had yet named Kate Leary. Two days later and two days too late, in a tragic accident of bad timing and good intentions gone astray, Michael McDermott's affidavit, collected five days earlier, was printed in the *Tribune*, finishing off Kate's former life once and for all. The affidavit, which sought to clear her name, instead attached that name—as "O'Leary"—to the Great Fire for all time. By publishing McDermott's report when it did, the comparatively conscientious *Tribune* had for all intents conspired with the shaggy, sensationalistic *Times* to render the city's impression of Kate Leary complete and final.

By the day of her interview at the second precinct, then, five weeks later, Kate Leary was already infamous. The Grosvenor murder and the mayoral election had deflected some of the attention, but the public clamor for hearings into the cause of the fire had brought her right back into the spotlight. By now she knew that what was entered into the record wouldn't matter. She wanted nothing to do with reporters, or police, or firemen, all of whom were in this room, circling her and her young son.

Very well, then. What she didn't know about this fire, what she had not the foggiest notion of, was the very thing everyone wanted to hear: how it started. The *Times* might have said she'd been milking her cow at nine thirty at night, but that was balderdash. No one milked a cow at nine thirty at night. Kate milked hers, all five of them, at five in the morning and then again at four thirty in the afternoon, every day. Her neighbors could and did mark time by it. That's what she'd done on the day of the Great Fire. A bit later, at seven, she'd fed the horse and put it in the barn for the night. Exhausted, she'd gotten into bed soon after dark, her foot sore. She needed to be up again the next morning at four thirty. It was the rhythm of her life. She and her husband owned a house. They rented to the McLaughlins. They each contributed to their family's living.

What did she know about this fire? Whatever thoughts she had or emotions she felt, this is what she said in answer to Chadwick's question:

> I was in bed myself, and my husband and five children, when this fire commenced. I was the owner of them five cows that was burnt and the horse, wagon, and harness. I had two tons of coal and two tons of hay. I had everything that I wanted in for the winter. I could not save five cents worth of anything out of the barn, only that Mr. Sullivan got out a little calf. The calf was worth eleven dollars on Saturday morning. Saturday morning I refused eleven dollars for the calf, and it was sold afterwards for eight dollars. I didn't save one five cents out of the fire.

That was that. That was her answer. But the commissioners persisted. They asked her about Daniel Sullivan, from across the street. Catherine Sullivan's boy, the one called Peg Leg for his wooden prosthesis, and that other young man, Dennis Ryan? Regan? Rogan? Daniel and Dennis had brought the fire to the Learys' attention, their shouts sharp and frightened in the yard, sometime just after 9:00 p.m. Then the scuffle of feet. Then Patrick, her husband, running back into the bedroom, shouting.

Chadwick had more questions. Did someone from the McLaughlins' party go in back, to the barn, to get milk for oysters? This was silly. How would Kate know? She'd been in bed. Things took a strange turn then, when Chadwick asked, "Had there been any rain of any account before that?" "That" meant the fire. She had trouble answering this one. The question made no sense. As every single last person in Chicago knew, there had not been a day of appreciable rain since just after Independence Day—by far the hottest, driest summer in the city's forty years of existence, certainly of her entire life in Ireland and America. Her answer—"Not for a very long time before that, sir"—communicated a fact well known to *everyone*.

That was also the end of the session's attempt to find out how the fire had started. When it seemed there were no more questions to ask, no more point to asking questions of her at all—hadn't she given her meager set of answers?—Thomas Brown and Robert Williams got in on the questioning. They'd sat there silent up to now as Chadwick had spoken. Now they asked, how fast did the fire engines get there? Leary was far too powerless, far too out of her element, far too caught up in events—she'd been lying in bed!—to be curt or short with them, or even amused, but what must she have thought?

How fast did the fire engines get there? Where was the closest fire hydrant? She gave what answers she could, reiterated the fact that she was in bed, and the session petered out. To close out the interview, one of the men posed the question everyone seemed to ask of anyone who lost anything in any fire in the city: "Had you any insurance upon your barn and stock?"

Why the men in charge of the fire department asked this, Kate didn't know. It did not seem like a sympathetic question. Rather, it served to put her in her place one more time. Her answer represented the last words she would ever put into the public record. She knew that she was being accused of something, yet again. In a more rational world, the fire department's efforts would be directed at the insured and the uninsured alike. But the fire department liked to help those who were already able to help themselves. It was an American creed, and it was strong in Chicago.

She might have surprised her interrogators now, because she had an answer ready. She roused a little and put an edge into her voice. "Never had five cents insurance," she said. "I had six cows there. A good horse there. I had a wagon and harness and everything I was worth. I couldn't save that much out of it"—and here Kate snapped her fingers, as eloquent an expression of her distress and her resistance as any words she might add—"and upon my word I *worked hard for them*."

After this interview, Kate Leary stepped out of the police station to find herself standing in the West Division four blocks away from the Chicago River. Six weeks earlier, the view to the east would have been dominated by the crowded verticality of the business district, the cupola of the courthouse above all of it, and a glimpse of Lake Michigan beyond. But no longer. Now the lake lay in full view, whipped up by the day's strong wind. In much of the rest of the country, the watchword was "reconstruction." But only here, in Chicago, was the word so literally apt. Four blocks away, the north branch of the Chicago River. Eleven blocks to the south, the house on DeKoven Street, one she had already left forever. Whatever direction Kate turned as she left the police station, she walked out of the story of the Great Chicago Fire forever. Never again did she grant a newspaper interview. Never again did she testify about her role, or lack of one, in starting the fire. Never again did she put herself forward into the public eye.

But in one important way, Kate Leary was still to make a lasting contribution to the public life and inimitable style of the city. Two years old on the day of the fire, her son James Patrick O'Leary—the boy who sat on Kate's lap during the commissioners' interrogation—went on to live a life that was as stereotypically and perhaps prototypically Chicagoan as could be. While still in his teens, Jim ran tickets and bets for bookies, before he set out to learn the ropes of the gambling business at his own book at an offtrack site near Indianapolis. By the time he was twenty-four, he was back in Chicago, owner of a saloon on Halsted Street, half a mile from DeKoven, that featured a restaurant, a bowling alley, a billiards parlor, and a Turkish bath for good measure.

His customers and fellow saloon owners started to call him Big Jim, in honor of his personality and his physical heft. And indeed, the latter part of his life was straight out of a silent film, fitted between the Chicago of the Great Fire and the Chicago of Al Capone. He ran an amusement park, a floating gambling emporium, several drugstores, and other businesses, some upstanding and some not so legal, many of which lasted for a short time. He was accused of a murder but never charged. He never spent a day in jail, though one or another of his gambling halls was every so often shut down by the police for the sake of appearances.

His was the very public life of a full-bellied, high-spirited man. Big Jim loved to tell stories: of gamblers with the greatest of nerve, or of big losses on big bets, or of narrow escapes from the law.

He was a philosophical man and a philanthropic one, armed with a raucous sense of humor and a booming laugh that made him beloved of his customers. And he was fiercely loyal to the poorer neighborhoods, the places that produced the kinds of people who worked the city's lumberyards, its stockyards, its slips and docks, its grain elevators. As he told the *Tribune* in an interview long after the Great Fire, "It is often the 'piker' that shows the real grit. The little he bets is all he has, and when he loses without whining he is showing nerve, but you might never know it. Nerve and pluck are funny propositions. They get by you even when you're looking for them. I know, because I've seen them go by."

In the way of many a gambling impresario, gregarious Big Jim was always ready with a tale, sometimes tall and sometimes true. But Big Jim never spoke about his parents and the Great Fire, other than to tell a single reporter on a single occasion, decades afterward, that his parents had "often told him that the story about the cow and the lamp was a monumental fake." One might without much of a stretch conclude that Big Jim made a legend out of his own life in order to push aside the one imposed on his mother. The effort wasn't entirely successful, but during his lifetime he came close enough to effacing his mother's notoriety that most of his obituaries mentioned the Great Fire only in passing. Like Kate Leary before him, he refused to give in to a city that wanted his family to stand in as a simple answer to questions that were, in the end, endlessly complex.

PART VI

Soup

≈ 25 ≈

WILLIAM BUTLER OGDEN returned to Chicago at the beginning of December, bone weary from his time surveying
the ruins of Peshtigo and eager to return to the quiet of
his Washington Heights home in New York and his beloved fruit
orchards there. Still, he tarried in the city for two weeks to complete
a more precise count of his losses and to lend his voice, in the form
of a newspaper editorial in advance of Joseph Medill's inaugura-
tion, to what he viewed as the most important challenge faced by
the next city administration.

"I find, on my return to Chicago," he wrote on December 3,
1871, "the question of the city fire limits and other matters growing
out of our great fire, attracting, very properly, considerable attention." He praised Illinois's governor, John Palmer, for calling a special session of the legislature to consider emergency state aid and
for deciding to reimburse Chicago for $3 million the city had spent
deepening the Illinois and Michigan Canal, money that for many
years now had been held back in a political dispute between city
and state and that would now be freed for payment of the interest
on the city's debt and, most important to Ogden, for the restoration
of public buildings in their original locations, "preventing a painful
and unfortunate scheming for change."

The rest of Ogden's editorial was given over to an argument
about wooden houses. He was aware of Joseph Medill's intention
to introduce draconian fire limits, and he disagreed with a ven-

geance. "We made our money generally in Chicago while living in cheap wood houses and stores," he wrote. In the face of the anticipated new fire limits, he argued, much of the North Side would depopulate as Germans and others migrated en masse to Chicago's outer suburbs, where they and their money would be much less connected to the downtown district. "Such action and effect would not only prove to be Chicago's first great mistake, but would be a great wrong at the same time."

He pointed out that the same groups of people who in normal times would have trouble affording masonry homes were also the least likely to be insured at all. Or, if insured, they had fallen prey to unethical outfits that withheld payment on technical grounds or couldn't now be found. All of this, said Ogden, added "permanency to their otherwise temporary misfortune and destitution." He argued that the city's most important task was to rebuild quickly and cheaply, which meant in wood, to allow its businesses to thrive, and then and only then could Chicago move on to the question of new, more restrictive fire limits.

Still, there was a hard ceiling to Ogden's empathy for the poor. He was an old and loyal Democrat, friendly on the surface to immigrants and laborers, but it was unusual for him to take such a vocal stance against the members of his own class. And in reality, he was aligned with them even now, viewing the recovery not through individual rights but through "the question of the manufacturing, mercantile, and commercial capacity and business of Chicago." As always, he saw the capital of the city in the aggregate, understood where and how money moved, and recognized that money spent on brick housing would circulate into the pockets of Chicago's businessmen far less than money spent on other things.

After publishing this last salvo, Ogden boarded a train and headed back to his home in New York, now the only permanent residence he possessed. His retirement was at hand, and he would return to Chicago on only a few more occasions in his life. Before he left, though, his words added fuel to an argument that was becoming more heated with each passing day. *The Chicago Times* professed polite amazement at Ogden's position:

He has done much, very much, that has contributed to the growth of Chicago. Few men have shown a more comprehensive foresight of its greatness, or greater boldness in the formation and execution of plans commensurate to the grandeur of an anticipated future. It is the more surprising, therefore, that in the matter of building a city of incendiary wooden shells, Mr. Ogden should manifest a disposition to cling to the follies of the past, instead of boldly grasping the necessities and realities of the future.

These are questions posed by every city, in every moment: How much attention should be paid to the past, how much to the future? Chicago had been visited by an unthinkable tragedy, but it had also been given a singular opportunity. So had Ogden's company town, and despite his promises he and Isaac Stephenson would never rebuild Peshtigo. Instead, they would put their money and remaining energy into the town of Peshtigo Harbor to consolidate their operation, reduce rebuilding costs, and streamline the entire shipping process. Over the next several years, Ogden's personal investments in Chicago and in the logging industry to the north would shrink, though never disappear, and the entire region would see far less of his personal involvement.

The Great Fire acted as a form of punctuation for Ogden, as indeed for many of Chicago's old guard. The era of the Old Settlers, "the indigenes," had passed, and a new one was about to begin. Old politics were now being replaced by new politics, the politics of the post-fire era, and as Ogden prepared to leave the city behind, a new council and a new mayor met to start the new political season and, as always in Chicago, to gird for battle.

Charles C. P. Holden and the other aldermen of the Common Council, after several brief stints in other temporary quarters, had settled into the West Side Masonic Hall, on Randolph Street. One year old, the building was outfitted for ceremony and grandeur at a moment when the decimated city was short on both. A sizable main-floor lobby let onto a grand staircase that led up to a meeting room on the second floor, a procession that provided an unusual sense of occasion during these provisional times. The meeting room, typical of Masonic chambers, was high ceilinged, gold walled, and bedecked with sheaves of wheat, trowels, surveyor's implements, and other assorted fraternal symbols.

Minutes before the first gathering of the new city council, on Monday, December 4, 1871, the ground-floor lobby of the building was packed with reporters, aldermen, and various sorts of spectators and favor seekers. Not since the urgent early days of the Civil War had a political assembly been held in Chicago with so many possibilities in the air. In the minds of the leaders of the Union-Fireproof coalition, everything they felt should happen in the city could begin to happen now. At the same time, Joseph Medill's statements about the fire limits had spooked many voters and aldermen in that loose collection of immigrant ward dwellers, old-line Democrats, and pro-Grant Republicans that had no name but still held on to a large portion of the city's power. If the actions of the Union-Fireproofers regarding the fire limits, the work of relief, and the policing of the city were any indication of their intentions, control of the city was at stake, and the bummers would not hand over that control in the form of a political monopoly to lawyers, bankers, and factory owners. For the opposition, council politics now became a shield to hold off private control of Chicago. Amid the ritualistic decorations of its newly located council chambers, the city would begin to remake itself, in one manner or another, and not without a battle.

At eight o'clock, the winter night fully dark, forty aldermen—twenty holdovers, twenty newly elected or reelected—made their way upstairs, along with a gaggle of reporters, clerks, and assorted functionaries. Holden took his customary seat at the head of the table, called roll, and turned the proceedings over to the outgoing mayor, Roswell Mason, for his valedictory address. "That the Mayor and the Council should sometimes differ in opinion is inevitable," Mason began, "but it is hoped and believed that nothing has occurred which has left behind it any bitterness of feeling."

These were just words, but they were expected. Mason also knew that he was handing over a much more powerful set of execu-

tive reins to Joseph Medill, and, insofar as the aldermen followed
Medill's lead, to the Union-Fireproofers on the council as well. The
Mayor's Bill that Medill had proposed at his election-night party
was now moving through the halls of Springfield in the hands of
the Illinois legislature and was certain to pass, though how soon
was anyone's guess. At minimum, the bill would allow the mayor
to enter nominations for all nonelected city positions, to preside
over council meetings and cast tie-breaking votes, to exert executive authority over the police and fire departments, and to wield
the power of a line-item veto over any ordinance passed by the
council. The new law might chip away at, or even do away with,
the perception in Chicago that the mayor was little more than a
ceremonial figurehead. An alderman aligned with the new mayor
could be forgiven for feeling that heady times lay ahead. The others
girded for a struggle.

Indeed, with his next sentence, Roswell Mason turned to the
subject of the Chicago Aid and Relief Society and the millions of
dollars that had poured into the city in the past two months. "It is
confidently believed that the expenditure of this world-wide bounty
will be more judiciously done," Mason said, "and accomplish more
good, than under any other organization, and that all will be sat-
isfactorily accounted for." He added a hasty note about the "great
exertions made by the Aldermen and other city officers, that is
now being made by the Chicago Relief and Aid Society," as if the
handover from one to the other had been orderly and amicable.
After that, Mason lauded the city's worldwide reputation and sat
down.

Holden wasn't about to concede everything to the Union-
Fireproof newcomers, and he wouldn't go quietly out of the
council president's chair. "Some hard things have been said of the
Council," he began, seeking to bring to mind, no doubt, some of
the hard things that had been said about *him* in the run-up to Election Day. Holden stood proudly on the council's record over the
past four years: a growing city, little evidence of waste, unblemished
civic pride, and a powerful enthusiasm for rebuilding. He added
"that the members have served their constituency faithfully," a con-

tention with which no one could disagree, even if Holden and the Union-Fireproofers didn't always serve the same group of voters.

Then, in a traditional ritual of comity, Holden left the president's chair at the head of the table and found his allotted seat as one of the Tenth Ward's two aldermen, a clear signal that a vote to decide on the new council president was in order. Upon reaching his seat, as was his prerogative, Holden put in his coalition's nomination, and with this act a new political season opened. John H. McAvoy was a canny choice for Holden and his allies. The Fourth Ward, which McAvoy represented and where he lived and worked, lay below downtown, in the middle of the fast-expanding far South Side, home to the city university where Theodore Treat had been a student, to General Sheridan and other prominent citizens, and to a great many of the owners of shops, services, small factories, and other enterprises that dominated the city's central business district. The Fourth Ward was nowhere near the West Side and North Side haunts full of the low-paid and hard-driven workingmen, most of them immigrants, whose politics were so friendly to Holden, dismantling any geographic objection from the Union-Fireproofers to McAvoy's candidacy.

Most important, the sight of McAvoy's three-story brewery and adjoining malt house along Lake Michigan twenty blocks or so south of downtown greeted visitors arriving by train along the Illinois Central breakwater and employed more than one hundred Chicagoans. McAvoy was an immigrant from Northern Ireland who'd risen from apprentice brewer to become a wealthy business owner. He was the made-good apotheosis of a native-born Protestant's ideal new American citizen, a naturalized white man of property, and he was well known for his partnership with an accomplished German brewmaster, which gave him additional credibility and cover with the city's other populous and politically vital ethnic group.

After the Election Day votes were counted, it was clear that eighteen or nineteen members of the council, including twelve holdovers, would most often vote with Holden. Another seventeen aldermen, new and old, were aligned with Medill and the Union-Fireproof bloc. This division left four or five members of the council as swing votes, an unpredictable and inconsistent group that was willing to make common cause with either side depending on the issue or the stakes. The contest for council president would be the first test of this new and precarious balance. One of the new Union-Fireproof councilmen countered Holden by introducing the name of the Fifth Ward alderman Peter Daggy, an active Methodist and Freemason, if a negligible force in city politics, who had once worked with Holden in the Illinois Central land division.

The first vote resulted in a 20–20 tie, followed by another that ended the same way. One of the South Side Union-Fireproof aldermen, Arthur Dixon, called for Joseph Medill, who was waiting in an adjoining chamber for his own introduction, so that the incoming mayor could break the deadlock in favor of Daggy. The clerk of the council, another Union-Fireproof man, piped up to agree that Medill possessed a tie-breaking vote, based on a key provision in the new Mayor's Bill. But the holdover aldermen weren't having it. "Sit down!" one yelled, and another added, "No games, Dixon!" A testy Holden pointed out that that Mayor's Bill was not yet passed, much less signed into law, then tabled the motion and called for a third ballot. This time the brewer McAvoy won twenty-one votes and the presidency of the council. Nothing in the council records indicates who changed his vote, or why. McAvoy gave a short, anodyne speech, pointing out the "great magnitude" of the work ahead of him, and then sent a delegation into an adjoining room to fetch the new mayor.

"The very brief period that has intervened since receiving notification," Medill began, referring to news of his election, "renders it impossible to furnish your honorable body with specific information on some subjects, or to make recommendations on others that require it." No one believed this. Medill had spent many years using his editorial perch at the *Tribune* to peer into the smallest corners of city government for the purpose of explaining how to set them right, and it was absurd for him to suggest he didn't know what he wanted to address, and accomplish, in his time as mayor. In truth, no one had ever come to the mayorship armed with a greater love of specific information or a longer list of specific recommendations.

For more than an hour, in fact, Medill conveyed nothing but "specific information." He began by running through tallies of the city's bonded debt and floating debt, and the interest coming due on each. He enumerated a long and numbing list of municipal fire losses, arriving at a gargantuan total of $2.5 million in damage. He recited a list of important documents lost in the fire that included every piece of paper from the mayor's office, the city comptroller's office, the city clerk's office, the city treasurer's office, the tax commissioner's office, the city collector's office, the Board of Public Works, the Board of Police and Fire, the Health Department, the police court, and the Board of Education. He lamented the city's inability to collect delinquent property taxes at a time of so much pecuniary need. He spent some time on a disquisition opposing the device of the special assessment, the municipal device that decreed public improvements be charged to nearby business owners rather than to a general fund, and he listed the seven separate legal cases that he felt best supported his opinion.

After this parade of numbers and facts, he got to the subject that more than any other had animated his willingness to be drafted as a candidate for mayor. That subject was neither unity nor fireproofing. Municipal reform, he announced, would be his administration's top priority, and it would begin with a bone-cutting regimen of financial austerity. "The fire-fiend came like a thief in the night and caught our municipal government living in excess of its income," Medill read, "with a loose discipline in some departments, inefficiency in others, and extravagance in all."

His focus as mayor, he said, would be to reform "luxurious tastes and expensive habits." He promised that "the services of hundreds of persons now on the pay-rolls can be dispensed with and their salaries saved to the Treasury; and that a multitude of expenses can be lopped off without detriment to the public interests." To begin with, he said, all municipal salaries, including those of the assembled aldermen, would be reduced by 20 percent for one year. And he sought to take all this work out of the hands of the city itself, proposing the formation of a special extra-governmental committee, made of prominent businessmen, to look into and implement every possible avenue of cost savings.

As Medill continued to introduce his prescription for financial oversight and discipline, Holden surely knew what was coming next. Boss Tweed's ongoing fall, now in full bloom on the front pages of Chicago's newspapers, would provide Medill with a perfect object lesson, and the mayor-elect pointed to the "evil example of the New York municipal rule that infected, to greater or less degree, all the municipal governments in the Union." Had Chicago escaped this pernicious influence? he asked the assembly. "I fear not," he answered. The solution was to be found not only in the passing of laws or creation of committees but also in the far more nebulous cultivation of good, moral government. "When the municipal rulers of a city are sober, upright, and honest men," he said, "they set an irresistible example for good before their fellow citizens."

Only at the end of Medill's address, after he'd outlined his vision of a new model of city government, built on equal parts moral uplift, thrift, and cold reason, did he come to the question that had been the entire point of nominating and electing him. He turned to the subject of the fireproofing of the city with another geyser of details he'd said he hadn't had time to gather. Medill knew as well as anyone that the upended poor of the city would want to rebuild in pinewood, unable to afford anything else, so he spent a few minutes trying to debunk the supposed myth of the great expense of brick construction. Then he lowered the boom, proposing that the city adopt and enforce the most comprehensive and restrictive fire limits possible.

"The outside walls and the roof of every building to be hereafter erected within the limits of Chicago should be composed of materials as incombustible as brick, stone, iron, concrete, or slate." He now raised his voice, his sole show of emotion in the meeting. "I am unalterably opposed, from this time forward, to the erection of *a single wooden building within the limits of Chicago.*" Perhaps William Butler Ogden's editorial of the previous week spurred Medill on to this uncharacteristic height of passion; he had not expected cross fire from a businessman of Ogden's prominence, after all. Should the council compromise by placing the imaginary line that would demarcate the ban on wood construction anywhere inside the city limits, the new mayor said, that line would be ripe for contraction by every subsequent city council. Make that line contiguous with the outline of the city, however, and it might stay clear and firm forever.

In these few paragraphs toward the end of his long introductory speech, Medill unwittingly lit a fuse inside his term as mayor. The municipal boundaries of Chicago were wide as American cities went—encompassing most residential neighborhoods of the city in its current form—while the insistence of its workingmen on rebuilding with wood was close to absolute. The current city limits encircled tens of thousands of burned wooden homes, thousands of burned wooden businesses, and many hundreds of burned wooden churches, grain elevators, train terminals, factories, warehouses, sheds, and shacks. More than 200,000 residents of Chicago, including all the denizens of Kate Leary's neighborhood, lived in wooden buildings, the majority without savings or insurance that might allow them to afford the extra cost of brick. Medill's fire limits would drive people out of homeownership and into duplexes, apartments, or even New York–style multistory tenements. Chicago's working class prided itself on its high rate of homeownership and would fight tooth and nail against anything that might make them into permanent renters.

No one neighborhood or type of business inside the city limits should be allowed an exception to rebuild in wood, Medill added, with a dollop of political sarcasm, because "special privileges are odious in a republican country." He pointed to the good fortune of other cities with extensive fire limits, including Brooklyn—failing to mention the far larger budgets allocated for fire protection in those cities—and proposed the construction of a system of underground reservoirs with multiple tap points, which was a fascinating idea but a bad fit with a regimen of financial austerity. He closed with some lines that might have been taken straight from any number of editorials his paper had written or published during the past two months:

Happily there is that left which fire cannot consume—habits of industry and self-reliance, personal integrity, business aptitude, mechanical skill, and unconquerable will. These created what the flames devoured, and these can speedily re-create more than was swept away. Under free institutions, good government, and the blessings of Providence, all losses will soon be repaired, all misery caused by the fire assuaged, and a prosperity greater than ever dreamt of will be achieved in a period so brief, that the rise will astonish mankind even more than the fall of Chicago.

On this note—the only uplifting rhetorical flourish in his entire address—Medill collected his papers and departed, without waiting around to hobnob with the aldermen.

After Medill left, a few items remained on the agenda. The rules of order from the last council were carried over to the present group by unanimous vote. The many and various suggestions in Medill's address were referred to many and various committees. A motion to adjourn was introduced, seconded, and approved. For a while, some of the aldermen lingered upstairs to speak to reporters, or descended downstairs to meander through the crowd still gathered in the lobby. Others dispersed into the night, climbing into waiting carriages or walking to the corner to catch late-night omnibuses to saloons or houses spread all over the city.

According to long-standing custom among Chicago's mayors, this would be one of the few times Joseph Medill would attend a city council meeting. He was confident enough in his personal reputation to believe that most of Chicago would see the logic and wisdom and plain sense of his observations and suggestions, that he would be perceived as the rational, nonpartisan solution to the city's problems. But in this hope—as in a great many other things—his optimism would prove to be unfounded and naive in the extreme. He was a pedantic, professorial personality who liked to explain things to people he viewed as less well informed, but he would soon be the one learning difficult lessons. And Chicago—the city he loved and liked to believe he knew better than anyone else—would do the teaching.

≈ 26 ≈

ON DECEMBER 12, 1871, eight days after Joseph Medill's inaugural address to the council, the city's police and fire commissioners released an eagerly awaited document titled *An Inquiry into the Causes and Progress of the Great Fire*. After six weeks of delay and four more of testimony, the Board of Police and Fire Commissioners—dubbed the "Smelling Committee" by *The Chicago Times*—had completed its investigation. Chicagoans craved sensation, but read their newspapers with a grain of salt, and this had been especially true in the days following the Great Fire, when the papers offered explanations for the blaze that included communist arsonists, flaming comets, or a vengeful Supreme Being. Few readers believed such theories; most simply saw a city burned down and a fire department that had been unable to do anything about it. And now they were going to get their explanation.

Except they didn't. They didn't learn how the fire started, and they didn't learn how it spread. Many questions that were important from a municipal standpoint—what new firefighting equipment was needed, what new precautions must be taken, how the watch and alarm system might be reformed—were also disregarded by the *Inquiry*. Instead of applying anything that might resemble a scholarly, scientific, or even journalistic methodology to their work, for two weeks the commissioners had asked a large variety of witnesses if, essentially, the fire department had *done the best it could*. And in almost every case, the answer supplied by the resulting document was yes.

The *Inquiry* included brief summaries of the Learys' and McLaughlins' testimony as well as that of Daniel "Peg Leg" Sullivan and others living in the DeKoven Street neighborhood. For the first time the public received an account of the sighting of the fire, the difficulty in determining its location, and the disagreement between Brown and Schaefer about calling in a second, more accurate box number. But most of the report consisted of interviews with a parade of rank-and-file firemen, a few shop owners, and a couple of policemen, forty-nine people in all. All were asked ad nauseam the same kinds of exculpatory questions. Did the men of the fire department do everything they could? (Yes.) How quickly did they get there? (Quickly.) Was the fire, at any point of progress, liable to yield to even the most diligent efforts to contain it? (No.) Was the fire hot? (Very.) Were the firemen drunk? (Not a bit.) Were the firemen exhausted from fighting in Red Flash the night before? (Yes.) Really, was there anything more anyone could have done?

Nothing in the published *Inquiry* went beyond material that had already appeared in every one of the city's major papers, all of which had provided daily updates on the commission's interviews. Those expecting surprising new conclusions or heretofore unpublished analysis found nothing. As the *Times* wrote, cynically, "The officers and members of the fire department are acquitted of drunkenness or other blameworthy conduct, and credited with all possible energy and efficiency." Two sentences in the *Inquiry*, and two sentences only, addressed the origin of the fire, and only to plead the department's everlasting ignorance. Leary and family, referred to in the report without the "O'" prefix, "prove to have been in bed and asleep at the time." The commissioners added that there was "no proof that any persons had been in the barn after nightfall that evening," the McLaughlins, the Learys, or otherwise. "Whether it originated from a spark blown from a chimney on that windy night, or was set on fire by human agency, we are unable to determine."

The notary Michael McDermott's sworn affidavit taken from the Learys on October 15, then, would stand to history as the most effective and official description of *when* the fire began. But no determination would ever be made as to *how*, because no serious investigation into that question would ever be made. The most logical explanation, in the hindsight of history, is that Peg Leg Sullivan and a friend—who were in the habit of using the Learys' barn for a smoke after dark and who were the first to alert the rest of the neighborhood to the blaze—had had a simple accident and were too frightened of the infamy that would fall upon them to own up to it. But the many small contradictions and telling elisions in Peg Leg's testimony that might have led to this conclusion went unprobed.

As for the fire department, the delay in conducting the inquiry served its purpose. The citizens of Chicago had moved on. Interest in the Great Fire, the legend, was still high, but interest in the actual blaze that had burned down a large part of Chicago had waned. More cranes and derricks now occupied downtown than charred brick walls. Business was coming back, as was politics as usual. Arguments over the fire had been replaced by other, more familiar arguments. And no argument so animated the political observers of Chicago, especially when a new administration took office, than whether the city's dependence on patronage jobs was criminal, uncouth, or simply business as usual.

On the same day the *Inquiry* was sent to the newspapers for publication, the lobby of the West Side Masonic Temple was, if possible, even more crowded than it had been the previous Monday. A festive, pressed-together crowd formed, made up of citizens seeking those dozens of vacated posts the new administration might have to offer. If the Union-Fireproof ticket had promised reform in city government, none of these men had gotten the message. And now they perched as so many "birds of prey," as one reporter called them, ready to swoop down on the various council members.

Naked, openly displayed office seeking was a venerable nineteenth-century pastime in Washington, D.C., and all across America, one that had been honed to a fine art during the Civil War. And in Chicago at least, it seemed that the smaller the post, the more brazen were the efforts to secure it. Money might change hands, or, more likely, money would be promised. The sums at play were nominal and never overlarge, expressing courtesy more than opportunities for wanton enrichment, and paled beside the numbers being reported out of New York City. In comparison to the revelations coming daily across the wires from the East, graft in Chicago was feeble and decentralized, exercised without much embarrassment or coordination because not all that much was at stake, not yet.

At seven, the council's sergeant at arms and a small squad of police began to clear out the assemblage, barking orders: "There, now, don't crowd!" "Stand back, you big fellow there!" "Gentlemen, you must keep back!" But "so closely did the visiting parties cling to the button-holes of the Aldermen, that to remove the former without the latter was almost impossible." As the council members began their work, they could hear a persistent buzz from below, evidence that everyone was prepared to wait out the entire meeting for news of their luck.

To the Union-Fireproofers, the entire scene offered proof that reform was needed, and to that end a West Side alderman and lumber merchant named Bolivar Gill led off the meeting by moving that the election of city officers be put off for at least another week. He accused the sitting members aligned with Holden of blackmail, graft, and accepting bribes "in the hundreds of dollars." Another alderman, an ally of Holden's, challenged Gill to substantiate his charges and name names. Gill did not. Motions were made to open various investigations, producing a raft of 20–20 ties.

Holden, more entertained than incensed, now stood to face Gill. "The alderman talks about bribery, corruption, and this sort of thing in our midst," he said to all assembled. "I would say that this is a Fireproof council. The word Fireproof carries with it honesty, so the papers say. There can be no dishonesty here for the reason that this is a Fireproof council." When Gill retorted that he had "positive information" that sums as high as $500 had been offered to aid in the selection of certain offices, most of the aldermen and the assembled spectators applauded—some in support of Gill, but more in support of the $500.

For all the accusations of graft, most of the offices received strong majority approval. The city clerkship was awarded, 35–5. The police justice of the South Division, 40–0. South Side justices were selected, by large majorities. South Side assessor, city weigher, boiler inspector, various clerks, the oil inspector, city sealer: all decided by large majorities. Then, just as the successful vote for West Side assessor was completed, another interruption occurred, providing a bit of real drama in a night that otherwise failed to deliver any. As reported the next day in the *Tribune*, "The hair—long, streaming, greasy, and highly combustible—of Mr. Langloth, reporter for the *Union*, became ignited from the gas jet, and blazed fiercely. A cry of 'Fire!' was raised, with additional calls of 'Put his head out!' when half-a-dozen men sprang excitedly to the spot and quenched the flame."

The excitement at an end, "the gentleman was quite unconcerned, and continued to converse with a friend opposite." After ninety minutes of rapid-fire voting, the council adjourned, and the aldermen pressed through the squabble in the lobby below. All of the city's sinecures had been filled, many promises had been made, and some money had surely changed hands under the table. Despite the Union-Fireproof coalition's vows throughout Medill's mayoral campaign to make the city safe from future fires, zero business had been transacted about the cleanup, the relief, or the fireproofing of the city. A lesson had been administered to all who were willing to absorb it: disaster and dislocation were temporary; politics and patronage were forever.

The fire department's inquest report, meanwhile, was read and discussed for a few days, after which it disappeared. December passed, and as the city made ready for the coming of a new year, the best evidence that people were moving on from hard questions about the fire, even more revealing than the indifference that greeted the *Inquiry* or the return to politics as usual, was the rapid and irreversible transformation of Kate Leary into Catherine O'Leary, from curiosity into legend, fact into myth, ordinary citizen into eternal scapegoat and pariah.

Under other circumstances, the *Inquiry*'s publication might have been expected to raise scrutiny of the courthouse-cupola errors of William Brown and Mathias Schaefer to a fever pitch, if not for the fact the public had already settled on its villain. Few Chicagoans cared any longer whether Kate Leary had started the fire or how. Instead, she became a universal emblem of the Great Fire and of Chicago's working class itself, a handy personification of persistent notions about the degeneracy of the immigrant poor. "She will be read of, and talked about," wrote the *Times,* "when the best known man or woman now in Chicago will have long been forgotten."

She would not only be read of and talked about: she would be bought; she would be *consumed.* On New Year's Day 1872, an advertisement for an illustration by L. V. H. Crosby appeared in the *Times* and the *Tribune* under the heading THAT OLD COW:

> With her last kick she started the fire which "wiped out" the better part of Chicago. Crosby was "on the spot" when she did it, and has faithfully depicted his great painting, the interior of the barn, showing the cow in the act of kicking, and the immediate effect upon the other domestic animals and Mrs. O'Leary. A ludicrous scene, showing the true "origin of the great fire."

Album-sized photographs of Crosby's painting were offered for sale for twenty-five cents. For a dollar, ten-by-twelve prints were available.

Crosby's tableau is remarkable for the sheer volume of kinetic action captured in a single small image. All at once the cow turns, looks, kicks. The lamp explodes; shards fly everywhere. Mrs. O'Leary reaches out one arm to shield herself against the cow's leg, the flames, and the heat, while in the same moment she uses the other arm to brace herself against falling. The milk pail capsizes, sending a small waterfall into a growing river of milk still pouring from the cow's teats. White smoke billows from the exploded lantern.

A veritable menagerie populates Mrs. O'Leary's preposterously

Origin of the Great Chicago Fire Oct. 8th 1871, from original painting by
L. V. H. Crosby, 1871

large and airy barn. A pig runs off the left edge of the frame, its
corkscrew tail about all the viewer can use for identification. A
cat arches its back and stares out of the painting. Birds of several
varieties have scattered in panic into the air above poor Catherine
O'Leary. There is no hint of the actual loft in the Learys' actual
barn where two tons of fresh timothy hay had been stored.

Catherine's face, meanwhile, is doing everything in the painter's
power to communicate the idea of "old hag" to the viewer. Her
nose juts straight out from her face as a cartoon witch's might, her
matted hair is colored jet-black, and her eye sockets are as dark and
deep as those of an old crone in a children's book.

Crosby's artwork makes clear that the reading—and buying—
public had reached its own conclusions about the "origins of
the fire." Dozens of other drawings and paintings of Catherine
O'Leary, her cow, and the supposed moment of ignition were sold,
most as insulting as Crosby's. Songs were written, commemorative
dinnerware issued. By the end of the year, no fewer than five instant
histories of the fire had been published, including one by Everett
Chamberlin that included his younger brother Ed's own narrative

of the fire as well as a passage about Kate Leary that was no more flattering—or accurate—than Crosby's painting:

> If the woman who was milking the cow had not been late with her milking, the lamp would not have been needed. If she had plied the dugs of the animal with proper skill, the lamp would not have been kicked at all. The blame of setting the fire rests on the woman who milked, or else upon the lazy man who allowed her to milk. We have no desire to immortalize the author of the ruin of Chicago at the expense of the noble and indefatigable pioneers whose work in the building of Chicago has been recounted in the preceding pages.

Here was Chicago's class hatred at its most virulent, heaping blame on a blameless immigrant woman while lionizing the "noble and indefatigable" Old Settlers whose city she had supposedly ruined. But even if Everett Chamberlin or the fire department's *Inquiry* had absolved the Learys, none of the public vilification of her and her family would or could have been prevented. The Great Chicago Fire was now a full-grown cultural phenomenon, uninterrupted and unaffected by any facts about its causes or fatal progress.

≈ 27 ≈

T HE FIRST DAY of 1872 broke cold and sharp, though as con-
solation the sun was out and the breeze mild. By morning's
light, many of the residents of the city were at work—New
Year's Day was not a holiday for most of Chicago—but still a crush
of people surrounded the new Tremont House hotel, one block
beyond the southern edge of the fire's zone of destruction. As the
size and restlessness of the crowd demonstrated, Chicago craved
the distraction provided by the presence of the grand duke Alexei
Alexandrovich, the first royal visitor from Russia that Chicago had
ever welcomed, an international curiosity of priceless appeal. "A
large crowd assembled on Michigan Avenue in front of the hotel,
and lined the roadway for a considerable distance," wrote the *Times*.
"The best of humor prevailed on all sides, and chaff and badinage
was freely engaged in."

Some of the gawkers had camped on the wooden sidewalks
through the night. Others had arrived in the darkness of early
morning, bundled in heavy coats and fur caps. Lively young women
made up a disproportionate portion of the gathering; the prince
was young and unmarried and rumored to be very fond of the
company of American girls. By ten o'clock "the crowd, noise, bustle, and excitement was excessive," wrote the *Tribune*. A worrisome
press of bodies developed at the main entrance, where "three or
four sturdy boys in blue tried their utmost to stem the torrent of
human bodies." When an indistinct human form passed by a third-
floor parlor window, a murmur ran through the crowd. Was it the

grand duke? Someone on the street shouted his name and others cheered.

It was not the grand duke, not yet. Inside, attuned to the noise on the street through the double-hung panes of the hotel's Presidential Suite, stood General Philip Sheridan and several of his aides, dressed in civilian coats and kid gloves. Beards and mustaches trimmed and groomed, the men enjoyed canapés as they chatted with Joseph Medill, the council president, John McAvoy, and a handful of other local leaders. A family of warmly dressed Russians stood stiffly by a door that led to the chambers upstairs, talking among themselves and paying little heed to the Chicagoans. The gathering was hosted by a doctor named Coudrin who stood in his own cluster with several other scientific and medical men, conversing in low tones. A jeweler moved around the room showing off a small replica of the courthouse bell that had purportedly been cast from the remains of the original itself, set in an elegant case of satin and red velvet and festooned with images of the Russian ducal arms and the Russian flag.

The guest of honor was late in coming down, but this was to be expected, and not only because Alexei Alexandrovich was still a young man just out of his teens. The nocturnal stamina exhibited by the grand duke during his tour of America had already become legend. He had come in late the night before, and the night before that, and the night before that, and on many of the nights over the last month and a half on a tour of the United States that by this point seemed never ending. All of Chicago had followed Alexei's progress across the country, from New York City to Niagara Falls, Philadelphia, Buffalo, Cincinnati, Milwaukee, and finally to Chicago and the Tremont. The grand duke's itinerary, in the works for a year or more, had not at first included Chicago—not until the Great Fire raged and moved the city to the top of the prince's list. Like everyone else, Alexei wanted to *see*.

At about half past ten, at last, the family of Russians at the door came to attention and barked out, "Hail Alexei, the grand duke of Russia!" in a "sudden explosion of gutturals, which seemed like the intermittent snapping of fire-crackers," so startling that it caused many in the room to jump. Next appeared a tall, bearish young man, dressed in a "shaggy overcoat of very heavy material," a black hat, polished shoes, and gloves. Alexei was young and looked young, with an expansive, bored, and boyish face covered by a rumpled beard and subdued by the early hour. Paying no attention to his countrymen by the door, he strode into the room and headed straight for General Sheridan, who, to no one's surprise, had over the past three days become the prince's best American friend.

Alexei was the fifth child and fourth son of the tsar Alexander II, the man who had freed the Russian serfs in 1861, a decree that had provided him with his nickname, the Liberator. The "Abraham Lincoln of Russia," the American papers called Alexander II, and for years the grand duke's father had been considered an enlightened liberal, at least as world leaders went, until an attempt on the tsar's life in 1866 had sharpened the edge of his rule. If Chicagoans knew anything else about the Liberator, it was that he'd sold Alaska to the United States in 1867, mostly to keep it out of the hands of the British.

The reasons for the grand duke's trip weren't discussed with his American hosts and weren't widely known. A lieutenant in the Imperial Russian Navy, the grand duke had already, by twenty, visited many a port and had many an amorous fling, but no love affair mattered to his father, the tsar, more than Alexei's connection with Alexandra Zhukovskaya, the daughter of a poet and a match far beneath his station. The affair, begun in 1870, had produced a child, also named Alexei, who existed in the tsar's eyes only as a stain on the family name. But because Alexei showed no signs of ending his relationship with Alexandra, despite considerable pressure to do so, his father in 1871 seized on a well-publicized visit to Russia by the American naval officer David Farragut as an excuse to propose a reciprocal gesture of goodwill. The Liberator would send his wayward son across the ocean on a long ceremonial visit to the United States, the first such visit ever by any member of the Russian royal family. And maybe, by the time young Alexei returned to Russia, his ardor for the poet's daughter would have cooled.

How much of this Joseph Medill or anyone else in the city knew is unclear. Probably none of it. But there is no doubt that the grand duke's visit to Chicago, which had been going on for three days now, did not represent Joseph Medill's favorite kind of mayoral duty. For a month now Medill had been mayor, and his first foray into political office was turning out to be less than gratifying. In December, Medill had been shifted into an ex officio role on the city's Board of Health, a rote and mostly pro forma commitment that soon became far more time-consuming when the city experienced one of its semi-regular outbreaks of smallpox. At the same time, he'd begun to dive into the minutiae of municipal reform, but his responsibilities were subdivided into so many increments that he could make little headway on anything. As a newspaper editorialist, he'd had the luxury of choosing each day's battles. Now the battles, no matter how small, chose him.

The annoyances had begun on his very first day in office, when he'd discovered that the outgoing mayor, Roswell Mason, had given away a large last-minute pile of commercial licenses in a rush, without collecting the usual fees, to just about anyone who had asked: teamsters, vehicles, peddlers, porters, junk dealers, detective agencies, and many others. Medill was trying to get the money owed the city by threatening to cancel the licenses, a pursuit that showed no sign of ending soon. Beginning on his first day, as well, he was asked to step in to adjudicate hundreds of vexing questions of land titles in the wake of the fire, when it had become far too easy to claim a piece of property, or a piece of a piece of property, as one's own in the absence of paper records. After winter arrived, several bitter arguments over snow clearance were brought to his desk. Two days after Christmas, he'd needed to issue a proclamation about mad dogs.

None of this work spoke to big ideas about remaking and reforming government or about reconstructing the physical face of the city, the kinds of ideas that sounded so clear and easy to implement when expressed in a newspaper column. Medill was learning that no matter what power the still-pending Mayor's Bill might soon grant him, there would be no escaping the ceremonial nature of his position. For a month now, he'd had to spend an inordinate amount of time preparing for this garrulous visitor from Russia who seemed an overgrown schoolboy, and the mayor was crabby about it—though in the case of Joseph Medill, crabbiness was sometimes impossible to distinguish from any other mood.

The city that hosted the grand duke, however, was in marvelous spirits. On this day, the start of the first new calendar year after the Great Fire, the sense of newness was invigorating. The turn of the calendar to 1872 was like no other new year the city would ever experience, a step into the future in a moment when the past had been obliterated. The winter had so far been exceptionally cold, but the sight of cleared lots full of piles of bricks and lumber ready for construction come spring lifted spirits. Some had wondered if St. Louis might seize the opportunity provided by the Great Fire to take away a large chunk of the city's business, but with the trains running again along the lakefront and the Mississippi River frozen down to Missouri's border and beyond, Chicago's worries faded fast.

Still, for all of this progress, the grand duke visited a city that was in some respects running in circles. Business leaders in the city and their journalistic organs tried to paint the rush of construction work as the harbinger of a new Chicago, but the truth is that Chicago as presented to its Russian visitor could best be described as a city trying to return to some sort of prelapsarian state. If the reconstruction continued as it had begun, in fact, a year hence a visitor might find herself convinced that the Great Fire had never happened. She would find not a New but an Old Chicago, the same board with the pieces shuffled. Or, in another metaphor more apt for the situation of businessmen downtown, she would witness the aftermath of a game of musical chairs.

Only a few of the city's business magnates—Marshall Field, Cyrus McCormick, and Potter Palmer above all—could count on insurance reimbursements and lines of credit sufficient to rebuild bigger than before. The story behind rebuilding for everyone else was about speed and ready cash: who had it, who didn't, who could buy or build on short notice, who could react the fastest to the news that a corner lot or a long undivided block was up for sale by a property owner whose insurance hadn't come through as hoped.

In a city infamous for corners on the market, street corners were the newest, most coveted form of currency, available only to a few, guaranteed to multiply in value if you could procure one *right now*.

Engineers poured in from all over, looking for work, as did builders and journalists, along with tens of thousands of skilled and unskilled laborers. In aggregate, the new buildings already erected downtown by January 1, 1872, had space for more than five hundred stores, and the scramble to get the best and most reliable tenants was intense. As for the buildings themselves, the entire effect was a restoration rather than a step forward. One observer wrote of the "new" downtown that it had "the effect of meeting an old and tried friend in a brand new Sunday suit." In a city that would soon become world famous for architectural innovation, there was none now. For now, as the calendar turned over to 1872, the city had to satisfy itself that a visitor was no longer bombarded with the sight of hulking walls of partially collapsed stone.

As for Chicago's economic fortunes, the grand duke's visit was the most glamorous example of a post-fire tourism boom that had overtaken the city and brought in a steady flow of cash to the city's hotels, shops, restaurants, and entertainment venues. Well into the new year, visitors from near and far continued to make their pilgrimages to the Learys' house, guided to the spot by hotel concierges, paperboys, or other obliging locals. A lucrative cottage industry grew up around tours of what everyone called the "burnt district"—carriage tours, walking tours, omnibus tours, even bicycle tours—and one invariable highlight was a stop along DeKoven Street and a retelling of the myth of Mrs. O'Leary and her cow.

Dignitaries came to Chicago in droves, including other cities' mayors and other states' congressmen and their wives. In November, Japan's ambassador to the United States had traveled out from Washington, D.C., to spend a few days riding a carriage around the ruins and ended his visit by presenting Medill with a $5,000 check to support the rebuilding effort. Whoever they were and wherever they'd come from, though, tourists expected to see ample evidence of both the destruction of the city and its rebuilding. One pole of the experience was meaningless without the other.

The entire party moved downstairs and through the main entrance, ears ringing with cheers and shouts on all sides. Swarmed on the steps, with the police shouting "Will you stand back?" at the crowd, they pushed through to their day's transportation. The ornate carriage of the new council president, John McAvoy, would hold the grand duke, McAvoy, Medill, and General Sheridan. Behind them followed eight more carriages, which departed to the sound of a small band and the noise of the delirious crowd.

The tour reached the University of Chicago before noon, and there the grand duke and his considerable entourage had fruit, cake, and coffee and inspected the institution's famous telescope, though the grand duke did not peer through the instrument, because it was daytime and he was told he wouldn't be able to view the Great Bear. The caravan continued through the South Side and late in the morning arrived at the Union Stock Yards, the eight-hundred-acre livestock-disassembly complex that stood to the rest of the world as Chicago's most fantastic and futuristic industrial innovation. They were shown the various animal pens, where Alexei commented that the prize hogs were bigger than he'd expected and the buffalo smaller. They witnessed up close the process of slaughter "from the last squeal to the final concealment of the meat in barrels ready for shipment." All the while, Alexei played the part of an amazed child in search of something to brag about back home, always eager to hear ever-bigger numbers. He was rewarded with the information that this season's swine kill in Chicago, from September until the end of the year, had added up to almost a million hogs, far and away the city's busiest-ever pace of slaughter and barreling, Great Fire be damned.

The grand duke and his entourage then decamped to the Transit House, the one luxury hotel in the stockyards complex, and ate for lunch "all kinds of meats, pastry, and luscious fruits of every variety," including pork from hogs that had recently been slaughtered a few hundred yards away. Alexei sat at the head of the table, Medill to his left. When the time came for a round of toasts, Medill stood and said, "May the rivalry between Russia and America be in the future what it has long been in the past, a rivalry to feed a hungry world." The grand duke agreed, and downed another glass of champagne as the Havanas were passed around.

The next stop on Alexei's itinerary was Dexter Park, which sat within the stockyards complex and encompassed a horse-racing track, a baseball field, and the Prairie Shooting Club, where Alexei—who had never shot, seen, or heard of the American double-barreled breechloader and who'd never seen a wild pigeon—received a quick lesson in the brand of shooting called pigeon popping. Proud of his hunting prowess, he picked up the heaviest gun on the site, missed his first live target, then killed the second one, to applause from the members of his suite, who were watching from seats in the balcony. "It was clearly evident that he enjoyed the fun," wrote a reporter, and indeed Alexei expressed genuine disappointment in every miss and exulted in every hit.

The next day Alexei visited a temporary wooden structure already erected at Washington and Market to house the Board of Trade, another so-called wigwam, where activity in commodity futures continued strong and a mood of optimism reigned. After a bit of encouragement, Alexei was persuaded to give a short speech to the merchants and traders. When he mounted the steps to the top of one of the trading platforms, and before he said a word, his audience cheered with abandon. Taking delight in the reception, the grand duke reciprocated the welcome in slow but steady English: "I am not in the habit of public speaking, but I must say that I am glad to meet you. I render you my warmest thanks for your cordial reception. I hope that before many years have passed Chicago will be as rich, as great, as prosperous, as she was at the time the great conflagration occurred."

The crowd applauded again, for a long while, not least because of the understanding throughout the room that Russia was an underexploited market for Chicago exports and imports. The grand duke had said nothing of substance, but in his earnest declaration of optimism he'd shown his Chicago soul. The young rough-and-tumble Russian prince and the young rough-and-tumble American city made a perfect match. His final evening in the city was reserved for a grand ducal levee, where he shook hundreds of hands belong-

ing to laborers and small shop owners, for whom the touch of roy-
alty would remain a singular event in their lives. This was followed
by a softer social soiree, where Alexei pointedly ignored the men in
preference to the young ladies.

On the morning of January 5, 1872, the grand duke departed
for a grand buffalo hunt along the Brule River in the Nebraska
Territory. The expedition had been in the works since July, and an
improbable number of famous people had been involved not only
in planning the hunt but also in persuading the skeptical grand duke
to undertake the trek onto the chilly January plains. The celebrated
landscape painter Albert Bierstadt had first suggested the idea to
the U.S. general in chief, William Tecumseh Sherman, who then
involved the Lakota chief Spotted Tail by way of the showman
Buffalo Bill Cody. The State Department, the War Department,
the Bureau of Indian Affairs, and seemingly every rail line between
Chicago and Omaha offered logistical or monetary support. Alexei
was apparently won over to the expedition sometime during his
Chicago stay by the prodding of Phil Sheridan and a personal visit
from Sherman, who bore the news that the famous Indian hunter
George Armstrong Custer would also join the group.

Over the next six weeks, Chicagoans read eagerly of the grand
duke's grand expedition, the "imperial party," as the papers called it:
a mob welcome in Omaha; a late-night dinner party on the Union
Pacific train to North Platte, where they were greeted by Buffalo
Bill in his trademarked buckskin costume; a camp on Red Willow
Creek, where Custer had bivouacked while pursuing Cherokee and
Cheyenne Indians in 1867; a stop at Medicine Creek for sandwiches
and champagne beneath a fluttering American flag; and then the
next day, January 14—the grand duke's birthday—Alexei's first kill,
aided by Custer riding his mare through the herd to separate a
particularly weak buffalo. The new year had started well, and the
diversion provided by the Russian prince seemed never ending—
that is, until the second Sunday after Alexei's departure, when an
equally compelling and far more troubling drama erupted much
closer to home and pushed everything else off the front pages.

≈ 28 ≈

O N MONDAY, January 15, 1872, nine days after the grand duke's departure, about a hundred men gathered in the street and on the wooden sidewalk on the North Side, in front of a small grocery store on the corner of Market and Illinois. A light rain fell on a cold and windy night. The crowd was restless, ready to move but forced to wait. Their next destination was the West Side Masonic Hall, where the city council was to hold its first vote on Medill's proposed fire ordinance. The language Medill had used in his first address to the council six weeks earlier—language that would make the fire limits absolute and coextensive with the city limits—was still in place in the proposed ordinance. The new limits allowed for no compromise and no special allowances, mandating construction in brick everywhere inside its boundaries.

After fifteen minutes of delay, nine more men rounded the corner from Michigan Street, bearing lamps suspended from long poles and freshly lettered transparencies, thin cloth or paper sheets emblazoned with words that popped into hard relief when lit from behind. NO FIRE LIMITS AFTER THIS CALAMITE, read one. LEAVE A HOME FOR THE LABORER, read another. A third was decorated with Masonic symbols and a scaffold, below which was written THE FUTURE OF THOSE WHO VOTE FOR THE FIRE LIMITS ORDINANCE. The largest transparency contained several messages: THE VOICE OF THE PEOPLE. DON'T VOTE ANY MORE FOR THE POOR MAN'S OPPRESSOR. HARMONY OF ALL NATIONS.

Another banner read THE RELIEF, TEMPERANCE, AND FIRE-

LIMITS SWINDLE MUST BE CUT DOWN. Appearing as it did not even four months after the Great Fire, this particular combination of words represented something brand-new in Chicago's political rhetoric and, for any member of the Union-Fireproof coalition, something ominous. The relief effort, the temperance movement, and the determination of fire limits were to Joseph Medill, and to most of those who had helped him to power, three very separate things. But to a great number of the city's ordinary people, they seemed a three-pronged offensive against the lives of laboring men and women. Many of the less well-off in Chicago were, for the first time, tying together a knot of grievances that would never come undone. The post-fire actions of Mayor Medill and of the forces that had helped him to office looked to them more and more like a cold-blooded and opportunistic grab for power and money, an unanticipated chance for the landed interests of the city to stick it to the working class and immigrant populations that did so much of the work to keep their factories, their lumberyards, and their slaughterhouses running.

Though the terms would only later become ideological flash points in a larger, more violent international struggle, Chicago was already in 1872 divided into two groups it called "capital" and "labor." But the distinction was never as simple as haves and have-nots. This gathering on an unassuming street corner just over the river on the North Side, on land first purchased and developed by William Butler Ogden, was no uprising of Europe-born revolutionaries or political left-outs. These were mechanics, merchants, factory foremen, saloon keepers, clerks. Fear of the rise of this kind of broad lower- and middle-class coalition was the reason Boss Tweed was mentioned so often by Medill and by the newspaper editors who were Medill's closest professional colleagues. The accusations of top-down Tammany-style machine politics thrown at Charles C. P. Holden, while invented, were more palatable to Holden's opponents than the truth that numbers were gathering from the bottom up, that the political ground was shifting underfoot, and fast.

The corner grocery was owned and run by Thomas Carney, one of the Eighteenth Ward's two aldermen and a stalwart member of the group aligned with Holden against the Union-Fireproofers. As many as could fit packed into the store. As their shoes left small puddles of murky water on the floor, Carney jumped on a countertop. "I want this procession to be orderly, respectable, quiet, peaceable, and law-abiding," he said, and while some in the crowd paid attention to him, most didn't. In fact, before Carney could say another word, the small group of men carrying the banners, lamps, and transparencies, still outside and getting wetter with every passing moment, hollered their impatience and started off down Market Street. A pack of young boys ran after them, trying to call them back, making enough noise that the departed men heard them and halted. But they did not turn around. They were willing to wait but not willing to return. They wanted most of all to move.

The crowd that milled outside Carney's grocery now numbered several hundred men and a few women. Within a handful of blocks an outpouring from the surrounding buildings, streets, and alleys swelled the number to more than a thousand. This count included fellow demonstrators, but more of them were spectators, skeptical and sympathetic, who walked on either side of the street beside the procession in anticipation of a night's rousing entertainment.

The main body of demonstrators marched for the West Side Masonic Temple in loosely organized rows of two, four, six, or eight. At the head of the procession rode on horseback two German businessmen, Charles Sporl and Henry Schmal. Just behind them a desultory band played a select few Civil War standards, including "The Battle Hymn of the Republic," over and over. When the players ran out of music, the crowd began to sing. A wagon decked with two giant American flags clattered in the middle of the advancing demonstrators. Some of the walkers carried German national or Union army flags. One man waved a flag decorated with a single large lager beer stein. A few torches dotted the scene, serving to emphasize the inky blackness of streets still mostly lined with packed-dirt lots where the rubble of the Great Fire had been partially cleared away.

If the council vote went against these marchers, many would find themselves adrift in their own city. As they understood the matter, their very identity as Chicagoans was at stake. Not to be able to rebuild out of wood meant that they would not be able to rebuild in their old neighborhoods at all. And they would not let that happen without voicing their displeasure to the aldermen in person. The "suburbs," as the new neighborhoods to the west of the West Side and the south of the South Side were called, were in their mind the homes of other people, later arrivals, heedless newcomers. The city was theirs. Carney's crowd felt that they were being less regulated than *examined*, told where they could live, told what they could do with their free time, told how much their participation in the making and remaking of Chicago was—or wasn't—worth. Whose Chicago had burned? seemed the question, and their answer was "ours."

Where Medill and the Union-Fireproof aldermen saw a pathway to a safer, more prosperous, more orderly, and more moral city, the demonstrators saw a smug and dangerous paternalism that aided a few at the considerable expense of the many. How much dictatorial control could and would be exercised by the business elite? Most workers in Chicago were familiar with William Butler Ogden's company town in Peshtigo—they'd read plenty of front-page accounts of its burning and of the work of reconstruction—and they knew that George Pullman, the Relief and Aid Society officer and inventor of the Pullman railroad car, was planning to build his own company town south of the city limits. The mood was not against these kinds of places—they supplied jobs, job security, and homes—but a man worked in such a company town by *choice*. They did not want all of Chicago to become such a place without their consent.

In the aftermath of the Great Fire, most workers' wages had been frozen, but rents had not been, and this disparity galled them. Any agitation for a general strike, they knew, was pointless in the face of a continuing stream of fresh labor entering the city, willing to work for almost any pay—not to mention how a stoppage would look in a city still full of homeless and destitute victims of the fire. The unfettered laws of supply and demand ground on without remorse: the constant supply of workers kept wages down while it pushed the price of housing up. Now the council was to vote on a measure that could put the price of housing forever out of reach of families that had called the central districts of Chicago home for many years. It was a point of pride with the working class that Chicago "contained a larger proportion of independent property-owners than any other great city of similar size," a fact demonstrated by thousands of families like the Learys, who in New York or San Francisco would have to live in overcrowded rental tenements instead of in homes they'd purchased themselves.

Turning off Market Street, the protesters marched east down Kinzie, then south to the entrance to the LaSalle tunnel, also called the North Side tube, where the entire procession stopped for a few minutes. "Form in columns of six!" one of the leaders yelled, hoping to make a show of order and organization, but no one paid any heed. As they passed through the tube underneath the main branch of the Chicago River, their voices resonated against the walls of the cylindrical passage, making such an "almost intolerable" din that their progress was heralded to the downtown district as if they'd all carried speaking horns. The hollering and cheering grew louder as the North Siders were greeted on the other side by another sizable crowd that had gathered from elsewhere in the city to await their coming.

Down LaSalle to Adams they went, then west several blocks, crossing over to the West Side, then north up to Randolph then west again until they stopped in front of the council's temporary Masonic home. There they found two prominent Germans waiting outside: Anton Hesing, publisher of the *Staats-Zeitung* and one of the most influential immigrants in the city, and his countryman Henry Greenebaum, the well-regarded banker whom Joseph Medill had nominated for mayor before accepting the candidacy himself. Hesing called out to the men bearing the transparencies to gather in the ground-floor lobby of the Masonic Hall, and then moved to go into the building himself, until the large numbers of Germans among the marchers began to call out, "Speech!" "Speech!"

As Hesing returned to mount a small platform someone had erected, he was gratified to see that the demonstration filled all of

Randolph Street in front of the building. Sunday night was a time of relative quiet, a day off for most, and more and more people continued to come out on the periphery of the commotion to listen, bracing themselves against the rain and cold. Hesing was famous in the city as an orator, and he spoke briefly and optimistically, expressing confidence that the show of unity and the size of the crowd would result in success with the council's fire-limits vote. His optimism was cheered. There was a meeting to attend, so Hesing closed, urging his listeners to forgo violence and maintain their belief in political solutions.

"Go home and tell your wives and little children that they shall have a home again on the lots bought with hard-earned money," he called out. "Be quiet and peaceable, and satisfied with what you have done. The legislators upstairs want peace and quietness to legislate for you and the city, and I know that your wishes will be gratified—that no such law will ever pass the City Council."

A cheer went up, the crowd began to shift, and then a strange thing happened. Another man, his name unrecorded by all the reporters at the scene, stepped up beside Hesing and made a loud remark in support of the temperance movement. This was something people did more and more these days, especially when the crowds were German or Irish. The teetotalers had a way lately of popping up just about anywhere. They were unsurprising interlopers, generally unpopular and lightly regarded, so the crowd laughed and pressed right past him and his words. Drinking was not the subject under discussion, after all, and besides, this was not a group in a mood to be told what they should or shouldn't be allowed to do. Still, the prohibitionists had reared their heads often enough in post-fire Chicago that a corresponding anti-temperance movement of sorts had formed—as made evident by the beer steins depicted on more than one of the banners fluttering overhead and the reference on one to a temperance swindle.

The crowd now started to surge into the building, heedless of their great numbers and the crush of bodies all around them. The men carrying the transparencies demanded that they be allowed upstairs and into the council chamber. Hesing would later argue with Medill and others in city administration that the assembly had been peaceful, if boisterous, and that in fact there had never been any threat to the men gathered in council one story above them. The view of the reporters inside the building attending the meeting, already well under way, was very different. "There was now terrible yelling below, as if the penitentiaries of the Union had disgorged their contents on the Common Council," wrote one. The sergeant at arms and two aldermen went down to see what was going on. Because Hesing and Greenebaum were still outside, the aldermen couldn't find anyone filling the role of an official spokesman in the lobby, where the crowd was growing unruly.

In truth, Hesing's admonitions for order could accomplish very little. This was a diffuse, many-minded crowd, some of whom had come to make a point about the fire limits, some to cause trouble, and many, as the *Tribune* put it, "simply to see the show on abstract principles." Upstairs, as the noise and tumult grew below them, one alderman made the suggestion that business be suspended for the day. Another alderman made the suggestion into a motion. The council clerk yelled above the increasing din, looking for someone to second the motion, but before that could happen, a banner and a large standard crashed through the door, which swung open on broken hinges. A Union flag and a lager beer banner fluttered into the chamber, followed by their bearers. Some of the aldermen broke into shouts, but still the council managed to operate by its rules of order.

Another motion was made, loudly, that the sergeant at arms remove the banners and their bearers by force. The aldermen could hear yelling in German beyond the door. Pressed close together, a small mob started to push into the room before the demonstrators and the sergeant at arms reached a quick compromise: admit the flags of the United States and of Germany but none of the others, not those with depictions of alcohol or various accusatory and confrontational messages. This proposal was agreed to, and in any case most of the flag bearers couldn't make it through the crowd, which was packed too thick in the lower lobby and on the stairs.

When the two national flag bearers squeezed in, their success drew huge applause and cheers from the lobby and a few hisses from within the chambers, "the disapprobation being not of the flags, but of their riotous accompaniments." Following the two flags, a steady stream of men managed to squeeze inside, some yelling, others beelining for individual aldermen to press their case against the fire limits. Some just ran around the room and whooped.

The council president, John McAvoy, the brewer who depended for much of his livelihood on the kinds of men now accosting the aldermen, banged his gavel and cried out, but no one paid him any attention. Finally, McAvoy shouted out an obvious observation, that "not being able to keep order and the further transaction of business being impossible, the Council is prorogued." There would be no vote at all on the fire ordinance, nor on any other council business. Some aldermen gathered in small groups according to their political proclivities and gestured with animation, at each other and at the mob, while others worked their hardest to slip out and away with minimal notice.

All the transparencies now moved into the room in one noisy and enthusiastic bunch. No longer did anyone play the role of leader or spokesman. Shouting broke out all over the room. The message, delivered over and over to no one in particular, was "*homes for our families!*" Voices rose and collided. As far as most of the demonstrators were concerned, delaying the vote was a success worth celebrating. The crowd kept pushing into the chamber, and soon someone figured out that the building itself might be in danger, that the mass of people jammed shoulder to shoulder might collapse the floor joists. A voice called above the din: the floor would give in with so many people packed into the room. But for many, there was no way now to move backward through the crowd.

Some began to call out in alarm. Others were elated or amused. Emerging now as the loudest voices among the crowd of speakers were James Conlan, a telegraph clerk and former alderman of the Fifteenth Ward, back in the spotlight, and Anton Hesing, who had come upstairs and now declared to one reporter in a tone of pride and amusement that he "cannot see anything disorderly in the proceedings." In a delighted tone, Hesing compared the crowd to the suffragists who had recently occupied the Capitol in Washington, D.C. The floor did not collapse, and soon all the aldermen were able to press through the crowd and head for home. Conlan mounted the speaker's platform and announced that the meeting, such as it had become, was over. He announced his satisfaction with the proceedings and lamented the "little difficulty at the door," but otherwise declared himself pleased, to more cheers.

In the absence of its intended target and purpose, the protest became a full-on political demonstration of a type the city had never seen before. Reporters from all the papers were more than happy to stay; this kind of chaos would fill the next day's front pages and more, and the scribblers with their pencils became the true audience. The North Side, Conlan told them, waxing poetic, was home to "the artisan, the mechanic, the toiler, the merchant." Most of these people could not afford brick, he cried, but some could, and to sunder neighbor from neighbor by way of an absolutist fire-limits law would be a great injustice. Together, he cried, the workers of Chicago made a single community. "If persons want fancy dwellings of brick," Conlan said, "let them have them. But let the fire limits on the North Side be where the people want them. The North Side people do not wish to be deprived of their homes."

The council lectern was next taken by Hesing. As always, he spoke past the front row, to the readers of the next day's newspapers. "Whatever my speech may be, it is pretty sure to be misrepresented in the papers in the morning," he said. A voice called back, sarcastically, "*Oh, no, no.*" His views were known to all, Hesing said, and he was not afraid to speak those views. He called out his past support for a powerful fire ordinance with clear and wide limits that would protect downtown businesses without throwing people out of their homes. But he averred that he did not understand the current form of Medill's ordinance, nor its unyielding and absolutist logic so dismissive of compromise. "Those who are trying to secure its passage *don't know the history of our cities.*"

This line got huge applause. Then Hesing ad-libbed a little and pointed out, for no obvious reason, that he had once declined positions in the administrations of Abraham Lincoln and Ulysses S.

Grant. "Gentlemen," he said, "I dare to face the music. I am not afraid to be intimidated." He inveighed against business owners and their architects for using so much wood to construct the "fire-proof" buildings whose husks now dotted the South Side. How could the men who had built and owned those buildings now demand that laborers build only out of brick? Medill and the Union-Fireproof aldermen were blaming workers for the business owners' own problems, or they were applying a standard of outrageous hypocrisy.

Hesing was gearing up now, but the good times and high spirits were about to come to an end. Before he could continue, he was interrupted by a loud shattering, and then shouting and screaming, and then another crash, as brickbats and cobblestones began to fly through the tall second-floor windows and into the council room.

"The first scattering shot became a storm of missiles," wrote one reporter in the next day's edition of the *Tribune*. "The front windows of the chamber looked like the windows of an old church in the country which had long been disused and the sport of rustic urchins." The crowd surged toward the rear of the room and then down the stairs, "like a great wave, carrying everything before it." Men jumped over desks, some crouched under them, some flipped the desks on their sides and huddled against them. "Men got down close to the floor, or crowded themselves into the corner, or between the windows." Some received injuries as the crowd trampled over them. Some of the remaining men dislodged the desks and pushed them forward as shields while they tried to escape. Soon, broken glass covered the floor as more bricks flew in through the windows.

"No one cared to hear any further oratorical display," wrote the *Tribune*, and "no one," for a change, included Anton Hesing, who ran out of the building along with the rest of the demonstrators. The entire evening had ended in comedy, chaos, crime, or farce, depending on one's point of view. No one had the foresight to suggest, however, that from such crude and modest beginnings could come big things—not least a seismic shift in the city's politics that would never be effaced.

On his hurried way out of the building, a janitor put out the lamps.

❧ 29 ❧

LESS THAN two weeks after the chaos at the city council meeting, while the fire limits continued to be debated, another new and unexpected front opened in the battle for post-fire Chicago. On January 26, 1872, the Relief and Aid Society's director, Wirt Dexter—he of the strictest adherence to the principles of scientific charity—published a public letter in the *Tribune* and in the *Times,* in order to discuss $100,000 committed by the Cincinnati committee to the relief of Chicago but not yet expended. By "discuss," he meant "commandeer." And by "expended," he meant "given to Wirt Dexter." He'd been prodded into writing his letter by a report conveyed to him, through the society's treasurer, George Pullman, that the Cincinnati delegation had made a decision that they could "better fulfill their trust by working through the volunteer societies, and in the increase of branches of the soup house," rather than by handing over their money to the Relief and Aid Society.

Cincinnati's wish to use its own money to continue to hand out its own soup was, alas, against Dexter's rules. Despite having no official position in Chicago's government, the society's director had persuaded Mayor Roswell Mason to issue a new charter stipulating that all money and supplies contributed to the city of Chicago for the relief effort be handed over to the society for the sake of "coordination and efficiency." Most cities had done so. And after three weeks of slapdash efforts at organization in October that had left many Chicagoans wondering when and if relief would ever appear, the society had found its footing and was now providing barracks,

homes, and work at an impressive pace—at least for every suppli-
cant their investigations deemed "worthy." Dexter and his fellow
board members had wrangled close to $3 million in donations and
more than $1 million worth of supplies. But Dexter was bothered
by the fact that they hadn't wrangled every last cent of it.

Much of his ire was directed at the Reverend Benjamin Frankland, who served as the public face and voice of Cincinnati's charity efforts in Chicago. A well-known Quaker, Frankland had for
years toured from city to city to speak on the question of "How can
Friends, in many places few in number, make their power felt?" or
similar themes. In answer to his own question, he'd put his missionary stamp on Cincinnati and then on Chicago, where he'd arrived
early in the year. In Ohio, Frankland had superintended the Bethel
House, part of a nationwide assistance network purposed with the
"temporal and spiritual elevation" of indigent sailors and dock-
workers, and he'd come to Chicago to head the same organization
there. Before leaving Cincinnati, he'd also been involved in efforts
to aid widows, "fallen women," orphans, and newly arrived Blacks.
His charity bona fides were impeccable, and his experience with
municipal officials and relief organizations was wide and deep. He
was a genial soul, but hardworking and—when he needed to be—
stubborn, even unmoving.

The previous week, Joseph Medill had spoken to Frankland to
express Chicago's satisfaction with Cincinnati's contribution. In
that conversation, Medill had told Frankland and a group of visitors from the Cincinnati city council that "nothing has been done by
any one or any city that is of as great benefit and as economical as
your soup-house." Frankland had presented the mayor with a led-
ger showing that the Cincinnati soup house to that point had served
24,600 portions of soup per week at a cost of $241.60, meaning
that each portion cost less than a penny. At that cost, the Cincinnati
effort could continue almost into eternity and never exhaust the
$100,000 they'd pledged. The precision of Frankland's accounting
and the thrift it displayed must have appealed to Medill's reformist
nature, and besides, given the current circumstances, charity, to the
mayor's mind, was charity.

Indeed, in the view of Medill, and of the editors at the *Tribune,* and even of many of the Relief and Aid Society's board members themselves, the five soup houses run by the Cincinnati delegation in various locations across the city served no ill purpose and created quite a bit of goodwill, at a cost that the city or the society couldn't hope to match. Medill was vexed by Dexter's habit of over-complicating every part of the relief effort, his dictatorial hand, his ham-handed way of communicating the society's goals, and his evident distrust of Chicago's populace. All these personality traits and tendencies, brought forward by Dexter in his open letter to the *Tribune,* were also the qualities that made the council's former president Charles C. P. Holden so dislike him. Reverend Frankland liked Dexter even less than did Holden or Medill, and found the society head's actions even more inexplicable. As a man, Dexter was easy to ridicule, but he carried considerable heft in the worlds of business and law, and his friends occupied the very highest of places. His methods could be laughable, as Frankland was learning, but his aims were anything but.

Dexter's open letter began by impugning the dignity of Chicagoans who used the Cincinnati relief stations. Soup, he wrote, was embarrassing. People didn't like soup and wouldn't eat it unless they had no other choice. "To compel these people to go daily to a soup-house, which is the only way soup can be distributed," he said, "is to put a deserving and worthy people temporarily rendered destitute by the fire upon the level of paupers." And even if the beleaguered citizens of Chicago didn't all harbor such ill feelings toward soup, Dexter continued, there was the larger question of the Cincinnati committee's unscientific methods. "So far as we can learn," wrote Dexter, "soup is given out at the houses contained by that Committee without either visitation or record." In other words, meals were given and *no record of the gift was kept.* Dexter's incredulity jumped off the page. This could not stand. Who received the soup? How much soup was given out? Had these people been measured and found worthy of the soup? He concluded his editorial by noting that "the dangers attending general, miscellaneous distribution are easily seen."

Cincinnati's reply to Dexter was published in the *Cincinnati Gazette* three days later, then reprinted in the *Tribune*. The response began with a lesson in recent history. Cincinnati's train had rolled into Chicago less than twenty-four hours after the quenching rain had fallen, they wrote. That same day, its delegation had visited the First Congregational Church and donated $35,000 worth of blankets to Charles C. P. Holden's original General Relief Committee. Within four days of the Great Fire, they had taken space in the Chicago and North Western terminal and began to serve their soup, *two weeks* before the society put any of its own citywide food-distribution systems in place. The time it had taken for the Relief and Aid Society to coordinate and launch its inspections and investigations had emphasized the need for instant, unconditional help, a need that Cincinnati had helped to fill. "The Cincinnati Committee," they wrote, "had clothed the naked and fed the hungry even before Mr. Wirt Dexter's Committee had an existence."

Contrary to Dexter's accusations, they continued, Reverend Frankland had not kept Cincinnati's money to himself, to spend if and when he chose. Rather, the entire balance of its funds had been given over that very first week to the Chicago Bethel House, which was charged with running the soup houses through the beginning of April. Cincinnati was only paying expenses; a Chicago entity was running the show, and its bank account held the money, even if that entity was run by Frankland himself. Besides, they pointed out, Mayor Medill had only good things to say about their efforts. Only Wirt Dexter, they added, "takes the extraordinary ground that soup is a humbug."

Now the Cincinnatians arrived at the crux of the matter: "The trouble with Mr. Dexter is, he wants to handle the money that remains in the hands of the Cincinnati Committee." They reported that Dexter had "repeatedly telegraphed" them for permission to draw on the Cincinnati funds on his own signature, a request that other cities had granted but one that the Cincinnati delegation refused: "He may slur the Committee, he may guore [*sic*] the soup-house, and he may continue to refuse to acknowledge what Cincinnati has done, but he cannot finger the money that remains in the hands of our Committee."

To another one of the society's criticisms, that the soup money was "unaccountable"—the society's favorite code word, though, because it was Cincinnati's money, it might seem that Cincinnati should decide on how it should or shouldn't be accounted for—they replied that Reverend Frankland would soon tally every penny in his own report. Considering the Chicago society's ongoing delay in producing its own first audit, they added, such a wait should be understandable. The Cincinnati committee ended its own open letter by going over Dexter's head and appealing straight to the mayor. If Joseph Medill "will inform the Cincinnati Committee that the soup-house is of no use, that that is no way to feed hungry people," they wrote, "it will, with all its branches, be suspended and the money will be used in some other way."

As Frankland understood well from his earlier conversation with the mayor, Medill was not about to close the soup houses. But by this point, the mayor surely wished he'd said nothing at all to the Cincinnati committee other than to offer his thanks. In private, he believed that Wirt Dexter's hunger to control all money given to the city of Chicago was absurd. Worse yet, all this sniping was a waste of time and energy in a city that had many needs that were best fulfilled through many different avenues. It was telling that when the ambassador of Japan and the grand duke of Russia, both of whom had visited since the Great Fire, made donations to the relief effort, Medill had passed those donations on to smaller relief organizations and not to the society, despite Dexter's rules.

Dexter, meanwhile, would not let go of the question of soup. On Tuesday, January 30, seven men accosted Frankland at the Cincinnati soup house on Peoria Street, where, "in very abusive language, they denounced the 'soup business' as a nuisance" and made a vague threat to rip down Frankland's temporary structures if they were not closed. That these men were there at Wirt Dexter's behest was not in doubt, given the uncanny repetitions in the rhetoric of the visitors who'd visited him and the language in Dexter's own public statements, which Frankland described as "almost similar in expression." Frankland asked them why, if the soup was as disgusting as they described, two thousand visitors came each day to have some. The men replied that the people of the neighborhood came for the crackers. Frankland went next door for a bowl of soup and brought it back for them to examine. One of the men tasted it, said it was good, but that the "other soup" they'd inspected wasn't from the same batch.

Exasperated, Frankland finally wondered, out loud, "Why are you even here?" After some hemming and hawing, the men replied that they'd heard—"somewhere"—that if the soup houses were closed, the society might instead distribute Cincinnati's money throughout the neighborhood. Furthermore, Frankland related, his visitors "seemed to have the impression that their share of it was about $10 each." This was too specific a rumor to be discounted, and after more probing, Frankland came to the conclusion that this money was Dexter's designated reward to these men for their help in closing the soup houses, payment to come after Cincinnati's money was transferred to the society. Still, instead of throwing the men out, Frankland promised to investigate the soup house himself and address any concerns he found as well as publish his findings. The men went away, their dreams of $10 rewards turned to dust.

Three days later, on Friday, February 2, those same seven men affixed their names to an affidavit published in the *Tribune*. Their accusations were lengthy and specific, and all were fabricated. "The soup is not fit for use and cannot be eaten, and is only taken from the Soup-House for the crackers which are eaten." They continued: the soup was taken away in barrels as feed for various sorts of animals; the soup contained maggots, hair, and dirt; the kettles, never cleaned, were coated with rust; the soup was under-cooked; the beans were hard. They concluded, "We think the money could be used much more advantageously for the use benefit of the poor in some other way than in the wholesale manufacture of soup for cows, hogs, and hunting dogs and for the flooding of vacant lots and filling of out-houses in the immediate vicinity."

The next day, Frankland published his reply in the *Tribune*. For someone Dexter had accused of not keeping sufficient records, he went into great detail regarding the soup's preparation and the sources of its ingredients. The meat, he wrote, was supplied at a discount by S. & W. Curtis and Company, which also supplied meat to some of the city's finest hotels, and was inspected for quality at each end of the day's delivery. Cincinnati's reputation was at stake, and that reputation would suffer a great deal if the soup was as rancid and unpalatable as the men had described. The soup was not cooked "in cold water for fifteen minutes," he said, but rather simmered seven hours overnight before leaving the Peoria station and was reheated—not heated—at its destination. As to the long hairs supposedly floating in the soup, Frankland invited any official of the Relief and Aid Society to visit his kitchens and talk with the chefs, all of whom were men, none long-haired.

Frankland addressed one final charge by Dexter and his proxies, the only credible accusation they'd made, that his soup was being used to feed animals. This, the reverend conceded, might happen sometimes. Whatever soup the delegation had left at hand at the end of the night, he said, was given away so that it would not sour. Leftovers were uncommon, but they were bound to happen. The alternatives, to make less soup than need called for, or to throw out good soup, ran counter to the delegation's mission and to the basic precepts of Christian charity.

But all this argument aside, Frankland wrote, "what in the world does this raid on the Soup Houses mean or amount to?" The money, he said, would never be Wirt Dexter's to control, and Dexter knew it. If the Chicago Relief and Aid Society demanded control of the $100,000 earmarked for the soup houses, Frankland assured his visitors that the money would be voted back to Cincinnati, thus denying Chicago any benefit from the contribution at all. He closed his report on the unexpected scrutiny of his soup houses by the society on an aggrieved personal note, acting as his own character witness. "I have, for the past eighteen years," he wrote, "been more or less actively engaged in Christian work, the aim of which was the amelioration of the condition of the poor, and I think it is the first time I have ever been charged with insulting the poor by offering them that which was unfit for use."

Frankland had one more card to play. For he knew that if there was one other group that stood apart from Dexter's heavy-handed, patronizing vision of charity work, it was Chicago's women. Two more of Wirt Dexter's rules were, first, that no materials received from out of state be distributed out of non-society organizations, much less out of private homes, and, second, that all materials donated in a particular ward of the city be distributed in that ward of the city. Many women's charity groups had formed within days of the Great Fire, and all ignored Dexter's rules with conspicuous unconcern. Several were associated with churches, including the First Congregational, where Charles C. P. Holden had housed the city's government in the days following the Great Fire and where Kate Medill and her daughters had worked long hours in support of Holden's initial relief efforts. The women's groups solicited their own contributions and donated where they wished, in friendly but firm defiance of the society.

What made this defiance especially sharp was the fact that the women involved were often friends of, or even married to, the men who ran the Relief and Aid Society. The wives of several of the society's directors, including Josephine Dexter, had after the Great Fire formed the Ladies' Relief and Aid Society as an adjunct of the larger organization. There was a certain cheekiness to the women's efforts, a tweaking of their self-important neighbors and husbands.

In a letter to a fellow worker, Katherine Medill left one of the few records of her feelings on the matter: "It would be a great satisfaction to be able to supply the wants I hear of every day of people who are in every way worthy and get beyond the Aid Society's Rules." She helped to form another charity, the Woman's Industrial Aid Society, and that organization now began to receive clothing, in her words, "to be distributed in violation of all general rules." At the same time, a third women's group formed, called the Good Samaritan Society and chaired by the wife of a former Chicago mayor, with an express charter to "afford immediate relief to deserving women who are unable to make known their wants."

Frankland now turned to the Good Samaritans and asked that they visit the soup house and tell the city what they found. The women responded with a speed and vigor that seemed to give away their own feelings about Dexter, if not the all-male Relief and Aid Society. They visited several branches of the soup house during the next two days and published their report on January 6 with the names and signatures of all fourteen members appended, including that of Hattie Pullman, wife of George Pullman, the railroad car magnate and Relief and Aid Society treasurer who had helped to open up the entire soup-house kerfuffle in the first place.

"We have eaten the soup," wrote the Good Samaritans, "and we pronounce it to be excellent; quite as good, in every respect, as that made in our own kitchens." The reference to their own hearths and homes was as potent a rhetorical tool as could be wielded in this day and age, but still they went further than eating the soup, fanning out to canvass the surrounding neighborhood. Their published report was full of carefully transcribed direct quotations from ordinary Chicagoans who had relied on Cincinnati's generosity: "Get the soup three or four times a week. Like it. Have never found anything wrong with it." "Comes in good for the children, and for ourselves, too. Never found anything in the soup. Have heard stories about it." "Get the soup whenever I want it. Do not want soup every day. The children like it. Some folks tell lies about it." "It is good, there's no mistake about it. Those who run it down eat it, too, you may be sure of that." "Splendid soup. Those who say they can't eat it are —— fools." "We like the soup. Get it every day. Could not get along without it."

The women of the Good Samaritan Society concluded with an emphatic confirmation of the strange rumor that Frankland had heard from his visitors of the day before, a corroboration that painted Wirt Dexter in a doubly damning light: "We infer that certain evil-minded persons have circulated the report that if the distribution of soup is discontinued, a large fund, now held in reserve by Cincinnati, will be divided equally amongst them." In a note appended to the report of the Good Samaritan Society and published in the *Tribune* the same day, Reverend Frankland expressed his satisfaction with the women's conclusions, writing, "I trust this is the last time I shall have to ask space in your columns on the Soup-House question; and, between this time and the 1st of April, when we expect to close up this brand of relief, our desire may be expressed thus: 'Let us have peace.'"

Joseph Medill, meanwhile, used the Good Samaritans' investigation as cover to make clear his own feelings on the case, in a letter read out at the next Cincinnati Common Council meeting and published in the *Tribune* on February 12. Wrote Medill, "That the soup-house has, since its establishment, done great good there can not be any question. For the next six weeks after the fire its value in relieving hunger can hardly be exaggerated." The rest of the letter responded in oblique but pointed fashion to Wirt Dexter's objections:

> There must be very many persons willing and anxious to labor, that are not on the Relief Society's rolls, and who experience the pinching of hunger this cold winter, to whom a free bowl of nutritious soup, proffered without ceremony or conditions, must be very acceptable and gratefully received.

Medill added, "The misunderstanding that exists between your committee and the officers of the Chicago Relief and Aid Society is a matter which I deeply regret." Medill presented himself as the soul of mediation and conciliation, while at the same time signaling his displeasure with Dexter's "conditions" and explaining his disbursement of those meager amounts of money under his personal control to women-run charities rather than to the society.

Not all compromises were to Medill's liking, however. The same day that his letter regarding the soup houses ran, February 12, 1872, the aldermen of the city council, as no one had doubted they would, approved the final form of their fire-limits measure by a vote of 26–6, with eight abstentions and absences. Medill's absolutist proposal, offered on the night of his election, had been rejected, and the more flexible position of William Butler Ogden and Anton Hesing had been adopted, further augmented by an impressive array of loopholes. Great sections of the German and Scandinavian portions of the North Side were exempted from new limits, and this was to set aside the thousands of pinewood homes that had risen within the proscribed areas during the months that the council debated the issue, which were allowed to stand. However, the fire limits for the first time did now include every block of the central business district on the South Side, as well as much larger swaths of the North and West Sides.

The political calculus was raw but honest. So long as a fire wouldn't destroy downtown, this was acceptable. Houses could burn, but business blocks must stand. As Ogden had argued, the total flow of the economy was what mattered, not its individual components. For his original proposal, offered on the night of his election, Medill had been vilified by Anton Hesing, Charles C. P. Holden, and many others, but in the end he had not made much of a fight out of it. The decision represented a defeat, but given the limited power Medill had to influence the aldermen's votes, he had reason to believe he'd gotten as much out of the effort as he could expect.

The fire-limits question would not go away because of a single vote of the council. The tussle over a soup house, on the other hand, would soon be forgotten. But the basic question raised by these battles—would a small group of wealthy and entitled men forever determine the way everyone else in the city was permitted to live?—would soon grow to deafening volume, and the city's arenas of conflict would continue to shift. The struggle for the soul of reconstructed Chicago would now take to its streets, its public spaces, and, most dramatically of all, to that most eminent expression of the city's raucous soul: its saloons.

≈ 30 ≈

MANY OF Chicago's immigrants, especially its Germans and
Swedes, held fond memories of the May Day celebrations
of their motherlands. But these rituals, steeped as they were
in eons-old agrarian cycles of decay and rebirth, had always been
tied to rural locales far more than urban, and by 1871 the traditional
observances—the dances around the Maypole, the crowning of a
May Queen, the collection of branches and flowers—had mostly
ceased in American cities. "With us the merry-making exists only
in song and chronicles," wrote one Chicagoan, but even so May 1
had lost none of its importance on the yearly calendar, particularly
for Chicago's poor and foreign-born. By 1872 the old-world traditions of May Day had been replaced by the new-world spectacle
of moving day, the day when as many as one-quarter of Chicago's
residents placed all their belongings in wagons and handcarts, and
on their backs, and left old lodgings for new. One kind of May Day
parade had been replaced by another, and this one, tied closely to
the climate, history, temperament, and economic arrangement of
Chicago, was religiously observed.

Housing in Chicago for recent arrivals took many forms: hotel
rooms and, for the better off, hotel suites; tenement homes of one
or two rooms, much like the one the McLaughlins rented from the
Learys; large, stately homes subdivided to become boardinghouses
of ten, twelve, even twenty rooms, often filled with young, single
workingwomen; and small bachelor apartments filling the top floor
of any number of downtown business blocks. For the most part

inexpensive and easy to find for newcomers, these options shouted "temporary lodgings," and newcomers discovered that even their first months in Chicago were often filled with an arduous and time-consuming search for new and better quarters. Inside the city limits, almost as a rule, leases ran for a year, and because moving a household between November and April was rolling the meteorological dice, May 1 became far and away the most popular date of occupancy.

Wednesday, May 1, 1872, the first moving day after the fire, was a fraught moment for many of the city's transplants. On the surface, everything seemed grand for a new transplant, of which there were tens of thousands. The weather in Chicago had warmed early in 1872, and by the middle of March the debilitating economic aftereffects of the fire had lessened as the pace of reconstruction accelerated. The year's first oceangoing vessel had docked in Chicago on March 9, weeks earlier than usual, and its arrival had been a symbol of much more than just the resumption of transatlantic commerce. Shipments of produce from midwestern and southern farming states and of livestock from the West were plentiful. With the hard frost out of the ground and the suck and slosh of wooden wheels slicing through thick mud once more the incidental music of Chicago, business was surging.

What this meant for Chicago's laboring class, though, was complicated. Even before the winter arrived, the supply of incoming workers had outstripped the boom in demand, and the competition for lodgings was fierce. Upward mobility was the ostensible point of moving day, and many of the families and individuals trundling their belongings through the streets were indeed making a move to better lodgings. But many weren't, as the *Tribune* recognized:

> This day, the first of May, Chicago takes its bed and kitchen furniture and seeks a new home, where it may have the inestimable blessing of paying twice as much rent as ever before for one-half of its usual comforts. This day, the pots, kettles, and pans, the crockery, pictures, and feather beds, the looking-glasses, bookcases, and sideboards, the vulgar necessities of the cellar and

the aristocratic luxuries of the parlor, with the owner proudly perched on top, will go in solemn procession through the streets, disclosing to the spectator those household secrets which have been kept sacred from the popular gaze for a year past.

The day was full of emotions, some joyful and some resentful. "Good-bye to the old house," continued the *Tribune*, "with its pleasant associations, its merry days and its jovial nights, its familiar nooks and corners, and cheap rent."

Goodbye to cheap rent, indeed. Transient workers, more than thirty thousand of them, had flooded the city since the Great Fire, and in response rents had increased while wages had remained stagnant or decreased for most jobs. The news was everywhere— nationally and internationally—that there was work in Chicago, for skilled and unskilled laborers alike. And the ramifications of this inflow of men and women looking for employment went well beyond a hyperactive housing market. With all the new workers arriving and willing to take whatever wages and jobs they were offered, the old labor order in Chicago was threatened as never before.

Five years earlier to the day, on May 1, 1867, a "Grand Eight Hour League" formed by Andrew Cameron, the Britain-born publisher of *The Workingman's Advocate,* had called a citywide strike that lasted for more than a week. In the decades after the Civil War, the fight for an eight-hour workday was a flash point like no other between workers and their employers, not least because it had been the loudest demand at the first congress of the International Workingmen's Association, held in Geneva in 1866, and had been authored by none other than Karl Marx himself. In the United States, in the wake of the war, with so many men returning to work with a newfound sense of independence and entitlement, the effort to pass an eight-hour law had gained particular traction.

For a moment, Chicago's laborers had won a victory. In April 1867, the Illinois state legislature had passed a law restricting shifts to eight hours before overtime pay was required. But the state's business barons had made sure the bill came with a single crucial and crushing caveat: if an employee signed an agreement forfeiting his right to an eight-hour day, an employer could offer any hours he pleased, and at the same time an employer was allowed to make that forfeiture a condition of employment for new hires. The exceptions not only killed the eight-hour movement; they also acted as a thumb in the eye of Chicago's entire working class.

The new law and its evisceration led directly to the Eight-Hour League's May Day walkout in 1867. *The New York Times* expressed the general feeling toward the movement among Chicago's Yankee elite when it opined that "the lower class of workmen, we think, will be nowise benefited by this new privilege. They will only the more frequent liquor-shops and work for politicians. Their new leisure will be a new temptation." In any case, the law's loophole and a healthy economy pushed most labor unions into weak compromises with their employers and spooked most workers at Chicago's larger manufacturing concerns into signing away their rights.

After this failure, membership in Chicago's unions had dropped and was only now picking up again. The lingering sting of defeat was strong, especially since in other quarters of the country the spring of 1872 was a season of successful strikes: housepainters in Richmond, horseshoers in Boston, copper miners in Michigan, carpenters in Brooklyn, mechanics in Philadelphia. As the season wore on, just about every trade in New York City struck or threatened to, in a cascade of discontent and political muscle flexing: pipe fitters, carpenters, cabinetmakers, plumbers, upholsterers, bricklayers, sash and blind makers, stonemasons, longshoremen, wheelwrights, blacksmiths, piano makers, marble cutters, and tin roofers, among others. The assumption in New York was that these unions would soon band together and call a general strike to revitalize the prospects of a comprehensive and effective eight-hour law.

The working class of Chicago, meanwhile, displayed no such unity as new arrivals continued to pour in by the trainful, most of them picking up jobs outside the structures of the trade unions. All the post–Great Fire departures and arrivals added up to a remarkable turnover of the city's population, a churning that brought in tens of thousands of new workers who had no connection to the city's customary ways of doing business. It was these newcomers that Chicago's unions sought to impress with what they called "a gala day—a day of recreation," scheduled for May 15, "to show the strength of the Trades Unions to the strange workmen now here, and to induce them to unite with their brethren." But all that the "boss builders" of the city heard was a call to get ready for an eight-hour strike, an issue they thought they'd settled for good in their favor just five years earlier. Once again, the class of men who made up the Union-Fireproof coalition assumed that whatever trouble happened in New York City would happen next in Chicago, and they would say and do anything to stop it.

In reality, the purpose of the demonstration would remain ambiguous up to and after May 15. Most likely, there was no single purpose. Some organizers were hoping to progress to a general strike, while others sought a simple show of strength. Some cared about the eight-hour movement; others simply wanted their jobs protected against the inflow of new workers unallied with any trade union. Andrew Cameron, writing in *The Workingman's Advocate* four days before the demonstration, framed it as a simple "plea" for higher wages and took his fellow publishers to task: "That a request for an advance of a dollar or fifty cents per day implies a riot, bloodshed, or a resort to violence is known to be false by the scoundrels who make the charge."

In the end, no one was sure if the day had been a success or not, not on either side of the divide between employers and workers. Only a fraction of the thirty thousand marchers hoped for by organizers turned out, so that perhaps four thousand men marched the winding route through the West Side from south to north. But a great many more than four thousand workers watched, thousands of them packing the parade's major intersections, many dressed in their Sunday finery and unusually, even strangely, subdued. A dozen unions were represented in the procession—including stonecutters, horseshoers, plasterers, carpenters, joiners, painters, lathe operators, and, in the largest numbers, more than a thousand bricklayers—along with policemen, a few aldermen, and several musical ensembles playing patriotic tunes. "The bands played, the men marched, and the people stood by and listened, but gave no sign of special interest or sympathy," wrote one watcher. The six-mile march began at eleven o'clock in the morning, and, though it was no strike, most of the city's labor did come to a halt, suspending construction work in the burned district for the day. In another sign that something serious was under way, there was little drinking by participants or bystanders.

The most peculiar thing about the peculiar event was the speech delivered by Joseph Medill atop a rickety scaffold erected in a large vacant lot at the corner of Harrison and Throop Streets, the end of the marcher's route. Andrew Cameron had asked Medill to attend and to speak ever since the first plans were laid for the demonstration, weeks earlier, but mayors were always asked to address trade-union gatherings and other local labor events, and they hardly ever said yes. Yet here Medill was, and no one seemed sure why he'd accepted, until he started to speak.

"It requires no figure of speech to justify me in calling this vast assemblage the bone and sinew of the city, for you are emphatically that," he began. Then, continuing in typically impolitic fashion, he added, "Whether my remarks will be pleasing or not depends on the correspondence of our views," and said that he proposed to "speak plainly and frankly—using no flattery and uttering no deceptive compliments." This opening might have confounded or amused many of his listeners, except that almost all of them couldn't hear him, given the congenital weakness of his voice, the size of the crowd, and the day's considerable breeze. As always, Medill spoke for the purpose of putting something into the written record. He could count on the *Tribune*, if no other paper, to reprint his speech in its entirety. To speak at great length in great detail, his voice an indistinguishable mumble, was part of the mayor's reputation, and he rarely disappointed.

For twenty minutes he rewarded the men who had invited him to speak not with a show of sympathy or friendliness but with threats and warnings. Referring to the rumors that the day of demonstration was the prelude to a general strike, as well as an effort to shanghai non-union men into the unions, he said, "I trust, for your

304 · SCOTT W. BERG

sakes, those reports and surmises are wholly false and baseless; and if there be any reckless persons in your organizations advocating such a course, that their proposition will be frowned down by an overwhelming majority." He followed with a slow and supercilious lecture on the principles of free contract wage labor, explaining that just as the workingmen had "the undoubted legal right to put your own price on your services," so too "the employer is not bound to offer more wages than he pleases, nor to accept the services of those he does not see fit to engage."

Medill's speech continued on a startling and ominous note. The right to free contract labor was one for which "every true patriot is willing to die," he said, and then he threw a rhetorical cannonball at the crowd:

> It is made the duty of the police officers to preserve the peace and arrest all persons committing breaches of it. This force may at any time be increased in accordance with the emergency; and the mayor may call on the governor for whatever military force is required to suppress any riot or disturbance, and he in turn may call on the president for the assistance of the army and the navy.

Medill did not use the name of Philip Sheridan, but he might as well have. Here was the threat of martial law all over again, but now, instead of a vision of a city cleansed of looters and incendiaries by federal soldiers, Medill's audience was provided a vision of those same soldiers turning on *them*.

The threat of labor unrest, he said, was un-American. It was the threat of the Paris Commune, of Karl Marx and the rising International, and, most of all, of the growing influence of immigrant populations in the city. "I am chiefly led to make the foregoing observations," he added, "for the information of strangers from foreign countries." In those foreign lands, he said, "Labor considers Capital its enemy, to be crippled and warred against."

Medill couldn't stop. He absolved Chicago's landlords of any wrongdoing in raising rents during the spring moving season and suggested that the best way to create more affordable housing was to build more houses: "Where there are ten houses for rent, and only nine families wanting them, rents will come down." If the cost of labor rose too high, he added, speculators would put off rebuilding, and as a result the city would suffer as a whole. Thus it was a patriotic duty, a duty to Chicago, to accept low wages and higher rent for the time being.

"How shall the condition of the laborer be improved?" he concluded. "No satisfactory answer has yet been given." He suggested that workers trust in the process of arbitration and appealed for cooperation, but outside of those vague and unimpressive remedies, he washed his hands of the matter and told the crowd to be more like Joseph Medill:

> I have nothing better to propose than the course I pursued myself: to work steadily at the best wages offered, practice economy in personal expenditure, drink water instead of whiskey, keep out of debt, put your surplus earning at interest, until you have enough to make a payment on a lot; build a cottage on it at the earliest day possible, and thus be independent of landlords; go with your wife to church on Sunday and send your children to school.

As Medill had promised at the start of his speech, there was nothing coded in this, nothing hidden. The assembled crowd heard the mayor tell workers to accept their fates, that in fact those fates were predetermined and inviolable according to the strict supply-and-demand laws of laissez-faire economics. They heard him say that the progress of his own life—progress that had relied at several points on well-heeled and well-positioned benefactors—was a usable model. They heard him suggest, as so many temperance crusaders had before, that their customary Sunday whiskey was one crux of the problem. And, most of all, they heard the mayor's threats of armed intervention.

The speech was not an effort at conciliation or "cooperation"; it was, rather, an accumulation of messages that seemed at odds with Medill's stated belief that the men gathered in a dirt-packed city lot on the West Side were the "bone and sinew of the city." But in the mayor's mind, there was no contradiction. He wanted to eviscerate the power of the city's trade unions to recruit new members and was willing to use just about any rhetorical tool to do so. Workers could flex their political muscles only so far as the city would not be harmed, at which point a line needed to be drawn. In no way did he believe that the interests of the working class and the interests of the city were the same thing. And draw a line he had.

PART VII

Beer

≈ 31 ≈

THE SUMMER of 1872 was notable above all for the frantic pace of rebuilding and the noise and mess that came along with it. Worries about a post-fire economic collapse, never realistic, had been forgotten. More buildings were now under construction downtown than had existed before the fire. By September, more people lived and worked in the city than before the fire. More money flowed into and out of the city than before the fire. The West Side was booming, and the plains beyond the West Side and to the far South Side were being cleared for new suburbs. Four train depots had burned, and all four had already been rebuilt. The Lull and Holmes planing mill, origin of the forgotten Red Flash fire of October 7, was back in business, now in a building made of brick and roofed with tin. Rain was falling in normal quantities. The mud had returned.

If the possibilities that lay latent in the new, post-fire Chicago were exemplified by one construction project, it was the work on Potter Palmer's new hotel. This was the second—and now sole—Palmer House, the contracts on which had been signed only weeks before the Great Fire. When the blaze caught downtown, the architect John Van Osdel—the same man who so many years earlier had designed William Butler Ogden's stately home on the northern banks of the main branch of the Chicago River—had run to the building site at State and Monroe, two blocks north of the original Palmer House, to gather his plans and instruments, much as Medill had tried to spirit out the complete run of the *Tribune* before its building burned down.

It turned out that Van Osdel had been craftier than Medill, or luckier, or perhaps just speedier. Believing his life's greatest work needed to live on, whatever his own fate, Van Osdel dropped the building's thick roll of blueprints deep into a hole on a corner of the lot. Then he'd covered the hole over with clay before dashing to safety. Four days later, the plans had been extracted intact, to the intense relief of everyone involved. The story was widely reprinted over the next several months and earned for Van Osdel the faith and loyalty of many a wealthy client going forward. It also gave the new Palmer House the kind of publicity that money couldn't possibly buy.

After the Civil War, Palmer had spent months in Europe cataloging its great hotels, and now he was more determined than ever to match their architectural grace, beauty, and sophistication in the middle of Chicago's reconstructed downtown. An engineering marvel touted as safe "from every accident save an earthquake of very respectable dimensions," its exterior would be clad in Amherst sandstone from Cleveland and graced with ornate French Renaissance ornamentation from ground to cornice. Forty-two varieties of polished marble would greet visitors on the walls in the ground-floor lobby, which would hold a thousand-prism chandelier 263 feet long and 63 feet wide, along with a sixty-two-foot-long marble counter. The stairs to the second-floor gallery would feature bronze griffins on newel posts, and the entire two-story space, the most public expression of the hotel's elegance, would be ringed with closely spaced gas lamps, an effect "recalling Byron's poem of Belshazzar's feast."

The second floor would contain the finest bridal chambers in America, each one fitted with a mantelpiece cut from a single block of Italian marble, topped with carvings of Venus and Cupid and wrapped in marble vines, the detail work so accomplished that "the feathers on the plumage of a tiny bird swinging in the vines are clearly visible." The third floor would be given over to four social parlors and six dining rooms. The five-thousand-square-foot kitchen would be housed in a separate building on the site to keep its steams and smells away from the guests. Five fifteen-person elevators would carry guests to seven hundred rooms.

For much of the next year, going downtown to watch the work being done on the Palmer House would become a popular pastime, especially when the workmen turned their spotlights on the building and worked until well after dark. "The structure seemed alive with men," wrote *The Land Owner,* a real estate periodical produced in the Tribune building, "their lanterns, like so many stars, glittering all about it, from roof, facade, basement, interior, elevators, etc., while teams of horses hauled the iron to the elevators, whence it was raised aloft and put by honest hands in its appointed place." As an added attraction, Palmer himself was sometimes found at the site encouraging the men, riding the elevator with a load of supplies, huddling with a contractor, or watching from the street.

A new county courthouse was set up in a temporary structure several blocks to the south of the original building, and while plans were made to reconstruct city hall on its old square in the center of downtown, more than a decade would pass until that happened. As a rule, public entities found what lodgings they could for quite some time, while high-profile private institutions rebuilt quickly. Perhaps even more than Palmer's new palace of a hotel, the reconstruction of the Chamber of Commerce, which also housed Chicago's Board of Trade, became the most visible symbol of the city's sense of rebirth. It seemed that politics could take place in any kind of setting, but the renewal of business required a sense of grandeur and permanence.

After the fire, the Chamber of Commerce and the Board of Trade had moved into their own temporary building—yet another "wigwam"—but then rebuilt at their original location, across from the courthouse square, with remarkable speed and in the same configuration: offices on the first two floors and upstairs a trading floor that was a model of elegant simplicity. Two-story Palladian windows provided ample light for the compact hall, which held two rows of tables against the walls and, at one end, three raised platforms, ironically named pits, where commodities and commodity futures were traded. The walls were decorated with large canvases depicting downtown Chicago before and after the Great Fire. Just as it had done before, the room buzzed with activity six days a week, Monday through Saturday, opening at seven o'clock and closing early in the afternoon. The city's commodities traders were capitalist swashbucklers, charismatic heroes and antiheroes of the business world. Chicagoans rich and poor alike looked on in wonder as the board's big operators tried to work the legendary "corner," that slippery device by which a purchaser could accumulate massive quantities of a commodity, along with enough futures contracts to dictate its value, and either hoard or dump the product to enormous financial gain for themselves and ruin for their competitors. "Corn futures" or "hog futures" didn't have the abstract elegance of the financial securities that gave lower Manhattan its cachet, but they did have a connection to the sight of fully loaded trains and oceangoing cargo ships that gave Chicago an ineradicable identity.

The business establishment of the city treated the Board of Trade as its unofficial headquarters, a sort of alternative city hall. At night, the building was often used as a forum where Chicago's elite met when deciding to do extra-governmental things, which made the trading floor a tidy symbolic counterpoint to the city council chambers. Holding a meeting in the Board of Trade contributed to the belief that any problem the council refused to take up, or took up with insufficient vigor, could be hashed out by the constant and strong-willed men of business instead of the variable and weak-minded men of politics.

One of the first such meetings at the new Board of Trade trading floor took place on the cold late-summer evening of September 12, 1872. For all the good news made visible in the buildings going up downtown, the city was still on edge. Worries of financial disaster or of another fire had diminished, and more immediate and personal fears had taken their place. If 1871 had been the summer of a hundred fires, the late summer of 1872 had seemed to be a season of a hundred murders. This was why the Board of Trade was full: many of the citizens of the city wanted something done about a crime wave of historic proportions, and they didn't trust

Chicago's government to solve the problem. The trading room was packed from wall to wall with various sorts of interested parties: "a large audience, many of them respectable citizens, and many of whom looked as if they were roughs who had looked in in order to find out what it was proposed to do with them."

By year's end, 1872's number of deadly incidents would not turn out to be unusually large. But so many of those incidents were compressed into August and early September that Chicago did indeed seem under siege. On the first day of August, a man had been stabbed in a dispute over presidential politics at Mack's saloon, on the corner of Kinzie and Rucker. Then, two days later, out to the southwest in the Irish neighborhood of Bridgeport, a woman who interfered with a neighbor beating his wife was herself almost beaten to death. Two days after that, on August 5, early on a Monday morning and also in Bridgeport, a policeman named O'Meara was shot dead on the streets. Five days later, on August 10, a Joliet businessman was found floating in the north branch of the Chicago River, perpetrator unknown. On August 25, on the outskirts of the city, a wealthy Winnetka farmer was found dead, the crime hours or even days old, his fatal injuries caused by pistol balls "and a stone." Seven days later, on September 1, a barroom brawl over a woman led to an exchange of fatal gunfire. On September 4, another quarrel in a different saloon spilled out into the street, where a man was beaten to death. On September 5, a woman named Mary Powers who lived in the Learys' old neighborhood died from wounds inflicted by her abusive husband two weeks earlier.

Finally, on September 10, on the same day that a man named Callahan was stabbed by two ruffians on the South Side, a group of civic leaders declared that they'd seen enough. A citizens' committee had been formed and the meeting at the Board of Trade announced. The September 12 gathering was led by Henry Greenebaum, the German banker well respected across political lines whom Joseph Medill had initially proposed as candidate for mayor on the Union-Fireproof ticket. Wirt Dexter was present, as was William Butler Ogden's brother, Mahlon. Several Holdens were there, including Charles C. P. Holden and his cousin Charles N. Holden, the city tax commissioner. Many other members of the city council were present, in a nongovernmental capacity. But the meeting was also open to ordinary citizens, and the early part of the proceedings was hijacked by an otherwise unremarkable man named Beasley, first name unrecorded. Given the floor, he unleashed a torrent of abuse on the police, the judiciary, the city council, and just about everyone else in a position of authority. "I see before me a field of upturned faces," he said. "And not one is safe this night."

When Beasley threatened darkly to visit violence upon accused murderers now awaiting trial—"If the courts do not right these things, the stout arms of those present will do it," he said—Henry Greenebaum spoke up to rebuke him. While many in the crowd hooted at Greenebaum in response, a single voice rose in support. This was Michael McDermott, the notary who had worked so diligently to exonerate Kate Leary, only to inadvertently kick-start the legend of her culpability. McDermott was as open-eyed and reasonable in this situation as he'd been in the case of the Learys. But he had no more luck now. Beasley yelled over the top of him, saying that McDermott "thinks me treading on dangerous ground, but as I gaze out on this honest sea of faces, I feel they will stand by me and guard their homes."

Many of the assembled citizens, like Beasley, were there because they were angry and upset, whipped up to no small degree by the breathless crime reporting of the city's newspapers, especially the *Times.* Participants voted on three resolutions. The first resolution was "that a Citizens Committee of Twenty-five be nominated by the Chairman and ratified by this meeting, whose duty it shall be to aid the authorities in the prompt arrest, speedy trial, and sure punishment of criminals." Though the proposal was probably unconstitutional, all present except for McDermott voted in the affirmative. The next resolution called for the creation of a subscription fund for rewards, detectives, and other costs related to extra-governmental crime fighting, and it passed. A third resolution mandated that the formation of the Committee of Twenty-Five happen immediately, at this meeting, and it too was successful.

That, then, was that. But then a physician named William

Tooke offered a "digression," an after-the-fact, unscheduled fourth resolution: "Resolved, that we commend to the authorities of this city the propriety of executing faithfully the Sunday Liquor law of this city." At this, the assemblage erupted. Many laughed, roared, or hissed in disapproval, but other voices called above the din: "Good!" "That's right!" "A dry city!" A motion to open discussion on the issue of Sunday drinking was made and shut down, to more shouts. The crowd left the Board of Trade building satisfied that first steps had been taken, but a new friction had emerged.

The new crime-fighting committee began its work five days later, on September 17, 1872, in the city hall office of the tax commissioner, Charles N. Holden. Only nine of the twenty-five members were present, but they included the unusual political grouping of Charles C. P. Holden, Wirt Dexter, Anton Hesing, and Henry Greenebaum. Also attending, as a guest, was Elmer Washburn, the new chief of police, a new and unpredictable part of the city's crime-fighting equation. The Mayor's Bill, passed earlier in the year, allowed Medill to remove and install the chiefs of fire and police without consulting the board of commissioners, and with this new authority he had appointed Washburn at the end of July, at the urging of Dexter and several other Union-Fireproof leaders, who had long considered the outgoing superintendent both inept and corrupt.

Washburn had been for many years the warden of the state prison at Joliet, which made him a particularly controversial choice in that he'd never been part of a police department at any level. His appointment from so far outside the rank and file was bound to cause trouble with the police force and its commissioners, and in the end it did. But for many in the Union-Fireproof bloc that was part of his appeal. And the reform-minded Joseph Medill liked the idea of new brooms sweeping clean. While Washburn would do himself no favors with his ham-handed management of the force— within days of starting on the job, he began meddling with his officers' working hours, precinct assignments, and uniforms—it was his bad luck that the concentrated pace of murders began shortly after his appointment.

Like many of the civic leaders at the previous week's meeting, Washburn blamed the summer's spate of violence on what he perceived as the city's revolving-door courts, the kind of charge one might expect from a former prison warden. He told the group that during his first few weeks on the job he'd heard his police officers saying that it was no use making arrests if the perpetrators weren't quickly and soundly punished. This wasn't entirely fair to the courts: murders and other violent acts tended to result in convictions, especially when backed by police testimony, but there was no doubt that the number of men in prison at any given time trailed the number of arrests in the city by a very wide margin.

The discussion next turned to the subject of graft and cronyism on the police force. For as long as a full-time, professional department had existed in Chicago, since 1855, a kind of gentleman's bargain had held: for the city council to release the police department's full appropriation, an expectation existed that its aldermen would be able to place a certain number of names into consideration for hiring. It was a little political machine, active in all twenty wards and across partisan boundaries, that didn't rise to the level of gross corruption. But neither did it produce an entirely professional force. No one disputed this.

Anton Hesing weighed in, saying that he'd had to pull strings to get criminal cops out of the department. Henry Greenebaum concurred with his fellow German that the force needed discipline and weeding. Then Hesing added that the city's policemen could stand to present a better personal appearance. The committee debated the issue of on-duty dress for a while—until another member of the Twenty-Five, the public works commissioner, Louis Wahl, who with his brother owned a Bridgeport glue factory and who was also an inspector of jails and a member of the Relief and Aid Society, offered a set of complaints that began to move the meeting away from its original purpose and drive a wedge between many of its most influential participants.

First, Wahl complained about omnibus racing on Wabash Avenue. Sometimes the buses raced four abreast, he said, and added that there was "never a policeman on that street." The others agreed that the drivers should be arrested. "There is another thing I want to say," Wahl announced. The resolution against Sunday liquor sales, hooted down at the citizens' meeting at the Board of Trade, he said, was "a valuable one." Whiskey, he added, "is at the bottom of nearly all the crime in the city." For good measure, he added, "it is always on or after Sunday that crimes are committed."

The Germans Greenebaum and Hesing had seen this routine before. Temperance movements were hardy perennials in nineteenth-century America. But what seemed to be the customary rhetoric of prohibition advocates was never customary if you were an immigrant. Both men understood Wahl's accusations, and the doctor Tooke's, to be an attack not on drinking per se but on German culture, all the more offensive because Wahl was German himself. The temperance forces were always far louder about beer in saloons than an after-work whiskey in a posh private residence, and beer, whether Wahl or anyone else liked it or not, was central to the German and Irish experiences in America.

Saloons and beer halls were far more than places to drink; they were restaurants, dance halls, lyceums, meeting halls, and gathering spots all in one. Most of all, they were a connection to old-country traditions stretching back centuries. Neighborhoods coalesced around drinking establishments, where personal connections were made and deepened. Business was decided. Politics was argued. For most of the laborers and small-shop proprietors of Chicago, Sunday was their only day off, the only day that belonged to them, theirs to do with as they pleased. Closing a saloon on Sunday was much more than an interruption of their drinking; it was tantamount to a constitutional violation, a denial of their freedom to assemble.

"The German who goes to church Sunday morning, and to a lager-beer garden in the afternoon, has a right to have his opinions respected," said Hesing. "We should teach the Puritanical element that Sunday afternoon can be pleasantly and orderly spent." Greenebaum pointed out, accurately, that only one of the murders that had precipitated the citizens' meeting had happened on a Sunday. Hesing added that if anyone wanted to examine the effects of excess drinking, they should first examine the problems of poverty and domestic abuse and not public lawlessness. "Burglars, pickpockets, and gamblers—such men as carried concealed weapons and committed the murders—are not drunkards," he said. He raised his voice and confronted Wahl face-to-face, saying that "nothing will be gained by restricting the saloon business."

Speaking for the overworked laborers who made up much of the German population, Hesing asked Wahl on what other day were they free to drink. Far more important to better regulate the saloons, he said, than to close them. Raise the price of a license and exercise the existing Illinois law that provided sanctions for "ill-governed" places of drinking. Those measures were sensible, and something his newspaper had always supported. But do not, he said, place any blame on ordinary working Chicagoans who just wanted a place to drink and talk and do business on their one day off.

There was so much heat in Hesing's part of the conversation that Wirt Dexter cut him off and asked everyone to leave aside the topic of Sunday drinking and stay focused on the real issues of judicial and departmental reform. Wahl retreated, but his was not a solitary voice, and what was the "real issue" was now in serious question. Like the doctor Tooke and like Beasley, the speaker whose anticrime harangue temporarily hijacked the meeting at the Board of Trade on September 12, Wahl, whatever his heritage, spoke for a large swath of the native-born population, the kinds of men and women who had populated the Know-Nothing Party in the 1850s and 1860s and who still felt that immigrant populations crowding drinking houses and speaking foreign languages were nothing but a recipe for violence and unrest.

For today at least, Wahl's voice was easily squelched. But others wouldn't be. A new temperance committee—or, as it called itself, the Committee of Fifteen—appointed itself after the mass meeting at the Board of Trade that had formed the Committee of Twenty-Five. Made up mostly of old-line Yankee Protestant clergymen, they represented one outpost of a temperance movement that held national meetings, formed local chapters, and operated a very active media machine for spreading the word far and wide. As many people pointed out even at the time, the temperance advocates were akin to the women's suffrage movement in their radical aims, canny use of the newspapers, and willingness to be patient. Dismissed with as much derision as those seeking the vote for women, the temperance people were just as determined and just as impossible to cow.

On the afternoon of October 2, 1872, three weeks after the meeting at the Board of Trade and one week before the first anniversary of the Great Fire, the members of the Committee of Fifteen packed themselves into Joseph Medill's office. Its title aside, the committee numbered twenty or so, and one by one they were introduced by their leader and spokesman, the Reverend Abbott E. Kittredge, pastor at the Third Presbyterian Church on the lower West Side. All were there to ask the mayor "how far the law would support temperance," meaning: Would Medill do what they felt was his job and order the city's saloons closed every Sunday?

Kittredge and his companions professed to speak for a progressive political movement, but also for the "moral men" of the city. In their quest to redeem souls, they said, they needed help from the strong arm of the city's government. The meeting at the Board of Trade might have concluded that judicial reform was the key to tamping down the recent spike in crime, but the men standing before Joseph Medill disagreed, believing that "the flood of violence and murder and vice" was the result of the "neglect of that law," meaning the Sunday-closing law, and of little else.

Medill too wanted morality to guide the affairs of Chicago. But that was where the similarity between himself and the men assembled before him ended. Medill believed that politics and religion could and should operate in their own spheres, the one offering enlightened policy and the other spiritual guidance on separate tracks, as it were. The mayor simply did not believe that a municipal ban on Sunday drinking would produce whatever outcome these men desired. He understood well that these men did not want *any* drinking at all and were going to start by trying to end Sunday drinking in saloons because ending Sunday drinking in saloons was the only measure available to them at this moment.

The mayor began by asking the assembled ministers if they'd read the law, because he, of course, had. Chicago's Sunday liquor statute, in place since 1845, mandated that saloons close on Sundays and contained two provisions for punishment: the mayor could fine someone for keeping a saloon open, or he could revoke the license. The law also allowed citizens to bring a charge against a place of business. Medill knew this, and he also knew that in the year he'd been mayor, the citizens of Chicago "had done nothing in any instance" to make any complaints. There were systems in place, trip wires available to the public to prevent Sunday drinking from getting out of hand, and the public had not seen fit to trip them. He told the temperance committee that "it is the duty of every good citizen to execute the laws: it was just as much a moral duty for them as it was for me."

When Medill felt himself in the right—as he did all of the time—he was happy to confront a group such as this, even enjoyed the experience. When addressing a large crowd in an outdoor space, he was sometimes so quiet as to be almost inaudible. It was not a style tailor-made to sway or inspire multitudes, but it was a splen-did style to use in smaller meetings with people whose opinions he held in low regard. The mayor's power in regard to the saloons, he told them, was not much greater than any citizen's. Medill nei-ther drank nor smoked, he said, and could in all honesty announce his sympathy with the temperance movement's credo of personal responsibility. But he also valued tangible results. Medill believed in the persuasion of voters followed by legislation, not through the absolute enforcement of laws the greater mass of Chicagoans wouldn't respect or obey.

One of the mayor's great strengths, born during his early days as a prospective student of the law, was his knowledge of the everyday particulars of any sticky political question. The penalties attached to the Sunday ordinance were the extent of his powers. A saloon could be punished for staying open on Sunday, he said, but no provision existed that could force it to close. An Illinois state law prohibited the "keeping of ill-governed tippling houses" and pro-vided for grand jury proceedings against any accused proprietor, but a saloon must be clearly established as "ill-governed" for such an action to be taken. And, Medill repeated, "there has not been, since I was elected, a solitary complaint against or conviction of a saloon-keeper at the insistence of a citizen."

No one could have argued against the proposition that the various social machineries of the city ran on alcohol. On the length of Randolph Street alone, the street Medill had walked on the night of the fire, there were 240 saloons in eight South Side blocks, an average of 30 saloons per block. Chicago's thirst for building, and now for rebuilding, went hand in hand with another kind of thirst. The mayor's answers were rich in sarcasm, winning him no friends in the room. "I think the police are strong enough to shut up the front doors," he said, "but they cannot prevent whiskey selling." When one of the ministers asked if everyone who went through the back door could be arrested, Medill responded, again, "We haven't force enough to do that." His exasperation showed through the entire conversation. Reverend Kittredge and the other representatives of the temperance committee wanted to believe that a police force made of fewer than five hundred men, as underfunded as the fire department had ever been, could enforce a sober population on Sundays by closing *three thousand* saloons.

Even closer to the mayor's thrifty, reformist heart, he was not eager to spend even a penny of the city's money to change the situation, much less the sums that would be necessary to fund a police force large enough to keep all the saloons closed all over the city. He cited the example of Brooklyn: with a far larger number of policemen, in a smaller city, they couldn't begin to halt Sunday drinking, as he'd seen firsthand on a visit in the era before the Civil War. "While the front doors were apparently shut," he explained, "the saloons were open and liquor flowed as usual," and after a six-week trial, after "a desperate and the severest effort ever made in this country to enforce a Sunday liquor law, it was given up in despair."

Medill could have talked all day, but after an hour Kittredge and the Committee of Fifteen went away, unsatisfied and not a bit dissuaded. One of Medill's chief weaknesses was that he overestimated the persuasive power of cold logic and clever rhetoric, a trait that was perhaps forgivable in an editorialist but caused him no end of difficulty as mayor. Six days later the temperance committee responded to him with a "report," published in the *Tribune*, the *Times*, and other newspapers, that vivisected Medill's leadership.

"The Mayor saw fit to administer a rebuke to the pastors and churches of the city for their failures in duty," they wrote. "The rebuke was ill-timed and wholly unmerited." The *Tribune*'s decision to publish the temperance committee's jeremiad against one of its own owners was not unusual. It was good press and it sold papers. Besides, as Medill knew it would, the temperance men's move to bring the argument onto his own journalistic ground played right into his hands and gave him a sizable advantage in fighting back. His rebuttal to Kittredge and the other clergy appeared in the *Tribune* three days later, but not in the form of yet another editorial. Rather, he framed his response as an interview with an impartial reporter, one summoned by Medill himself. The questions came in just as the mayor wanted them to come in, and he had his answers ready:

> The fundamental error of these gentlemen is, in placing their trust entirely in carnal weapons or on physical force to reform habits of inebriation and cure the appetite for alcohol, which shows a sad deficiency of faith in moral and spiritual agencies, in combatting evil. The Inquisition was based on the same lack of faith in the efficiency of these means to cure heresy in dogma.

Something in the demands of the clergy of the temperance committee, much like the demands of Wirt Dexter, stirred up the latent Irish in Joseph Medill. The mayor wanted a point proven and knew how he would do it. Having compared the opponents of Sunday drinking to Roman inquisitors, he surprised every one of the temperance men by calling their bluff. He would accede to their request. In a directive aimed at the police commissioners, who were well understood to want no part of trying to close every saloon in the city, Medill wrote, with undisguised sarcasm, "I am happy to learn that you anticipate no difficulty in stopping liquor drinking in

the saloons on Sunday if an order is issued to that effect. I, therefore, and hereby issue said order, and ask your Board to enforce
Section 4, of Chapter 25, of the city ordinances, and all other ordinances related thereto."

As a teetotaler himself, Medill might have preferred the idea of
a dry city, but above all he was a Chicago man, every bit as much as
William Butler Ogden or Charles C. P. Holden or Marshall Field.
He wasn't as wealthy as many of his friends, and he didn't spend
his Sundays drinking with the city's laborers or anyone else, but
he knew his home city well and he knew that closing the saloons
was not going to work. But the proof, as so often for Medill, would
have to rest in the pudding. He wanted resolution, and if making
his point needed the exertion and exasperation of a fruitless effort,
so be it.

"The experiment," he wrote, "will be tried on Sunday next."

THE MUSIC most associated with the German population was orchestral, one indication of their superior social standing among immigrants. And the most famous musician in America—as famous in his own way as Charles Dickens—was a charismatic, precocious thirty-six-year-old German named Theodore Thomas. At fourteen, Thomas had toured the United States, performing Bach and Brahms on the piano. As his fame grew, he'd formed his own orchestra and toured as his own ticket agent, acting as a master of ceremonies as much as a conductor and playing most of the piano solos himself. On the Monday night of the Great Fire, he was to have opened the renovated Crosby's Opera House with a gala concert. Crosby's had burned with the rest of downtown. Now, one year later, Thomas was back.

His venue was the newly opened Aiken's Theatre on the south edge of the burned district downtown, a much smaller space than Crosby's, but one possessed of the cardinal virtue of being open. Its exterior was still unpainted, but its seats were upholstered, its boxes carpeted, and its lobby finished, and this made it the most glamorous concert hall in the city. The announcement of Thomas's appearance, published just a week earlier, had led to a mad rush at the box office for tickets, and the conductor didn't disappoint. For more than three and a half hours, he supplied three virtuoso helpings of Wagner—an artist he'd brought to prominence in America—three of Beethoven, two each of Strauss and Schubert, and a sampling of Liszt, Schumann, and Weber.

The concert was only one marker of the Great Fire's first anniversary. The city reveled in its progress. The figurative reconstruction of the country was not going well—news of the violent rise of the Ku Klux Klan in South Carolina appeared in Chicago newspapers every day—but the physical and metaphysical reconstruction of Chicago was, to all outward appearances, a smashing success. "At last the revolving seasons have brought around the anniversary of that day, more memorable than all others in the history of Chicago," crowed the *Tribune*. "The years of its prosperity will be numbered from the hour when it was believed that it was ruined, that its site was to remain desolate, and its trade and commerce to be parceled out among the neighboring communities." Not a single soul believed that such an absolute danger had existed, but it sounded good.

Not to be outdone, the *Times* opined that "a winter's snows soon fell upon our ruins, but a summer's sun warmed them into life again, and the first anniversary of that great event exhibits to the world a resurrection more wonderful than was the city's taking off." Wednesday, October 9, was a day of tale-telling: "Everyone had an experience to relate, and everybody related it." Numerous American flags bedecked numerous construction derricks. Churches held celebratory services, bells tolling. The entire week was treated for hundreds of miles in every direction as a sort of regional holiday, and the city hosted an influx of visitors from single-day railroad destinations—Milwaukee, St. Paul, Cincinnati, St. Louis—who rode and walked around the city and gawked. Residents too rode the streets or hired carriages, acting as tour guides for out-of-towners.

With the city in such a spirited and celebratory mood, it was strange that snuffing out public gatherings would be its next item of attention, but on the morning of October 13, Medill's Sunday-closing "experiment" was to begin. The impetus behind enforcement of the old and moribund law might have come from the temperance committee, but the mayor would receive the credit, for good or for ill. His day began when a "noted liquor-dealer, proprietor of an extensive West Side billiard parlor," called at the mayor's office to offer Medill a bargain: the liquor dealer would present himself at the police court every Monday morning and hand over $100, "on condition that the police authorities would not interfere with him, or prevent his keeping his establishment open on Sunday."

The dollar amount was not random; this was the maximum fine for a first violation of the existing Sunday-closing ordinance. Whoever this unnamed "liquor-dealer" was, his gesture managed to make three points all at once. First, the penalties under the current law, wielded by the mayor in an unmediated executive capacity, were a ripe opportunity for graft. Second, the offer was a marker of the amount of money to be made selling liquor on a single day; in effect, the man visiting the mayor's office was offering to pay the city a $5,200 sin tax each year to keep the liquor pouring. If Medill could have found ten such men—and this would have been easy to do—$52,000 in additional money for the city would have been more than enough, for one example, to pay for a year's worth of necessary repairs to the fire department's engines, hose, and telegraph system. Third, the offer made the point that no one, outside the temperance groups, was taking the situation all that seriously.

Besides, the city had been through all this before. Memories were short in Chicago, but a little remembering might have served the opponents of Sunday drinking well. What was soon to happen on the streets of the city could be called many things—a celebration, a protest, a demonstration, a carnival—but what had happened seventeen years earlier had been an urban crisis. The Lager Beer Riot, it was called, and it had been one of the signature events in a city whose history had now been partly effaced by the Great Fire.

In 1855, Chicago's mayor, Levi Boone, a distant cousin of Daniel Boone, had taken dead aim at the growing influx of immigrants by trying to enforce an old and never-used prohibition on Sunday drinking that had stood since 1845. For years new German arrivals had skirted fines and prison by locking the front doors of their saloons on Sundays, entering the back, and keeping the blinds drawn, until Boone decided to fight back by raising the annual cost of a saloon license from $50 to $300, well out of the reach of most immigrant proprietors. The Germans and Irish rioted. One policeman was shot and had to have his arm amputated, while one of the rioters was killed. The violence shocked the city, and the issue of Sunday saloon closings was pushed far into the political background, where it had remained for another seventeen years—until now.

Sunday, October 13, the first day of Medill's order, was light on news. To untutored eyes, in fact, the mayor's experiment seemed to be a rousing success. The Committee of Fifteen and its supporters roamed the drinking districts of the city bearing tablets of paper, writing down the names of saloons that stayed open—nabbing only a few—and noting a greater number that pretended to be closed while leaving a back door ajar. "Some few places were really closed, while many others had their blinds closed, shutters up, curtains drawn," wrote the *Times*. "In some places the keyholes were carefully stuffed with paper, or in other equally significant ways suggested that the latch string of the back door was hanging out for the benefit of old customers." Still, even if Saturday the twelfth had been a heavier drinking night than usual, Sunday the thirteenth saw the vast majority of the city's saloons go dark. The temperance groups spent the week congratulating themselves and praising the mayor, believing that they had achieved a victory.

The next Sunday told a very different story. As it turned out, the previous weekend had been for the saloon keepers and regular drinkers of Chicago a reconnaissance, not the battle. The Committee of Fifteen had not been testing the saloons, but the opposite. On October 20, the weather was "warm and genial," unlike the thirteenth, which had been wet and chilly. In the West Division, Zenieschek's saloon, one of the largest and best known in the city, kicked off the festivities at three o'clock in the morning by opening its doors wide and lighting a string of lanterns to ward off the dark, "the design of the proprietors evidently being to make their defiance of the law as complete as possible." The police came by before dawn, took statements and names from witnesses—most of whom were temperance advocates—and went away.

By dawn, crowds filled streets all over the city. The counter-protest to the temperance effort for many was to get as drunk as

possible as soon in the day as they could. The display of defiant ine-
briation was impressive, and before noon "men staggered or were
helped up the stairs, and rolled along the streets." As if coordinated
by a central committee—coordinated in a way no other activity
could be in the city, except perhaps the disassembly of hogs at the
Union Stock Yards or the assembly of reapers at McCormick's—
the drinkers of Chicago made an awesome show of solidarity.

At ten in the morning, five hundred saloon keepers gathered
at the far end of Milwaukee Avenue on the western edge of the
North Side, where the largest concentration of German beer halls
was located, for a procession. At their head rode an express wagon
topped with several very large kegs. Every block or so they stopped
and passed out free beer to the populace, who had gathered on
the sidewalk to proffer their glasses, mugs, and cups. The Sunday-
closing ordinance forbade the *sale* of beer *inside* any saloon, so these
saloon keepers were twice covered, in that they were giving out *free*
beer very much *outside* their establishments. The *Tribune*, disgusted
with the drunken display if mostly opposed to the effort to close the
saloons, noted that "the donors cannot be expected to have made
money by their mockery of municipal law," demonstrating that
while the *Tribune* was a pro-business paper, it didn't know everything
about business.

Legal loopholes were the undisputed heroes of the day. The
Sunday-closing law was a *city* ordinance, and so another several
thousand people participated in the age-old dodge of crossing
boundaries to a place where drinking was allowed. Groups of boisterous young men hitched teams and wagons and drove out to the
north, toward the separately incorporated town of Evanston, arriving at disreputable places called Sunnyside and Downing's. At the
terminus of the North Side Railway, also in Evanston, sat four or
five drinking houses, and hundreds more flooded these establishments and the surrounding streets.

On the South Side, rebellion took on a different cast. Here the
proprietors sat closer to power, were more wary of causing disrup-
tions on a large scale. Several saloon keepers downtown, interested

both in law and order and in healthy sales receipts, had advised their customers on Saturday to buy extra beer that day and take it home. A saloon called Phil Conley's, on Clark Street within view of the courthouse square, was open at the back, its front door locked and its windows blocked with curtains made of newspaper. Nearby, the bar at Burke's European Hotel operated as normal, but quietly. At a Dearborn Street establishment, only steak, oysters, ham, and eggs were listed on the menu, "but by 'tipping a wink' to the courteous clerk, presto, change, and a drink appeared" with "the suddenness of a stroke of lightning, and was swallowed with record speed."

As Medill knew well, the rank-and-file police wanted no part of trying to curtail the drinking habits of an entire city by way of an unloved and obsolete law. Wrote the *Tribune* of the beleaguered police officers and the Sunday-closing ordinance, "Many of them complained of the absurdity of its passage, and intimated that its appeal was merely a question of time." Even the hardiest temperance supporters couldn't expect the police to start breaking down the front doors of hundreds of German-owned establishments. "Mysterious disappearances of Teutonic gentlemen in alleys at various points," wrote one reporter, "and their reappearance at intervals ranging from three to ten minutes, inclined one to the opinion that the beer saloons were in some way accessible." The first arrest was made in the late afternoon, but the charge was public drunkenness, which was much more often enforced, especially in the more genteel sections of town, than the prohibition against being open.

Customers at Zenieschek's drank so much that the saloon, left with nothing more to sell, closed at 1:30 in the afternoon and rushed to procure more beer. The festive spirit was high and made the entire day a sort of bookend to the Great Fire. They called it the Great Reopening. Even those who obeyed the law found ways to contribute to the fun. One West Side saloon owner, in a version of many other signs in many other establishments, posted a notice that read, "Closed for the day. Grand matinee at 12 o'clock to-night. Free Lunch, Clam Chowder, and Plenty of Beer." The next morning, thousands of revelers went off to their jobs hungover and happy with the roles they'd played in a mass assertion of civic unity and civil disobedience.

There had been no fires. And no murders. As had become clear even before daybreak on this second Sunday of Medill's "experiment," the threatened enforcement of the Sunday-closing ordinance would have the opposite effect of the one intended. In their zeal to condemn the consumption of alcohol, the Group of Fifteen had created the biggest citywide celebration of drink they could have managed, or imagined—in the *Tribune*'s formulation, "a concentrated eruption of what was sought to be repressed." Sunday, October 20, was, in many ways, the best day the city had had in the past year—the day Chicago looked and felt most like itself at any time since the Great Fire. The temperance movement would not be cowed by a single day's demonstration, of course. But its political path, rocky before, now climbed uphill. Fifty years later its ideological descendants would achieve a Pyrrhic victory with the arrival of Prohibition, a victory that would do nothing in the slightest to reduce the crime and violence that had supposedly been the largest point of the effort. But for now, the city had beat the reformers back, seemingly as a single organism.

Medill's experiment had ended as he'd expected it would, but, as always, credit for the insight would elude him. Coming on the heels of the Relief and Aid Society's "investigations" of the Great Fire's victims and the bitter fight over fire limits, the Great Reopening represented far more than a day of cutting loose. It was part of a slow tectonic shift that rode underneath the city's frantic pace of rebuilding, exposing the schisms that separated the great mass of working Chicagoans from a leadership that seemed to think it knew better in every instance, that behaved as if it had the right in every instance to dictate how their lives might best be lived. As so often in Chicago, the means employed might be crude and even comic, but the ends were utterly serious.

ᴗ 33 ᴗ

O N THE MORNING of October 30, 1872, Joseph Medill and Charles C. P. Holden, among many others, boarded a train at the Kinzie Street terminal of the Chicago and North Western Railroad depot for a ride twenty-six blocks to the west. Ahead of them lay an afternoon of civic posturing that would include a long Masonic ceremony and a longer parade of self-congratulatory speechifying. In eleven cars rode Ellsworth's Zouaves in their red-and-gold chasseur caps, a delegation from the Knights Templar, several brass bands, and eight complete lodges of Masons in full regalia. With them traveled the ubiquitous German banker Henry Greenebaum and a large assortment of insurance executives, park commissioners, utility barons, real estate brokers, lawyers, and other businessmen of note.

The free ride furnished by the Chicago and North Western rail line left the station at 11:30 a.m., and within fifteen minutes it had reached its destination, a new public space named Central Park in homage to New York City's greensward of the same name—even if Chicago's version was a fraction of the size of the original and its location was nowhere close to "central." This new green space had been placed well out to the west at the end of Washington Street, past the city limits, with a view in one direction of empty suburban house lots and in the other of swaying prairie grasses. Six days a week, for six months, laborers had excavated dirt to create a man-made lake and had made that dirt into a "miniature mountain" that still dominated the setting. On the south side of the park was a copse of oak trees beside an excavation for a future lawn, while to the west were several giant holes in the ground, other ponds in the making. This was one of three new parks created under the dominion of Holden, in his capacity as West Side park commissioner, and stood as one of the city's most prized planning initiatives.

Medill, Holden, Greenebaum, and their fellow passengers disembarked from the local platform on Washington Street on a wet day, their finery hidden under dark umbrellas and dark jackets. An oversized American flag flew over the station. In the center of the emerging park stood a derrick with a large pyramidal stone hanging from its chain. About two hundred guests followed behind a procession of Masons, who fanned out around the derrick in concentric circles, with the Illinois lodge in the center, Templars in the next ring, and the members of several city lodges in the third. Many ladies had arrived in carriages, and now they emerged, umbrella-bearing servants at their sides. The mayor, the park commissioner, and the other local dignitaries "took up the best positions they could find" as spectators, and watched as the Masons stood stock-still for several minutes so that a photographer could expose a series of commemorative plates.

The idea for this entire day, in a manner appropriate to the spirit of Chicago, had been born a year earlier out of the *Tribune*'s sarcastic suggestion that the city make a monument to the Great Fire out of the safes it had charred and melted. As the mayoral election had entered its final stretch, the paper had equated these objects to the "confessedly worthless" Charles C. P. Holden and his "bummer" coalition, but the joke, it turned out, was on the newspaper—if only for a short time. For even in 1872 there were unconventional thinkers in Chicago. One of them was Holden, who certainly would have relished throwing the *Tribune*'s own snide words back at it from such an unexpected direction. Another was the architect and engineer William Le Baron Jenney, who saw that the charred safes of the city might operate not as a mockery of the city's recent trial by fire but instead as its most fitting symbol.

The idea to embed the Great Fire itself in the monument—in the form of the safes it had charred and warped—was brilliant, as was the idea of building something meaningful out of the ruin of the city. Jenney's design for a fused and stepped stack of safes and other objects saved from the fire presaged in its form the design of many of the skyscrapers that would later so distinguish the city, an achievement in which Jenney would have an important hand. The monument design also echoed and amplified the public's fascination with "relics," the reverence attached to the fire's stubborn leftovers: pieces of the courthouse bell, bits of shredded metal, children's toys found in the ruins, giant iron machinery still standing like sentinels.

William Le Baron Jenney's first design for a proposed fire moment, from the frontispiece of *The Lakeside Memorial of the Burning of Chicago*, 1872

There was a real poetry and a muscular art to Jenney's design. It was beautiful and utilitarian, in the best Chicago sense. It echoed across classes and across experiences, blending blunt realism and provocative symbolism into a single arresting and memorable form. It would have become something uniquely and memorably specific to Chicago.

In spite of its affinity with the city's own image of itself—or because of it—Jenney's design stood no chance. The decision makers of Chicago were too timid and artistically conservative to approve such an unconventional form of monument. Holden's fellow park commissioners heard Jenney out, considered his proposal for a few weeks, and then asked him to design something "classic" instead. He responded with an idea for a forgettable and uninspiring columned arcade inside which would rest marble tablets bearing a list of the names of cities that had donated to the relief effort and, in true Chicago fashion, "the sums donated." Above the arcade would rise a Gothic spire topped with "a female figure holding aloft in both hands a flaming torch," reminiscent of Thomas Crawford's *Statue of Freedom*, which had been raised to the top of the U.S. Capitol dome nine years earlier.

This tame and unoriginal second design was what Medill and Holden were here to help commemorate. Not that they could perceive the eventual shape of the structure, for all they saw was the single large capstone hanging from a chain. The new monument was nowhere close to fruition. The excursion was an exercise in pomp and circumstance and little else, an excuse to gather, celebrate the anniversary of the fire, and brag about how big that fire had been. The grand master of the Illinois lodge opened with a speech that sought to put Chicago's tragedy into a rather broad historical perspective: on October 30, 1003, BC, he said, King Solomon had dedicated a temple at Jerusalem, and now, 2,875 years later, the collected Chicagoans were "assembled to lay the cornerstone of a monument to commemorate the most direful calamity that ever befell a people."

Robert Collyer, grand chaplain of the Illinois lodge, pastor of the Unity Church, and fervent Union-Fireproof supporter, offered a prayer. Then the grand treasurer of that same lodge brought out a large box and listed its contents, all of which were to be entombed within the monument as a time capsule to mark the era of the Great Fire. The collection of items included many planning documents from Holden and the other West Side park commissioners. Photographs of the stone itself were included, along with the eleventh annual report of the Board of Public Works. The box also held a small piece of cast iron from the courthouse bell that had fallen into the basement of the building, copies of several newspapers, the initial report of the Relief and Aid Society, maps of the city showing the burned area, a narrative of the city's history up to 1872, and, for good measure, a record of the current volume of railroad traffic into and out of the city.

The eclectic hodgepodge of objects made an odd kind of sense, serving as it did as a representation of the city's mania for planning, counting, and building. Words were spoken, the box was inserted in the stone, and then the stone was lowered to the ground, where it sat like a large toad lost atop an unfamiliar pond. Jenney, responsible for the design of the park and of the fire monument, gave the stone a swipe of cement and then presented the trowel and other tools to the grand master. Much ceremony followed as the stone was festooned with corn, symbol of nourishment; wine, symbol of plenty; and oil, symbol of joy. A gavel was struck three times. Then a song:

> *Heavenward point the shaft,*
> *Prov'd by the Ancient Craft;*
> *While loftier spire,*
> *Tells from a deeper base,*
> *How love, with saving grace,*
> *Came promptly to efface*
> *Chicago's Fire.*

The Masonic portion of the ceremony complete, Medill now stepped forward to provide an uncharacteristically short contribution. "People are apt to forget the most stupendous of events," he

said. "In one short year half the horrors of the fire have been obliterated, and at the end of another no trace will be visible to the eye
of the destruction that swept over the city on that eventful October
night." He praised the design of the monument and finished by
speaking of a fight against forgetfulness:

> In other cities monuments are raised to keep green in the minds
> of the people the great deeds of heroes and statesmen which
> would otherwise be forgotten, and here will stand that noble spire
> pointing over the plain, to perpetuate the triumph of energy and
> enterprise, an example worthy of emulation to the end of time.

In a cynical piece of commentary published the next day, the
Tribune cast doubts on the prospects for the monument's eventual
completion: "The day and hour when the last brick shall be laid,
the last nail driven, and the Western metropolis, finished and complete, shall rise to her full stature without one stain of the ashes of
the conflagration upon her garments, we will not attempt to determine." In the end, Medill's paper would be proven right. The monument would never be completed. Chicago was full of landmarks
that told people where they were and helped them to get where they
were going, but the idea of monuments—a record of where they
had been—held little appeal. No more than 50 people out of the
300,000 who lived in the city had seen Chicago when it was still a
trading post and an onion bog and little else. Yet that moment in
history had passed less than forty years earlier. And given the city's
youth, it was easy to view the Great Fire as the beginning of everything and not the end of anything.

Commemoration, however, was not the same thing as nostalgia. Chicago, full of people who had left one way of life behind to
embrace a headlong rush of constant activity, always had plenty
of room for nostalgia. Just a few hours after attending the dedication of the never-to-be-built memorial, Medill received a rare and
treasured respite from his official duties when he acted as host for
the annual meeting of the Western Press Association and Western Union telegraph association. Here was a bittersweet reminder

of a treasured pre-fire, preelection life that must have seemed fifty years away rather than one. Twenty men sat in a smoky room and talked of the growth of Chicago, talked about the current reach of the telegraph, and then got to drinking and reminiscing about "the early days of the telegraph as applied to news-transmission." These were all old-line editors and newspapermen, who, like frontiersmen ruing the advance of civilization, fondly remembered a time when their presses were powered by ponies rather than by steam engines, when a single paper could be as important to a town as its church, bank, or city hall. It was a sign of something that Medill wrote the *Tribune*'s small notice about the association's meeting himself. He had not been born into privilege, and his fondness for his early days never left him.

Things—telegraph wires, a line of type, the feel and texture of newsprint—mattered to Medill in direct proportion to their ability to communicate and spread ideas. To that end, proximity to power mattered, but there was something about being *in* power that never sat right with Medill; he was animated not by the mechanisms, policies, and dictates of government but rather by what those things might accomplish, and he had no comfort at all with the job's ceremonial aspects. The Mayor's Bill had given him more executive authority, but it pained him that it hadn't made him any less of a figurehead.

The next day the mayor was reminded yet again of his discomfort with the job when he was vilified in several meeting halls by the clergymen of the Temperance Union speaking to small but enthusiastic crowds. The barrage was led by the Reverend Abbott Kittredge, front man for the Committee of Fifteen, who was still stinging from Medill's sarcastic dismissal of him at their audience in the mayor's office one month before. Referring to Medill's statement that the Sunday liquor law would be enforced only so far as the people of Chicago demanded it, Kittredge said, to cheers, that "so cowardly a so-called proclamation could not be found in the annals of any city," adding, "I do not know the mayor and perhaps the mayor does not want to know me." Then the pastor offered a most unchristian admonishment: Medill, Kittredge cried, had missed the chance to "make his reputation for all time" by "plant-ing cannon in the streets" on the day of the liquor protests. "The good mayor will come up to the scratch, gradually but firmly."

No matter how much he would allow the temperance advocates their say—no matter to what degree he was a temperance advocate himself—Medill would never come up to scratch in the eyes of the forces of moral reform in Chicago, not on the issue of beer. Soon, the mayor would ask that the whole question of Sunday closings be passed along to the voters of Illinois, helping to draft a statewide referendum on the question. In the simplest and broadest possible language, Chicagoans, and the residents of every Illinois town and city, should be asked to vote "for the sale of intoxicating liquor on the Sabbath day or night" or "against the sale of intoxicating liquor on the Sabbath day or night." The vote would be binding in the absolute: if "for," it would thereafter be against the law for any city council in the state to pass any law regulating saloon hours on Sundays, and in addition any existing such laws—including Chicago's—would be rendered null and void.

Medill's new proposal was designed not to force closure of the saloons on Sunday but to ensure the issue left him alone. Most of the smaller cities and towns in the state, including Springfield, where the legislature met, had no concerns about Sunday drinking and would vote "for" in large numbers. Medill knew from close experience that the temperance groups in Chicago were a vocal lot, but he also knew that they were smaller in number than their volume made them appear and could not wage a fight against all of Illinois. Though he would never have phrased it in this way, he was conducting a holding action for the German and Irish saloon goers of the city. But even if the immigrant communities of Chi-cago understood this, their appreciation was muted. The freedom represented by their single day of assembly in the city's drinking establishments was to them an inviolable right, not a question in need of political solutions. Medill, they felt, didn't understand this point and didn't understand them. And they were beginning to wonder if they'd made the right choice to put him in office.

≈ 34 ≈

T EMPERANCE WAS not the only subject of conversation in Chicago. The new fall fashions from Paris had come in. Many miles of new railroad track were being laid, in and out of the city, promising a quick return to the city's usual lucrative bustle. The customary stream of complaints about filth and odors was referred to the Board of Health. A new public library was due to open before the end of the year, a symbol of culture and civic seriousness second to none in nineteenth-century America—if the city's leaders could agree on a place to put it. A new Western Union telegraph office opened. A convention of Universalists came to town. On November 9, 1872, a commercial warehouse in Boston caught fire and the fire spread, destroying sixty-five acres. This was less than 10 percent of the size of Chicago's blaze, but still Medill joined the rest of the northern half of the country in sending an expression of utmost sympathy and a generous promise of aid.

Meanwhile, something was wrong with the horses. They called it the "Canada disease" because it had been traced to horses transported from Toronto in the fall of 1872 that spread the affliction among their new stablemates in America, beginning on the East Coast. Chicago's animals started to take sick in late October 1872, and in just four days of transmission the Canada disease stopped all streetcar business and carriage transportation in the city. The mail shifted to hand delivery, and the city slowed to a frontier-times pace. Chicago became a walking city, and the horses coughing in their stalls created a cacophony that seemed to emerge from nowhere and everywhere all at once.

The malady was a form of equine laryngitis, and by itself it wasn't catastrophic. Transmission was rapid among horses, dogs, cats, and goats, though cows and rats seemed immune. The disease swelled and narrowed the top of the trachea, not enough to be fatal, but enough that horses couldn't work for as long as two weeks. But earlier in the year, in New York and several other cities to the east, the coughing had been the precursor to the much more serious purpura hemorrhagica, a frightening and sometimes fatal dropsy-like malady that could cause swelling of the head, belly, and limbs, in addition to flaking skin, lameness, madness, or various combinations thereof.

In the end, Chicago avoided all of the worst scenarios. A few horses died, but within six weeks the numbers of affected animals began to drop at a reassuring pace and the mail moved on time again. Carriages clattered and pedestrians once more found themselves at constant risk. Under certain rare and unpredictable circumstances, however, the purpura could be passed to humans. While the rest of the city thawed through the optimistic spring of 1873, while Lake Michigan turned azure again, a pall fell over the home of the former council president Charles C. P. Holden. His wife, Sarah, was very ill.

In October 1871, in fine health, Sarah had worked at the First Congregational Church along with Katherine Medill and others to make sure clothes and other supplies got to the victims of the Great Fire as fast as possible. In early 1872, she'd made a visit to the Holden family seat in Will County, Illinois—to the farm where she and Charles had first met many years earlier—where she fell sick with a cough that turned violent and left her exhausted and unable to return to Chicago. For the rare, exceedingly unlucky human sufferers of purpura hemorrhagica, the "horse disease," the sensitivity to touch became so acute that bedsheets and all but the softest clothes were forsaken. Sarah's temperature rose, as did her pulse rate. From that time forward, her illness subsided, then returned, again and again. Charles received reports of his wife's come-and-go agony all through the fights over the fire limits and the Sunday-closing law.

Then, in October 1872, Sarah felt better and came home to Chicago. For a time, through November, she felt well. But she was never the same as she had been before her trip to Will County. In December, her case manifested itself anew as a painful disease of the bladder. A halting recovery in the new year of 1873 was followed by the purpura's return in the spring, and this time her deterioration was swift and irreversible.

As the city continued to grow stronger, Sarah wasted away. And as she did, her husband and Joseph Medill, once friends and then enemies, performed a public dance of reconciliation. In late April 1873, the new police chief, Elmer Washburn, raised the temperature of the temperance argument tenfold when he issued General Order No. 20, which dispensed with Medill's pragmatic approach and gave the force's officers the power to nail up saloons and arrest their owners. In doing so, Washburn managed to infuriate most of the city's ethnic communities, of every nationality, and at the same time alienate its police force, which drew many of its members from those same neighborhoods. The police commissioner, Mark Sheridan, a politically powerful Irishman who was well liked by many in the force, had fought Washburn's elevation from the start, which put Medill in a bind: he didn't approve of Washburn's actions, but he'd appointed him and needed a way of appeasing the police without giving in to Mark Sheridan, who was his sworn opponent.

In a moment of epiphany that Abraham Lincoln would have appreciated, the mayor realized that a nomination of Charles C. P. Holden as Sheridan's replacement might be a good way to prevent a rank-and-file law-enforcement mutiny while at the same time providing himself with some political cover in the immigrant communities that were most upset by Washburn's heavy hand. For two months he importuned his former electoral adversary. But in June 1873, with Sarah dying, Holden turned down Medill's offer for the last time. It was not the only position Holden refused after his retirement from the council. From the outside, his withdrawal from view was hard to understand: here was a public servant who for decades had seemed happy immersed in the rough-and-tumble of an engaged civic life. But soon enough news spread of Sarah's condition, and the wondering ceased.

On the morning of July 26, 1873, Sarah Holden's body gave out. She had had a long time to get ready for her passing, as had Charles, and she had taken solace in a newfound embrace of religion. The following Monday morning, Sarah's funeral was held in the Holden house. It was a small and quiet affair, attended by family, family friends, and a select few aldermen and other civic figures. She was only thirty-seven when she died, but she and Charles had been married more than half of her life.

It was ironic that Charles had said a firm goodbye to Chicago's elected politics by this point, because the winds were once again blowing in his direction. By the time of Sarah's funeral, it was already clear that the next election would be very bad for the Union-Fireproof coalition. Medill had done himself no favors with his original stance on the question of fire limits, and he was still the subject of hard feelings resulting from his threat-filled talk at the May 15 trade unions demonstration the year before. And though his compromise positions on Sunday closings, the Cincinnati soup houses, and the Relief and Aid Society had sometimes leaked into public view—positions that, closely examined, often aligned with opposition views as much as with the business aristocracy, or at least spoke to his willingness to seek useful compromises—Medill would forever be branded by association.

The perception among Chicago's poor and foreign-born residents, one supported by most of the available evidence, was that the Union-Fireproof coalition had promised one thing and then, once in office, pursued quite another, much broader agenda. They had presented themselves as an apolitical, multi-partisan collection of accomplished city managers, ready and able to guide Chicago back to its strong, confident self, and then they'd drawn stark sides in an effort to take whatever power they could away from the city's working class, which relied on the city council and its various boards for whatever influence it could muster. The Union-Fireproofers had also spent a lot of time talking about Boss Tweed and graft without providing much concrete evidence of the same in Chicago, and this galled them as well.

Politics not only made strange bedfellows; it could also alter one's relationship to the familiar ones. In July 1873, one week before Sarah Holden's death, Medill made the formal and all but customary announcement that he wouldn't run for reelection. One day after that announcement, Anton Hesing, Medill's old friend and fellow editor, turned the world of journalism in Chicago upside down by publishing in his paper, the German-language *Staats-Zeitung*, a blistering condemnation of Medill's mayorship and a clarion call to Germans to reject the Republican Party in the next election.

It was not enough for Hesing that Medill would not run again. Medill's entire party needed to be repudiated, and this made the terms of Hesing's condemnation severe:

> [Medill] is the principal representative of that weakness and perfidy which, in its yielding to a family of base fanatics, and Know-Nothings, and common hypocrites, contracts and oppresses personal and social freedom in Chicago, and at a time when harmony among the citizens is more indispensable than ever before, has substituted, in the place of the good feeling and the tolerance which formerly prevailed among the different nationalities of Chicago, the opposites, of bitterness and discord.

Just two years earlier, Hesing and his *Staats-Zeitung* had endorsed Medill's run for mayor, a personal and journalistic affirmation that had gone a long way to assure Medill's margin of victory among the Germans, and therefore in the election itself. Now Hesing charged that Medill had contradicted himself and his ideals in the service of a base ambition for higher office, though, he added, "what particular jewel Medill has in his eye, he does not say." This was a sea change in the politics of the city, and Chicago's German community began in 1873 to fall away from the Republican Party they had supported so loyally since Lincoln's nomination for president thirteen years earlier. More ominously for the Republicans, Hesing began for the first time to coordinate with Dan O'Hara and the

344 · SCOTT W. BERG

other Democrats who made up the city's Irish political leadership, nurturing a heretofore impossible partnership.

The entire scenario, in a different season, would have been a perfect vehicle for Charles C. P. Holden to assert his relevance anew, either as a candidate for mayor or as the force behind a handpicked proxy. Fireproofing seemed to be a concern of the past, and the idea of "union" had proved a chimera. With prosperity and a sense of normality returning, with the rebuilding city providing jobs in abundance, with the Relief and Aid Society's barracks dismantled and the city dotted from one end to another with rebuilt pinewood houses, the clamor for public relief had all but vanished. What had seemed a summer of murder now seemed in hindsight more like the city's usual ration of arbitrary violence, unconnected to the question of whether saloons were or weren't open on Sundays. But as the state of crisis receded, one overarching impression remained for many of Chicago's less well-off voters: using the excuse of the Great Fire, Medill's administration, and even more so the Union-Fireproof leaders who had lifted him to power, had tried to push the city's hardworking bedrock population out onto the prairie, had tried to close their saloons, and had tarred them as shiftless, lazy layabouts. A new group of business leaders, organized by the indefatigable and widely disliked Wirt Dexter, was already beginning to constitute itself as a "law and order" party. A transparent sop to the temperance crusaders, theirs was a losing message.

By late summer 1873, as Sarah Holden was laid to rest, it was becoming clear that in November Chicago's working-class neighborhoods would vote with a vengeance. The Germans and Irish and Bohemians were well housed and employed, thanks to the construction boom and the continued influx of tourists and business visitors to the city. Their saloons remained open on Sunday, and there they talked about the need for political change, providing the city's working-class neighborhoods with an ever more expansive and more secure sense of unity and community. Primed by the fights of the past eighteen months, those neighborhoods were ready to vote, and not for anything called a "law and order" ticket.

It was a deep irony, then, that Medill's own political reckoning went hand in glove with the end of electoral politics for Charles C. P. Holden, who would go on to a productive career in real estate, finance his own business and real estate ventures, and play an instrumental role in the making of the Chicago and Illinois River Railroad. Holden stayed on the job as West Side park commissioner and would later take a post with the Cook County Board of Commissioners. But all of this was tame, unexciting fare for a man whose political battles had for so long been fought at the center of the action.

In Holden's exit from the front pages of Chicago's newspapers, he had some interesting company. All at once, it seemed, a group of once highly visible men began to recede, as if the Great Fire and its attendant arguments had erased them from view. The most notable was William Butler Ogden, who had already returned to New York City, to his orchards and his view of the Hudson River, and would seldom be seen in Chicago again. In 1875, Ogden would marry for the first time, to a wealthy widow named Marianna Tuttle Arnot, twenty years younger than him, a perfect social and temperamental match. Two years after that he would be dead of kidney failure, and in the absence of any children his personal fortune would be dispersed to several dozen people and institutions, most of them not in Chicago.

Most surprising of all, though, was the sudden and complete retreat of Joseph Medill from public life. When he announced his decision in the summer of 1873 not to run again for mayor that November, he'd already decided, privately, to take a much more dramatic step. Medill was worn out by the mayorship, so worn out that he'd decided to quit before the end of his term. And, having decided to quit, he also decided to abandon Chicago altogether.

PART VIII

Fire

❧ 35 ❧

ON AUGUST 1, 1873, six days after Sarah Holden's passing, a young woman walked into a South Side police precinct and asked to speak with the police commissioner, Mark Sheridan. It turned out that she had a lot to say about the fire marshal, Robert Williams. Williams was the man who had run all over the Learys' neighborhood on the first night of the Great Fire trying to coordinate the actions of a few damaged and late-arriving engines, to no avail. He had been the man with the most to gain from the whitewashed departmental inquiry, and indeed, he was the biggest beneficiary of the ceaseless attention paid to Kate Leary's fictional culpability. Williams was still called a lot of names in the press, but anyone in charge of anything in Chicago was called a lot of names in the press. Through it all, he'd kept his job and even flourished—until now.

The woman's name was Uphemia Hallock, and her husband had until recently been a fireman. She said her piece to Sheridan, which led the commissioner to call for Williams himself. After a short wait, then, Hallock told her story in front of the fire marshal, two police commissioners, and a reporter for the *Times*. Williams called her a liar and blackmailer, in response to which she produced an affidavit sworn before a notary public that outlined, in detail, the history of Williams's carnal relations with her. The details included regular trips to "an assignation house," a diagnosis of venereal disease, and regular payments of hush money. "I love him yet," she added, "though I try to hate him."

Williams protested, but Commissioner Sheridan happened to be in possession of a similar letter from the wife of another fireman, and it was—apparently—a rule in Chicago that one accusation against a public official of Williams's stature might be ignored, but not two. For good measure, Hallock offered to provide the names of other firemen's wives "whom he has seduced," and took an oath before a notary that the fire chief had, "during the past three years, been holding carnal intercourse with me, having promised to keep and protect, and never leave me." Inquiries to a bank that same evening confirmed Williams's payments to the woman—and evidence of such payments to other spouses of other firemen. The chief, who had several drivers at his call and access to every fireman's weekly schedule, was well known for his travels around the city—travels now revealed as something more suspicious than simple visits to the force's various engine houses.

The next morning, Joseph Medill fired Robert Williams. Then he sent a note to Mathias Benner informing him that he was appointed acting fire marshal, effective immediately, until such time as the mayor could put in a new nomination for the permanent position. For Benner, this was a lot to absorb. That morning he'd awakened as assistant marshal, a position he'd held for years with no immediate expectation of advancement. By noon, he was chief of the entire force. And, most improbably of all, before the night was through, he would be tested as no brand-new department chief had ever been tested—for it was time for Chicago to have another big fire.

Field & Leiter's new retail building had begun to rise in May 1873, after the season's ice and snow had melted and the lot on the corner of State and Washington was cleared of debris. A lease was signed later in the summer with the Singer sewing machine company, which bought the lot from Potter Palmer for an astonishing $350,000. Groundbreaking was delayed by a wrangle with the insurance company regarding the building's proposed mansard roofs, which held and trapped heat in dangerous ways that made fighting a fire far more difficult. In the end, practicalities won out:

no mansard roofs. That insurance tussle most likely saved the day for Marshall Field, and it might even have saved Benner's new job.

The best guess as to the cause of the Field & Leiter fire of August 2, 1873, is that a roofer had left his small soldering fire burning and that a hot coal had fallen on the exposed lath below. There were consolations to a fire starting on the roof of a tall building, even the tallest building in the city. For one, the smoke from the building was visible almost instantly, which allowed for the quick evacuation of workers in the surrounding blocks and little confusion as to where the fire engines should go. In addition, post–Great Fire repairs and modifications to the system of telegraph relays had made it hum with efficiency so that when the alarm box was sounded, engines from all over the South Side were dispatched within seconds rather than minutes. Still, by the time Benner rode up to the building in his marshal's cart at about five o'clock, barking his orders through his speaking horn, a dismaying effusion of smoke was pouring up and out of the building's uppermost story.

The structure's magnificent height, six stories, also had its drawbacks. Several hoses burst trying to carry water to the top of the building from the top of the hook and ladder, and for the first thirty minutes of the fight a single stream played on the building, without much effect. The smoke began to thicken, a bad sign. But soon the firemen succeeded in hauling a single line of hose all the way up to the top of the building so that its stream didn't have to leap several stories to work on the flames but could be poured down from above instead.

Benner's satisfaction at this development was interrupted by a pack of boys and girls who decided to run in the doors of the burning building "in a spirit of bravado worthy only of the most thoughtless and desperate." Some in the crowd shouted alarm, some tsked, and others cheered. The police superintendent, Elmer Washburn, arrived, followed by a squad of men, and they ran into the building after the children even as the firemen worked far above them. Some of their quarry escaped; others were removed by force.

As so often at a big blaze, the chaos on the surrounding streets was just short of unmanageable. South of the new construction, at the end of the rebuilt city track, fifty or so streetcars unable to get out of their berths—and blocked in any case by the supply hose lying across the track—were pressed together in a bunch. One conductor jumped his vehicle off the rails and got it moving in the other direction, to the south. Most of the passengers stuck in the logjam got out and walked, though some stayed in their seats and watched through the windows, content to pay their fare for a longer-than-anticipated trip home, given the unexpected bonus of a big fire. Others climbed aboard the motionless omnibuses to watch. Should they wait in their seats long enough, they might even receive a free ride through the city that night.

Next door to the burning building, one of downtown's several dozen brand-new business blocks was rising. By the time the second alarm was called in, hundreds of spectators had moved into that unfinished shell of a building. Some sat in the window openings on the side facing the burning store, waving to friends below. Piles of wood, brick, and other building materials sat on the surrounding streets and empty lots, and men and women and children filled every available space. A carriage flew past the scene at a dangerous speed, but two alert laborers grabbed the pair of spooked horses by their heads and forced them away from the crowd, cursing the driver's incompetence as they did so.

Despite the blessed absence of so much as a light breeze, the first challenge of Benner's tenure as chief was a big one. The space between the ceiling of the sixth floor and the roof was narrow and enclosed, and the fire was trapped within, getting hotter and hotter by the minute and threatening to blow the lid off Field & Leiter's. Such an explosion could kill many of the firemen on the roof and a number of the spectators below at the same time. So Benner improvised. Though he was later blamed for taking too long to form a plan—even on his first day on the job he must have understood that he would always be blamed for something—once the idea came to his mind, it worked so well that it served as a vindication of his elevation to the top post in the department.

He ordered his men to cut small holes in the roof and jam their pipe ends in tight to create an improvised sprinkler system. When this maneuver seemed to produce success, he had some of his men go below and cut into the ceiling of the top floor in the same manner, but they gave up when they were showered with sparks and flames on their first attempt. Hoses draped along the side of the building continued to burst, and each time one did, it gave the spectators below a shower. The affected engine would then shut down, attach new hose, and the hook and ladder would extend again—an anxious dance of approach and retreat. Firemen emerged on the roof in short shifts through a second and then a third alarm, which brought every available engine and hose cart in the city to the fire.

Starting at six o'clock, an hour or so after the fire was called in, the supply of water began to surge in the lines as the downtown buildings emptied out for the day. The resulting increase in pressure was bane and boon: bane, because the hoses would be even more likely to rupture, boon because a pipeman's spray of water could fly all the farther. By the time Benner himself ascended to the roof, his worry was less that the building would be engulfed or explode than that it would collapse, a jewel of the rebuilding city cracked and then crumbled on his first full day on the job. No touring musician or stage actor had ever performed an opening night in Chicago with so much at stake. The audience for Benner's debut stretched around the block and building grew to as many as ten thousand firebugs.

As Benner started to feel a sense of control, the *Little Giant* arrived from the West Side, led by the foreman Billy Musham, who would never for the rest of his life stop telling people he had been the first to arrive on the scene at the Great Fire and who would forever blame Benner for the flames' fateful jump across Taylor Street, one half-block north of the Learys' alleyway. With a theatrical flourish, Musham addressed the crowd, promising to send a stream from the street up to the blazing cornice, ninety-four feet in the air. His team promptly delivered on the boast, to the whoops and cheers of the assembled watchers. Wrote one observer in wry appreciation, "It was the first exhibition of really high water-throwing that had been shown at a fire in some time."

In the end, it was a good show. Benner and his men put out the last of the flames less than four hours after the first alarm had sounded. People began to disperse at eight o'clock, when they knew that the fire department had won. The Fire Insurance Patrol went in after ten, fifty men with brooms who spent all night sweeping away the water, pushing it toward the stairways where it poured down "with a sound like a mountain gorge" into the basement, to be pumped out the next morning.

As the men swept, Mathias Benner's engine companies collected and reeled hose, separating the burst lengths from the intact. Later that night, they would go through their checklists with care, restoke their boilers, and repair what hose they could. After all, there might be another big fire the next day. In the end, the building suffered $100,000 in damage, about one-fifth of its total value. Five of the six floors of the building were salvaged, and though Field would have to push back the retail emporium's opening date, the publicity surrounding the fire would turn out to be yet another marketing coup for a man who didn't need any.

Plastering, woodwork, windows, and roofing needed replacement. But the marble fittings and statuary already gracing the main hall had been left undamaged, and no expensive carpets or shawls had yet been moved in. The Singer Company carried its own financial liability and gladly paid the bill, which it knew it would recoup after only a year or two of rent payments. Even before the last of the water had been swept away and the last hose cart wheeled off to its station, the manufacturers of the building's galvanized iron cornices were on the site and writing up a new contract for replacements.

Marshall Field and Levi Leiter had escaped disaster, and this was a good omen. The city was in high spirits. The two hundredth anniversary of Jacques Marquette's first visit to the future site of Chicago in the fall of 1673 was at hand. A national exposition was planned for September 1873, to be housed in a palace of glass built near Lake Michigan beside the Illinois Central terminal, and such an event seemed the perfect vehicle for a vigorous dose of boosterism at just the right time. People with money from west, east, and south, and from across the oceans, would descend on the city. They would fill the hotels, shop at the city's stores, drink in its saloons, and plant the legend of Chicago's miraculous recovery in newspapers across the country.

Or so went the thinking in the late summer of 1873 as Marshall Field surveyed the damage to his new building and made plans to keep the work on track. But the relentless boom-and-bust pattern of life in any American city would have the final say. In the nineteenth century, disasters came fast one upon the next and kept changing their form—sometimes "natural," sometimes man-made, most often a combination of the two. If the Civil War that consumed the first half of the 1860s had been one kind of continuous, rolling human catastrophe, followed in October 1871 by the biggest urban disaster the country had ever known, the financial calamity that hit at the end of 1873 would be no less memorable or consequential. Fire, beer, wood and brick housing, sick horses—all of these were in their own ways local concerns. The next disaster, which would punctuate the entire post-fire era, would not be.

❧ 36 ❧

IN THE END, Anton Hesing and the *Staats-Zeitung* had taken sloppy aim. The German publisher had charged that Medill sought to use his tenure as mayor to put himself in position for a run at governor or senator, and that this ambition was behind the mayor's attempts to subject the city to draconian rules about fire limits and saloon closings. But as had been proven, Medill lacked the necessary political skill and fervor to push those rules through. Whatever ambition burned inside him was not and never would be directed at electoral office. Not one year earlier, Medill's foes in the temperance movement had made the same accusation—in reaction to what they perceived as Medill's *opposition* to the saloon closings—but it wasn't true then or now.

Medill's candidacy for mayor in 1871 had been a response to an emergency, an unlikely political ascendancy born of a city in crisis. But it turned out that the scope of that crisis as imagined by the Union-Fireproof coalition had been exaggerated. Chicago's credit was never in trouble, its business was never going to St. Louis, and its workers were never going to shut down the city with a strike, at least so long as jobs overflowed. Crime continued at its usual pace, no better or worse than before. Neither Joseph Medill nor Charles C. P. Holden nor anyone else could have done much to slow or, for that matter, speed up the freight train that was the post-fire economy of Chicago. The city moved forward of its own accord. All that was left for Medill as the end of his term came in sight was old-fashioned politics, and he had proven himself an atrocious politician, accomplished only at producing results that represented the opposite of his aims.

Every day Medill continued as mayor, in fact, he discovered that his true influence over the course of Chicago would always be far stronger outside politics than inside. He never made a recorded statement about his reasons for relinquishing the mayor's chair before his term was complete. But whatever those reasons were in the particulars, it was clear that the unholy mess of city politics seen up close was too much for him. What he viewed as the levelheaded and logical subtleties of his approach to the questions of relief, fire limits, and Sunday closings left little permanent mark on Chicago's brash and blunt-nosed approach to resolving conflicts. Medill had sat and listened to what seemed innumerable empty speeches at innumerable public events and had discovered that his own efforts at administration and reform felt, in their own way, equally empty. He'd hoped for a Chicago re-created in what he viewed as his own image: rational, frugal, abstemious, logical, upstanding, receptive to the power of debate. But Chicago didn't like a debate; it liked a fight. And Medill was in no mood to take part in one.

A small notice in the newspapers on August 12, 1873, served as Medill's first public announcement of his intentions: "Mrs. Mayor Medill and daughters left the city last evening for Ohio, en route for Europe. His Honor will join them in New York in about two weeks, and accompany them to the Old World." A week later a more informative item appeared, with an unusual caveat. Medill would not be seen in Chicago for the rest of his term. But at the same time, "he has not resigned the office of Mayor, and will not do so." He would return to the city, he said, only if the council chose an "unfit person for the office of Acting-Mayor." Medill had no doubt that the Union-Fireproof coalition, which was already beginning to transform into a self-styled "law and order" party with a single-minded fixation on the issue of Sunday saloon closings, would lose the mayorship and the council in November. But he would not allow the opposition to take control of the city a single minute sooner.

On Monday, August 18, 1873, Medill made his final trip to the council chambers, in order to inform the aldermen of his intention to leave Chicago. Before broaching the topic of his departure, however, he offered the aldermen a lengthy view of the recent Field & Leiter fire and its implications for firefighting in the coming era of ever-taller and more vulnerable buildings. Even on his way out the door, he had lost none of his fervor for numbers, nor his faith in technology. He noted that the new chief Mathias Benner's official report indicated that eighty-three lengths of hose had burst in the effort to reach the roof of the Singer building, adding up to more than a mile's worth of lost hose. Medill's solution was to propose a mandate that owners of buildings four stories tall or taller "erect iron stand-pipes of suitable diameter inside of the exterior walls, fronting on the streets and alleys, with proper hose couplings and stop valves, on each of the upper floors, and projecting above the roof."

The ordinance made good sense. Almost two years into his time as mayor, finally, Medill had offered a concrete, practical, and public expression of the "Fireproof" portion of the Union-Fireproof coalition that elected him. Before the turn of the next century, internal sprinkler systems of many sorts, including the type Medill proposed, would become the norm in tall buildings. But after he offered his proposal, the idea was referred to the council's Committee on Fire and Water, where, for reasons of cost alone, everyone knew that it stood no chance of implementation before the next election. Then Medill announced that he had secured a suitable building for a new public library, after which he read out the announcement of his intention to leave the country and asked for a vote on his choice for acting mayor.

His nominee was the lawyer and Union-Fireproof alderman Lester L. Bond, who won out among three other nominees after a series of voice votes. The final bit of friction in Medill's term in Chicago now occurred when one of the other nominees for acting mayor, a solidly Democratic member of the council named James J. McGrath, accused Medill to his face of prearranging Bond's votes via private communications in which the mayor disparaged McGrath's fitness for the job. In response, Medill, "greatly enraged, stated that the Alderman was a falsifier; that he had never written a line against him to anyone, challenged any person to show anything of the kind, and authorized any Alderman to show anything of the kind if he had it."

No alderman produced any such evidence, and that night Bond was sworn in as acting mayor. The next day, at 5:00 p.m., Medill boarded a train at the Illinois Central depot for New York City, where he would lay over a week before embarking for Ireland on the steamer *Algeria*. A few hours before leaving Chicago, he told a reporter that "he goes for rest, and the only thing approaching labor he will engage in while absent will be writing an occasional letter upon something not given in the guidebooks." In the coming months and years, his term as mayor would be ridiculed by some, lionized by others, and forgotten by many. But whatever people praised or damned him for, in this moment he was not a politician but rather the son of an Irishman headed for the land of his ancestors.

Indeed, the luck of the Irish seemed to be with him. By leaving the country when he did, Medill proved once again that though he might not be a master of city administration, he was a master of timing. On the morning of September 19, 1873, less than two weeks after Medill caught his first sight of Ireland's coast from the rail of the *Algeria*, the news exploded across Chicago and across America that the New York–based firm of Jay Cooke, the most well-known and influential banker in the country, had collapsed, defaulting on all of its obligations.

The news was calamitous, but it wasn't a surprise to all. In May, the Austrian stock exchange had crashed, followed by the German market. Chicago had played a small but decisive role in this carnage, because one of the many causes of the European economic collapse was an influx of cheap American wheat in England—much of it routed through Chicago River grain elevators via Chicago-based rail lines—that had helped to cripple European grain exports to the point that bankruptcies began to spread across the Continent. When the countries of Europe responded by curtailing their international investments, American railroads—a popular home for overseas dollars—were left undercapitalized and exposed. And no one was more exposed than Jay Cooke, who had housed a reckless percentage of his bank's capital in the Northern Pacific line, which now had no way to pay him back, neither principal nor interest. A thousand other intertwined financial companies, partnerships, and instruments suffered in a swift chain reaction. By the end of September, numerous other rail lines were bankrupt. Every branch of Cooke's bank closed, with other banks soon to follow suit.

The telegraph had run across the ocean to Ireland since 1866. Despite his absence from Chicago, Medill understood as fast as anyone what Cooke's failure would mean to the city. For months afterward, well into 1874, his partners at the *Tribune* would do their best to pretend otherwise, to tell their readers that no full-blown financial panic was on the horizon. That all was well. But Medill, even from afar, was ever the realist. In a letter dated September 22, 1873, and posted in Edinburgh three days after the news struck, he penned a grimmer and much more accurate prophecy:

> I took in the situation at a glance when I read of the fall of Jay Cooke. I saw that he would pull down with him scores of others, and send the shock of a fiscal panic throughout the United States. It is obvious there will be a general distress and a stringent money market for some time to come, and Chicago must feel the effect as severely as any other city in America, on account of the vast sums her people owe in consequence of the sudden rebuilding of the city.

True to form, Medill wrote to the city comptroller, advising him that "there is only one course to pursue under the circumstances of the case, and that is to shorten up expenditures." His understanding was that the debilitating panic of 1857 was about to be repeated, "and Chicago is in no condition to escape unscathed."

He was right. As the winter of 1873 approached, infrastructure projects big and small all over the country stalled or were canceled, shipments of raw goods began to slow to a crawl, and Chicago's economy began to shed workers by the thousands. In response, new political alliances grew stronger. Medill was in France in November 1873 when Chicago's voters denied the new law-and-order ticket the reins of power by a 61–39 percent majority and installed a bona fide immigrant-friendly administration, the first of its kind in Chicago, that had no intention of siding with the city's business elite. The new coalition had started to form back in April, two days after the police chief, Elmer Washburn, issued General Order No. 20, the directive that allowed for the forcible closure of saloons and the arrest of owners. Irish and German leaders met to decide on a response and decided to form an unprecedented political alliance across ethnic and party lines. The entire effort was a mirror image of the bipartisan coalition that had formed in the month after the Great Fire, to the point that Henry Greenebaum, the man first floated by Joseph Medill as the Union-Fireproofers' candidate for mayor, was now a leader of the opposition. By the middle of May, they'd given themselves a name—the People's Party—and had enlisted every Irishman and German of any political significance with the purpose of kicking the Yankee elites out of power.

Formed to fight back on the issue of saloon closings, the People's Party had no trouble adding the considerable woes produced by the economic crisis of the fall of 1873 to its list of grievances. The November vote was in many ways a rebuttal of the decisions Medill had made during his twenty months in office, but at heart it was a response to a response, an angry repudiation of the entire program of intimidation and diminishment they felt had been perpetrated on them by the Union-Fireproofers in lieu of a genuine effort to make things right after the Great Fire. Politics could move at the speed of lightning in Chicago, and after the election of 1873 city hall was populated not by government reformers or established business interests or pious temperance crusaders but by an administration antagonistic to all three. Opportunity provided by disaster cut both ways. The show of force undertaken by the members of the city's business establishment after the Great Fire returned on them in spades.

The council was swept of many of its Union-Fireproof members, especially in the German wards, tipping its balance of power toward the new People's Party mayor, Harvey Doolittle Colvin. If Medill's tenure produced a single political legacy, this surge of power and cohesion displayed by Chicago's working class was it. His term had begun in an elevated, bipartisan spirit, because many Irish Catholics and Germans united with him, but it ended with Catholics and Germans united against him. The demand printed on the banner at the infamous fire-limits protest of January 1872— THE RELIEF, TEMPERANCE, AND FIRE-LIMITS SWINDLE MUST BE CUT DOWN—had become prophecy. In the fall of 1873, twenty-five months after the Great Fire, the poor and immigrant neighborhoods voted to do just that.

The result was full of ironies for Joseph Medill. Of the three most vexing points of contention during his term, only in his support of wide and absolute fire limits had he stood in clear opposition to the popular will. He had nothing to do with the handover of the relief effort to Wirt Dexter, and his instruction to enforce the Sunday-closing law was designed only to demonstrate that law's weakness. But these were ironies that few voters cared to notice. He had been given the lever of the Mayor's Bill three months into his term, and with this power he'd tidied a few corners of government, had fired some people, and had imposed a limited brand of austerity. These things had been important to the city, but they did not make a usable platform for a new election, not in the face of the worldwide panic that arrived in the wake of Jay Cooke's collapse. It was an irony of even greater proportions when, one week after the 1873 contest, David Gage, the outgoing Union-Fireproof treasurer, was caught red-handed with $50,000 of city funds in his own personal accounts. Had Medill still been in the city and still mayor, the painful discovery would have sliced straight into the inner chambers of his reformist's heart.

It hadn't helped the electoral prospects of the "law and order" party at all that its new and far smaller coalition of elites—shorn of most of its immigrants and also of the bipartisan spirit it had displayed two years before—was driven along by the Relief and Aid Society's director, Wirt Dexter. By election night in November, as the effects of the fall of Jay Cooke began to cut deeply in Chicago, relief was once again on the minds of Chicago's workers. It was one thing for them to face a Great Fire—an identifiable and well-known, if arbitrary, menace. It was another thing altogether to try to understand why their jobs could drift away because a bank in New York had collapsed.

The panic of 1873 was, for most Chicagoans, the decade's biggest disaster. Wages collapsed as inflation rose. Anyone in debt, an individual or a company, found their creditors less accommodating of late or missed payments, even as interest rates soared. The building boom of 1872 sputtered and then went bust. Many a suburban development, wholesale firm, and business block went bankrupt. Public projects, including several parks, were canceled. The influx of unskilled workers who'd arrived after the fire stayed in the city even as jobs evaporated—where else would they go to escape a depression affecting the entire country?—and this only added to the city's woes. As far as the working class in Chicago was concerned, the scenario Dexter's Relief and Aid Society had prepared for by not spending all of the money donated to the city was here in force. The society had withheld $600,000 of the millions given to it in October 1871; now, surely, that money must be given out.

As the panic of 1873 took hold, Chicago's workers were filled with foreboding and anxiety, but also with a growing sense of their own political strength. In their post–Great Fire political battles, beginning with their fire-limits protest at the city council, the gathering that had ended with a fusillade of bricks through the windows, they had savored the first taste of an increased influence they would never relinquish. In the aftermath of the Great Fire, Chicago's lasting reputation as a town full of stiff-necked, broad-shouldered, politically powerful working men and women first took root as its poor and foreign-born citizens began to refute the city's historical insistence on using people, especially immigrants, as anonymous, interchangeable parts. They'd marched to keep their right to build affordable homes, with success. They'd filled the streets to mock a government that felt it could dictate their drinking habits, and they'd won an election on the issue of Sunday saloon closings. Now their jobs were in jeopardy, so they marched about jobs.

Everything the Relief and Aid Society had done since the day in October 1871 that it finagled control of the relief effort from Charles C. P. Holden had been built on one proposition: that its money would never serve as a *general* relief fund, that it would always be earmarked for special relief in extraordinary circumstances. Wirt Dexter and his fellow society administrators believed, in earnest, that leaving $600,000 of the money earmarked for disaster relief unspent was not the failure of a public trust but rather the very essence of trust itself, a promise of financial stability in the face of *future* disasters. Fair enough, then: Chicago's jobless believed that the panic of 1873 was very much that future disaster.

A resolution was passed by the new city council demanding that the society release the money it had held back the previous year, and a committee of five aldermen was designated to ensure that the money was disbursed. On the day after Christmas 1873, a meeting was held at the Relief and Aid Society's new headquarters, which were far larger and more imposing than its modest old haunts and filled the third and fourth floors of a new office building on LaSalle, near city hall between the Chicago River and the courthouse ruins. In response to the council's delegation, the society's superintendent Charles Truesdell expressed his conviction that "a great many of the able-bodied men who are loafing about the streets could get something to do if they were not too lazy to look for it." Wirt Dexter added his opinion that in the end Mayor Roswell Mason's edict of October 14, 1871, still held: the society had been given charge of all relief money donated for the Great Fire and could disburse the money when and as it wished. It was not obligated to give the money to anyone and was not answerable to the city council when it did so.

Two days later, on December 28, 1873, hundreds of jobless men stuffed themselves into the lobby of the society's new building while thousands more shivered in the bitter wind outside. The fire-limits protest and the trade unions' day of demonstration in 1872 had involved perhaps a thousand marchers at most; now the crowds of protesters included many times that number. Change had come to Chicago.

Dexter and his colleagues at the society were much less expe-

1875 worker demonstration at Chicago Relief and Aid Society's headquarters (similar in size and character to the demonstration of December 28, 1873), from *Frank Leslie's Illustrated Newspaper*, March 20, 1875

rienced than the aldermen of the city council in addressing the frenzied energy of a mass of people, and when it came to public relations, they had no savvy at all. As a first salvo, Superintendent Truesdell announced to the crowd packing the lobby that the first requirement for receiving employment or any other aid would be proof of vaccination for smallpox, which had flared in the city in recent months. Anyone could come back and fill out an application—once they'd received their scrape. In response, the crowd roared, hooted, and pressed forward. One older German workingman near the front turned and shouted back to the crowd, "That is the way the Society means to treat us! Monday they will tell us to come Wednesday, and then to come Sunday, and so on until the winter is over, and we and our families have died of starvation." Someone opined in another shout that if they had revolvers, they would be successful. Someone else pointed out that they couldn't do that, because they'd sold their derringers and Colts to pay for bread.

The shouts and bitter laughter continued, but the crowd was far more disciplined than the fire-limits or Sunday-closing protesters of the previous year. The working class of Chicago was growing in numbers and as a political force, and most ominously for the business barons of the city it was learning patience. The gathering dispersed, but ward-level meetings took place all over the city the next day, and the day afterward, and many days after that. Some of these meetings called for socialism, some for communism. Other meetings denounced both but still, at the same time and for the first time, railed openly against the liberal-Republican, no-holds-barred, laissez-faire, noblesse oblige capitalism that had animated Medill and the Union-Fireproofers and that seemed to be a religion in the plutocratic power centers of the city.

As the society continued to withhold its surplus fund—it would only ever disburse a fraction of what it'd kept, even as the panic of 1873 continued into 1874—the political demands of the new working-class bloc sharpened. At their ward meetings, some speakers demanded that the Relief and Aid Society's board admit working-class members of the German, Scandinavian, and Irish populations of the city so that it might better represent and understand the people most in need of aid. Some called for general strikes. Some called for violence, though most often these voices were shushed. Whatever their various positions, though, never again would the working people of Chicago go away quietly because they were told to do so by their employers.

In the long run, Medill's term as mayor represented the last time Chicago's old business aristocracy could claim dominance in city politics. As the calendar turned over to 1874, these men and their wives began a more or less permanent retreat from city politics, led away by such august couples as Marshall and Nannie Field, Wirt and Josephine Dexter, and Potter and Bertha Palmer. Some turned their attention to exclusive social clubs and fraternal organizations, while others looked to national politics and the courts, where they fought an increased emphasis on public welfare and industrial regulation with some of the most expensive lawyers in the country. They suffered little financial damage as they departed the political scene; in Chicago, the rich stayed rich even as the men and women they employed took more or less permanent possession of the city's majority vote.

Yet even in the hardest of times, the city was characterized by a rough, raw symbiosis between classes. Some were called builders, some did the actual building, but all of them made Chicago. The old Yankee elite might have depended on the poor and foreign of the city to stack their lumber, disassemble their livestock, and load their grain into railcars, but the poor and foreign of the city also depended on the rich to keep money and jobs flowing, and to do their part to make Chicago one of the country's most impressive and extraordinary cities, one that all of them claimed with pride as their own. Despite the growing distrust and enmity between the city's working class and its businessmen, even the men and women out of work weren't about to gainsay the power of the resurgence of the city itself, especially when it was expressed so visibly in iron, brick, glass, and wood.

In many ways, architecture—for those who owned it and for those who built it—became the most evident shared source of Chicago's sense of self and a kind of neutral meeting ground for people from all walks of life. "Such a season of building activity was never known in the history of civilization," wrote the *Tribune* of the years 1872 and 1873. And those outward signs of better times might for a while have saved the city from greater turmoil. The count for the first year of reconstruction alone had included 51,619 linear feet of new buildings and around $50 million in expenditures. Fifty thousand men had arrived in the past two years to work in manufacturing and construction, more than the entire number employed in those jobs before the Great Fire.

Just as Chicago liked to believe its disaster was the greatest in human history, it also liked to pretend that everything it built was the greatest of its kind. "These buildings were all of a superior order, in point of finish and architectural beauty," crowed the *Tribune,* but this wasn't true. In fact, the panic of 1873 did slow construction for many years. But it didn't bring a complete halt to the work, and whatever troubles might be brewing beneath the surface, the con-

368 · SCOTT W. BERG

tinuing sound of hammers, saws, and riveting guns provided an air
of optimism that few other cities were able to feel. Chicago's downtown and the neighborhoods consumed by the Great Fire continued to rebuild because, in a sense, they *had* to, and this gave the city
a rare vitality and momentum at this moment in history.

As Chicago's politics got messier, as its urban melting pot began
to move from simmer to boil, the discipline of architecture would
continue to provide the city with the greatest measure of its importance on the world stage. Early in November 1873, as the People's
Party took power, the new Palmer House opened to rave reviews,
offering lodgings at a discount because not all of the hotel's public
spaces and amenities were ready for use. Later that same month, all
but unnoticed, the city received the first glimpse of its future fame
when a precocious young architectural apprentice named Louis
Sullivan, seventeen years old, rode into town with his family on
the breakwater tracks of the Illinois Central. Sullivan would go on
to become the most influential architect in the city's history, if not
quite its most famous. He represented another, new sort of immigrant in Chicago: an artist eager to use the city itself as his canvas,
someone come to the city because of its enormous pull as a symbol,
as a muse, as an inexhaustible source of human energy.

Sullivan's Transportation Building, with its colossal Romanesque Golden Door entryway, would be the most unique and
remarkable structure in the famous "White City," site of the 1893
World's Columbian Exposition. In 1899 he would design the seven-
story Schlesinger & Mayer department store and office at State and
Madison, the first expression of Sullivan's very Chicagoan notion
that "form should follow function," that a retail palace could be
substantial *and* beautiful, solid *and* sophisticated, its own aesthetic
pleasures equal to the lure of the goods sold within. He would also
design the last of the city's magnificent old-school masonry buildings, the Auditorium Building, where the conductor Theodore
Thomas, whose gala concert had been postponed for a year by the
Great Fire, would eventually helm the Chicago Symphony Orchestra. And most famously, Sullivan would take on as an apprentice

the young Frank Lloyd Wright, turning the key, as it were, on the opening of Chicago's greatest artistic glory.

The moment of Sullivan's arrival along the Illinois Central breakwater—as told in his autobiography, which he wrote in the third person—is perhaps the greatest paean to the lure of Chicago that has ever been written. In the early winter of 1873, the city, for all its crowing about "resurrection," was in certain ways the same coarse frontier post it had always been, just much larger and louder. But as it weathered the panic of 1873 and continued to rebuild itself with both eyes fixed on the future, the city thought of itself less in terms of what was there than in terms of what yet wasn't.

It was this sense of glorious unfinishedness, fed by the destructions of the Great Fire, that so excited young Louis Sullivan as he rode into town along Lake Michigan. In his enthusiasm and awe he echoed all the fortune seekers yet to come and spoke for an entire American generation of architects, writers, activists, business barons, and laborers who would over the last quarter of the nineteenth century make Chicago one of the world's biggest, greatest, most turbulent, and most fascinating urban places:

> The train neared the city; it broke into the city; it plowed its way through miles of shanties disheartening and dirty gray. It reached its terminal at an open shed. Louis tramped the platform, stopped, looked toward the city, ruins around him; looked at the sky; and as one alone, stamped his foot, raised his hand and cried in full voice: THIS IS THE PLACE FOR ME!

A S YOUNG LOUIS SULLIVAN approached his destiny, as dreamy and full of Chicago fever as anyone could be, Joseph Medill was far away in body, if not quite in mind. After rejoining his wife and daughters in Ireland, he stayed true to his word and sent letters back home that hinted at literary skills he seldom had reason to display as an editorialist or mayor. He was a publisher at heart, with a deep respect for the reporter's tools, but it is still a surprise to realize how far his ability with a pen could exceed the power of his reedy, monotone voice.

Medill's description of Cork, Ireland, published in the *Tribune* in September 1873, drew a sharp contrast with the city he'd left behind:

> As a whole, the population were well-dressed, orderly, respectable, and decent-looking. But nobody seemed to have much of anything to do. The town is finished; not a new house is being built nor an old one repaired in all Cork. To the eye, it does not seem probable that a house has been erected for 100 years.

To drive home the divide between the place he'd left and the place he'd come to, Medill added, "I could not hear that a fire had ever broken out in this city. I can see little use for either engines or insurance." As much as anything he'd done in his career—as much as his role in engineering Abraham Lincoln's nomination, his effort to save the history of the city as printed in the pages of the *Tribune*, or his term as mayor—this last comment revealed Medill as a tried-and-true Chicagoan. He had traveled all the way to the Emerald Isle to talk about insurance and fire engines.

His sojourn in Europe would last for almost a year and would take him to Ireland, Scotland, England, France, Italy, and Germany. On the family's return to Chicago in the fall of 1874 he would find the People's Party in charge of the city and the Union-Fireproof coalition nowhere to be seen. Soon after his return, Medill used the occasion of the dedication of a new monument to Abraham Lincoln in Springfield, Illinois, to give a long talk on the creeping spread of corruption in American politics since his late friend's assassination.

For a while, in fact, this was mostly what Medill did: he lectured, on municipal reform, sometimes, but also on Roman history, on the Irish landscape, on continental politics, all peppered with anecdotes from his recent tour of Europe. Soon he decided that he wanted to do one thing above all: buy the *Tribune* outright and become its sole owner. He began to accomplish this goal in November 1874 by way of a $250,000 loan from none other than Marshall Field, a necessary piece of finance that bedeviled Medill for many years, in the form of Field's constant intrusions into the paper's management practices, until the note was repaid nine years later.

By 1883, when the paper became his and his alone, twelve years after the Great Fire, Medill was sixty years old, and Chicago had become the center of radical agitation in America, which pushed Medill into ever more xenophobic postures, believing as he did that the Republicans' dream of free contract labor—of an employer's right to bring on an individual worker at whatever terms that worker would accept—had been forever soiled by the influence of unions and the desire of unskilled laborers to rise above their stations. His Calvinist Scotch-Irish roots showing through more than ever, he railed against the tides of immigration, especially Catholic immigration, with all the force and bile of the Know-Nothings he'd once opposed.

In the end, Medill's legacy would be mixed, full of genuine accomplishments and missed opportunities. He was a superb newspaperman, but he was never going to make a good mayor, impeded as he was by his dour personal style and lack of political imagination. His life story included significant moral failings, but also surprising moral triumphs. During the run-up to the Civil War, he and the *Tribune* had run ahead of Abraham Lincoln and most of Congress on many of the most incendiary racial arguments of the day. Day after day, in editorial after editorial, Medill had defended his paper's support of abolition and emancipation against all comers. During the Civil War, Medill had been an early and adamant advocate of the creation of Black Union regiments, describing prospective "colored soldiers" as "able-bodied, robust, and brave."

In 1872, as fights over relief, temperance, and fire limits had dominated the public's attention, Medill quietly pressed for and approved the hire of the city's first Black police officer. And later that same year, when the fire department had added three new engine companies as part of a small post–Great Fire bump in spending, Medill supported the establishment of one of the new firehouses as a Black fire company. Opposition to the new firemen was immediate and fierce from many of the force's rank and file, who saw in the three new stations three dozen or so new jobs and didn't want any of them going to a group of Black men. But Medill, who under the terms of the new Mayor's Bill had final say on the hires, held his ground. In September 1872 he signed off on the staffing of Engine 21: six Black firemen, though still under the supervision of a white foreman, engineer, and captain.

Engine 21 was stationed in the midst of the city's only sizable concentration of Blacks, part of a neighborhood on the South Side called the Cheyenne district, where they lived intermixed with a Jewish and poor German population. The firehouse was surrounded by brothels and gambling houses, in a set of blocks where the rent was affordable and the police presence on the streets negligible. The *Tribune* described the neighborhood as "that compactly built, and densely settled district where fire comes laden with all of its terrors, since it strikes those who, though they lose a little, lose everything."

Three new steam engines were ordered for the department, and the Black firemen were given one of the oldest ones, the *Winnebago*. When Engine 21 received press, good or bad, the new recruits were reduced to a laughably limited range of characteristics. They were called "fast," "agile," and "maniacal." They were referred to as "speedy" and "acrobatic" firemen who could be counted on to persevere all night but who couldn't be trusted to understand how to attack even the smallest blaze. Often they were labeled "monkeys," and when their work was described, much was made of the way they "clambered" and "leaped" and "climbed," their voices always "howling" and "hollering."

On July 14, 1874, thirty-three months after the Great Fire, the *Winnebago* was the first engine to arrive at a fire at a nearby drugstore, most likely started by a discarded cigarette or a stray spark landing in a pile of turpentine-soaked rags in an oil factory and rag shop next door. The new blaze blossomed into another all-out catastrophe as it jumped from building to building and street to street on a southwesterly path, scattering the frightened residents of the Cheyenne district in all directions and drawing the customary swarms of firebugs by the thousands.

So much in front of the eyes of these spectators resembled the early progress of the Great Fire. The sights of hotel guests fast emptying their quarters. The sounds of intermittent explosions and the screams of horses and cows burned to death in their stalls and stables. The scenes of saloon keepers dispensing free drinks. The problems trying to quench a fire raging through buildings made of wood that housed businesses that worked with wood: cigar and match factories, mills, flour stores, lager-beer saloons, a vinegar works, a gun shop, even a hay-press and lard-oil factory across from the *Winnebago*'s engine house. Wrote the *Times*, evoking the memory of October 1871, "There was the same jam of loaded vehicles, the same half-crazed horses, the same wrathful, excited, and avaricious drivers, the same anxious, indescribable mixture of excited humanity, household furniture and general depravity, and the same general hubbub."

Echoing the desperate efforts of October 1871, twenty of the fire marshal Mathias Benner's men formed a line in front of a distillery, only to fall back to a millinery and then fall back again to the German Methodist Church at Third and Polk, where the superheated air soon gave the bell a booming ring, "although there was nobody in the church at the time." Women roamed the streets looking for their children and wailed. A madam named Annie Stafford, "pale and trembling with fright," told anyone who would listen that the late captain Hyman, who had recently died in her brothel, had appeared to her in a prophetic dream: there would be another conflagration and she was to die in it. One estimate of the number of prostitutes who lost their places of business was five hundred. All were presumed to have suffered heavy losses, "for the majority of them had the most costly and elegant fittings and wardrobes."

In one crucial way, however, the new conflagration was very different from the Great Fire of 1871. It started not on the West Side but on the South Side, one mile away from Lake Michigan instead of two miles away, which meant that there was much less of the city to be found in the path of a fire driven by a dry wind again blowing hard from the southwest—a wind that became Mathias Benner's ally as much as his enemy as it pushed the blaze away from the center of downtown and toward the lake. All the while, the residents of the Cheyenne district watched their homes and businesses burn. Many of them filtered northward into the still-rebuilding portions of the South Side and spent the night "on the heaps of rubbish which yet remain to tell the tale of the fire of 1871." One reporter described the flow of "nondescript fugitives who spoke all the languages of Babel":

> The wretched inhabitants of the long line of South Clark Street dens that fell before the flames formed a contingent by themselves, and made the air heavy with maledictions on their evil fortune. Beds and bedding lay around in profusion. Old women scolded; young women cried and wrung their hands. Babies screamed in a grand chorus.

Many of the Black residents of the neighborhood had spent the day on a Sunday-school picnic on the Michigan Southern Railroad, and these revelers came home en masse about seven o'clock, while the fire was still burning at its height. "The men looked sadly at the devastated spots which they called their homes when they left," reported the *Tribune*, "and silent tears ran down their cheeks: the women were more demonstrative, and loudly lamented and bewailed their losses, refusing to be comforted by sympathetic friends, who offered them temporary shelter." As the night went on, a new group of watchers joined them. These were Black waiters from the downtown restaurants, who trickled in after their shifts ended, one by one or in small groups. They formed a large crowd of their own, still dressed in their crisp button-downs, some with towels slung over their shoulders, some still wearing their aprons. No reporter interviewed them.

In the end, the new fire's footprint took up about one-twentieth of the size of the Great Fire's, and its monetary cost and the number of buildings lost were smaller in similar proportions. The West Side and North Side escaped. But the loss was still large enough that the city could once again wax poetic about its impressive scale. In the customary search for instant meaning, much was made out of the fact that the northern line of the fire of 1874 matched up with the southern line of the fire of 1871:

> It has come to complete the work of 1871, and to scoop out of existence another broad belt of wooden buildings which menaced the new structures which have sprung up in the business quarter of the South Division. It has shaken hands with the fire of 1871 and, reaching the ground its predecessor conquered, has stopped, not satiate, and yet satisfied. Well it may be for the palaces that line Madison Street that yet another strip of brick and stone is to be piled up between them and the menacing frame structures that lie beyond, and yet we cannot help reflecting that this security of the future has been bought by too great a sacrifice.

Several of Chicago's newspapers, true to form, tried to blame the blaze on a single family of careless immigrants—in this case, on Polish Jews, whom the *Tribune* libeled as insurance fraudsters and absentee landlords. The *Times* spread its own blame among what it described as "a swarm of Jew peddlers and junk dealers." But unlike the tarring of Kate Leary, these assignations of infamy didn't stick. No songs would be written, no commemorative coins issued, no paintings produced, no myth made.

As for the returning picnickers and waiters, they would soon have to abandon their decimated neighborhood. In August 1874 there were about three thousand Black residents in a city that would one day house more than a million. These displaced Black home-owners, these Black firemen, these Black waiters, began a dias-pora throughout the city, birthing other neighborhoods. Over the next four decades many of those neighborhoods would grow into the South Side's Black Belt as Chicago became a key end point of the Great Migration from the rural South to the urban North. Six decades further along, in the 1960s and 1970s, a stark series of high-rise apartments called projects would rise in many of the same locations. And four more decades later, when ideas about what cit-ies owed to their most disadvantaged residents shifted yet again, those projects would come down, in sensational and well-publicized demolitions.

Of course, in 1874, the men of Engine 21 trying to keep their neighborhood from burning, and the waiters and picnickers watch-ing it burn, had no idea what Chicago, their city, would become. In 1874, they moved away from their homes because the fire made them move. Or they moved because the fire allowed them to move. They moved because the city was changing. They moved because the insurance companies, still vulnerable as a result of the panic of 1873, had had enough.

What Joseph Medill and the Union-Fireproofers hadn't been able to accomplish after the Great Fire, a unified front of influen-tial insurers in Chicago and across the country now did by raising premiums so high that many of the homeowners and smaller busi-nesses that surrounded downtown had no choice but to go elsewhere to rebuild. The city council followed by expanding its fire limits and making wood construction illegal everywhere inside those limits, abandoning its previous objections and exceptions in the face of a new national pressure, which accelerated the departure of poor and middle-class citizens from the city's oldest wards. Many of Chicago's wealthiest families moved to Prairie Avenue on the South Side, near Marshall Field's new mansion, while immigrants of all nationalities relocated to the far South and West Sides, where they gave birth to new and long-lasting ethnic enclaves of their own.

The city's newspapers tried to give the July 1874 fire a name it could carry into history—the Little Chicago Fire, the Little Big Fire, the Second Chicago Fire—but none of them stuck, and in the end the "Fire of 1874" had to serve. In many ways, the new blaze was remembered only as a stunted version of the fire of October 1871. In other ways, though, the fire served as a reminder of the city's divisions, as well as a glimpse of the city's future and a seeding of its strength.

Over the next dozen years Chicago would become a crucible of socialist, communist, and anarchist agitation that, along with a proportionally overheated response, brought the city a different kind of notice. The showdown between the city's "better citizens" and its poor and foreign residents didn't end with post-fire politics. In 1874 and 1875 private militias formed: on the one side, the Citizens' Association's First Illinois State Guard, funded by the same stratum of men who helmed the Relief and Aid Society, and on the other the Irish Clan-na-Gael Guards and the German Lehr und Wehr Verein. To Chicago's Great Fire of 1871 were added violent railroad strikes in 1877 and 1894 and the Haymarket bomb blast of 1886 that killed eleven people and resulted in the sensational show trial and hanging of several of its alleged perpetrators.

The great unheeded lesson of the aftermath of the Great Fire for men as varied in outlook and personality as Joseph Medill and Wirt Dexter was that their fear of Chicago's mildly corrupt aldermen and the immigrant neighborhoods that voted for them—a fear expressed in a set of punishing policies that used the conflagration as a paper-thin pretext—helped to usher in the pitched class conflict they dreaded, leading in turn to a lasting era of working-class agitation, ward bosses, and, eventually, full-blown machine politics. Chicago in 1870, one year before the Learys' barn caught fire, had still been in many ways an overgrown frontier outpost in which a small group of men made a lot of money while making most of the decisions. Chicago, two years later, was fast becoming a hothouse of populist democracy, a locus of political power and ambition for a much wider swath of the citizenry than had ever been imagined before. In this manner—and in a dizzyingly short period of time after the Great Fire—Chicago became a modern American city.

"A concentrated eruption of what was sought to be repressed," the *Tribune* had written of the citywide celebration of drinking that had greeted Medill's attempt to enforce the Sunday-closing law— but the formulation could apply to every measure taken by the city's Yankee elite and their allies in the business establishment in the months following the Great Fire. The show of political and financial force represented by the election of the Union-Fireproofers failed to produce even short-term gains for the men who had supported them. What it did was to create a new and permanent political awareness among the city's less fortunate residents. Though by 1871 any adult male citizen could vote, it was the Great Fire that finally fully enfranchised residents of all the city's neighborhoods, rich and poor alike. Between 1879 and 1893, the Democrat Carter Harrison Sr., backed by the ever broader and stronger coalition of working-class immigrants that had first formed in response to the "relief, temperance, and fire-limits swindle," was elected mayor five times.

With little interruption, the population of Chicago continued to grow at a pace that seemed impossible: from 330,000 people at the time of the Great Fire to more than 1 million less than two decades later. Over the last quarter of the nineteenth century, the real estate vacuum created at the center of Chicago by the elimination of so much housing stock in the wake of the fires of 1871 and 1874 helped to make downtown a hothouse garden for all kinds of entrepreneurial and architectural innovations. Montgomery Ward & Company, founded in Chicago in 1872 as a small mail-order shipping company, would grow by leaps and bounds to become one of the country's most recognized and respected mercantile firms, inspiring a raft of competitors that soon came to include Sears, Roebuck, and Company. Marshall Field would buy out his partner, Levi Leiter, and soon expand his retail and wholesale department store empire to encompass three thousand employees and $30 million in annual sales. The new Palmer House would become a national landmark and Chicago's best-known destination for famous visitors in politics, business, and the arts well into the next century. And most famously, in 1893, in the midst of yet another international economic panic caused by over-leveraged railroad corporations, the Chicago World's Fair drew more than twenty-seven million visitors, proving again the special resistance the city seemed to have to hard times.

Hundreds of new and exhilarating buildings went up in downtown in the 1880s and 1890s in a frenzy of urban construction unique in American history: giant auditoriums, resplendent department stores, vast warehouses and factories, and in 1885 the world's first skyscraper, the Home Insurance Building on Adams and LaSalle, four blocks straight south of the site of the county courthouse atop which Mathias Schaefer first spied the beginnings of the Great Fire. Unlike the courthouse, or the Tribune building, or the first Palmer House, all of which advertised themselves as "fireproof," the new generation of tall buildings deserved the title. Wood and brick were replaced by metal and glass, and firemen trying to raise sewn-together hoses up the sides of buildings were replaced by sophisticated internal water-delivery systems. As the new century approached, these new structures rose higher and higher and higher, so much so that visitors felt a strange new kind of claustrophobia, pinned between shadowy canyon walls made of glass and steel.

As the Gilded Age came and went and the twentieth century marched on into the twenty-first—as the myth of Mrs. O'Leary, her cow, and a broken lantern took root ever deeper and became a piece of permanent Americana—fears of all-devouring citywide fires ebbed. Other fears became more pronounced: drought, earthquakes, tsunamis and floods, nuclear war, suicide bombers, chemical weapons, cyberattacks, climate change. If great urban fires still occurred, most often they were a by-product of other disasters, second-class citizens in the gruesome hierarchy of catastrophe. But in this time and in this place, at this moment in 1871 between the Civil War and the coming of a series of world-shaking technological revolutions, fire reigned supreme. Fire destroyed. Fire created. Fire entertained and fire terrified. And always, fire transformed.

Acknowledgments
and a Note on Sources

Long live the archivists, those keeping the physical record of history intact and accessible and those preserving that record in electronic form. For every archivist in a library reading room who handed me a bound volume of rare newspapers or a wound reel of microfilm, there is an unseen digital archivist making the work of scholarly inquiry and historical narrative far more open and accessible than it has ever been. Thanks to all of them, but in my case especially those working at the Chicago History Museum, the Library of Congress, the National Archives, the Newberry Library, and the First Division Museum at Cantigny in Illinois.

The Chicago History Museum's resources on the Great Fire form the core of any investigation into the subject. The complete set of fire department inquiry transcripts kept there, in the Chicago Fire Department collection within the Chicago Fire of 1871 collection in the Archive and Manuscript holdings, is crucial to describing the progress of the fire, especially its first nine hours. The museum's entire Chicago Fire of 1871 collection—which also includes dozens of individual narratives of the fire, some available elsewhere and some not—contains far more material than any one researcher could encompass in a single project, however lengthy. *The Burning of the World* tells a particular tale through a particular set of lenses; any number of other points of entry into the story are available, and the hope, as with all histories, is that other writers eventually use them.

The Great Chicago Fire and the Web of Memory website at

greatchicagofire.org/web-of-memory, curated by Carl Smith, is an impressive and invaluable online resource—especially for a book written, in part, during a pandemic. I thank the Chicago History Museum and the Northwestern University Information Technology Department of Academic and Research Technologies for supporting that work. The website chicagology.com is another marvelous online encyclopedia of people, places, and events from the city's history. Many documentary sources, some hard to find through other channels, are transcribed there. Both websites are also repositories of a rich range of images dating from the time of the Great Fire and are worth browsing for that reason alone. In addition, archive.org and Google Books were important online resources. And if you love maps, as I do, the complete set of 1868–69 Sanborn fire insurance maps of Chicago, available in ultrahigh resolution through the Norman B. Leventhal Map & Education Center at the Boston Public Library, is a joy.

Chicago's newspapers from the period 1871–74, taken all together, are a vital, vigorous, and sometimes confounding collection of viewpoints. Many documentary records burned during the Great Fire, while many of the city's most notable citizens were more concerned with keeping accurate ledgers than with leaving behind personal recollections, so the city's not always entirely well-behaved newspapers have become an irreplaceable record of events and of attitudes. In part because one of my central subjects, Joseph Medill, was a part owner, and also because it was Chicago's de facto newspaper of record during this time period, the *Chicago Tribune* provided the narrative spine of my story and is heavily cited. While the *Tribune* was not always perfectly reliable, and its editorial judgments were unapologetically biased, its reportage certainly presents a more trustworthy historical record than, say, *The Chicago Times*, which nonetheless contains much of value thanks to its boisterousness and strong preference for journalistic tools such as dialogue and dramatic scene making. I accessed the *Tribune* online via George Mason University's subscription to the searchable ProQuest Historical Newspapers database, without which the book would not have been possible. I accessed the complete run of the *Times* and the *Evening Post* from 1871 to 1874 via microfilm through the Newspaper and Current Periodical Reading Room at the Library of Congress—without which, again, the book would not have been possible. The Chicago Foreign Language Press Survey, an online resource housed at the Newberry Library, provided translations of a wide range of key source material published in languages other than English.

In the years since 1871, many histories of Chicago and of the Great Fire have appeared, each with its own new and important perspective on the place and event. All are valuable, but any research into these subjects must begin with Carl Smith, the dean of Chicago Fire scholars, whose *Chicago's Great Fire: The Destruction and Resurrection of an Iconic American City* presents a wonderfully comprehensive, even encyclopedic, overview of the event. Karen Sawislak's *Smoldering City*, the best scholarly work on the immediate aftermath of the fire, raises a raft of questions about the political realignment of the city that were formerly submerged beneath layers of feel-good mythmaking. Among modern-day scholars, in addition to Smith and Sawislak, Perry R. Duis, Robin L. Einhorn, John B. Jentz, Donald L. Miller, Ross Miller, Dominic A. Pacyga, and Richard Schneirov have all provided crucial contributions to my understanding of the role of the Great Fire in the creation of a new kind of Chicago, and by extension, a new kind of American city. Cynthia A. Kierner's *Inventing Disaster* and Rebecca Solnit's *Paradise Built in Hell* provided well-timed and eye-opening discussions of what Kierner calls America's "culture of calamity." Finally, I highlight Richard F. Bales, whose *Great Chicago Fire and the Myth of Mrs. O'Leary's Cow* is a remarkable example of dogged historical detective work that should be read by anyone seeking a deliciously granular analysis of the fire's first moments along DeKoven Street. Those names listed above are, of course, a fraction of the writers and researchers who have produced excellent scholarship about Chicago and the Great Fire. I hope that my bibliography has not overlooked too many of them.

Finishing a book during a global pandemic and its aftermath has made the explosion in online resources a godsend, but at the same time it has also fostered a refreshing reliance on more local communities and resources. I've had a strong community of writers and scholars at George Mason University to lean on for crucial scholarly, professional, and personal support. Out of the many, many colleagues who asked interesting and insightful questions about my project and who provided help in myriad ways, I thank by name Zachary M. Schrag, historian and author of *The Fires of Philadelphia,* for his enthusiasm and support, as well as for a thorough read through of a draft version of the manuscript; Douglas Luman, a poet and book designer now in the department of computer science at Allegheny College, for his excellent work on the book's maps; George Oberle, history librarian; Gregg Wilhelm, the director of creative writing, for his always-on enthusiasm and friendship; the members of the leadership team of Watershed Lit: Center for Literary Engagement and Publishing Practice for creating and nurturing a vital community of writers and readers on campus and far beyond; the department chairs Debra Lattanzi Shutika and Tamara Harvey for their steady and inventive leadership; and many other colleagues inside and outside English. I also want to express my appreciation for Linda Hall and the other present and former staff at Stillhouse Press, an independent literary teaching press run by GMU alumni, graduate students, and undergraduates, where I act as publisher and editorial adviser. I'm not as young as I used to be, but they are, and being in their company and watching them work always reminds me of how much books matter.

Now that I've been publishing narrative histories for more than twenty years, I've come to recognize how lucky I was to enter into a particular set of partnerships early in my career. First at William Morris Agency, then at Fletcher and Company, and now at United Talent Agency, Eric Lupfer has from the start been my biggest supporter, as well as a razor-sharp agent and ultra-perceptive sounding board. And it may be customary for authors to thank their editors for their patience and their discerning eye, but I truly believe that my editor, Edward Kastenmeier, is the gold standard. Editing is both a dynamic, ever-changing profession and a subtle, finicky art, and Edward always manages to go far, far beyond my expectations. Also at Penguin Random House, Pantheon, and Vintage, I thank Lisa Lucas, Dan Frank, Chris Howard-Woods, Rose Cronin-Jackman, Sarah Pannenberg, Altie Karper, Romeo Enriquez, Nicole Pedersen, Cassandra Pappas, Lauren Peters-Collaer, Kelly Blair, and Lisa Kleinholz. This book may have a single name on the front cover, but like all published works it is very much a "we" proposition.

Writing books really is an unpredictable and unsteady endeavor and, without the forbearance and good humor of those in its orbit, close to unsustainable. With that support, however, it's a good life. I can only hope I've accommodated my parents, Margaret and Roger, brother, David, wife, Cory, and sons, Carter and Elliot, half as much as they've accommodated me.

Finally, a nod of appreciation to the city of Chicago. For those of us who grew up in Minnesota's Twin Cities and made frequent visits over the years, Chicago was, simply, our New York, every bit as alluring and amazing. Its successes and failures are legendary, its reach enormous, its energy undeniable and forever thrilling. It's been a privilege to spend time trying to understand how this great American city came to be in the crucible of the Great Fire, and I hope my book will serve as one useful piece of fuel to feed our never-ending fascination with the world's urban places.

Notes

To balance the need for documentation with space concerns, I've provided citations for all quoted material in the book, while primary and secondary sources of particular use have been listed under the corresponding chapter headings below. When using source material in the text, I have lightly edited spelling and punctuation for consistency and ease of reading.

· PROLOGUE ·

The story of the fire in Red Flash was built on reporter Ed Chamberlin's personal narrative, as published in Colbert and Chamberlin, *Chicago and the Great Conflagration*, as well as accounts of the blaze contained in Andreas, *History of Chicago*, vol. 2, and the *Chicago Tribune* of October 8, 1871.

xviii "poor old woman": *Chicago Tribune*, Oct. 8, 1871.

· 1 ·

The inquest testimony of William Brown and Mathias Schaefer provides a detailed chronology of the first sighting of the Great Fire. Cronon's *Nature's Metropolis*, perhaps the best book of history ever written about Chicago, is an engaging and comprehensive guide to the city's myriad commercial and economic connections to the rest of the United States and the rest of the world.

13 "I can't alter it now": Brown inquiry testimony, Chicago Fire of 1871 Collection, Chicago Fire Department Collection, Chicago History Museum.

· 2 ·

The story of the fire's origins on DeKoven Street was drawn from the inquest testimony of, most prominently, Catherine O'Leary, Patrick O'Leary, Daniel Sullivan, and Catherine McLaughlin, and from the detailed analysis presented in Bales, *The Great Chicago Fire and the Myth of Mrs. O'Leary's Cow*.

14   "a *terra incognita* to respectable Chicagoans": Colbert and Chamberlin, *Chicago and the Great Conflagration*, 226.

14   "thickly studded with one-story frame dwellings": Ibid., 226–27.

15   "an honester woman": Catherine McLaughlin fire testimony, Chicago Fire of 1871 Collection.

18   "shin-dig": *Chicago Times*, Nov. 25, 1871.

20   "not five cents": Catherine O'Leary fire testimony, Chicago Fire of 1871 Collection.

20   "The wind blowed every way" and the following quotations: Ibid.

· 3 ·

The most useful narratives of the initial response of the Chicago Fire Department to the Great Fire are found in the sometimes contradictory inquest testimony of many different firemen, along with a long article written in 1940 by H. A. Musham, son of the *Little Giant*'s foreman, Billy Musham, and published in *Papers in Illinois History*. While written by an author who clearly had an ax to grind against his father's superiors on the force, Musham's analysis of the early spread of the fire is well researched and extremely detailed.

27   "was under such fierce headway": Andreas, *History of Chicago*, 2:711.

28   "One thousand dollars would have paid": Ibid.

30   "pass the fire on their way": Musham, "Great Chicago Fire," 101, 161.

30   "on their taps and on top of the fire": Robert Williams inquiry testimony, Chicago Fire of 1871 Collection.

31   "Is it going to do any harm": Schimmels inquiry testimony, Chicago Fire of 1871 Collection.

· 4 ·

37   "Private interests impel men": Report of the Board of Police in the Fire Department, 3.

38   "Robert, fire" and the following quotations: Robert A. Williams inquiry testimony, Chicago Fire of 1871 Collection.

42   "the whole fire was a mistake": *Chicago Tribune*, Oct. 9, 1893.

42   "Can't you work north of this?": Cromie, *Great Chicago Fire*, 52.

43   "beer and whiskey were running like water": *Chicago Tribune*, Oct. 9, 1893.

43   "Men were harnessed to trucks": Ibid.

45   "I couldn't sleep": Ibid.

· 5 ·

Joseph Medill waited decades to publish his tale of the valiant and quixotic attempt to save the Tribune building, contributing to two articles in the

Tribune in the early 1890s. The fire narratives of William Bross and Horace White were helpful. For my portrayal of Medill, I relied on the papers held at the First Division Museum at Cantigny and several excellent secondary sources listed in my bibliography, especially McKinney, *The Magnificent Medills.* No definitive biography of Medill has yet been written, but he and his times deserve one. Achorn, *The Lincoln Miracle,* published in 2023, provided a full and just-in-time account of Medill's machinations at the 1860 Republican National Convention. Finally, volume 2 of Kinsley, *The Chicago Tribune: Its First Hundred Years,* offers a lively narrative of the newspaper's editorial positions during the fifteen years after the Civil War.

47   "Here comes a woman": William Gallagher fire narrative, Chicago Fire of 1871 Collection.

47   "the great crowd that filled the bridge": *Chicago Tribune,* Oct. 9, 1893.

49   "There are no old men here": Sawislak, *Smoldering City,* 8.

51   "He wrote countless editorials": Junger, *Becoming the Second City,* 21.

53   "I *know,* and you know I wouldn't promise": Ibid., 47.

53   "neutral in nothing": *Chicago Daily Journal,* June 10, 1847.

55   "For days past alarm has followed alarm": *Chicago Tribune,* Oct. 8, 1871.

· 6 ·

Like many of his fellow businessmen in Chicago, Marshall Field left behind very few personal papers, but he did leave behind ledgers and business correspondence available at the Chicago History Museum that, read closely, provide a surprisingly robust portrait of his personality. Tebbel, *Marshall Fields,* and especially Wendt and Kogan, *Give the Lady What She Wants,* were helpful secondary sources.

58   "Regard a fixed bad habit": Tebbel, *Marshall Fields,* 17.

60   "Brilliantly lighted from garret to basement": *Chicago Tribune,* Oct. 13, 1868.

61   "Few credits and those only on short time": Tebbel, *Marshall Fields,* 30.

· 7 ·

71   "The city and county officers and police": *Chicago Tribune,* Oct. 9, 1893.

74   "the plastering was then dropping down": Schaefer inquiry testimony, Chicago Fire of 1871 Collection.

74   "The strong southwest wind": Loesch, *Personal Experiences,* 10.

· 8 ·

76   "it is constructed of Athens (Illinois) marble": *Harper's Weekly,* May 22, 1869.

76   "I found the printers at work": *Chicago Tribune,* Feb. 1, 1891.

77 "I had a bird's-eye view of the ravages": *Chicago Tribune*, Oct. 9, 1893.
79 "to organize a corps": Ibid.
80 "There were half a dozen chimneys": Ibid.
81 "a castellated monstrosity": Sturgis, *Oscar Wilde*, 227.
81 "I saw the wooden palings": *Chicago Tribune*, Oct. 9, 1893.

· 9 ·

83 "All solicitude for the remaining portion of the city" and the following quotations this chapter: Colbert and Chamberlin, *Chicago and the Great Conflagration*, 227–34.

· 10 ·

92 "melted into a mass": *Chicago Tribune*, Feb. 1, 1891.
93 "The printing of any papers": Ibid.
93 "there was no time to coax a man to get up": Ibid.

· 11 ·

Holden's narrative of his activities in the wake of the Great Fire, along with a great deal of important context, is found in Andreas, *History of Chicago*, vol. 2. Andreas's impressively illustrated three-part history of the city, which covers the years up to 1885, is full of documentary sources presented in lightly edited form and makes a superb source for those interested in any aspect of the city's life during its first forty-eight years of existence.

102 "mission of observation": Andreas, *History of Chicago*, 2:762.
103 "harvest of death" and the following quotations: Ibid.
107 "rude log hut": *History of Will County*, 842.
109 "Action, immediate action": Andreas, *History of Chicago*, 2:762.

· 12 ·

111 "a nucleus, or headquarters": Andreas, *History of Chicago*, 2:762.
111 "was the city, in its corporate capacity": Ibid.
112 "as if by instinct": Ibid.
112 "and not to return without him" and the following quotations: Ibid., 763.
115 "PROCLAMATION": Ibid., 764.
117 "Barrels and boxes came pouring in": Ibid., 765.
118 "Hundreds and thousands of people": Cassius Milton Wicker fire narrative, Chicago Fire of 1871 Collection.
118 "some nuns marshaling a long line": Ada Rumsey fire narrative, Chicago Fire of 1871 Collection.

· 13 ·

Several well-researched biographies of Sheridan exist and are listed in my bibliography. Sheridan's own memoirs, sadly, leave off less than a month before the Great Fire, but they are still an invaluable record of his life, times, and thought. The official account of his post-fire activities (*Report Made by Lieut. General P. H. Sheridan*), while hardly unbiased, was useful in establishing chronology.

121   "Not an ounce of superfluous flesh": Greiner, *General Phil Sheridan*, 309.
121   "chunky little chap": Morris, *Sheridan*, 3.
121   "Under his spurning feet the road": Read, *Poetical Works*, 266.
126   "Where is General Sheridan?": Andreas, *History of Chicago*, 2:735.
126   "great strength, an easy gait": Greiner, *General Phil Sheridan*, 402.
129   "It was my earnest desire": Sawislak, *Smoldering City*, 55.

· 14 ·

Invaluable details regarding the early life of Bertha Honoré and her courtship with Potter Palmer are found in Ross, *Silhouette in Diamonds*.

130   "One after another, all hands turned up": Goodspeed, *History of the Great Fires in Chicago*, 63.
131   "In the midst of a calamity": *Chicago Tribune*, Oct. 11, 1871.
131   "was bright, cheerful, pleasant": *New-York Tribune*, Oct. 14, 1871.
133   "any hotel west of New York": *Chicago Tribune*, Aug. 28, 1870.

· 15 ·

Like Joseph Medill, Potter Palmer, Bertha Honoré Palmer, and Marshall Field, William Butler Ogden deserves far more consideration as an important figure in American history. Harpster's *Railroad Tycoon Who Built Chicago* is the only full-length biography, and as such was a godsend.

142   "Men, women, and children huddled together": Andreas, *History of Chicago*, 2:765.
143   "every imaginable article fitted to aid the sufferers": Ibid., 766.
150   "The burning district had no lamps": Ogden to Charles Butler, Oct. 11, 1871, William B. Ogden Papers, Chicago History Museum.

· 16 ·

153   "man of far above the ordinary size": *Chicago Tribune*, Oct. 12, 1871.
154   "a morbid curiosity": Ibid.
155   "drunken man": *Chicago Tribune*, Oct. 11, 1871.
155   "charred trunk of a human body": Ibid.

155 "skull and limbs": *Chicago Tribune*, Oct. 13, 1871.

155 "notorious cracksmen": *Chicago Tribune*, Oct. 17, 1871.

155 "The wife and two children of Chaz. Herzog": *Chicago Tribune*, Oct. 11, 1871.

· 17 ·

159 "An excited crowd gathered round": *Chicago Tribune*, Oct. 11, 1871.

159 "Whether the report is or is not correct": Ibid.

159 "We hear that a fellow": *Chicago Evening Post*, Oct. 11, 1871.

160 "responsible for peace and order": Sawislak, *Smoldering City*, 55.

161 "There can be but one hand in this": Ibid., 56.

162 "The preservation of the good order and peace": "Military Rule in Chicago," greatchicagofire.org.

162 "here the head of the city": *Chicago Tribune*, Oct. 12, 1871.

165 "I have deemed it best" and the following quotations: Andreas, *History of Chicago*, 2:769–71.

169 "Persons wishing soup will bring buckets": *Chicago Tribune*, Oct. 18, 1871.

· 18 ·

Gess and Lutz, *Firestorm in Peshtigo*, is a satisfying telling of a catastrophe that for many Americans remains obscure or unknown.

175 "efforts said to have been made": *Chicago Tribune*, Oct. 16, 1871.

175 "of the early history of the city": Ibid.

177 "I was born close by a sawmill": Arnold, *William B. Ogden*.

180 "We will rebuild this village": Gess and Lutz, *Firestorm in Peshtigo*.

180 "At daylight in the morning he was up": Ibid.

181 "he was cheerful and pleasant": Ibid.

· 19 ·

The murder of Colonel Grosvenor by the unfortunate Theodore Treat is covered aptly by several different sources, including Andreas, *History of Chicago*, vol. 2; *The Chicago Times* and the *Chicago Tribune;* and *The Volonte*, the newsletter put out at the time by the University of Chicago. The subsequent controversies and arguments regarding martial law in Chicago are covered in detail in *Special Message of Governor John M. Palmer.*

182 "*The prevention of evil is always better than the cure*": *Spider and the Fly*, x.

183 "independent of Government or municipal control": *Edwards' Annual Directory*, 719.

183 "Any person Stealing": Image collection, greatchicagofire.org.

183 "The doubter must remember": *Chicago Tribune*, Oct. 14, 1871.

188 "Go to hell": *Volonte*, Feb. 1872.
189 "Oh God, oh God": *Chicago Tribune*, Oct. 21, 1871.
189 "The boy sentinel": *Chicago Times*, Oct. 23, 1871.
189 "Who is General Sheridan?": *Chicago Times*, Oct. 22, 1871.
189 "Never did deeper emotions of joy": Andreas, *History of Chicago*, 2:734.
190 "thoughtless manner in which": *Chicago Tribune*, Oct. 22, 1871.
190 "It excited the greatest surprise": Andreas, *History of Chicago*, 2:776.
191 "I would like your opinion": Colbert and Chamberlin, *Chicago and the Great Conflagration*, 500.
191 "If Your Honor deem it best": Ibid., 501.
192 "The extraordinary circumstances": Andreas, *History of Chicago*, 2:777.

· 20 ·

194 "the red flames that blotted out Ninevah": *Chicago Tribune*, Oct. 31, 1871.
196 "obligatory by a municipal enactment": Ibid.
198 "throwing pell-mell into the heart of the city": Ibid.
199 "Facts alone are wanted in life": Dickens, *Hard Times*, 1.
199 "The intention and desire": *Chicago Tribune*, Oct. 18, 1871.
200 "some reliable and well known citizen": Ibid.
203 "he believed that a ticket of the very best": *Chicago Tribune*, Oct. 24, 1871.

· 21 ·

207 "change their ticket daily": *Chicago Tribune*, Nov. 1, 1871.
207 "The Democrats and sorehead Republicans": *Chicago Tribune*, Oct. 31, 1871.
207 "Dem-i-Reps": *Chicago Times*, Nov. 5, 1871.
208 "anxiety for office in the present emergency": *Chicago Times*, Nov. 1, 1871.
210 "LET US COMMEMORATE": *Chicago Tribune*, Nov. 10, 1871.
212 "Chief Caucus Packer Holden": *Chicago Tribune*, Nov. 6, 1871.
212 "If it costs him $240 a week": Ibid.
213 "in his breeches pocket": *Chicago Tribune*, Nov. 4, 1871.
213 "Holden," it wrote, "says he is made of 'steel'": *Chicago Times*, Nov. 5, 1871.
213 "nature will assert itself": *Chicago Tribune*, Nov. 6, 1871.
216 "Chicago Tammanyites": *Chicago Times*, Nov. 3, 1871.

· 22 ·

218 "other such brutal sports": *Chicago Tribune*, Feb. 1, 1871.
219 "The speculators eventually made their calculations": *Chicago Tribune*, Nov. 3, 1871.
220 "wealthy old widower": *Chicago Tribune*, Nov. 8, 1871.

220 "Among the prodigies of pluck" and the following quotations: *Chicago Tribune*, Nov. 7, 1871.
222 "The store was thronged with ladies": *Chicago Times*, Nov. 7, 1871.
223 "It will be a gratifying item": *Chicago Tribune*, Nov. 7, 1871.

· 23 ·

224 "I do not believe that God": *Chicago Tribune*, Nov. 7, 1871.
225 "endeavor to-day to relieve themselves": Ibid.
225 "I think he has no equal": Ibid.
227 "one whose moral influence": *Chicago Tribune*, Nov. 8, 1871.
227 "The affairs of this city": Ibid.
228 "I would feel at liberty to resign": Green and Holli, *Mayors*, 3.
228 "As its requirements during the next two years": *Chicago Tribune*, Nov. 8, 1871.
229 "To have found a Holden man": Ibid.
229 "every candidate, entrusted this day": Ibid.
231 "For a time men were unreasonably cheerful": Olmsted, "Chicago in Distress."

· 24 ·

235 "smiled good-naturedly": *Chicago Times*, Nov. 25, 1871.
236 "having failed in their duty": *Chicago Tribune*, Nov. 15, 1871.
236 "If, as is generally believed": *Chicago Evening Journal*, Nov. 21, 1871.
237 "the investigation be thorough and complete": *Chicago Evening Journal*, Nov. 11, 1871.
237 "for employing a man so totally unfit": *Chicago Times*, Nov. 14, 1871.
237 "What do you know about this fire?": Catherine O'Leary fire testimony, Chicago Fire of 1871 Collection.
238 "have been known to me personally": *Chicago Tribune*, Oct. 20, 1871.
238 "An honester woman I would never ask to live with": Catherine McLaughlin fire testimony, Chicago Fire of 1871 Collection.
240 "The fire broke out on the corner": *Chicago Evening Journal*, Oct. 9, 1871.
240 "How these flames originated": *Chicago Evening Post*, Oct. 10, 1871.
240 "at 9:30 a small cow barn": *Chicago Tribune*, Oct. 11, 1871.
241 "The contemptible cow barn": *Chicago Times*, Oct. 18, 1871.
242 "on the corner, owned by the old hag": Ibid.
243 "I was in bed myself": Catherine O'Leary fire testimony.
246 "It is often the 'piker'": *Chicago Tribune*, Jan. 3, 1914.
246 "often told him that the story about the cow": Ibid.

· 25 ·

Narrative accounts of the meetings of Chicago's Common Council were entered faithfully into the pages of the *Chicago Tribune*, not least because an owner of that paper was mayor of the city. In this and several other chapters, digital copies of the council's proceedings, available through the HathiTrust Digital Library and the Newberry Library's online holdings, were crucial in the attempt to make sense of Chicago's ever-shifting and not always easily parsed political arguments and alignments. I've cited the newspaper but corroborated with the council proceedings. Here and elsewhere, Einhorn, *Property Rules* (which expands on the scholarship of Jentz and Schneirov, also found in my bibliography), was my essential guide to the history and mechanisms of the city's municipal administration. Finally, chapter 5 of Rosen, *The Limits of Power*, provides an excellent analysis of the course and resolution of the arguments regarding Chicago's post–Great Fire fire limits.

249 "I find, on my return to Chicago": *Chicago Tribune*, Dec. 3, 1871.
251 "He has done much, very much": *Chicago Times*, Dec. 6, 1871.
252 "That the Mayor and the Council": *Chicago Tribune*, Dec. 5, 1871.
253 "Some hard things have been said": Ibid.
255 "Sit down!": *Chicago Times*, Dec. 5, 1871.
255 "great magnitude": *Chicago Tribune*, Dec. 5, 1871.
255 "The very brief period" and the following quotations: Ibid.

· 26 ·

260 "Smelling Committee": *Chicago Times*, Dec. 12, 1871.
261 "The officers and members of the fire department": Ibid.
261 "prove to have been in bed and asleep": *Chicago Tribune*, Dec. 12, 1871.
262 "birds of prey": Ibid.
263 "There, now, don't crowd!": *Chicago Times*, Nov. 12, 1871.
263 "so closely did the visiting parties" and the following quotations: *Chicago Tribune*, Dec. 12, 1871.
265 "She will be read of, and talked about": *Chicago Times*, Oct. 9, 1871.
265 "With her last kick": *Chicago Tribune*, Jan. 1, 1872.
267 "If the woman who was milking the cow": Colbert and Chamberlin, *Chicago and the Great Conflagration*, 201.

· 27 ·

Chicago's newspapers were obsessed with the visit of Russia's young grand duke to America, before, during, and after his stop in their city. Farrow, *Alexis in America*, is an excellent book-length recounting. Wade, *Chicago's Pride*, offers the best description of the Union Stock Yards in this era.

268 "A large crowd assembled on Michigan Avenue": *Chicago Times*, Jan. 3, 1872.

268 "the crowd, noise, bustle, and excitement": *Chicago Tribune*, Jan. 3, 1872.

268 "three or four sturdy boys": *Chicago Times*, Jan. 3, 1872.

269 "Hail Alexei": *Chicago Tribune*, Jan. 3, 1872.

273 "the effect of meeting an old and tried friend": *Chicago Tribune*, Dec. 5, 1871.

274 "from the last squeal": *Chicago Tribune*, Jan. 3, 1872.

274 "all kinds of meats": Ibid.

274 "May the rivalry between Russia and America": Ibid.; *Chicago Times*, Jan. 3, 1872.

275 "I am not in the habit of public speaking": *Chicago Tribune*, Jan. 3, 1872.

· 28 ·

In this and later chapters, my understanding of the role of the Great Fire in forging a more active and visible working-class constituency in Chicago owes a great deal to Einhorn, *Property Rules*; Jentz and Schneirov, *Chicago in the Age of Capital*; Sawislak, *Smoldering City*; and Smith, *Urban Disorder and the Shape of Belief.*

279 "I want this procession to be orderly": *Chicago Tribune*, Jan. 16, 1872.

281 "Form in columns of six!": Ibid.

281 "almost intolerable": *Chicago Times*, Jan. 16, 1872.

281 "Speech!" "Speech!" and the following quotations: *Chicago Tribune*, Jan. 16, 1872.

286 "Gentlemen," he said, "I dare to face the music": *Chicago Times*, Jan. 16, 1872.

286 "The first scattering shot": *Chicago Tribune*, Jan. 16, 1872.

286 "Men got down close to the floor": *Chicago Times*, Jan. 16, 1872.

286 "No one cared to hear": *Chicago Tribune*, Jan. 16, 1872.

· 29 ·

Chicago's competing models of public assistance, as well as the considerable divide between its male-dominated and female-dominated charities, are the subject of Flanagan, *Seeing with Their Hearts*, and McCarthy, *Noblesse Oblige.*

287 "better fulfill their trust": *Chicago Times*, Jan. 26, 1872; *Chicago Tribune*, Jan. 26, 1872.

287 "coordination and efficiency": *Chicago Tribune*, Oct. 14, 1871.

288 "How can Friends, in many places few in number": Rhoads, *Friends' Review* (supplement), i.

288 "temporal and spiritual elevation": *Eighth Biennial Report*, 272.

288 "nothing has been done by any one": *Chicago Tribune*, Jan. 21, 1872.

289 "To compel these people to go daily": Ibid.

289   "So far as we can learn": *Chicago Tribune,* Jan. 26, 1872.
290   "The Cincinnati Committee": *Cincinnati Gazette,* Jan. 29, 1872.
291   "in very abusive language": *Chicago Tribune,* Feb. 3, 1872.
292   "The soup is not fit for use": *Chicago Tribune,* Feb. 2, 1872.
293   "in cold water for fifteen minutes": Ibid.
293   "what in the world does this raid": Ibid.
294   "It would be a great satisfaction": Flanagan, *Seeing with Their Hearts,* 16.
294   "afford immediate relief to deserving women": Ibid., 18.
295   "We have eaten the soup": *Chicago Tribune,* Feb. 6, 1872.
296   "That the soup-house has": *Chicago Tribune,* Feb. 12, 1872.

· 30 ·

Duis, *Challenging Chicago,* is a treasure trove of street-level detail and contains a fascinating analysis of the meaning of "moving day" to the average Chicagoan. Jentz and Schneirov, *Chicago in the Age of Capital,* is an irreplaceable source of information and insight regarding the relationship between employers and employed in nineteenth-century Chicago, and includes an illuminating section on the May 15, 1872, "day of recreation."

298   "With us the merry-making exists": *Chicago Tribune,* May 4, 1860.
299   "This day, the first of May": *Chicago Tribune,* May 1, 1872.
301   "the lower class of workmen": *New York Times,* May 22, 1872.
302   "a gala day": *Chicago Tribune,* May 4, 1872.
302   "That a request for an advance": *Workingman's Advocate,* May 11, 1872.
302   "The bands played, the men marched": *Chicago Tribune,* May 16, 1872.
303   "It requires no figure of speech" and the following quotations: Ibid.

· 31 ·

Chapter 4 of Mitrani, *The Rise of the Chicago Police Department,* contains an excellent analysis of what the author calls the "Protestant elite's bid for control" and offers helpful context for Chicago's supposed crime wave of 1872, as well as for the troubled tenure of Elmer Washburn as police chief.

310   "from every accident save an earthquake": *Chicago Tribune,* Oct. 9, 1873.
310   "the feathers on the plumage": Ibid.
311   "The structure seemed alive with men": *Land Owner,* May 1873.
313   "a large audience": *Chicago Tribune,* Sept. 13, 1872.
313   "and a stone": *Chicago Tribune,* Aug. 27, 1872.
314   "I see before me a field of upturned faces" and the following quotations: *Chicago Tribune,* Sept. 13, 1872.
315   "Good!": *Chicago Times,* Sept. 13, 1872.
316   "never a policeman on that street": *Chicago Tribune,* Sept. 18, 1872.
317   "The German who goes to church": *Chicago Tribune,* May 21, 1872.
318   "Burglars, pickpockets, and gamblers": *Chicago Tribune,* Sept. 18, 1872.

319 "how far the law would support temperance": *Chicago Tribune,* Oct. 3, 1872.

322 "The Mayor saw fit to administer": *Chicago Times,* Oct. 8, 1872; *Chicago Tribune,* Oct. 8, 1872.

322 "The fundamental error of these gentlemen": *Chicago Tribune,* Oct. 11, 1872.

322 "I am happy to learn": Ibid.

323 "The experiment," he wrote, "will be tried": Ibid.

· 32 ·

325 "At last the revolving seasons": *Chicago Tribune,* Oct. 9, 1872.

325 "a winter's snows soon fell": Ibid.

325 "Everyone had an experience to relate": *Chicago Tribune,* Oct. 10, 1872.

325 "noted liquor-dealer": *Chicago Tribune,* Oct. 14, 1872.

327 "Some few places were really closed": *Chicago Times,* Oct. 14, 1872.

327 "warm and genial" and the following quotations: *Chicago Tribune,* Oct. 21, 1872.

· 33 ·

Chapter 5 of Miller's excellent *The Great Chicago Fire* (originally titled *American Apocalypse*) contains an insightful analysis of the iconography of William Le Baron Jenney's abandoned design for a monument to the Great Fire.

331 "miniature mountain": *Chicago Tribune,* Oct. 31, 1872.

332 "took up the best positions": Ibid.

332 "confessedly worthless": *Chicago Tribune,* Nov. 10, 1871.

334 "the sums donated": *Chicago Times,* Oct. 31, 1872.

334 "a female figure" and the following quotations: *Chicago Tribune,* Oct. 31, 1872.

337 "so cowardly a so-called proclamation": *Chicago Tribune,* Nov. 1, 1872.

338 "for the sale of intoxicating liquor": Ibid.

· 34 ·

Moret, "Purpura Hemorrhagica in Man," helped me understand the nature and progress of Sarah Holden's fatal disease.

343 "[Medill] is the principal representative": *Illinois Staats-Zeitung,* July 17, 1873.

· 35 ·

349 "an assignation house": *Chicago Times,* Aug. 2, 1873.

350 "during the past three years": Ibid.

351   "in a spirit of bravado": *Chicago Tribune*, Aug. 3, 1873.

353   "It was the first exhibition": Ibid.

· 36 ·

White, *The Republic for Which It Stands*, provided a cogent overview of the fall of Jay Cooke.

357   "Mrs. Mayor Medill and daughters": *Chicago Tribune*, Aug. 12, 1873.

357   "he has not resigned the office of Mayor": *Chicago Tribune*, Aug. 18, 1873.

358   "erect iron stand-pipes of suitable diameter": *Chicago Tribune*, Aug. 19, 1873.

358   "greatly enraged": Ibid.

359   "he goes for rest": *Chicago Tribune*, Aug. 20, 1873.

360   "I took in the situation": *Chicago Tribune*, Oct. 9, 1873.

360   "there is only one course to pursue": Ibid.

364   "a great many of the able-bodied men": *Chicago Tribune*, Dec. 23, 1873.

365   "That is the way the Society means": *Chicago Tribune*, Dec. 28, 1873.

367   "Such a season of building activity": *Chicago Tribune*, Oct. 9, 1873.

367   "These buildings were all of a superior order": Ibid.

369   "The train neared the city": Sullivan, *Autobiography of an Idea*, 197.

· 37 ·

370   "As a whole, the population were well-dressed": *Chicago Tribune*, Sept. 23, 1873.

372   "able-bodied, robust, and brave": Baldino, *Family and Nation Under Fire*, 150.

372   "that compactly built, and densely settled district": *Chicago Tribune*, July 15, 1874.

373   "There was the same jam": *Chicago Times*, July 15, 1874.

374   "although there was nobody in the church" and the following quotations: *Chicago Tribune*, July 15, 1874.

376   "a swarm of Jew peddlers": *Chicago Times*, July 15, 1874.

378   "A concentrated eruption": *Chicago Tribune*, Oct. 21, 1872.

Selected Bibliography

Abbott, Carl. "The Location of Railroad Passenger Depots in Chicago and St. Louis, 1850–1900." *Railway and Locomotive Historical Society Bulletin* 120 (April 1969): 31–47.

Achorn, Edward. *The Lincoln Miracle: Inside the Republican Convention that Changed History.* New York: Atlantic Monthly Press, 2023.

Ahern, M. L. *The Great Revolution: A History of the Rise and Progress of the People's Party in the City of Chicago and County of Cook, with Sketches of the Elect in Office.* Chicago: Lakeside, 1874.

Album of Genealogy and Biography: Cook County, Illinois. Rev. ed. Chicago: Calumet Book & Engraving Company, 1896.

Andreas, A. T. *History of Chicago: From the Earliest Period to the Present Time.* Vol. 2, *From 1857 Until the Fire of 1871.* Chicago: A. T. Andreas, 1885.

———. *History of Chicago: From the Earliest Period to the Present Time.* Vol. 3, *From the Fire of 1871 Until 1885.* Chicago: A. T. Andreas, 1886.

Andrews, Wayne. *Battle for Chicago.* New York: Harcourt, Brace, 1946.

Arnold, Isaac N. *William B. Ogden; and Early Days in Chicago.* Chicago: Fergus, 1881.

Baldino, Georgiann, ed. *A Family and Nation Under Fire: The Civil War Letters and Journals of William and Joseph Medill.* Kent, Ohio: Kent State University Press, 2018.

Bales, Richard F. *The Great Chicago Fire and the Myth of Mrs. O'Leary's Cow.* Jefferson, N.C.: McFarland, 2002.

Barber, Eunice Miena. *The Wright-Chamberlin Genealogy: From Emigrant Ancestors to Present Generations.* Binghamton, N.Y.: Vail-Ballou, 1914.

Barth, Gunther. *City People: The Rise of Modern City Culture in Nineteenth-Century America.* New York: Oxford University Press, 1980.

Black, Hope L. "Mounted on a Pedestal: Bertha Honoré Palmer." PhD diss., University of South Florida, 2007. scholarcommons.usf.edu/etd/637.

Bluestone, Daniel. *Constructing Chicago.* New Haven, Conn.: Yale University Press, 1991.

Boehm, Lisa Krissoff. *Popular Culture and the Enduring Myth of Chicago, 1871–1968.* New York: Routledge, 2004.

Boyer, Paul. *Urban Masses and Moral Order in America, 1820–1920.* Cambridge, Mass.: Harvard University Press, 1978.

Brown, M. Craig, and Charles N. Halaby. "Machine Politics in America, 1870–1945." *Journal of Interdisciplinary History* 17, no. 3 (Winter 1987): 587–612.

Bubnys, Edward. "Nativity and the Distribution of Wealth: Chicago 1870." *Explorations in Economic History* 19 (1982): 101–9.

Callow, Alexander B., Jr. *The Tweed Ring.* New York: Oxford University Press, 1966.

Chamberlin, Joseph Edgar. *The Ifs of History.* Philadelphia: Henry Altemus, 1907.

The Chicago Fire and the Fire Insurance Companies: An Exhibit of the Capital, Assets, and Losses of the Companies, Together with a Graphic Account of the Great Disaster, Accompanied by Maps of Chicago Showing the Burned District. Chicago: J. H. and C. M. Goodsell, 1871.

Chicago Relief: First Special Report of the Chicago Relief and Aid Society. Chicago: Culver, Page, Hoyne, 1871.

Colbert, Elias, and Everett Chamberlin. *Chicago and the Great Conflagration.* Chicago: J. S. Goodman, 1871.

Condit, Carl W. *The Chicago School of Architecture: A History of Commercial and Public Building in the Chicago Area, 1875–1925.* Chicago: University of Chicago Press, 1964.

Connely, Willard. *Louis Sullivan as He Lived: The Shaping of American Architecture.* New York: Horizon Press, 1960.

Connolly, James J. *An Elusive Unity: Urban Democracy and Machine Politics in Industrializing America.* Ithaca, N.Y.: Cornell University Press, 2010.

Cook, Frederick Francis. *Bygone Days in Chicago: Recollections of the "Garden City" of the Sixties.* Chicago: A. C. McClurg, 1910.

Cromie, Robert. *The Great Chicago Fire.* New York: McGraw-Hill, 1958.

Cronon, William. *Nature's Metropolis: Chicago and the Great West.* New York: W. W. Norton, 1991.

Currey, J. Seymour. *Chicago: Its History and Its Builders: A Century of Marvelous Growth.* Vol. 2. Chicago: S. J. Clarke, 1918.

Dante, Harris L. "The *Chicago Tribune*'s 'Lost' Years, 1865–1874." *Journal of the Illinois State Historical Society* 58, no. 2 (Summer 1965): 139–64.

Dickens, Charles. *Hard Times.* Oxford: Oxford University Press, 1955.

Downard, William L. "William Butler Ogden and the Growth of Chicago." *Journal of the Illinois State Historical Society* 75, no. 1 (Spring 1982): 47–60.

Duis, Perry R. *Challenging Chicago: Coping with Everyday Life, 1837–1920.* Urbana: University of Illinois Press, 1998.

Edwards' Annual Directory of the City of Chicago. 14th ed. Chicago: Richard Edwards, 1871.

Eighth Biennial Report of the Board of State Commissioners of Public Charities of the State of Illinois. Springfield, Ill.: H. W. Rokker, 1885.

Einhorn, Robin L. *Property Rules: Political Economy in Chicago, 1833–1872.* Chicago: University of Chicago Press, 1991.

Erwin, Robert. "Having It All." *Massachusetts Review* 51, no. 2 (Summer 2010): 286–93.

Farrow, Lee A. *Alexis in America: A Russian Grand Duke's Tour, 1871–1872.* Baton Rouge: Louisiana State University Press, 2014.

Field, Walker. "A Reexamination into the Invention of the Balloon Frame." *Journal of the American Society of Architectural Historians* 2, no. 4 (Oct. 1942): 3–29.

Fire Ordinances of the City of Chicago, Published by Order of the Board of Public Works, March, 1872. Chicago: Jameson & Morse, 1872.

Flanagan, Maureen. *Seeing with Their Hearts.* Princeton, N.J.: Princeton University Press, 2002.

Foner, Eric. *Reconstruction: America's Unfinished Revolution, 1863–1877.* New York: Harper-Perennial, 2014.

Foner, Philip S., ed. *Wilhelm Liebknecht: Letters to the Chicago "Workingman's Advocate," November 26, 1870–December 2, 1871.* New York: Holmes & Meier, 1983.

Gess, Denise, and William Lutz. *Firestorm at Peshtigo.* New York: Henry Holt, 2002.

Goodspeed, E. J. *History of the Great Fires in Chicago and the West.* New York: H. S. Goodspeed, 1871.

Green, Paul M., and Melvin G. Holli, eds. *The Mayors: The Chicago Political Tradition.* Rev. ed. Carbondale: Southern Illinois University Press, 1995.

Greiner, Captain H. C. *General Phil Sheridan as I Knew Him, Playmate-Comrade-Friend.* Chicago: J. S. Hyland, 1908.

Haeger, John Denis. "Eastern Money and the Urban Frontier: Chicago, 1833–1842." *Journal of the Illinois State Historical Society* 64, no. 3 (1971): 267–84.

Hahn, Steven. *A Nation Without Borders: The United States and Its World in an Age of Civil Wars, 1830–1910.* New York: Penguin Books, 2016.

Harpster, Jack. *The Railroad Tycoon Who Built Chicago: A Biography of William B. Ogden.* Carbondale: Southern Illinois University Press, 2009.

Hayes, Augustus Allen. "The Metropolis of the Prairies." *Harper's New Monthly Magazine,* Oct. 1880.

Hazen, Margaret Hindle, and Robert M. Hazen. *Keepers of the Flame: The Role of Fire in American Culture.* Princeton, N.J.: Princeton University Press, 1992.

Hirsch, Eric L. *Urban Revolt: Ethnic Politics in the Nineteenth-Century Chicago Labor Movement.* Berkeley: University of California Press, 1990.

The History of Will County, Illinois. Chicago: Wm. Le Baron Jr., 1878.

Hoffman, Dan G. "An Irish Broadside on the Great Chicago Fire." *Journal of American Folklore* 63, no. 249 (Sept. 1950): 362–63.

Holli, Melvin G., and Peter d'A. Jones, eds. *Ethnic Chicago.* Grand Rapids: William B. Eerdmans, 1984.

Holt, Glen E. "The Birth of Chicago: An Examination of Economic Parentage." *Journal of the Illinois State Historical Society* 76, no. 2 (1983): 82–94.

Hoyt, Homer. *One Hundred Years of Land Values in Chicago.* New York: Arno Press, 1970.

Hubbard, Gurdon Saltonstall. *The Autobiography of Gurdon Saltonstall Hubbard.* Chicago: R. R. Donnelley & Sons, 1911.

Hutton, Paul Andrew. *Phil Sheridan and His Army.* Lincoln: University of Nebraska Press, 1985.

Jentz, John B., and Richard Schneirov. *Chicago in the Age of Capital: Class, Politics, and Democracy During the Civil War and Reconstruction.* Urbana: University of Illinois Press, 2012.

Junger, Richard. *Becoming the Second City: Chicago's Mass News Media, 1833–1898.* Urbana: University of Illinois Press, 2010.

Karamanski, Theodore J., and Eileen M. McMahon, eds. *Civil War Chicago: Eyewitness to History.* Athens: Ohio University Press, 2014.

Keil, Hartmut, and John B. Jentz, eds. *German Workers in Chicago: A Documentary History of Working-Class Culture from 1850 to World War I.* Urbana: University of Illinois Press, 1988.

———. *German Workers in Industrial Chicago, 1850–1891: A Comparative Perspective.* DeKalb: Northern Illinois University Press, 1983.

Kinsley, Philip. *The Chicago Tribune: Its First Hundred Years.* Vol. 2, *1865–1880.* Chicago: The Tribune Company, 1945.

Kirkland, Joseph. *The Story of Chicago.* Chicago: Dibble, 1892.

Klatt, Wayne. *Chicago Journalism: A History.* Jefferson, N.C.: McFarland, 2009.

Kogan, Herman, and Robert Cromie. *The Great Fire: Chicago, 1871.* New York: G. P. Putman's Sons, 1971.

The Lakeside Memorial of the Burning of Chicago. Chicago: University Publishing Company, 1872.

Lamb, Martha J. *Spicy: A Novel.* New York: D. Appleton, 1873.

Lewis, Lloyd, and Henry Justin Smith. *Chicago: The History of Its Reputation.* New York: Harcourt, Brace, 1929.

Lewis, Robert. *Chicago Made: Factory Networks in the Industrial Metropolis.* Chicago: University of Chicago Press, 2008.

Loesch, Frank J. *Personal Experiences During the Chicago Fire, 1871.* Chicago: privately printed, 1925.

Lowe, David Garrard, ed. *The Great Chicago Fire: In Eyewitness Accounts and 70 Contemporary Photographs and Illustrations.* Mineola, N.Y.: Dover, 1979.

Luzerne, Frank. *The Lost City! Drama of the Fire-Fiend! or, Chicago, as It Was, and as It Is! And Its Glorious Future!* Chicago: M. A. Parker, 1872.

Mack, Adam. *Sensing Chicago: Noisemakers, Strikebreakers, and Muckrakers.* Chicago: University of Illinois Press, 2015.

Madsen, Axel. *The Marshall Fields.* Hoboken, N.J.: John Wiley & Sons, 2002.

Mayer, Harold M., and Richard C. Wade. *Chicago: Growth of a Metropolis.* Chicago: University of Chicago Press, 1969.

McCaffrey, Lawrence J., Ellen Skerrett, Michael F. Funchion, and Charles Fanning. *The Irish in Chicago.* Urbana: University of Illinois Press, 1987.

McCarthy, Kathleen D. *Noblesse Oblige: Charity and Cultural Philanthropy in Chicago, 1849–1929.* Chicago: University of Chicago Press, 1982.

McGovern, John. *Daniel Trentworthy: A Tale of the Great Fire of Chicago.* Chicago: Rand, McNally, 1889.

McKinney, Megan. *The Magnificent Medills: America's Royal Family of Journalism During a Century of Turbulent Splendor.* New York: Harper, 2011.

McLear, Patrick E. "The Galena and Chicago Union Railroad: A Symbol of Chicago's Economic Maturity." *Journal of the Illinois State Historical Society* 73, no. 1 (1980): 17–26.

———. "William Butler Ogden: A Chicago Promoter in the Speculative Era and the Panic of 1837." *Journal of the Illinois State Historical Society* 70, no. 4 (1977): 283–91.

Meroney, Robert N. "Fires in Porous Media: Natural and Urban Canopies." Paper presented at the NATO Advanced Study Institute, "Flow and Transport Processes in Complex Obstructed Geometries," Kiev, Ukraine, May 5–15, 2004.

———. "Fire Whirls and Building Aerodynamics." Paper presented at the Eleventh International Conference on Wind Engineering, Lubbock, Tex., June 1–5, 2003.

Merriner, James L. *Grafters and Goo-Goos: Corruption and Reform in Chicago, 1833–2003.* Carbondale: Southern Illinois University Press, 2004.

Miller, Donald L. *City of the Century: The Epic of Chicago and the Making of America.* New York: Simon & Schuster, 1996.

Miller, Ross. *The Great Chicago Fire.* Urbana: University of Illinois Press, 2000.

Mitrani, Sam. *The Rise of the Chicago Police Department: Class and Conflict, 1850–1894.* Urbana: University of Illinois Press, 2013.

Monkkonen, Eric H. *America Becomes Urban: The Development of U.S. Cities and Towns, 1780–1980*. Berkeley: University of California Press, 1980.

Montgomery, David. *Citizen Worker: The Experience of Workers in the United States with Democracy and the Free Market During the Nineteenth Century*. Cambridge, U.K.: Cambridge University Press, 1993.

Moret, J. "Purpura Hemorrhagica in Man." *Iowa State University Veterinarian* 4, no. 3 (Spring 1942): 135–36.

Morris, Roy, Jr. *Sheridan: The Life and Wars of General Phil Sheridan*. New York: Crown, 1992.

Musham, H. A. "The Great Chicago Fire, October 8–10, 1871." In *Papers in Illinois History and Transactions for the Year 1840*, 69–149. Springfield: Illinois State Historical Society, 1941.

Naylor, Timothy J. "Responding to the Fire: The Work of the Chicago Relief and Aid Society." *Science and Society* 39, no. 4 (Winter 1975/1976): 450–64.

Nelson, Bruce C. *Beyond the Martyrs: A Social History of Chicago's Anarchists, 1870–1900*. New Brunswick, N.J.: Rutgers University Press, 1988.

Nelson, Otto M. "The Chicago Relief and Aid Society, 1850–1874." *Journal of the Illinois State Historical Society* 59, no. 1 (Spring 1966): 48–66.

Olmsted, Frederick Law. "Chicago in Distress." *Nation*, Nov. 9, 1871.

Pacyga, Dominic. *Chicago: A Biography*. Chicago: University of Chicago Press, 2009.

Palmer, John M. *Personal Recollections of John M. Palmer: The Story of an Earnest Life*. Cincinnati: Robert Clarke, 1901.

Pauly, John J. "The Great Chicago Fire as a National Event." *American Quarterly* 36, no. 5 (Winter 1984): 668–83.

Phelps, Egbert. "The Tale of a City." *Lakeside Monthly*, July 1873.

Pierce, Bessie Louise. *As Others See Chicago: Impressions of Visitors, 1673–1933*. Chicago: University of Chicago Press, 1933.

———. *A History of Chicago*. Vol. 1, *The Beginning of a City, 1673–1848*. Chicago: University of Chicago Press, 1937.

———. *A History of Chicago*. Vol. 2, *From Town to City, 1848–1871*. Chicago: University of Chicago Press, 1940.

———. *A History of Chicago*. Vol. 3, *The Rise of a Modern City, 1871–1893*. Chicago: University of Chicago Press, 1957.

Proceedings of the Common Council of the City of Chicago for the Municipal Year 1869–70, Being from December 6th, 1869, to December 1st, 1870. Chicago: Republican, 1871.

Proceedings of the Common Council of the City of Chicago for the Municipal Year 1870–71, Being from December 5th, 1870, to November 27th, 1871. Chicago: J. S. Thomson, 1872.

Proceedings of the Common Council of the City of Chicago for the Municipal Year 1871–1872, Being from December 4th, 1871, to November 30th, 1872. Chicago: Rand, McNally, 1872.

Proceedings of the Common Council of the City of Chicago for the Municipal Year 1872–1873, Being from December 2nd, 1872, to November 24th, 1873. Chicago: Jameson & Morse, 1874.

Ranalletta, Kathy. "'The Great Wave of Fire' at Chicago: The Reminiscences of Martin Stamm." *Journal of the Illinois State Historical Society* 70, no. 2 (May 1977): 149–60.

Randolph, Charles. *Thirteenth Annual Report of the Trade and Commerce of Chicago for the Year Ending December 31, 1870*. Chicago: Horton & Leonard, 1871.

Read, Thomas Buchanan. *The Poetical Works of Thomas Buchanan Read*. Vol. 3. Philadelphia: J. B. Lippincott, 1867.

Report Made by Lieut. General P. H. Sheridan of the Condition of Affairs in the City of Chicago, Occasioned by the Great Fire of October 8th and 9th, 1871. Chicago: Headquarters Military Division of the Missouri, 1871.

Report of the Chicago Relief and Aid Society of Disbursement of Contributions for the Sufferers by the Chicago Fire. Chicago: Chicago Relief and Aid Society, 1874.

Report of the Chicago Relief and Aid Society to the Common Council of the City of Chicago. Chicago: Horton & Leonard, 1872.

Rhoads, James E., ed. *Friends' Review: A Religious, Literary, and Miscellaneous Journal.* Vol. 31. Philadelphia: Friends' Review, 1877.

Roe, E. P. *Barriers Burned Away.* New York: Dodd & Mead, 1872.

Rosen, Christine Meisner. *The Limits of Power: Great Fires and the Process of City Growth in America.* Cambridge, U.K.: Cambridge University Press, 1986.

Ross, Ishbel. *Silhouette in Diamonds: The Life of Mrs. Potter Palmer.* New York: Harper & Brothers, 1960.

Sawislak, Karen. *Smoldering City: Chicagoans and the Great Fire, 1871–1874.* Chicago: University of Chicago Press, 1995.

Schneirov, Richard. *Labor and Urban Politics: Class Conflict and the Origins of Modern Liberalism in Chicago, 1864–97.* Urbana: University of Illinois Press, 1998.

Sewell, Alfred L. *"The Great Calamity!": Scenes, Incidents, and Lessons of the Great Chicago Fire of the 8th and 9th of October, 1871.* Chicago: Alfred L. Sewell, 1871.

Sheahan, James W., and George P. Upton. *The Great Conflagration: Chicago: Its Past, Present, and Future.* Chicago: Union, 1871.

Slap, Andrew L. *The Doom of Reconstruction: The Liberal Republicans in the Civil War Era.* New York: Fordham University Press, 2006.

Smith, Carl. *Chicago's Great Fire: The Destruction and Resurrection of an Iconic American City.* New York: Atlantic Monthly Press, 2020.

———. *Urban Disorder and the Shape of Belief: The Great Chicago Fire, the Haymarket Bomb, and the Model Town of Pullman.* 2nd ed. Chicago: University of Chicago Press, 2007.

Smith, Richard Norton. *The Colonel: The Life and Legend of Robert R. McCormick, 1880–1955.* Boston: Houghton Mifflin, 1997.

Sparling, Samuel Edwin. "Municipal History and Present Organization of the City of Chicago." University of Wisconsin, 1898.

Spears, Timothy B. *Chicago Dreaming: Midwesterners and the City, 1871–1919.* Chicago: University of Chicago Press, 2005.

Special Message of Governor John M. Palmer, to the Twenty-Seventh General Assembly, Transmitting the Official Correspondence Between General Sheridan and His Superior Officers, and the Correspondence Between Gov. Palmer and the President of the United States, Concerning the Military Occupation of Chicago, December 9th, 1871. Springfield: Illinois Journal Printing Office, 1871.

The Spider and the Fly; or, Tricks, Traps, and Pitfalls of City Life by One Who Knows. New York: C. Miller, 1873.

Sturgis, Matthew. *Oscar Wilde: A Life.* New York: Knopf, 2021.

Sullivan, Louis. *The Autobiography of an Idea.* Mineola, N.Y.: Dover, 1956.

Taylor, Charles H., ed. *History of the Board of Trade of the City of Chicago.* Vol. 1. Chicago: Robert O. Law, 1917.

Tebbel, John. *An American Dynasty: The Story of the McCormicks, Medills, and Pattersons.* Garden City, N.Y.: Doubleday, 1947.

———. *The Marshall Fields: A Study in Wealth.* New York: E. P. Dutton, 1947.

Tonning, Wayland A. "The Beginnings of the Money-Back Guarantee and the One-Price Policy in Champaign-Urbana, Illinois, 1833–1880." *Business History Review* 30, no. 2 (June 1956): 196–210.

Twombly, Robert. *Louis Sullivan: His Life and Work.* Chicago: University of Chicago Press, 1986.

[Untitled.] *The Volonte* 1, no. 2 (February 1872): 4–5.

Wade, Louise Carroll. *Chicago's Pride: The Stockyards, Packingtown, and Environs in the Nineteenth Century.* Urbana: University of Illinois Press, 1987.

Wendt, Lloyd, and Herman Kogan. *Give the Lady What She Wants: The Story of Marshall Field & Company.* Chicago: Rand McNally, 1966.

Wheelan, Joseph. *Terrible Swift Sword: The Life of General Philip H. Sheridan.* Cambridge, Mass.: Da Capo Press, 2012.

White, Richard. *Railroaded: The Transcontinentals and the Making of Modern America.* New York: W. W. Norton, 2011.

———. *The Republic for Which It Stands: The United States During Reconstruction and the Gilded Age, 1865–1896.* New York: Oxford University Press, 2017.

Wilkie, F. B. *"Walks About Chicago," 1871–1881.* Chicago: Belford, Clarke, 1882.

Wittke, Carl. *Refugees of Revolution: The German Forty-Eighters in America.* Westport, Conn.: Greenwood Press, 1952.

Woody, Robert H. "A Description of the Chicago Fire of 1871." *Mississippi Valley Historical Review* 33, no. 4 (March 1947): 607–16.

Zukowsky, John, ed. *Chicago Architecture, 1872–1922: Birth of a Metropolis.* Munich: Prestel, 1987.

Index

Page numbers in *italics* refer to maps and illustrations.

ILLUSTRATION CREDITS

A NOTE ABOUT THE AUTHOR

Born and raised in the Twin Cities, Scott W. Berg holds a BA in architecture from the University of Minnesota, an MA from Miami University of Ohio, and an MFA in creative writing from George Mason University, where he now teaches publishing, writing, and literature. He is the author of *Grand Avenues: The Story of Pierre Charles L'Enfant, the French Visionary Who Designed Washington, D.C.* and *38 Nooses: Lincoln, Little Crow, and the Beginning of the Frontier's End.*

A NOTE ABOUT THE TYPE

This book was set in a version of Monotype Baskerville, the antecedent of which was a typeface designed by John Baskerville (1706–1775). Baskerville, a writing master in Birmingham, England, began experimenting around 1750 with type design and punch cutting. His first book, published in 1757 and set throughout in his new types, was a Virgil in royal quarto. It was followed by other famous editions from his press. Baskerville's types, which are distinctive and elegant in design, were a forerunner of what we know today as the "modern" group of typefaces.

Composed by North Market Street Graphics,
Lancaster, Pennsylvania

Printed and bound by Berryville Graphics,
Berryville, Virginia

Designed by Cassandra J. Pappas